B 1198
A5 1971

30064

Anderson, Fulton Henry

The philosophy of Francis Bacon

DATE DUE			
NOV 28 1973			
OCT 29 1975			
DEC 17 1975			
JAN 3 1989			
6/7/94			
OCT 18 2002			

WITHDRAWN

Waubonsee Community College

THE PHILOSOPHY
of FRANCIS BACON

THE PHILOSOPHY *of* FRANCIS BACON

By

F. H. ANDERSON

Professor of Philosophy in the University of Toronto

1971

OCTAGON BOOKS

New York

Copyright 1948 by The University of Chicago

Reprinted 1971
by special arrangement with The University of Chicago Press

OCTAGON BOOKS
A DIVISION OF FARRAR, STRAUS & GIROUX, INC.
19 Union Square West
New York, N. Y. 10003

LIBRARY OF CONGRESS CATALOG CARD NUMBER: 72-120224

Manufactured by Braun-Brumfield, Inc.
Ann Arbor, Michigan

Printed in the United States of America

PREFACE

THE matter contained within the pages which follow was collected and organized initially to satisfy the author's curiosity about the sort of philosopher Francis Bacon was. It is now published to fill partially what is obviouslly a gap in Baconian exegesis. New ground has been broken, and this, the author believes, will repay further cultivation by those who desire an understanding of seventeenth-century thought.

The study aims primarily at an ordered statement of that philosophy which is contained within thirty-odd of Bacon's extant works. Unlike many other expositions of Bacon, it does not presume to say what he should have written or done. Nor does it undertake an assessment of the value of his specific conclusions. Nor yet does it criticize Bacon's account of other writers, such as Plato, Aristotle, Paracelsus, Telesius. It may, for instance, occur to the reader that an interpretation of Aristotle's three theoretical sciences according to successive grades of abstraction is not Aristotle's own, but rather one derived from medieval commentaries. Yet this traditional alignment is the one which Bacon has in mind when he criticizes Aristotle. To argue the problems involved in this and other comparable interpretations by Bacon would result in throwing several chapters of the present work out of perspective. In any event, Bacon's understanding of other historical thinkers deserves a place in the history of learning along with his own recorded "reform" of knowledge.

Most of Bacon's philosophy is written in a seventeenth-century Latin which cannot always be read with easy assurance. One cannot readily determine whether a "classical" or a "medieval" construction is intended; and one cannot always conclude whether or not the word employed is really English in Latin form. In making translations and paraphrases, the author has not hesitated to draw freely on such renderings as are available, especially when these have parallels in Bacon's English writings. The translations which follow are, generally speaking, free, though not so free as those, for example, in the Spedding, Ellis, and Heath edition of the *Works*. Statements crucial to argument are rendered as literally as possible. Of terms whose meanings have changed considerably in the history of the Latin language, those senses in which they are used by Pliny and others, upon whose writings Bacon on occasion heavily relies, have usually been preferred.

The author is indebted to many of Bacon's biographers and commentators, especially to the painstaking Spedding and, in a lesser degree, to Ellis. On this occasion he would make public his gratitude to Professor R. F. Jones, at whose side he worked for several summers in the British Museum and through whose bibliographical knowledge, generously given, he became acquainted with many writings which have brought perspective to his reading of seventeenth-century authors. He thanks two of his colleagues, Professor J. R. O'Donnell and Dr. R. F. McRae, for aid. Professor O'Donnell's wide and varied Latin scholarship has helped on several occasions in the construing of obscure terms and phrases. Dr. McRae has liberally given time and energy to the reading of proof.

CONTENTS

I.	Politics and Learning	1
II.	Suing for Science: Attack upon the Universities	13
III.	Bacon's Philosophical Writings: Their Classification	31
IV.	Bacon's Revival of Materialism: His Interpretation of Fables	48
V.	Bacon's Materialism: Atoms and Motion	70
VI.	The Earlier Formulary of Interpretation	80
VII.	The Vanities and Errors of Learning	91
VIII.	Idols or False Phantoms	97
IX.	First Review of Extant Philosophies	106
X.	Bacon on the Pre-Platonists	112
XI.	Bacon and Plato	124
XII.	Of the Post-Aristotelians	132
XIII.	Classification of the Sciences respecting God and Nature	144
XIV.	Classification of the Sciences respecting Man	165
XV.	The New Method of Science: Introduction	181
XVI.	Bacon contra Aristotle. I	190
XVII.	Bacon contra Aristotle. II	204
XVIII.	The New Logic: The First Vintage of Discovery	217
XIX.	The New Logic: Aids to the Senses	224
XX.	The New Logic: Aids to the Intellect	229
XXI.	The New Logic: Aids to the Furthering of Operation	242
XXII.	Natural History: Rules and Topics	259
XXIII.	Natural History: The Data	270
XXIV.	Ladder of the Intellect: Forerunners of the New Philosophy: The New Metaphysics	279
XXV.	Bacon's Influence	292
Index		305

CHAPTER I

POLITICS AND LEARNING

THE pages which follow contain an account of Francis Bacon's contribution to learning and philosophy. The reason for their writing will furnish a clue to their design. For some years the writer has been preparing materials for a history of British philosophy in the latter half of the seventeenth century. In the works of some two hundred authors which have been brought under review no name is mentioned and no writings are quoted more often than those of Bacon. It had been thought possible to avoid a minute reading of Bacon's works—since investigation must have limits—by using available exegesis and commentary. This having been assumed, the surprising discovery was made that neither historians nor commentators had included within their published books many of the doctrines which readers in a generation succeeding Bacon's, when his influence became ascendant, had found central to his thought. It was thereupon decided to make a study of the thirty-odd philosophical pieces which were written by Bacon himself. What follows is part of what has been learned from this.

The exposition of Bacon's thought has been undertaken mainly by "literary" persons who are content to indicate, and do not care to expound, his philosophical terms and tenets; by scholars who seem unaware of the history of philosophy with which their author deals in large measure; by biographers who consume their pages in an attempt to fit a courtier of the reigns of Elizabeth and James into the pattern required for a modern office-holder in Whitehall and Westminster; and by those who compile histories of philosophy. Of these four the last have done least justice to Bacon. They have either merely glanced at his works or subjected his thought to that "Hegelianizing" practice whereby an author appears as an incident in a philosophical "tendency." Bacon, accordingly, has emerged from their treatment variously as a hesitant exponent of that empiricism which culminates in Hume, as flotsam and jetsam on an inductive tide which reaches its full flow in Mill, as an Aristotelian or at least a medievalist. Actually Bacon is no empiricist. His methodology of science is hardly comparable to the logic and epistemology of the author of the five famous canons of induction. And one would have to search far indeed to find a systematic philosopher more unlike a Peripatetic. What Bacon is, in himself, will be seen presently from his own testament within his works.

We are calling this study "the philosophy of Francis Bacon," because, while it treats in large measure of the author's reform of knowledge, the plan which this reform takes, as the Great Instauration, is designed and motivated according to the requirements of a specific type of systematic thought. All the issues involved, whether they be academic, educational, or scientific, are dependent upon the method, presuppositions, and dogmas of a "new" philosophy. In exposing his writings we shall try to hold to the text and not to amplify or to distort or to embroider with the ideas and the idioms of other thinkers what he himself has left on record. The exposition will be limited to what our author has had to say. It may lack much that is required for a complete philosophy, but it will, so far as lies in our power, be just to his outlook and intention.

The plan of the study is a simple one. First, we shall mention sufficient incidents of Bacon's life to give perspective to his scheme for the reform of learning and the sciences. Then we shall trace his efforts to obtain the means for its establishment in fact. Next, we shall undertake to classify the author's writings according, first, to the Great Instauration of learning which he hoped to bring to pass and, secondly, to the several projects which he found subsidiary, yet necessary, to this Instauration. Then we shall attempt to expound the major ideas which these writings contain. And, finally, we shall attempt by way of conclusion, to show that Bacon's philosophy marks the parting of the ways between ancient and modern thought. His legion of followers are led in a new way through (1) his attack on "learning"; (2) his separation of philosophy from various types of theology; and (3) his philosophical materialism which is based on (*a*) a new logic, (*b*) a "modern" interpretation of nature, and (*c*) the identification of metaphysics with generalized physics.

Francis Bacon was born on the twenty-second of January, in the year 1561, the son of Sir Nicholas Bacon, Lord Keeper of the Great Seal. He died on the ninth of April, 1626. His mother was Anne Cooke, daughter of Sir Anthony Cooke and sister of Lady Cecil—wife of Sir William

Cecil (Lord Burghley in 1571). Bacon was by these circumstances brought under two influences, first, religious "reform," and, secondly, the personages and the practices of the Court. His grandfather, Sir Anthony Cooke, was associated with those seeking changes within the established church; and his mother, a woman of erudition and spirit, was a puritanic Calvinist, given to the advising of her sons in matters which affected their faith and conduct. And, however much Francis Bacon may have resented the strict regimen of the Cookes, to the principles of these forebears must be credited in no small measure his revolt from the forms of thought in the English church which retained continuity with those of the Church of Rome, and his refusal, when philosophizing, to mix carnal learning with the revealed wisdom of the inspired Word.

The other influence which was to determine the beginning, the middle, and the end of Bacon's career was the Court. He was born and cradled in its shadow. He early frequented the haunts of the great and was at times in the august presence of his sovereign, Elizabeth, who was given to calling him her "young Lord Keeper" and took delight in "proving" him with questions to hear his grave replies. He lived from his boyhood onward among those who directed and changed from year to year the course of England's constitutional affairs. And he spent much of his energy and most of his life trying to be one of the chiefest among them.

In his twelfth year (1573) Francis Bacon went with his brother Anthony to Cambridge, where he remained until the end of 1575. When sixteen (1576), he, along with his brother, was admitted as an ancient of Gray's Inn; that is to say, he received a relatively senior status as the son of a judge, the society consisting of benchers, ancients, barristers, and students under the bar. In 1582 he was admitted as an utter barrister and in 1586 as bencher. In 1577 he went to Paris as one of the suite of Sir Amyas Paulet, the Queen's ambassador to France. He remained two years in France, living in Paris, Blois, Tours, and Poitiers. He tells us in the *De augmentis* that during his sojourn there he invented a new method of writing in cipher; and on one occasion he was intrusted with the task of carrying a "message" to the Queen. In 1579 he was called home because of the sudden death of his father and found himself the possessor of a small inheritance—one-fifth of his father's personal estate, his parent not having completed an intended provision for him through the purchase of a portion of land.

Bacon faced the world at the age of nineteen with a "head, tongue, pen," but a "narrow portion" and great ambitions. He had relatives and an occasional friend among the great; and he had the ear of the Court. But he had to prove his worth and show himself useful to leaders in a society of opportunists. He was a nephew of one Cecil, Lord Burghley, Lord Treasurer of great power during the reign of Elizabeth; and he was a cousin of a second Cecil, Lord Salisbury, Secretary of State under Elizabeth and chief adviser to James I. With these relatives he and his brother Anthony had greatly to reckon. Anthony called the elder Cecil "the old fox," and Francis, when he reflected on his relationship to the younger Cecil, regarded himself as "a hawk tied to another's fist that might sometimes . . . . proffer, but could never fly." Neither of the Cecils seemed anxious to advance Francis Bacon's cause. To them he appeared too arrogant of mind and manner, too incessant in his suit for place, and too precipitous in his political undertakings. They noted with apprehension his eagerness for innovation. Nor was their suspicion laid when Bacon insisted that any changes which he hoped to bring to pass touched only human learning and the established universities; that reform in science and revolution in the state were two things differing in origin, nature, and consequence; and that a new sort of solid learning could be of very great use to settled governments.

It is true that the elder Cecil helped Bacon obtain in 1584 a seat in the House of Commons, where he was to have a continuous and active career before going to the House of Lords. And to this uncle he was indebted—partly, at least—for the gift of the clerkship of the Council of the Star Chamber. This grant, received in 1589 and carrying an emolument of £1,600, was given by reversion; and Bacon was not to reap its profits—although he borrowed money on the promise of it—until the year 1608. Bacon dubbed it a "dry reversion" and compared it to "another man's buttailing upon his house, which might mend his prospect, but it did not fill his barn."

Bacon was befriended by Essex, the favorite of Elizabeth. To Essex, Bacon became a private and frank counselor; and the Earl, in return, supported Bacon's suits for place with a zeal which amounted almost to "violence." In the year 1593, for example, Essex demanded of all and sundry that Bacon, who was still in his early thirties, be given the senior office of attorney-general which had become vacant. The Cecils insisted that Bacon should be more than content with the solicitor-generalship.

The Queen, having suffered annoyance at a speech of Bacon's in Parliament against the largeness of a subsidy sought by her government, banished him from her presence. Bacon received neither appointment, and in 1595 Coke, an older man and one better read in the law, got the coveted attorney-generalship. Essex thereupon presented Bacon, who was then, as always, pursued by creditors, with land worth £1,800. On the rejection of his suit which he had pursued with conniving and servility, Bacon fell into despair; bewailed his "exquisite disgrace"; and threatened to leave the service of the Court and to retire to studies at Cambridge. On this occasion Bacon's mother wrote to her son Anthony, "I am sorry your brother with inward secret grief injureth his health. Everybody saith he looketh thin and pale. Let him look to God and confer with Him in godly exercises of hearing and reading. . . . . I had rather ye both, with God His blessed favour, had very good health and well out of debt, than any office." Bacon wrote the Queen in acknowledgement of God's providence toward him "that findeth it expedient for him to *bear the yoke in his youth.*" And for his comfort he heard that Elizabeth was of the opinion that Mr. Francis Bacon was beginning "to frame very well." He received one further grant of public office from this sovereign. He was appointed a learned counsel—this without patent or written warrant. In discharging the duties of this office, it became Bacon's unfortunate lot to be a prosecutor of Essex on the charge of treasonable action against the sovereign Elizabeth.

When James I came to the throne, Bacon hoped for an early improvement in his political status. As a result of entreaty to his uncle Cecil, he was dubbed a knight in company with some three hundred similarly honored two days before the King's coronation. He found that his name was omitted from the list of learned counsel reappointed on the accession of the new sovereign. His nomination under Elizabeth had been without official patent, and his name was probably overlooked. However, in 1604 he formally received a patent as king's counsel. He immediately took measures to impress the King both by conciliatory dealings, as a member of the Commons in controversy with the Lords, and by shrewd advice concerning the union of the kingdoms of England and Scotland. He supported the King in his plans and arranged as well as he could compromises with the King's opponents.

By 1607 Bacon found his efforts rewarded. He obtained the office of solicitor-general. In the following year the secretaryship of the Council of the Star Chamber, which he had long held by reversion, became his in fact. This he filled by deputy. The duties of the solicitor-generalship he found most exacting, so much so that he characterized the office one of the "painfullest places in the Kingdom." In 1612 he was made judge of the Court of the Verge. In 1613, when his old rival, Coke, was made chief justice of the King's Bench, Bacon obtained the place upon which he had long set his heart, that of attorney-general. Four years later, as the result of continued entreaties to the King and to the King's favorite, Villiers (created Duke of Buckingham in 1623), Bacon was made Lord Keeper; and one year thereafter (1618), Lord Chancellor. In the middle of the same year he was created Baron Verulam of Verulam, and in 1621 he was made Viscount St. Albans. Three days after the last honor was conferred, Parliament met, and Bacon's political enemies, of whom he had gathered not a few in his upward career, accused him of bribery. He was found technically guilty and deprived of office. He had acted according to the practice of the time and had accepted presents from litigants in the courts where he sat. He contended, and likely in honesty, that he had never had "bribe or reward in his eye or thought when he pronounced any sentence or order." And, while acknowledging that in conforming to custom he had condoned a vicious practice, he put himself on record—to quote from a commonplace book of Rawley's—thus: "I was the justest judge that was in England these fifty years. But it was the justest censure in Parliament that was these two hundred years."

Throughout his political career Bacon avowed continuously that the high position and the emoluments belonging thereto which he sought were not primary and final but secondary and instrumental, within the scheme of his ambition. He maintained that the main passion of his life was the good of mankind and the relief of the misery which belongs to man's present estate, that his political pursuits were motivated by the desire to gain the wealth or the influence which would render actual a new sort of science through which these ends might be acccomplished. And, if he sought personal advancement at the Court of James with a servility common to aspirants, it must be said in fairness to him that while pursuing his philosophic designs he employed similar means when dealing with the great in church and state and also made uncommonly candid demands upon his sovereign.

Bacon could never forget—notwithstanding his temporary threats to retire to contemplation and studies in relative poverty, when honors did not quickly come his way—that by birth and breeding he was destined to high station; nor could he entertain for long the thought of seeking truth in modest circumstances without high living, pomp, and great circumstance. The crown of his ambition was the direction from a great place with magnificence and magnanimity of widespread and expensive scientific operations. Little of this desire was satisfied. He could obtain neither a college nor a royal foundation, nor even a patron, and the scientific work which he initiated lapsed for a generation after his death. He sought wealth and died in debt. Indeed, it was his lot never to be out of debt, always to be pursued by creditors, and never to use his income to pay assistants for the collecting of the scientific data upon which his new sort of learning was to depend. He received large stipends from the state and lived lavishly. At the time of his death accumulated debts amounted to £20,000, and his estate to £7,000; and his last attempt to serve the cause of science by providing in his will, made a few months before he died, for lectureships in Cambridge and Oxford on "natural philosophy and the sciences thereupon depending" came to nought.

By choosing a political career, Bacon consigned his energy, which might have been used in furthering the cause of science, to intrigues for place and to the compiling of manifestoes for James and his advisers in a battle waged between King, Court, and Lords, on one side, and the Commons and courts of common law, on the other. His pen, which might have been employed in the writing of the several parts of that Great Instauration of knowledge on which he had set his hope for humanity was given over to the recording of shrewd suggestions in defence of the schemes of an arbitrary monarch who hatched new plots, sometimes from year to year, sometimes from day to day. The majority of his reflections on human learning were set down in intervals between sessions of Parliament, court-sittings, connivings for place, and advices to the King and the King's favorites. Many works in philosophy were begun; none was completed according to its design. Most of them remain tentative in statement, inconclusive in structure, and fragmentary in detail. Indeed, Bacon's political watchings and recordings were so unceasing that one wonders not at the incompleteness of his Great Instauration but at the survival of any of its portions. Cowley, in a poem of salutation to the Royal Society in praise of Bacon, well asks,

> "For who on things remote can fix his sight
> That's always in a Triumph, or a Fight?"

Throughout his political life Bacon entertained a distrust of his capacity for affairs and a firm belief in his native aptitude for learning and science. As early as 1592 he described himself to Burghley as a man not "born under Sol, that loveth honour; nor under Jupiter, that loveth business (for the contemplative planet carrieth me away wholly)." In 1597 he wrote to his sickly brother Anthony, "I sometimes wish your infirmities translated upon myself, that her Majesty might have the service of so active and able a mind, and I might be with excuse confined to these contemplations and studies for which I am fittest." Eight years later he told Sir Thomas Bodley, "I do confess since I was of any understanding, my mind hath been absent in effect from that I have done; and in absence are many errors which I do willingly acknowledge; and amongst the rest this great one that led the rest—that knowing myself by inward calling to be fitter to hold a book than to play a part, I have led my life in civil causes, for which I was not very fit by nature, and more unfit by the preoccupation of my mind." He was to bewail in his *De augmentis* of 1623 his carriage by destiny against the inclination of his genius into active affairs. And there can be no doubt of the sincerity of the prayer he made to his Maker on his desertion by the Court and overthrow by political enemies, "I confess before thee that I am debtor to thee for the gracious talents of thy gifts and graces, which I have neither put into a napkin, nor put (as I ought) to exchangers, where it might have made most profit, but misspent it in things for which I was least fit; so as I may truly say my soul hath been a stranger in the course of my pilgrimage."

Bacon's estimate of himself seems well-founded. He could write sagely and well. Clear reflection and apt statement became habitual. But the machinations of practical politics never took on the ease of a second nature. He had not the gift of a born politician, and the task of training himself to be one lay beyond his powers, even though he could set down in writing when and where to smile or frown at great men and little men, whom to flatter, to praise, to blame—like a theoretical teacher trying to impose a rule of action on a pupil ill-disposed by nature to pursue a course of conduct. Usually he moved through the mazes of politics with precipitous ambition, as one anxious quickly to arrive at a place from which he might authoritatively announce his philosophic designs. His very precipitancy revealed his lack of political sense. He could connive; but his political plots remained too evident, and his enemies perceived the design. He possessed a capacity for cunning, but he lacked stealth and sureness, and the political prizes ultimately escaped him. Much of his career may be figuratively described in his own words, "like a child following a bird, which when he is nearest flieth away and lighteth a little before, and then the child after it again, and so on *in infinitum.*"

Because of his interpretation of the circumstances in which he found himself, or at least of those with which he felt himself obliged to cope, Bacon determined to pursue both politics and learning. Of the two, he avowedly esteemed the latter greater than the former. In 1592, when he wrote Cecil concerning the "meanness" of his estate, he set in contrast his "moderate civil ends" with his "vast contemplative ends," and hoped that through his uncle's good offices he might obtain some place which would "carry" him. "For," he explained, "I have taken all knowledge to be my province: and if I could purge it of two sorts of rovers, whereof the one with frivolous disputations, confutations, and verbosities, the other with blind experiments and auricular traditions and impostures hath committed so many spoils, I hope I should bring in industrious observations, grounded conclusions, and profitable inventions and discoveries; the best state of that province. This, whether it be curiosity or vain-glory, or nature or (if one take it favourably) *philanthropia,* is so fixed in my mind as it cannot be removed. And I do easily see, that place of any reasonable countenance doth bring commandment of more wits than a man's own, which is the thing I greatly affect..... And if your Lordship will not carry me on, I will not do as Anaxagoras did, who reduced himself with contemplation unto voluntary poverty, but this will I do.... I will sell the inheritance I have, and purchase some lease of quick revenue, or some office of gain that shall be executed by deputy, and so give over all care of service, and become some sorry book-maker, or a true pioneer in that mine of truth, which (he said) lay so deep."

Throughout his days Bacon continued to affirm that it is in the pursuit and attainment of knowledge that man achieves his sovereignty, dignity, and "memory and merit of the times succeeding." In 1593 he announced in the device *Conference of Pleasure,* "The sovereignty of man lieth hid in knowledge wherein many things are reserved which kings with their treasure cannot buy, nor with their forces command; their spies and intelligencers can give no news of them; their seamen and discoverers cannot sail where they grow." And in another device, *On the Queen's Day,* in 1595, he contended, "the monuments of wit survive the monuments of power." This theme he repeated both in his *Advancement of Learning* of 1605 and in his *De augmentis* of 1623: "By learning man ascendeth to the heavens and their motions where in body he cannot come;.... the dignity and excellency of knowledge is that whereunto man's nature does most aspire;.... to this tendeth.... the strength of all other human desire. We see then how far the monuments of wit and learning are more durable than the monuments of power or of the hands" (*Bacon's Works,* ed. Spedding, Ellis, Heath [New York, 1869], VI, 168; II, 171).

What is perhaps the most informative statement of his attitude toward knowledge is contained in his fragmentary *De interpretatione naturae prooemium,* written early and not published during his life. This runs as follows:

> Considering myself born for the service of mankind, and interpreting the care of the common weal as one of those things which, like the air and water, are of public right accessible to all, I investigated thoroughly what might contribute the most to humanity, and deliberated on what I was myself best fitted by nature to perform. Now I discovered that nothing is of such benefit to the human race as the discovery of and devotion to new truths and arts by which the life of men is cultivated..... And above all if a man should bring forth no particular invention, even though quite useful, but were to kindle a light in nature which from its very beginning would illumine the confines which hold within their grasp facts already discovered, and once raised aloft would straightway lay open and bring into view the most hidden things, that man seemed to me to be the propagator of man's empire over the universe, the protector of liberty, and the conqueror of necessities.
>
> And for myself, I found that I was constructed more for the contemplation of truth than for anything else, as having a mind agile enough to recognize the resemblance of things (and this is the most important), and sufficiently steadfast and eager to observe the refinements of their diversity; as possessing the desire to seek, patience to ponder, fondness to meditate, slowness to assert, readiness to reconsider, carefulness to set in order. Such was I that I neither affected the novel nor admired the ancient; indeed I hated all imposture. For this reason I decided my nature had an intimacy and kinship with truth.
>
> Nevertheless, because by birth and education I had been absorbed with affairs of state, and inasmuch as I was not yet a man and I sometimes gave way to fancy, and thought that I owed a special debt to my country which did not extend equally to all other interests, and because I hoped that if I obtained any place of honor in the state, I should be able to perform by a greater resourcefulness of ability and industry what I had determined upon; I learned the civil arts and, as far as modesty and the safeguard of my birthright would

allow, I sought the favor of such of my friends as had any influence. And in addition to this, because those things, of whatever kind, do not penetrate beneath the circumstances and attainments of this mortal life, the hope gradually suggested itself to me that I (born in conditions unfavorable to religion) might manage, if I undertook civil offices, something useful for the salvation of souls. But when my zeal was taken for ambition, and my years had already matured, and my impaired health warned me of my unfortunate tardiness, I thereupon reckoned that I was by no means discharging my duty, when I was neglecting that by which I could of myself benefit man, and was attaching myself to that which is dependent upon the pleasure of others.... and in keeping with my earlier resolution betook myself wholly to this work.

Nor is my resolution diminished because I descry in the condition of the times the decline and fall of the science and learning which is now in use. For although I have no fear of the inroads of Barbarians (unless perchance the Spanish Empire should become strong and should oppress and weaken others by arms, and itself buy the burden); yet from civil wars which seem to me about to spread through many countries—because of certain ways of life not long since introduced—and from the malignity of sects, and from those compendious artifices and precautions which have stolen into the region of learning, no less an assault seems to be imminent on letters and the sciences, and against these misfortunes not even the Printing Office will be able to suffice. And that pacific learning which is nourished by leisure and flourishes by praise and reward, and furnishes no means of support to the ardor of expectation, and is deluded by artifices and impostures, is overwhelmed by the impediments I have mentioned. Far otherwise is the way of knowledge whose authority is secured by utility and works. Concerning the violences of the time I have little care, and I am assuredly untroubled about the injustices of men. If indeed anyone should say that I was being wise to an excessive height, I reply simply, in civil affairs there is a place for modesty, in contemplations there is room only for truth.

Now if any one resolutely demand works, I say without any imposture, that I—a man not old, of weak health, engaged in civil pursuits, attacking the most obscure of all subjects without guide or light—have made sufficient advance if I have constructed the machine itself and the art, though I may not have set it in motion and kept it at work. And with the same candor I avow that the legitimate interpretation of nature should in the first ascent, before a certain stage of generality is reached, be kept pure and segregate from all application to works. And in fact I know that all those who have in any one respect committed themselves to the waves of experience have in the beginning, because they were insufficiently steadfast of purpose and desirous of display, immoderately sought after the pledges of works, and thereafter have suffered overturning and shipwreck. On the other hand, if any one demand at least specimen assurances beforehand let him consider that by the science which is now in use men are not sufficiently instructed even to wish. And what is a matter of less moment, if any of the politicians, whose custom it is to appraise things one at a time according to personal calculations or to draw inferences from the examples of a similar undertaking, presume to thrust his judgment into a matter of this sort, I offer him the old saying "the lame man on the course came before the runner off the course," and the information that no reflection upon precedents is required, for the matter is without precedent.

The design for publishing these things is this, that such of them as conduce to the capturing of the correspondence of men of wit and the cleansing of the threshing-floor of minds be popularized and spread abroad by word of mouth, and that the remainder be handed down with selection and discretion. Nor does it escape my notice that it is a common and trite artifice of impostors to keep from the public things which are not a shred superior to those absurdities they do hand over to the multitude. However, without any imposture .... I foresee that the formula of interpretation itself and the discoveries by means of it will be more active and secure when contained within legitimate and select capabilities. And indeed I exert myself in behalf of those things to the hazard of others. For I have at heart nothing which is dependent upon externals. I am not hunting for fame, nor do I take pleasure in founding a sect after the fashion of heresiarchs; and to seek to obtain any private gain from such an undertaking I consider ridiculous and base. Sufficient for me the consciousness of well-deserving and that very effecting of things with which fortune itself cannot interfere [*Works*, VI, 446–50; cf. VII, 132].

CHAPTER II

SUING FOR SCIENCE: ATTACK UPON THE UNIVERSITIES

BACON'S maneuverings to gain high position in the state have been discussed and debated time and time again. It will be appropriate on this occasion to record in some detail his suit for science and his struggle to found a new sort of learning. This suit has exerted more influence on the history of Western thought, belief, and action than any political ambition he ever entertained. If it does not succeed according to its author's precipitous intention with Elizabeth and James and those who wield influence in their courts, its essence and implications are to compel the imagination of thinkers in a generation succeeding Bacon's own and are to change the face and the character of European learning and education for centuries to come; for it identifies learning with philosophy and philosophy with empirical science. The substance of learning becomes experimental knowledge, and the instrument of education becomes technical information for the satisfaction of man's need through the invention of "works."

The scheme of knowledge on which Bacon has set his heart is such that it can be established only by the amassing of large natural histories within or without a "college." Bacon indicates the character of his "new" learning as early as 1592 in a letter to Cecil, in which he speaks of "industrious observations." In the device *Gesta Grayorum* (1594), presented for the entertainment of Elizabeth at Gray's Inn, he asks for "a model of universal nature made private"; and in the *Valerius Terminus* of 1603 he undertakes a critical treatment of "particulars and history," tabulating a list of errors which have been made by such persons as have already "descended and applied themselves to experience, and attempted to induce knowledge upon particulars." His *De interpretatione naturae prooemium* (1603) contains, as we have seen, the announcement that the author has made ready a new organon of scientific induction. He has been able to provide the machine; he now awaits from others the stuff of natural history on which alone it can operate. In his *Advancement of Learning* (1605), as in the *Novum organum* and *Parasceve* (1620), the *Historia naturalis et experimentalis* (1622), and the *De augmentis* (1623), natural history is explicitly specified within a classification of human learning and made the *sine qua non* of such an interpretation of nature "as shall be operative to the endowment and benefit of man's life." This interpretation is to proceed out of a natural history collected according to the great scale of nature itself. The history may be considered as the "basis" of that scientific pyramid which has physics in the center and metaphysics at the apex. Natural history will record "the *variety of things;* Physic the causes, but *variable or respective causes;* and Metaphysic, the *fixed and constant causes*" (*Works,* VI, 182, 184–88, 218).

In each of the documents mentioned above, where history is made the basis of the sciences, there is evidence of the author's solicitation of the Court for aid in its collection. And, in fairness to Bacon, it should be said that he is ready in the interests of his new interpretation of nature to hazard, while still seeking high office in state, a direct appeal to the head of the established church and the sovereign of the realm for a scheme of science which contains a thoroughgoing materialistic philosophy and is calculated to revolutionize the structure and practice of established institutions of learning.

In 1592 Bacon reminds Burghley, "the Atlas of the Commonwealth," that "place of any reasonable countenance doth bring commandment of more wits than of a man's own." In the *Gesta Grayorum* of 1594 he makes manifest his confidence that he may even approach the throne itself in his seeking the command of nature through what he considers a revolutionary knowledge and invention. Here the Second Counsellor addresses the Prince:

It may seem, most excellent Prince, that my lord, which now hath spoken, did never read the just censures of the wisest men, who compared great conquerors to great rovers and witches, whose power is in destruction and not in preservation. Else would he never have advised your Excellency to become as some comet or blazing star, which should threaten and portend nothing but death and dearth, combustions, and troubles of the world. And whereas the governing faculties of men are two, force and reason, whereof the one is brute and the other divine, he wisheth you for your principal ornament and regality, the talons of the eagle to catch the prey, and not the piercing sight which seeth into the bottom of the sea. But I contrariwise will wish unto your Highness the exercise of the best and purest part of the mind, and the most innocent and meriting conquest, being the conquest of the works of nature; making this proposition, that you bend the excellency of your spirits to the searching out, inventing, and dicovering of all whatsoever is hid and secret in the world; that your Excellency be not as a lamp that shineth to others and seeth not itself, but as the Eye of the World, that both carrieth and useth light.

Antiquity, that presenteth unto us in dark visions the wisdom of former times informeth us that the [governments of] kingdoms have always had an affinity with the secrets and mysteries of learning. Amongst the Persians, the kings were attended on by the Magi. The Gymnosophists had all the government under the princes of Asia; and generally those kingdoms were accounted most happy that had rulers most addicted to philosophy. The Ptolemies in Egypt may be for instance; and Solomon was a man so seen in the universality of nature that he wrote an herbal of all that was green upon the earth. No conquest of Julius Caesar made him so remembered as the Calendar. Alexander the Great wrote to Aristotle upon the publishing of the Physics, that he esteemed more of excellent men in knowledge than in empire.

And to this purpose I will commend to your Highness four principal works and monuments of yourself. First, the collecting of a most perfect and general library, wherein whatsoever the wit of man hath heretofore committed to books of worth, be they ancient or modern, printed or manuscript, European or of other parts, of one or other language, may be made contributory to your wisdom. Next, a spacious, wonderful garden, wherein whatsoever plant the sun of divers climates, out of the earth of divers moulds, either wild or by the culture of man, brought forth, may be, with that care that appertaineth to the good prospering thereof, set and cherished; this garden to be built about with rooms to stable in all rare beasts and to cage in all rare birds, with two lakes adjoining, the one of fresh water, the other of salt, for like variety of fishes. And so you may have in small compass a model of universal nature made private. The third, a goodly huge cabinet, wherein whatsoever the hand of man by exquisite art or engine hath made rare in stuff, form, or motion; whatsoever singularity, chance, and the shuffle of things hath produced; whatsoever nature hath wrought in things that want life and may be kept, shall be sorted and included. The fourth, such a still-house, so furnished with mills, instruments, furnaces, and vessels as may be a palace fit for a philosopher's stone. Thus, when your Excellency shall have added depth of knowledge to the fineness of [your] spirits and greatness of your power, then indeed shall you be a Trismegistus, and then, when all other miracles and wonders shall cease, by reason that you shall have discovered their natural causes, yourself shall be left the only miracle and wonder of the world.

In spite of such entreaties as these, direct and indirect, to great persons, Bacon, during the reign of Elizabeth, gets no patron or helpers or financial grant toward the amassing of the data of natural history. In the *Prooemium* of 1603 he complains that when he had sought the aid of such friends as had influence for a place of honor, in which he might have had a larger command of aid to help him in his work, his efforts proved to be of no avail, because his zeal had been mistaken for ambition.

With the advent, in 1603, of James to the throne, England is ruled by a sovereign "who speaks Latin like a scholar," and whose literary work *Basilikon doron* Bacon is himself to quote in his writings (*vide Works,* II, 315; III, 28; IX, 19, 209; XIII, 412). Bacon now entertains a new hope that this instructed prince may prove a benevolent Alexander to a modern Aristotle who, like his early predecessor, has taken all knowledge for his province. Bacon arranges a collection of topics and observations under the title *Valerius Terminus of the Interpretation of Nature: with the Annotations of Hermes Stella.*

The title of this document, which Bacon does not publish, is of considerable interest. The word "terminus" probably indicates the "limits and end" to which investigation may proceed. The *Annotations,* of which "none are set down in these fragments"—to quote a statement written on the manuscript by Bacon's hand, are to throw light as by a star (*stella*). Now "star" is the symbol used by Bacon in the *Gesta Grayorum,* the *Advancement of Learning,* and the *De augmentis* to represent the Sovereign. And the significance which he attaches to the word "Hermes" is evident from his address to King James in the Introduction to the *Advancement of Learning.* "There is met in your Majesty," says Bacon, "a rare conjunction as well of divine and sacred literature as of profane and human; so as your Majesty standeth invested of that triplicity which in great veneration was ascribed to the ancient Hermes; the power and fortune of a King, the knowledge and illumination of a Priest, and the learning and the universality of a Philosopher." Bacon is, or pretends to be, greatly impressed by James's learning: "To drink indeed", he says, "of the true fountains of learning, nay to have such a fountain of learning in himself, in a king, and in a king born, is almost a miracle." And it would appear that he hopes at the beginning of James's reign—long before he suffers disillusionment respecting this sovereign's interest in the advance of "solid" knowledge—that, whether or not he can obtain a greater position of state beyond that allotted to him by Elizabeth, he may be enabled to have the modern Hermes, king of the realm and head of the church, and a literary man of no mean fame and importance, annotate a subject's work on the new science. James, when he has done this, may well be prevailed upon to make provision for the operation of the new method of knowledge either by subsidizing helpers or by placing at the author's disposal old or new foundations of learning (*Works,* II, 175, 180; VI, 90, 172; VIII, 396, 401).

Whatever may have been the intention behind Bacon's choice of title for his first considerable work on the limits and method of science, his design in addressing directly his next piece and first philosophical publication, the *Advancement of Learning,* to James is unmistakable. It is to bring to the attention of the Sovereign the suggestion that "if Alexander made such a liberal assignation to Aristotle of treasure for the allowance of hunters, fowlers, fishers and the like, that he might compile an History of nature; much better do they deserve it that travail in Arts of nature" (*Works,* VI, 172, 175, 177).

Bacon publishes this work in English. It is the only philosophical work published by him in any language but Latin. His use of his native speech in this instance becomes the more significant when we recall his distrust of modern tongues and his translating into Latin those of his nonphilosophical writings which he deems worthy of survival. "These modern languages," he says, "will at one time or other play the bankrupts with books." He addresses the work on a new philosophy as an Englishman to an English king, who is head of a church which has broken historical continuities. He hopes, as a result of its publication, to summon to his aid both his sovereign and others of preeminence in state, church, and institutions of learning. He uses English, not to announce a new era of knowledge to the "common people"—a concept he despises—in opposition to the learned, but to enlist a particular ruler, a particular court, churchmen of his own country and authorities of English universities in the reform of the old learning and the inauguration of a new science and a new invention. Later he is to look further afield and to publish this English work—with additions and discreet deletions—in Latin, but only when aid and helpers near at hand have failed to respond to his earlier plea.

Bacon sends a copy of the work to Salisbury with a flattering message and adds, "Sure I am, the argument is good, if it had lighted upon a good author. I shall content myself to awake better spirits, like a bellringer which is first up, to call others to church." James he addresses as a "temporal monarch.... learned in.... literature and erudition, divine and human." He informs the King of the hope that when the "excellency of learning and knowledge" and the "defects and undervalues" of the "particular acts and works which have been undertaken for the advancement of learning" are noted, his Majesty may be moved personally to suggest things for the improvement and the propagation of knowledge. These, Bacon urges, "may be done by many, though not by anyone;.... may be done by public designation, though not by private endeavours" (*Works,* VI, 89, 91, 182).

Bacon, in making his proposals, is well aware that he is seeking aid from the head of an established church and a somewhat unsettled government for the introduction of a scheme of knowledge which is both materialistic and revolutionary. He, accordingly, before presenting for royal approval his account of learning, shrewdly instances certain "discredits" learning has received, "in the zeal and jealousy of divines" and in the "severity and arrogancy" of politicians. There are divines, he says, who caution against natural knowledge with the warning "that knowledge hath in it somewhat of the serpent, and wherefore where it entereth into a man it makes him swell." And this, they declare, "demonstrates how learned men have been arch-heretics." Such divines as these, however, Bacon argues, fail to distinguish the proper use of men's natural faculties, which are limited by their Creator to a knowledge of natural things, from their unwarranted extension into preternatural domains. The Creator in his wisdom has set "bounds and limitations whereby human knowledge is confined and circumscribed." "These limitations are three: The first, That we do not so place our felicity in knowledge as we forget our mortality. The second, That we make application of our knowledge to give ourselves repose and contentment, and not distaste or repining. The third, That we do not presume by the contemplation of nature to attain to the mysteries of God" (*Works,* VI, 91–95).

Turning from religion to affairs, Bacon cites certain imputations which are brought against learning by politicians: that learning softens men's minds and makes them unfitted for the exercise of arms; that it perverts the dispositions of citizens in matters of government and policy, by encouraging curiosity and irresolution through too great variety of reading and too much reflection on examples in different ages and circumstances; that it diverts men from action into a liking for "leisure and privateness"; that it engenders in states a relaxation of discipline, making every man "more ready to argue than to obey and execute." In reply he argues, with citations from history, that "when kings themselves, or persons in authority under them, or other governors in commonwealths.... are endued with learning" sound knowledge produces and maintains with great efficacy civil merit, military prowess, the arts of peace, peaceable government, and public and private virtue. Learning rids the mind of "wildness and barbarism"; purges it of levity, insolence, and fear; restores it to health and increases its growth. It makes a man a ruler of himself; and gives a law to his will (*Works,* VI, 97–106, 146–67).

Having thus prepared the way for the real business in hand, namely the procuring of a foundation for the pursuit of a new sort of learning, Bacon goes on to examine the universities. Aware that James considers himself a "learned" man, he proceeds with caution. He promises to limit his remarks to "an instance or two, for example's sake, of the things that are most obvious and familiar." He tells James that "the removing of.... defects formerly enumerate.... are *opera basilica* (works for a king); towards which the endeavours of a private man may be but as an image of a cross-way, that may point at the way but cannot go it"; and that among kingly acts "there is not any more worthy than the further endowment of the world with sound and fruitful knowledge." And with some understanding of the character of this learned and conceited king, he poses the question, "Why should a few authors stand up like Hercules' Columns, beyond which there should be no sailing or discovery, since we have so bright and benign a star as your Majesty to conduct and prosper us?" He reminds him that "all works are overcome by amplitude of reward, by soundness of direction, and by conjunction of labours. The first multiplieth endeavour, the second preventeth error, and the third supplieth the frailty of man. But the principal of these is direction" (*Works,* VI, 171–72, 178–80).

Bacon's attack on the universities in the *Advancement of Learning* and in its Latin translation, the *De augmentis,* appears strangely mild when we consider his belligerent attitude to the traditional learning which prevails within these foundations. He is somewhat more outspoken in his other pieces, especially in the *Filum labyrinthi sive formula inquisitionis,* the *Cogitata et visa,* and the *Novum organum.* His criticisms, whether mildly or severely stated, are, however, all of a piece. And it would seem that his attitude toward the practices of universities undergoes no marked change from his younger days, when he revolts against the belated Peripateticism of Cambridge.

Bacon recognizes the utility of universities as cisterns for the preservation of the "excellent liquor of knowledge." But their office, he finds, is in traditional practice mainly that of a repository for inoperative relics. The fact that their customs have been anciently determined in times of ignorance by men weak in science is by itself sufficient to derogate from their authority. Their inhabitants are content with the production of new editions of authors, more correct impressions of ancient texts, more profitable glosses, more diligent annotations. Their works and acts are "rather matters of magnificence and memory than of progression and proficience," and "tend rather to augment the mass of learning in the multitude of learned men than to rectify or raise the sciences themselves."

As for the exercises of the colleges: Scholars engage when far too young in the practices of school logic and rhetoric, and are required to undertake disputation without their first having accumulated the matter of knowledge. Scholastic argumentation, which presumably is designed to enlighten the mind, "degenerates into childish sophistry and ridiculous affectation." Speeches are either completely memorized or extempore; whereas in "life and action" there is use for "intermixtures of premeditation and invention, notes and memory." Universities consequently provide no "image of life." Those who are trained within them become ill-fitted for active professions and civil occupations. Their inhabitants generally are inimical to the sciences and prejudicial to states. Princes find a lack of able men to serve them because the universities are not places where persons so disposed may occupy themselves with such subjects as history, modern languages, "books of policy and civil discourse, and the like enablements unto services of estate."

The administration and ordering of universities manifest "great contrariety" to scientific discovery. Study in the main is restricted to a few authors—chiefly Aristotle. If any man dissents from these, he is "thought a turbulent person," refused the company of other scholars, and made to suffer in his fortunes. "Whereas it be well advised, there is a great difference to be made between matters contemplative and active. For in government change is suspected, though to the better; but it is natural to arts to be in perpetual agitation and growth; neither is the danger alike of new light, and of new motion or remove."

Experimental pursuits are rendered subsidiary to practice in the professions. And, so far as university authorities hold that science is to be referred to action, they judge well. Action and operation, however, should follow upon well-founded theoretical science. The prevailing procedure in experimentation is to seek practice immediately. One is reminded of the ancient fable in which the other parts complained that the stomach did nothing, because it performed the office neither of locomotion nor of sensation; notwithstanding that it is the stomach which carries on digestion and distributes nourishment to all the rest. Those who think "philosophy and universality" are idle studies forget that it is from these alone that any profession can be supplied with strength and efficacy (*Works,* II, 178; VI, 174; VII, 110; VIII, 399).

A few means for observation and experiment have been furnished by the universities. Botanical gardens are provided for the study of certain medicinal herbs; arrangements are made for the dissection of bodies; while globes, spheres, and astrolabes are now available for those who pursue astronomical and cosmographical studies. Certain alchemists exhort men "to sell their books and to build furnaces, quitting and forsaking Minerva and the Muses as barren virgins, and relying on Vulcan." But the provisions by learned foundations pertain to but a few things; while the unguided experiments of the alchemists are scattered and without significance—like the straws of a broom without a string (*Works,* II, 177, 183; VI, 176–77, 180–81; VIII, 400–401, 405).

Bacon, addressing James directly, reminds him, "It is one of your Majesty's own most wise and princely maxims, *that in all usages and precedents, the times be considered wherein they first began;* which if they were weak or ignorant, *it derogated from the authority of the usage, and leaveth it for suspect.* And therefore in as much as most of the usages and orders of the universities were derived from more obscure times, it is the more requisite they be re-examined." He tells the King that not least among matters requiring remedy is the "intermission or neglect in those which are governors in universities of consultation, and in princes or superior persons of visitation; to enter into account and consideration, whether the readings, exercises and other customs appertaining unto learning, anciently begun and since continued, be well instituted or no; and thereupon to ground an amendment or reformation in that which shall be found inconvenient."

The universities, continues Bacon, would be well advised to make designation of persons to report on such parts of knowledge as are, and such parts as are not, sufficiently advanced; and a census should be undertaken by them of those areas in which knowledge is really poor and destitute, no matter how rich it may seem to be—"for the opinion of plenty is amongst the causes of want; and the great quantity of books maketh a shew rather of superfluity than lack." Foundations should, accordingly, add to their readers in extant knowledge "writers or inquirers concerning such parts of knowledge as may appear not to have been already sufficiently laboured or undertaken"; and send forth secretaries, who, even as the emissaries of princes bring intelligence respecting affairs of state, would report on the acts of nature. And, finally, cooperation should be sought with scientific societies throughout Europe for the exchange of information gained through observation and experiment. Nature creates brotherhood in families; the mechanical arts occasion fraternities of another sort; the anointings and vows of religion make brotherhoods among clergy and bishops. Why then should there not be brought into being a generous brotherhood among men by the light of scientific learning under the paternity of God himself, "who is called the Father of illumination or lights" (*Works,* II, 175–83; VI, 173–81, 424–26; VIII, 396–405).

In presenting his proposals to James for the reform of existing universities Bacon undoubtedly guards his pen, lest his plans should appear too revolutionary for a "learned" monarch to entertain. His design is nevertheless clear. He wants a new sort of foundation in which natural knowledge will be begun and increased in stature and use through continuous and widespread observation and experiment. The King, on their receipt, manifests no interest in the project entailed. But James is not unmindful of the author. He is quite aware that this innovator, even if he has more than a yearning for the unsettling of learned institutions, has a ready pen as well as a demonstrated capacity for calming the Commons on occasions of turbulent opposition to the exercise of prerogatives assumed by the King. James bestows political favors upon him; and two years after the publication of the *Advancement of Learning* Bacon finds himself solicitor-general, and one year later clerk of the Star Chamber. Bacon's political star is in ascendancy; and he hopes, once more, that his plan for the "commandment" of wits through a "place of reasonable countenance," which many years before he mentioned to the elder Cecil, may now become a reality. It is apparent that neither James nor his political satellites will undertake, either by visitation, edict, or less direct means, to revolutionize the general character and the practices of the universities. Perhaps, then, as an alternative, Bacon hopes, it may be possible to gain control for his purposes of one or more of the existing colleges. He sets down in his private diary, *Commentarius solutus,* July 26, 1608, a plan "for a place to command wits and pens, Westminster, Eton, Winchester, specially Trinity College in Cambridge, St. John's in Cambridge, Magdalene College in Oxford, and bespeaking this betimes with the King, my Lord Archbishop, my Lord Treasurer." He makes a list of probable backers: Russell, the chemist; the Court physicians, Poe and Hammond; Harriot, the mathematician; Harriot's patron, the Earl of Northumberland; Chaloner Murray, treasurer to the Prince; Bishop Andrews—"single, rich, sickly, and professor to some experiments"; the Archbishop of Canterbury—desirous of reputation; and "Sir Walter Raleigh in the Tower."

The foundation which he seeks will contain "labories and engines, vaults and furnaces, terraces for insulation." Its inhabitants are to collect a history of "marvels" in nature and of works in the mechanical arts; and, while compiling data of their own through observation and experiment, will engage in correspondence with such societies about the world as are given over to similar investigations. Provision is to be made for "giving pensions to four, for search to compile the two histories *ut supra.* Foundation of a college for Inventors. Two galleries with statuas for Inventors past, and spaces, or bases, for Inventors to come. And a library and an Inginary."

The entry in the diary includes the additional topics: "Query, of the order and discipline, to be mixed with some points popular to invite many to contribute and join. Query, of the rules and prescripts of their studies and inquiries. Allowance for travelling. Allowance for experiments. Intelligence and correspondence with the Universities abroad. Query, of the manner and prescripts touching secrecy, tradition, and publication. Query, of removes and expulsions in case, within a time, some invention worthy be not produced. And likewise query of the honours and rewards for inventions. Vaults, furnaces, terraces for insulation, workhouses of all sorts."

In his enthusiasm over the prospect of a new type of college, Bacon puts pen to paper and "devises," sometime after 1608, "a model or description of a college instituted for the interpreting of Nature and the producing of great and marvellous works for the benefit of men, under the name of Solomon's House, or the College of the Six Days' Works."

The piece is originally left unfinished and is brought to a partial completion only toward the end of the author's life. Its plan includes a "frame of laws of the best state or mould of a commonwealth" as well as a model for establishments of learning. Only the latter is set down. Under the title, the *New Atlantis,* the work is published posthumously by Rawley, Bacon's chaplain, confidant, and editor. By the middle of the century it furnishes a pattern for curricula proposed by those who would supplant university learning by technical training. Its content serves to indicate in large measure why James and other "learned" contemporaries turn a deaf ear to Bacon's entreaties for the control of established colleges. The importance of this model of learning for future European thought can hardly be overestimated. It introduces a new type of education—at its worst, mere skill in manifold trades; at its best, scientific humanism—which is to contend with, and not seldom to overwhelm, classical reflection and letters.

Bacon describes his new sort of foundation as "the noblest.... (as we think) that ever was upon the earth." Its end, he says, is the knowledge of causes and the secret motions of things, and the enlarging of the bounds of human empire to the effecting through inventions of all works that are possible. The foundation contains instruments for works, assigns functions to its fellows, and prescribes ordinances and rites. Among its instruments are caves of several depths, called the Lower Region, segregated from the sun and common air. These are used for refrigeration, induration, and coagulation and conservation of bodies; for the imitating of natural mines and the producing of new sorts of metals; and for the cure of certain diseases. Other instruments are natural mineral baths and artificial wells and fountains, made in imitation of natural baths, which serve to cure disease and prolong life; and dispensaries, which provide all the known natural simples and artificial drugs.

Lakes, both fresh and salt, are employed for the observation of fish and fowl, the immersion of bodies during experiment, and the transferring of water from a fresh or a salt condition into its respective opposite. Cataracts and streams aid in the study of lively motions. Means are provided for the creation of artificial snow, hail, rain, thunder, and lightning; for the production of lusters, dyes, and the like; and for the collecting, making, or exhibiting, as the case may be, of glasses, crystals, fossils, and precious stones, both natural and artificial. In special brewhouses, bakehouses, and kitchens are prepared drinks, breads, meats; wines from grapes; and other beverages from fruits, grains, roots, honey, sugar, pulp of canes, and sap of trees.

Rare beasts are available for study in parks and other inclosures. Dissections of animals are practiced. Experiments are made in continuing life, even when organs which might be regarded as indispensable for vitality are removed; in the resuscitating of the seemingly dead; in the increasing and the decreasing of stature; in the changing of structures, colors, and functions. Cross-breeding of organisms is pursued to the production of new types of beast, bird, and fish; and the creatures thus engendered are not found to be barren, as, according to the opinions of the Peripatetics, they should be. Here cross-breeding is not subject to mere chance but is controlled by ascertained knowledge in prediction of the nature of the resultant creatures. It is pursued with excellent effect by those seeking the improvement of the character of such useful organisms as silkworms and bees.

In the case of orchards and gardens examination is made of soils and manures in order to determine their suitabilities for the growing of different trees, herbs, berries. Through the grafting of trees, both cultivated and wild, according to the rules of art, fruits of relatively earlier ripening, better taste, odor, color and shape, and herbs of great medicinal value are produced in increasing quantities.

Engines are used to manufacture—in some cases purely mechanically—heats of all sorts and degrees. And there are shops for the manufacture of clocks, supporters of swimmers, instruments of war, unquenchable fires, boats which travel under water, ships which imitate birds in the air, and instruments without end.

The College contains a mathematical house in which are found those instruments which are of use in geometry and astronomy. It includes also perspective-houses, in which are produced lights and colors of various sorts—such, for example, as are found in rainbows, gems, and prisms. Here deceptions of sight in matters of distance, magnitude, figure, line, color, and shadow are demonstrated. Glasses enable observers clearly to see great objects, such as planets afar off, and, through magnification, minute things near at hand, such as insects, grains, and flaws in gems.

Perfume-houses provide means for experimenting on odors in conjunction with taste. In sound-houses all sorts of sounds are produced; here instruments, which when attached to the ear help hearing, are examined. Experiments are made with quarter-tones, harmonies unrecognized by musicians, sounds in vocal representation of written letters and words or in imitation of the noises of birds and beasts, echoes and amplified sounds, and sounds produced in pipes.

Inquiry is made into the deception of the senses by feats of juggling, false apparitions, illusions and the like. Impostures, however, are generally discouraged. The fellows of the College are forbidden under threat of ignominy and fines to increase any natural event through adornment or affectation. The works of nature are in themselves great enough to satisfy those who are ready to behold them (*Works,* V, 398–409).

So much then for the "instruments" of Solomon's House; as for the offices of its members, certain of its fellows, called Pioneers or Miners, undertake new and promising experiments. Others, known as Mystery-men, assemble such inventions as are made in the mechanical arts and liberal sciences. Still others undertake journeys periodically to foreign lands and report on the state of the sciences, arts, manufactures, and inventions in these parts. These last fellows, called Merchants of Light, return with books, abstracts, and patterns of experiment. Still others, called Depredators, make a collection of the experiments contained in these documents.

Compilers set down the findings of these four sorts of fellows under titles and tables and thereby furnish "the better light for the drawing of observations and axioms out of them." Dowry-men or Benefactors undertake to educe out of established experiments things of use for life and practice. That is to say in effect, to an understanding of causes they add knowledge of works.

When the various fellows have performed their several respective duties, all assemble to consider the information acquired. Three of their number, designated Lamps, now proceed to direct such further experiments as may enable them to penetrate yet more fully into the nature of things. Other three again, the Inoculators, execute the experiments thus directed, and report their findings. Whereupon still three others, called Interpreters of Nature, "raise" these findings "into greater observations, axioms, and aphorisms" (*Works,* V, 409-11).

The "ordinances and rites" of the College are few. The House possesses two galleries; and in one of these extant inventions are kept; in the other, statues of discoverers and inventors of ordinance, for example, of ships, of gunpowder, music, letters, working in metal, glass, silk of the worm, wine, corn, bread, sugar, and other "excellent works."

Circuits of the principal cities of the kingdom are made for the publishing of new and profitable discoveries, as well as for the diagnosis and remedy of diseases, plagues, swarms of hurtful creatures, scarcities, tempests, earthquakes, inundations, and divers like things.

Finally, hymns and services are sung daily in praise of God for his marvelous works, and prayers of invocation are uttered for the illumination and the turning to good and holy uses of scientific labors (*Works,* V, 411-13).

Whether Bacon ever really expects to acquire the sort of foundation described in his diary, or hopes for an early actualization of the imaginary College of the Six Days' Works remains conjectural. Certainly nothing comes of his attempts to obtain and renovate an existent college or of any comparable project in the years of his great political successes between 1608 and 1618, during which he both becomes the Lord Chancellor and attains a barony. And in 1620, while high in office and great in power, he is once more supplicating, in the dedicatory epistle of the *Novum organum,* his sovereign in behalf of his history of nature. On this occasion he presents James with the petition that His Majesty will bring under his care and command the collecting and perfecting of a natural and experimental history liberated from book learning, so that, at length, after many ages of mankind's history, philosophy and the sciences may not be left suspended in the air but set on the firm foundation of experience of every kind, and this well weighed. He again reminds the King that he has provided the machine for discovery, and that the stuff for its operation must be obtained from things themselves through the help of many workers.

Throughout the work of 1620 there is evident realization of the magnitude and the incompleteness of his scientific work. He reiterates for all who care to read that his project for a new sort of knowledge is "not an opinion to be held but a task to be performed." He calls upon readers everywhere "to come forward and take part in what work is to be done." And he stresses, both in the *Novum organum* and the *Parasceve,* that the required collection of natural and experimental history is a work of great proportions and involves very great labor and expense. The materials are so widely spread that the gathering of them lies beyond the power of any one mortal. Agents and merchants must be deputized to search them out and bring them in.

Bacon has virtually reached the conclusion that James, who has suffered repeatedly from the truculent mood of the Commons, is not prepared to encourage further insurrective designs even in such matters as learning. He attempts to convince the King and others that he is not seeking to pull down and demolish the traditional arts and sciences and the practices which prevail in universities. On the contrary, he esteems, so he says, their cultivation, because of their supplying matter and ornament for discourse, as well as conveniences for professors and persons in civil life. They serve as common coinage everywhere received. The faithfulness of his affection and good will toward the received sciences, he says, is publicly declared in his published works, especially the *Advancement of Learning;* and, therefore, he will not attempt "to demonstrate it further by words" (*Works,* I, 197, 198, 334; II, 44; VIII, 18, 24, 159–60, 354).

Bacon sends the King a copy of the *Novum organum,* in which his reform of knowledge is publicly announced and its method explained, with a letter "The why I have published it now." He tells James, "One part of the work, namely the compiling of a Natural and Experimental History, which must be the main foundation of a true and active philosophy .... is a body of clay, whereunto your Majesty, by your countenance and protection may breathe life." James sends a polite reply, promising to "read it through with care and attention," and to "give a due commendation to such places in my opinion shall deserve it." What he thinks of the work he never tells Bacon. To his friends he describes it as being "like the peace of God, which passeth all understanding."

In 1623 Bacon repeats in the *De augmentis* the plea to his sovereign which he has made some eighteen years before in the *Advancement of Learning* that His Majesty reform the universities and make provision for the collecting of scientific data. But one year before this in the

Preface to his *Historia naturalis et experimentalis* his appeal for aid toward the saving of his Instauration from oblivion is directed not to his own king or countymen but specifically to "capacious, unshackled, lofty, subtle, solid, and constant wits scattered throughout Europe." Finally, in 1625, the year before his death, Bacon tells the Venetian Fulgentius, "The third part of the Instauration that is, the Natural History, it is plainly a work for a King or a Pope, or for some college or order, and it cannot be performed by private industry as it should."

The aid which Bacon thus persistently seeks does not come during his lifetime either from those within or from those without his own country. And not until a quarter of a century passes do men give heed to his entreaties. After that, "virtuosi," both within and without the Royal Society, whose character he greatly influences, compelled both by his words and his example, bring the tribute of numberless natural experiments and histories to his memory and hail him as, what he undoubtedly believes himself to be, the "liberator of learning" and the "modern Aristotle" (*Works*, II, 175, 180; III, 207–8; VI, 172; VIII, 396, 401; IX, 372).

As early as 1608 Bacon has become painfully aware of solitude in his undertaking. He writes in his *Redargutio philosophiarum* (Harleian MS.), "I move in complete solitude." There is no one, he says, to whom he can speak freely and without reserve on the subject and no sympathetic hearer to whom he can expound the matter and thus quicken his mind. By this time he has reached the conclusion that he must make the attempt to provide by himself enough historical matter to enable him to demonstrate to others how the inductive method which he has promised may be put into effective operation. In his *Commentarius solutus* under the entry of July 26, 1608, he mentions "The finishing of 3 Tables, De Motu, De Calore et Frigore, De Sono." The issue of these plans is *Inquisitio legitima de motu, Historia et inquisitio primo de sono et auditu,* and *Calor et frigus*. Some years later he prepares the *Descriptio globi intellectualis,* with the *Thema coeli,* and the *De fluxu et refluxu maris*. None of these pieces, however, is deemed worthy of publication by their author. The first is no more than a list of types of motion and of inquiries to be pursued. The second and third are collections of observations without significant order or interrelation, the one superseded by the collection of data on heat in the second part of the *Novum organum* of 1620, and the other, by the second and third "centuries" of the late *Sylva sylvarum;* while the *De fluxu et refluxu maris* is theoretical and bookish and includes "history" only by way of a list of subjects for inquiry.

The astronomical observations of the *Thema coeli* immediately give way to the construction of a theoretical treatise on "the universe." In the *Descriptio globi intellectualis* a distinction is drawn between two sorts of natural history "according to its use and end." It may be employed, "either for the sake of knowledge of the things themselves.... or as the primary material of philosophy." The latter is its "noblest" use, for it is then made the "stuff and matter of true and legitimate induction." The author promises to illustrate this second sort of history by an exemplary account of the heavens. But having given this undertaking, he proceeds to discuss "philosophical questions" concerning "celestial Bodies." And the promised history is not included within the extant work, which is abruptly broken off. Indeed, Bacon seems never able before 1622 to prepare any history which he deems apt to illustrate his reform of knowledge (*Works,* VII, 57-58, 290-98, 344; X, 409-18, 463).

CHAPTER III

BACON'S PHILOSOPHICAL WRITINGS
THEIR CLASSIFICATION

DESPITE his varied political tasks Bacon finds time to write more than thirty pieces of philosophical literature. His reflections finally take definite form somewhere about 1620 in the design of his Great Instauration of learning, a scheme for the complete regeneration of human knowledge. This is published by way of an introduction to the *Novum organum*. According to an entry in his diary, *Commentarius solutus* (July 26, 1608), Bacon assigns himself the task of finishing the aphorisms, *Clavis interpretationis* ("Key of Interpretation"); and between this time and 1620 he makes a consistent effort to provide the details of what he considers to be a completely revolutionary method for the obtaining of scientific knowledge.

Bacon's design for the reform of knowledge begins, however, to take shape much earlier than 1608. Its first plan is mentioned in the earliest of his specifically philosophical pieces—disregarding for the time being incidental references to science in the "devices." This early fragment, *Temporis partus masculus,* written before 1603, lists three objects for accomplishment: (1) the Refinement and Direction of the Intellect; (2) the Light of Nature, or Method of Interpretation; and (3) Nature Illuminated, or the Truth of Things. The next specification of a scheme of learning is found in the *Delineatio* of 1607. The plan as there set down is to include six books. The first of these is not even mentioned and has to be inferred from the listing of a second, a third, fourth, fifth, and a sixth book. The second book will present a new method for the interpretation of nature. The fifth will have to do with such "anticipations" as may be reached through the ordinary use of the human understanding and may serve for practice until such time as they are submitted to that strict and thorough regimen which is imposed by the new method of inquiry described in the second book. The subjects of the third, fourth, and sixth books are not given. Only the subject of the second book is discussed, this in considerable detail.

In another piece the *Cogitata et visa,* which is at least partially written by 1607, Bacon gives an indication, without a specific listing of parts, of what he intends to include within his new scheme for learning. "A review," he says, "should be made of the modes of discovery in use." The purpose of this is "to guide the powers of human wit and understanding to the invention and improvement of arts and sciences." What he intends by this latter statement is made plain in the pages which follow. The end and test of sound science is not contemplation but operation. Its pledge is the inventions which it provides—printing, gunpowder, the compass, engines, silk, and the like; "for truth is shown and proved by the evidence of works rather than by argument, or even sense." Accordingly, "modes of demonstration should be reviewed; for demonstrations are by a certain potency philosophy." Next, "a collection and body of material, sufficient for information from its number, kind, and certainty or subtilty may be collected and amassed from natural history as well as mechanical experiments." "This mass should be reduced and digested into Tables and order, so that the intellect may work upon it and perform its office." Then particulars thus arranged should be set forth by way of "example." And, finally, "we should not suddenly pass from particulars brought together into Tables to the investigation of new particulars—this is nevertheless a useful thing and as it were a kind of Learned Experience [the fifth stage of investigation], but first ascend to general and large comprehensions"—which is the concern of the sixth part. In the last of these practices caution should be taken to avoid the vicious habit of proceeding immediately to first principles and then deducing the middle and the lower propositions from these. The correct procedure is to move from lower propositions to the middle and afterwards to the higher by a proper scale or ladder of ascent (*Works,* VII, 123, 125, 139–43).

In the light of the content of the *Cogitata et visa* Bacon's failure even to mention the first part of his sixfold scheme, while listing the other five parts in the fragment *Delineatio et argumentum* is significant. By the time he writes the latter he is attempting, it would seem, to reach a decision on a choice between two approaches to the question of extant science, two criteria of truth, two alternate designs for the first part of his Instauration. In the *Valerius Terminus* of 1603 and in the *Cogitata et visa* operation is placed before contemplation, and workability alone is made the test and pledge of truth. In the *Delineatio* the operative and the contemplative parts of discovery are placed side by side; but in the *Novum organum* of 1620 the former is rendered inferior to the latter. According to both the *Valerius Terminus* and the *Cogitata et visa* one stage of the reform of knowledge is to consist of a listing of "inventions" suitable for the use of man—this, according to the former piece, being "the Inventory, or an enumeration and view of inventions already discovered and in use, together with a note of the wants and nature of the supplies." However, sometime between 1607 and 1620 the calculating of available "works" gives way before a review of theoretical learning which is now assigned to the first part of the sixfold scheme of the Instauration, and by 1623 the list of useful "inventions" is relegated to an appendix of a chapter within the *De augmentis* and made one division among some fifty-one desiderata appended to a survey of the prevailing conditions of the sciences (*Works,* II, 302; III, 188; VI, 51, 62–63; VII, 41, 131; VIII, 516; IX, 361).

The Great Instauration, according to the final plan announced in 1620, is to consist of six parts: the classification and review of the sciences; a new inductive method; natural history, the "stuff" on which this method is to operate; tables in exemplification of discoveries made through the use of the new method; tentative doctrines gathered from mere experiments, which may be accepted for use provisionally until such time as they are subjected to rigorous induction; and a philosophical synthesis based upon tables inductively established.

The sixfold plan of the Instauration is set forth in an introduction to the *Novum organum*. This work is published mainly in representation of the second part, that is, of the new method. The first of the two books of aphorisms which constitute the chief part of the work is given over, however, to a critical review of traditional philosophies and is therefore preparatory to the whole sixfold scheme. The second book exhibits the method, but only in part; for its author, having described the earlier stages of induction, hurries on to provide rules for the compilation of natural history, which is to constitute the third part of his scheme. These rules he includes in the *Parasceve,* which is published along with the *Novum organum.* And having prepared these two pieces with the acknowledgment that the method—which he considers the most important part of his plan—is yet far from complete, he realizes that among his several manuscripts there is none which measures up to the strict requirements set down in the published announcement of his sixfold plan. One piece only is partially an exception. This is the early work of 1605, the *Advancement of Learning,* which he believes is "a general and faithful perambulation of learning, with an inquiry what parts thereof lie fresh and waste, and not improved and converted by the industry of Man." To this work he turns in some desperation—since time is short, and nothing better is to be got—renovates it by addition and deletion, has it turned into Latin, and publishes it, more or less as a makeshift, under the title *De augmentis scientiarum* in representation of the first part of his scheme. He is still without that aid from patrons or fellow-workers which he believes necessary if his Great Instauration is to reach anything like a fulfilment during his lifetime—or is, indeed, to be given even an exemplary representation sufficient to insure its survival. And he hastens to compile typical natural histories which will provide some representation of the third part of his design. Having prepared these, he is unable to bring more of the fabric of his Instauration, beyond introductions to two of its parts, into existence before his death.

The writings which Bacon leaves in representation of his Great Instauration are not many; and none of them is both complete and adequate. To the first division belongs *De dignitate et augmentis scientiarum* ("Of the Dignity and Advancement of Learning"), 1623; and to the second division, *Novum organum sive indicia de interpretatione naturae* ("The New Organon or True Directions concerning the Interpretation of Nature"), 1620. The third is represented by the introductory *Parasceve ad historiam naturalem et experimentalem* ("Preparative toward a Natural and Experimental History") with *Catalogus historiarum particularium secundum capita* ("Catalogue of Particular Histories by Titles"), 1620, and by a number of pieces containing natural history. The most important of these, in Bacon's view, is *Historia naturalis et experimentalis ad condendam philosophiam: sive phenomena universi* ("Natural and Experimental History for the Foundation of Philosophy: Or Phenomena of the Universe"), 1622. This work is designed to include six titles to be published consecutively in as many months. The first of these, *Historia ventorum* ("History of Winds"), which includes a general preface to history, a preface specifically its own, and prefaces to other designed histories, is published in 1622. *Historia vitae et mortis* ("History of Life and Death") is published in 1623. *Historia densi et rari: necnon coitionis et expansionis materiae per spatia* ("History of Dense and Rare or the Contraction and Expansion of Matter in Space") is published posthumously by Rawley in 1657. *Historia gravis et levis* ("History of Heavy and Light) has been—we learn from Rawley's Life of Bacon—"lost." Gruter, however, has seen a manuscript of Bacon's on the subject. Of the remaining histories announced in 1622, namely *Historia sympathiae et antipathiae rerum* ("History of the Sympathy and Antipathy of Things") and *Historia sulphuris, mercurii, et salis* ("History of Sulphur, Mercury, and Salt"), only the prefaces included within the original *Historia naturalis et experimentalis* of 1622 survive.

To the third part of the Instauration belong also *Sylva sylvarum* ("A Forest of Materials"), the last of Bacon's works, published by Rawley a year after its author's death (1627); *Inquisitio de magnete*, ("Inquiry concerning the Loadstone"), one of the last of the fragments written by the author and published by Rawley in 1658—a brief list of preliminary experiments and observations; and another fragment, *Abecedarium naturae* ("The Alphabet of Nature"), which Bacon intends to add to the *Historia ventorum*. Rawley says that this is "lost." It is recovered and published, however, by Tenison in 1679. One fragment of Bacon's is difficult to classify; this is *Topica inquisitionis de luce et lumine* ("A Topic of Inquiry concerning Light and Illumination"), the last but one, according to Rawley, of Bacon's writings. It is published by Gruter in 1653 and by Rawley—from another manuscript—in 1658. The piece consists mainly of a set of questions preparatory to the composition of tables, which marks a stage of the new induction described in the earlier portion of the second book of aphorisms in the *Novum organum*. This piece opens with questions respecting Tables of Presence, Absence, and Degrees and includes the preliminary procedure in the preparation of a "table." Its inquiry into method does not, however, proceed as far as that of the earlier *Novum organum*. The document, which contains also directives for history, is thus not "pure" history. But then Bacon's extant histories, as their author admits, are not consistently "pure," but are "mixed." Since the work in question has to do with a specific investigation of natural philosophy and is written late, the probability is that the author intends to find a place for the matter it contains within his sixfold scheme. The incompleteness of the method which is set forth in the second part of the Instauration—that is to say, in the *Novum organum*—and the mixed character of the writings generally left in exemplification of the third part render it impossible to determine the division to which the fragment in question belongs.

Of the fourth and fifth parts of the Instauration only respective prefaces survive under the titles *Scala intellectus sive filum labyrinthi* ("Ladder of the Understanding or Thread of the Labyrinth") and *Prodromi sive anticipationes philosophiae secundae* ("Forerunners or Anticipations of the New Philosophy"). As to the exact dates of the composition of these, no crucial evidence remains. They are published by Gruter in 1653. Nothing of the sixth part of the Instauration is extant.

These, then, are the works which may be assigned with considerable assurance to the several sections of Bacon's Great Instauration. And it is to these that we must look for a final statement of the author's positive philosophy. The list contains all the philosophical works, except two, which are prepared by Bacon between the announcement of the Instauration and the end of his life, during the period, that is, when he is attempting desperately, against circumstances and time, to leave enough of the great scheme, in which his lifelong ambition culminates, to assure its survival. The two pieces which are omitted are *De principiis atque originibus* and *New Atlantis*. The second of these is a work of the middle period, reshaped for publication because it may prove useful toward the survival of the Instauration. The former is not listed independently by Rawley among the later writings of Bacon and is probably no more than a document prepared for the revising of the *De sapientia veterum,* a semi-philosophical work, published in 1609 and widely read during the author's lifetime—a task which, according to Rawley, Bacon undertakes toward the end of his life.

This list of titles, when considered as the record of Bacon's ambitious scheme for the reform of human knowledge, appears relatively scant; and the more so when placed beside the thirty-odd extant documents which constitute his philosophical writings. Yet we cannot agree with those editors who are disposed to find places for more—if not for all—of the author's pieces within the Instauration. The primary objection to the inclusion of more titles than those we have listed is the simple fact that neither the author, even in his anxiety to have his Instauration represented as adequately as possible, nor Rawley, his confidant and editor, who knows Bacon's literary plans and hopes as well as any man, gives any assurance that the earlier writings other than those which we have named are to be placed in the respective divisions of the final sixfold scheme. Unless, then, conjecture or divination be deemed sufficient direction, outside these the other writings should remain. Conjecture is especially precarious in this instance because the Instauration as designed is dependent upon a method according to whose requirements the contents of the several parts are to be furnished and attested; and this method is never fully set down by its author. Moreover, several of the author's writings demand classification under headings which are not to be found within the sixfold scheme; while the contents of many of them run counter to the directions for those respective divisions into which they could conceivably be placed. If it is argued that the last of these objections can be raised against Bacon's own assignment of works in representation of the six parts—especially of the third—of his Instauration, in that case any opinions on the part of the commentator must give way before the authority of the author himself. Certainly it is one thing for the author to include, because of the exigencies of the circumstances, more than he can fully accommodate to the stated structure of his own design, and it is quite another for an expositor to include what the author himself by omission rejects.

We shall assume, then, that the extant statement of Bacon's mature philosophical teachings is to be found in the writings which he prepares in representation of his Instauration and shall accordingly segregate these for treatment by themselves.

We have thus initially classified Bacon's philosophical writings simply, after the indication of the author himself and of his editor and confidant Rawley, under two headings—pieces which fall within and pieces which fall without this Great Instauration. And, indeed, any further classification of the writings presents considerable difficulty. The definite character of the several divisions of the Instauration is not determined until many of his works have already been written. The authority of his criticism of extant learning and his validation of permissible knowledge are made finally dependent upon a method whose invention and exposition are not accomplished until some six years before the author's death. Not a few of the writings are begun and then suddenly suspended, sometimes to be incorporated into later documents. Most of the earlier pieces are tentative in character; hardly any are complete. When considered together, they are seen to abound in cross-reference and repetition. And as we have seen, the author, because of public duties, physical infirmity, and anxiety to publish some pieces in representation of parts of the Instauration, finds it necessary to amend or to combine for publication earlier writings in lieu of more satisfactory works.

Yet we cannot disregard those writings which fall outside the Instauration, nor can we confine the exposition of the author's philosophical reflections over a period of many years to an interpretation of works which fall within this Instauration, whose plan is complete only six years before the author's death. It so happens that the earlier writings often present Bacon's opinions in a manner which is more telling because the statement is less diplomatically restrained for the purpose of winning an audience, royal, courtly, learned, or continental. Many of the earlier pieces reveal the working of the author's mind toward the shaping of conclusions. Often a later document separates with informative perspectives statements formerly considered in combination and sometimes unites with a measure of modification doctrines previously set forth independently or in disparate contexts. Occasionally the early works treat of subjects which are not to be found in the writings of the Instauration proper; and generally they throw not a little light on the growth of Bacon's philosophical designs. Most of the author's specific doctrines suffer but little change throughout his literary career, yet some of them, such as those respecting ancient philosophers, traditional sects, and method especially, undergo, as we shall have occasion to note, a considerable development. Occasionally conclusions respecting the same subject vary from work to work, even—as in the case of the vacuum, for example—to the point of contradiction.

The estimation of the doctrinal content of the earlier writings must, of course, be governed by one consideration: Any of the opinions contained within these which may prove inconsistent with those of the writings included within the mature Instauration must be rejected from Bacon's final philosophy. All that seem to go beyond the statements of the later pieces on any topic are to be held in suspicion; and where alternative conclusions present themselves, those of the Instauration are to be given priority.

Let us proceed, then, to find a basis for a further and second classification of Bacon's works. In Bacon's judgment the future of human knowledge is to depend on the Great Instauration of the sciences. The components of this and the method on which it is to depend he publicly announces in 1620; and throughout the remainder of his life he attempts to bring the plan into operation. During the many years from 1592 onward, through several of which the scheme for the reform of learning is taking shape and substance, Bacon entertains various plans and means for its inauguration. These become manifest in four projects which are in some respects essential for, and in others subsidiary to, the Instauration itself. The first of these four is the supplanting of prevailing doctrines in the Platonic and the Aristotelian traditions by those of a Democritean sort. It should not be supposed that Bacon, despite his incessant emphasis on observation of the "facts," approaches philosophic questions without predispositions and preferences. Certainly in both his early and his later writings there is everywhere evident a disposition to set the bounds of inquiry and to pose questions for investigation in the interests of a thoroughly naturalistic and materialistic philosophy.

In the second place, Bacon finds it necessary to invent and expound a new method of investigation. With high hope he writes, as we have seen, in his *Proem* of 1603, that the method is ready. Actually, at this time it exists, as the *Valerius Terminus* shows, only in a most rudimentary form. The first invention is superseded by another in 1607, and both by the new organon of 1620.

Thirdly, Bacon considers it imperative to collect a large and varied natural history either without or within, preferably within, a new sort of learned foundation. His continued efforts toward this end have already been described.

And, fourthly, in order to obtain for his own philosophy a hearing and reception from the learned, he finds it necessary to undertake a refutation of the methods, prepossessions, and doctrines which prevail in traditional learning.

All these four projects are manifest, with varying emphases, within the *Valerius Terminus, Of the Proficience and Advancement of Learning, Divine and Human,* the *Novum organum,* and the *De augmentis.* Specifically toward the furthering of the first of them Bacon writes several sections of *Cogitationes de scientia humana* ("Thoughts on Human Knowledge"); considerable portions of *Descriptio globi intellectualis* ("Description of the Intellectual Globe") and *Thema coeli* ("Theory of the Heaven"), 1612; *Cogitationes de natura rerum* ("Thoughts on the Nature of Things"), 1604 or *ca.* 1609; *De sapientia veterum* ("Concerning the Wisdom of the Ancients"), 1609; *De principiis atque originibus, secundum fabulas cupidinis et coeli: etc.* ("Concerning Principles and Origins, According to the Fables of Cupid and Coelum: etc."), 1623–24.

His attempts to invent a new method of investigation are recorded in the *Valerius Terminus of the Interpretation of Nature; with the Annotations of Hermes Stella*, 1603; *Partis instaurationis secundae delineatio et argumentum* ("Outline and Argument of the Second Part of the Instauration"), 1607; *De interpretatione naturae, sententiae XII* ("On the Interpretation of Nature, XII Judgments"), 1608–20; and *Aphorismi et consilia, de auxiliis mentis et accensione luminis naturalis* ("Aphorisms and Counsels, concerning the Mind's Aids, and the Kindling of Natural Light"), 1608–20.

Toward the furthering of the third project, the obtaining of natural history, either within or without a learned foundation, Bacon writes, in part, *De interpretatione naturae prooemium* ("Of the Interpretation of Nature: Proem"), about 1603, several of the sections within *Of the Proficience and Advancement of Learning, Human and Divine*, 1605, and its Latin version *De dignitate et augmentis scientiarum*, 1623; *Filum labyrinthi, sive formula inquisitionis* ("Thread of the Labyrinth, or Rule of Inquiry"), ca. 1607, and its enlarged Latin version *Cogitata et visa: de interpretatione naturae, sive de scientia operativa* ("Thoughts and Impressions: Concerning the Interpretation of Nature, or concerning Operative Science"), 1607–9; sections of the *Novum organum* (in preparation, 1609–20); *Filum labyrinthi; sive inquisitio legitima de motu* ("Thread of the Labyrinth; or the Legitimate Investigation of Motion); *Calor et frigus* ("Heat and Cold"); *Historia et inquisitio prima de sono et auditu, et de forma soni, et latente processu soni; sive sylva soni et auditus* ("History and First Investigation of Sound and Hearing, and concerning the Form of Sound, and the Latent Process of Sound; or the Material of Sound and Hearing"); *Phaenomena universi; sive historia naturalis ad condendam philosophiam* ("Phenomena of the Universe or Natural History for the Foundation of Philosophy"), all ca. 1608; a part of *Descriptio globi intellectualis* and *Thema coeli;* the *New Atlantis,* written in the middle period, revised ca. 1624; and *De fluxu et refluxu maris* ("Of the Ebb and Flow of the Sea"), *ante* 1620, possibly *ante* 1616.

"Refutations" of traditional philosophies are provided mainly in *Temporis partus masculus* ("The Masculine—or Fertilizing—Birth of Time"), a very early work; sections of the *Valerius Terminus; Filum labyrinthi sive formula inquisitionis; Cogitate et visa;* the historical portions of the *Advancement of Learning* and of the *De augmentis; Redargutio philosophiarum* ("The Refutation of Philosophies"), 1608; and the prefaces, plan of the Instauration, and the first book of aphorisms within the *Novum organum.*

It will be noted that specific dates or periods have been indicated for many of the Baconian works, and neither periods nor dates for others. Actually some of these writings are prepared over a period of years. A few are compiled from notes on varied subjects which are set down on several occasions. Others contain no clues to the times of their composition beyond the internal evidence of style and doctrine; and, generally speaking, they can be classified into early, middle, and late on this evidence, after comparison with works of known date.

The *Novum organum,* which is published in 1620, is under preparation for more than a decade. It incorporates the matter and statement of the fragments *De interpretatione sententiae XII,* and *Aphorismi et consilia,* the latter of which manifests a much closer approximation in order and form to relevant sections of the mature work. *Cogitationes de scientia humana* is a collection of sketches on such varied topics as the boundaries of human knowledge, early fables, natural history, the dignity of observing the lowly and common things in nature, rest and motion, the fixity of the quantity of matter. Nearly all its varied observations are to be found within other pieces of several dates, the *Valerius Terminus,* the *Advancement of Learning,* the *De sapientia veterum,* the *Cogitationes de natura rerum,* and the *De augmentis. Phaenomena universi* is a preliminary draft of writing for the third part of the Instauration.

The *Valerius Terminus* is clearly an early work. On the cover of the collection of papers which it contains are written astronomical signs and the date 1603. This year probably indicates the time of the original writing of some of its unfinished chapters and the date of the compilation and arrangement of some of the collected fragments which survive under the title. Several of its pages read like preliminary statements of doctrines which are more fully developed in the *Advancement of Learning.* The latter work is under preparation from 1603 until 1605.

An unfinished manuscript of *Cogitata et visa,* an amplified version in Latin of the English *Filum labyrinthi sive formula inquisitionis* is shown to Sir Thomas Bodley in 1607, and a copy, likely a more "finished" product, is sent to Bishop Andrews in 1609. *Partis instaurationis secundae delineatio et argumentum* contains, along with the first statement of Bacon's sixfold scheme for the reform of the sciences, an exposition of the second "book" on method. As a presentation of method it lies between the early *Valerius Terminus* and the *Novum organum*. Its statements are not incorporated within the *Novum organum* as are several of those of the *Cogitata et visa* of 1607–9 and of the *Aphorismi et consilia*. There is no word of its projection in the *Commentarius solutus* of 1608 as there is of the *Aphorismi*. Most likely, then, it should be placed before 1608, when the later *Aphorismi et consilia* is in preparation, and after 1605. Perhaps 1607 is the most likely date.

In Bacon's *Commentarius solutus* there appears under the date of July 26, 1608 the entry, "Discoursing scornfully of the philosophy of the Grecians, with some better respect to . . . . the utmost antiquity and the mysteries of the poets." Presumably this note portends the writing of the *Redargutio philosophiarum* and the *De sapientia veterum*. Also under the same date is written, "The finishing of three Tables, De Motu, De Calore et Frigore, De Sonu. The finishing of the Aphorisms, Clavis Interpretationis." The aphorisms indicated here, which have to do with method as the "key" to interpretation, are in all probability those of the *Aphorismi et consilia,* while *De motu, De calore et frigore,* and *De sonu* obviously refer to three of the natural histories which bear these titles. The period *"circa* 1608" has been deemed apt for the pieces indicated within the *Commentarius solutus,* since it cannot be assumed with assurance that Bacon is able to bring the several pieces even to the incomplete stage in which they remain during the year 1608.

Between 1609 and 1620 Bacon makes preliminary drafts of the *Novum organum* and finally publishes it along with the *Parasceve* in 1620. This is the third piece of a distinctively philosophical nature which Bacon makes public, the others being the *Advancement of Learning* of 1605 and the *De sapientia veterum* of 1609. During the period of some twelve years before 1620 he writes, but does not publish, the *De fluxu et refluxu maris,* part of the *New Atlantis,* the *Descriptio globi intellectualis* and *Thema coeli*—really two incomplete parts of one incomplete treatise. The *New Atlantis,* according to Rawley, is one of the latest pieces on which Bacon works. There is an earlier draft, however; and it may be concluded that at the later period, indicated by Rawley, the author is attempting to put the original piece into shape for publication.

The date of the *Descriptio globi intellectualis* is indicated by the author's reference to a new star in Cygnus "twelve years hence"—the star made its appearance in 1600. *De fluxu et refluxu maris* is sometimes assigned to a period before 1616, on the ground that it contains no reference to Galileo's theory of tides announced in that year. One cannot be sure, however, that because of this omission the work is written previously to that date. There is a possibility that Bacon's preoccupation with political affairs and his own philosophic schemes keep him unaware, for some time at least, of the details of Galileo's theory, and even of the theory itself. A somewhat similar problem arises when an attempt is made to determine the date of *Cogitationes de natura rerum*. This piece, when assessed according to the statement of its subject matter, certainly seems to belong to the middle period of Bacon's writing. Yet it is possible to argue, after Ellis, that, since a new star appeared in Cassiopeia in 1572 and one in Ophiuchus in 1604 and since Bacon here mentions the former and not the latter, whereas in the *Globi intellectualis* he mentions both, it should be presumed that Bacon is not aware of the second new star when he writes *Cogitationes de natura rerum* and that the document is consequently to be placed in a period prior to 1605. This argument, however, takes no account of the possibility that Bacon does not choose on the occasion concerned to employ a twofold illustration and is content with the naming of one star. Moreover, by reasoning of the sort used by Ellis here, it could be argued that the work in question is written by 1600 because it makes no mention of the new star in Cygnus which is first observed in that year!

Scala intellectus is a preface to the fourth part of the Instauration, and *Prodromi* a preface to the fifth part. No date may be assigned with any assurance to either. Both, of course, belong to a period after Bacon's determination of the sixfold character of his reform of knowledge by 1607. The *Scala intellectus* does contain one hint of relatively early composition: the divisions of the new scheme of knowledge are called within it "books" and not "divisions" (*libri* and not *partitiones*), the earlier designation being used in the *Delineatio* and the latter in the *Novum organum*. The general content of the fragment indicates a writing somewhere within the thirteen years which elapse between the *Delineatio* and the *Novum organum*. *De principiis atque originibus* seems to be a late document, containing as it does ideas and phrases which are to be found in the mature *Novum organum*. In all probability the author writes the piece during his preparations for a revision of *De sapientia veterum*, one of Bacons latest undertakings. Rawley informs us that *Historia densi et rari* is composed about the same time as *Historia vitae et mortis*, which is prepared in 1623. He also lists among the latest writings of the author *Inquisitio de magnete* and *Topica inquisitionis de luce et lumine*, and *Sylva sylvarum*.

The date of one work has been a question of debate. This is *Temporis partus masculus*. We have left it to the end partly for purposes of emphasis; for commentators, beyond recording the title, are inclined to disregard its content. The piece, however, is important, because it shows in a striking way Bacon's disposition toward prevailing philosophers at that stage of his career in which his attitude to learning is being determined. Some commentators are disposed to identify the piece with a work which Bacon mentions under another name in a letter written to Fulgentius in 1625. "I remember," Bacon says in this letter, "that about forty years ago I composed a juvenile work . . . . which with great confidence and a pompous title I called *Temporis partus maximus*." Here he intimates to Fulgentius that he has had definite designs for the reform of learning since his twenty-fifth year. It is tempting to think that with the passing of years Bacon grows sufficiently modest to change the name —if not the intemperate content—of the piece, from the "Greatest Birth of Time" to the "Masculine—or Fertilizing—Birth of Time." That the *Temporis partus masculus* is both pompous and full of youthful confidence there can be no doubt, and that it is an early work seems clear; however, apart from the similarity of titles, its identification with the *Temporis partus maximus* remains a matter of pure conjecture.

As to the period during which Bacon sets down the absurdly violent statements of the *Temporis partus masculus*, editors and commentators are neither clear nor in agreement. Spedding recognizes the piece as one which stands apart from the author's other writings in its lack of respect for the authors it mentions and in its "entering abruptly into the subject in a spirit of contemptuous invective, not to call it presumptuous and insolent." Yet he is inclined to place the date of the first and briefer part of the fragment, which has to do with method, later than that of the

Valerius Terminus, and to assign the second chapter, which contains a vitriolic and uninformed attack on philosophers past and present—the fragment consists of a short introduction and two chapters, to a period as late as 1608, if not later. His opinion is based on three considerations. First, the title and the first chapter of the fragment—compiled, incidentally, by Gruter from loose sheets—are mentioned at the end of the manuscript of the *Valerius Terminus* with the legend, "The first chapter of a book of the same argument, written in Latin, and destined to be separate and not public." Secondly, the philosophies which exemplify what Bacon calls "Idols of the Theatre" are subjected, in the second chapter, to rigorous review, and this, Spedding says, is a practice which postdates the *Advancement of Learning* of 1605. And, thirdly, the tone of the writing is deliberately chosen by the author for the purpose of gaining an audience, after the failure of the *Advancement of Learning* to accomplish this end, and following the author's intention, recorded in the *Commentarius solutus* of 1608, of *"discoursing scornfully* on the philosophy of the Grecians, with some better respect to .... the utmost antiquity and the mysteries of the poets .... *taking a greater confidence and authority* in discourses of this nature."

From the legend on the manuscript of the *Valerius Terminus* Spedding argues respecting the piece in question that "the design and commencement of the work may therefore, in default of other evidence, be safely referred to the time when Bacon revised the manuscript of the *Valerius Terminus.*" But surely both and not only one of these incomplete pieces may have been written previous to the compiling or the transcribing or the revision of the *Valerius Terminus.* It is obvious from the character of the fragmentary chapters and the unorganized character of the *Valerius Terminus* that Bacon is assembling papers already written on various topics. Under the title he includes a collection of sketches, some more, some less, complete on various subjects converging toward the problem of a method of investigation. These sketches he apparently subjects to his own editing. There is every probability that while he selects pages for inclusion within the *Valerius Terminus,* presumably as a step toward the publication of a new method, he also reserves certain of the remaining pages for inclusion under the title *Temporis partus masculus.* And, so far from publishing the latter for the purpose of gaining an audience, he expressly determines to keep them "separate and not public" from his learned contemporaries—and for good reason, as we shall have occasion to see when we come to note their content.

In the next place, Spedding's implication that Bacon's attack on those philosophies which he is to call the "Idols of the Theatre" occurs subsequent to 1605 is absurd. We find him stating, for instance, as early as 1593 in the *Conference of Pleasure* (*The Praise of Knowledge*) that the philosophy "of the Grecians hath the foundation in words, in ostentation, in confutation, in sects, in auditories, in schools, in disputations. The Grecians are, as one of them saith, 'you Grecians ever children'..... That of the alchemists hath the foundation in imposture, in auricular traditions and obscurity....."

Again, the direction set down in the *Commentarius solutus* of 1608 respecting the ideas of ancient poets, "of utmost antiquity," and of ancient philosophers are definitely not carried out in the second chapter of the *Temporis partus masculus*. This work contains no matter on the poets and great antiquity. The writings which Bacon has in mind when he writes the direction are undoubtedly the *Redargutio philosophiarum* and the *De sapientia veterum*.

Further, it seems inconceivable that Bacon could design such a piece as the *Temporis partus masculus* for the purpose of gaining an audience. Its violence, its lack of reflection, and its absurd perspectives could only be calculated to alienate from the author men of learning or of good sense, even among such as might be zealous for the reform of learning. Its very language is scurrilous. Galen, for example, is described as *canicula,* a small female dog, or, perhaps, as we suggest, as a star within the baleful constellation of Canis. A thinker who has hit upon some isolated part of knowledge is represented as a sow making an accidental imprint upon the earth with her snout. Paracelsus is called a braying ass; and all past and present philosophers are dubbed lunatics.

Indeed, it seems impossible to account at all for the tone and the composition of the *Temporis partus masculus* except by the unreflective ignorance and precipitant arrogance of an extremely precocious youth. That Bacon is precocious is obvious from his early political services and writings. That he is precipitous is evident from his suits for place. And that as a youth he is arrogant is well attested. For instance, as early as 1586 his uncle, Lord Burghley, complains of his nephew's vanity, and

Bacon in reply construes his "arrogancy" as the bashfulness of those who live *"in umbra."* Some years later Essex, too, finds it necessary to explain Bacon's "only natural freedom and plainness which he had used with me, and, in my knowledge, with some other of his best friends."

Such considerations as these apart, there are at least three other good reasons for assigning the fragment in question to a very early stage of Bacon's literary career. First, Bacon in a *Letter and Discourse touching Helps for the Intellectual Powers* to Henry Savill, provost of Eton, includes among authors for serious study Agrippa and Ramus. The former of these is described in the *Temporis partus masculus* as a trivial buffoon and irrational animal, and the latter is called a lurking-hole of ignorance! And it so happens that this *Letter and Discourse* is written before 1604; for it is addressed *Mr.* Savill "in the two most authentic manuscripts"—to quote Spedding; and Savill, appointed provost of Eton in 1596, becomes Sir Henry in 1604.

Secondly, the *Temporis partus masculus* announces (*a*) a tactful presentation of old knowledge in conjunction with the new and (*b*) the illumination of knowledge by a new method. These promises are fulfilled, respectively, by the *Advancement of Learning* written between 1603 and 1605, and the *Valerius Terminus* of 1603 (*Works,* VII, 9–18; XIII, 293, 302).

Thirdly, when we compare the treatment of historic philosophies in the *Temporis partus masculus* with that in the *Advancement of Learning* (1603–5), the *Cogitata et visa* (1607–9), and even the *Valerius Terminus* of 1603, we find the former full of ignorance, disproportion and philosophic ineptitude; while the latter manifests evidence of information, balanced criticism, and apt thoughts. The former consists of a series of jottings by a daring and quite young man in early revolt from university manuals and exercises and quite unaware of the facts and the purposes inherent within historic systems of science and philosophy. The latter is the writing of a person who has acquired information and attained philosophical reflection.

CHAPTER IV

BACON'S REVIVAL OF MATERIALISM: HIS INTERPRETATION OF FABLES

WE HAVE now before us four concerns of Bacon which serve his Great Instauration. One of these, his attempt to provide a natural history, has already been considered. The remaining three are, to repeat, the preliminary statement of a philosophy of nature, the institution of a new method for the examination of the data of knowledge, and the ridding of the mind of such prepossessions as are either inherent in its nature or bequeathed to it as a heritage from the past. These we shall discuss in some detail before going on to an exposition of the Instauration itself.

It is Bacon's avowed intention to merge metaphysics with physics and to promulgate a materialistic philosophy. His predisposition in favor of this type of philosophy is evident from his early works. In the *Temporis partus masculus* he intimates that the pre-Socratic thinkers Anaxagoras, Empedocles, Pythagoras, and Democritus, who do not separate philosophy from physical science, are more weighty in their doctrine than are their successors who do. In the same fragment Democritus is singled out as a person to be respected for his opinions. In the *Valerius Terminus,* the *Advancement of Learning,* the *Cogitata et visa,* and the *Redargutio philosophiarum* pre-Socratic philosophy is held to be the soundest and Democritus the most penetrating thinker of all who have gone before; for Democritus rejects final causes, leaves mind out of nature, avoids abstract forms, and accepts positively formed matter as the source of all things and their activities (*Works,* VI, 42, 224; VII, 26, 29, 67, 70, 72–73, 112, 117).

Bacon is quite aware that a naturalistic and materialistic philosophy is not the sort which is likely to receive a welcome from learned inhabitants of colleges, from prelates and others in high places, or from a sovereign who combines in one person the headships of both church and state. And he knows that to offend any of these personages is to bring a general denunciation from the rest. For even as the colleges control learning, so does the church dominate learned foundations. Schemes of philosophy are involved with tenets of faith, and tenets of faith are matters of the gravest state concern. Nevertheless, it is Bacon's bold design to announce a revival of the theories of Democritus. Indeed, it is his optimistic hope that these theories, if properly understood in a new and adequate classification of the sciences, so far from being made the object of suspicion and contempt—not to mention overt attack as atheistic and sensual—will be hailed by contemporary men of faith and learning as a sound philosophy and one agreeable to the furthering of the cause of religion and human welfare. And what is more, this philosophy, when it has supplanted prevailing doctrines, will, Bacon believes, take possession of the old foundations of learning.

Bacon is thoroughly aware, however, that his chosen philosophy will initially meet with great opposition. Many among the religious are opposed to philosophical innovation in any respect, and most emphatically where it has to do—as his undoubtedly will have—with scientific knowledge, faith, and questions respecting the relationships between these two. Others of the clergy are fearful lest the search for knowledge may unsettle men's minds and new discoveries in science may issue in assaults upon religion. Certain religious thinkers, especially the Aristotelians, have so thoroughly united religion and philosophy that they deduce the tenets of the one from the doctrines of the other.

The new materialistic philosophy will have to compete with three types of prevalent thought, namely Aristotelianism, Platonism, and a meager sort of dialectic which ends in philosophical negation. These three are interpreted in various ways and with varying degrees of understanding by different groups. Generally speaking, the first is affirmed by many of those who retain intellectual, if not episcopal, continuity with the pre-Reformed church. The second is vigorously pursued by others who return for their doctrines to certain of the Church Fathers, especially Augustine; and the third is preached by certain Fanatics who separate the truths given in revelation from the carnal opinions of the "fallen" and therefore degenerate human mind.

The Aristotelians identify the Being of their metaphysics, as well as the First Mover and Supreme Final Cause of their natural theology, with the God of Christian revelation. They have merged their philosophy so thoroughly with the Christian religion that it has been well observed concerning the Council of Trent: "We are beholding to Aristotle for many of the articles of our faith." The result of this union, says Bacon, is superstitious philosophy and heretical religion (*Works,* I, 300–301; VI, 27–33, 91–97, 421; VII, 69, 108; VIII, 125–26; XIII, 385).

Platonism has been given a pre-eminence through the revival since the Reformation of an interest in Patristic texts. "Martin Luther," recounts Bacon, "in discourse of reason finding what a province he had undertaken against the Bishop of Rome and the .... traditions of the Church, and finding his own solitude .... was enforced to awake all antiquity, and to call former times to his succours to make a party against the present time; so that the ancient authors, both in divinity and in humanity, which had long time slept in libraries, began generally to be read and revolved."

Whether Bacon's interpretation of Luther's motive be correct or not, the historical fact is clear that post-Reformation Protestant thinkers turned to the early Church Fathers for an authoritative statement of Christian doctrine. Post-Reformation England witnessed an intense revival of interest in Patristic, as distinct from Scholastic, literature. Between the years 1475 and 1640 some sixty titles, not a few of them elaborately edited, of "that mirror of religion and learning, St. Augustine," were published in England; and during the same period—if we may accept the findings of the editors of the *Short Term Catalogue*—not a work of the Aristotelian Thomas Aquinas came off an English press. Patristic texts were edited and re-edited, sometimes in a scholarly, and not seldom in a propagandist, fashion by both Reformers and their Roman Catholic opponents. In these writings Protestant theologians found the means of relating their own doctrine to the teaching of the early church; and from them they gathered doctrines for a militant weapon in controversy against Scholasticism.

The Fathers, both those who accepted and those who rejected the findings of reason, were, in their use of philosophy, mainly concerned with Platonic concepts and arguments; while the most renowned of them all, "the saintly and sagacious Augustine," was in his systematic thought recognized as a thoroughgoing Platonist. Reasons for the reading of the Fathers are not difficult to find. To begin with, the teachings of the Church of Rome were set forth in terms of Scholastic learning, and the Reformed church desired a theology which was distinctive in both content and form. Moreover, in seeking a continuity of doctrine with a continuous church, Protestant theologians turned to the writers of the earlier church as teachers more authoritative because nearer to its Founder. Many, if by no means all, within the Reformed church saw the Kingdom of God primarily as something within the hearts of men rather than in ecclesiastical organizations, orders, and teachings. Some went so far as to deny the presence of revelation and its counterpart, faith, in promulgated doctrines, offices, fastings, and hearings, and considered them both as a unique, personal experience of a literally enthusiastic union with Christ. Those who, as true Enthusiasts, accepted the doctrine of a continuous personal revelation were by no means agreed on the portrayal of God's presence to the man of faith. Two opposing schools of interpretation appeared, one Platonic and the other Fanatical. For the former the Divine Nature present in the act of saving and sustaining grace is intellectually recognizable through the thought of rational man and, since cognitively perceivable, capable of intelligible statement and communication. The Fanatics, on the other hand, believed that the nature of revelation, because of a uniquely immediate, private character, is rationally unintelligible and incommunicable in the form of logical propositions. Indeed, those of the latter type rejoiced in "mysteries, and paradoxes, and senseless propositions"; they boastfully damned and despised, as the evil fruit of "carnal reason," everything that could be "understood"; and they placed scientific knowledge, if not within the domain of Satan, at least beyond the pale of religious significance.

The former group found the writings of Augustine ready to hand. And in these works they read the words of a redeemed man who was not afraid to make use of the doctrines of pagan Plato—did not God use wicked men to build the ark, and could not he use a pagan Plato, or a Pilate, to accomplish his purpose "in the fulness of time?" According to this pagan philosopher the Sun, in the realm of sense, is the object as well as the cause of sight; and analogously in the intelligible realm, the Good is both the object and the cause of intelligence, an activity in which the intellect perceives forms. In perceiving these forms one knows reality and in a measure thinks the thoughts of God, for the forms are "exemplars" according to which the particulars in the created world are made and through which these particulars are intelligible. Again, for Plato, desire is not a blind impulsive stirring, but the pursuit of a perceivable object; and, as a consequence, the grade of a man's desire is directly dependent upon the degree of his enlightenment.

Augustine takes over these Platonic doctrines and remolds them in accordance with the "wisdom" born of the love of God, received through revelation as the free gift of the "Father of Lights," and lived by men in charity. The Sun and the Good of Plato, Augustine supplants by God the Creator, Sustainer, and Redeemer, who manifests in a measure himself and his thoughts as objects of rational cognition and whose providence is made evident in the care of things as lowly as the sparrow and in its crowning manifestation in the incarnation and death of his Son. Through the last of these the Cross becomes the central fact of history, by which all events before and after become properly significant. Providence, for Augustine, is a continual causal creation, and saving knowledge is an illumination in warmth and light unto faith and deed. Through the vouchsafed grace of God man is enabled in a new way to function in understanding and desire. Even in his awareness and hatred of sin as sin there is evidence of the presence of God's grace; for he has been enabled to perceive and to desire what before he could not see.

Man as a creature is a remembering, desiring, perceiving agent. In a state of nature he has these functions; and he continues to have them in a state of grace. When God comes to him in grace, he does not lose his memory of past deeds but is made the more acutely aware of them. He does not lose his rational perception and his desire; rather, in his new awareness through illumination he turns from love of creature to love of God. God is the cause of his illumination. Yet man continues to act through his native human capacities. Of the faculties bestowed upon earthly creatures, the highest is the distinctively human one, reason; and it is through this that the redeemed sinner comes to perceive what before he could not perceive, to desire what before he could not desire. Moreover, it is through this, in the function of the rational cognition of commonly intelligible objects, that individual men are enabled to possess a church with a commonly recognized doctrine, an ascertainable rule of life, and a rational theology.

Those who, in opposition to the Augustinians, taught a private "fanatical" way of faith entertained no such explicit doctrine. They dismissed all philosophies, as well as "the logic of the Schools," as pagan and barren. Rational principles they shunned as carnal works. Even the terms of coherent speech they scorned as things tainted by human imagining. Much of their statement was negative, especially so in the condemning of truths palatable to the natural human understanding. Ethical rules of life they suspected as judgments dictated by the worldly wisdom of worldly men. The church they regarded as an assembly of individuals with private communications from the Most High, an assembly united "in spirit" and emphatically not through a common body of rationally promulgated truths. They acknowledged no *science* of theology and arrayed the "statement" of their faith sometimes in highly figurative, sometimes in warmly sensuous, phrases, sometimes in philosophical terms which appeared in the doubtful garb of quotation marks, indicating thus that what was said was not being said.

Between the respective views of these two groups Bacon takes a middle position. He recognizes as a supreme rule of conduct the Augustinian principle of charity which, like Augustine, whose phrases he often uses, he finds in the writings of Solomon and Paul. He refuses, however, to construe his doctrine in Platonic terms. He contends that man may properly philosophize and through his philosophy may know as much of the goodness and power of God as is set forth in God's created works. But Bacon is unable to see in the human creature any natural faculty or faculties capable of discerning either the inner thoughts or the nature of God. He opposes the Platonic teaching which regards forms as both the content of human cognition and the knowledge of the Divine Nature. He maintains that wisdom respecting the Supreme Being cannot be attained by reason and sense but only through the revelation contained within his inspired Word. He thus separates revealed theology from all philosophy discovered through the efficacy of human functions. This separation is fundamental to Bacon's philosophy of nature, man, and God. His sharp separation of revelation—with its counterpart, faith—from reason may have been occasioned by the circumstances of his upbringing. Yet, had he not been the son of a Calvinistic parent, he could not, his philosophy being what it is, have escaped the issue involved. Certainly the cleavage is found throughout his early, middle, and late writings. It holds a fundamental and initial place in such works as the *Temporis partus masculus,* the *Valerius Terminus,* the *Advancement of Learning,* the *De sapientia veterum,* and the *De augmentis scientiarum.* There is no good reason, then, to suggest, as commentators are sometimes prone to do, that the doctrine is merely an incidental device calculated by a fearful Bacon to mislead ecclesiastical and state authorities!

The Platonists in their rational theology identify the pagan Good of Plato with the God of Christian revelation, causal in preservation and illumination. And, for them, the Divine Being accordingly becomes the apt object of human cognition, his nature and his thoughts being given an epistemological correspondence to the forms which are the proper objects of rational human perception. With this conclusion Bacon cannot agree any more than he can bring himself to identify the Supreme Final Cause and the Prime Mover of Aristotle's natural theology with the God of revelation, because, for him man remains a creature of limited capacities shut within his senses; the objects given to sense manifest the power of God but not his will and essential nature. It is true that, on one occasion at least, Bacon uses language which suggests extreme Platonism, when, in contrasting false mental images with the true mental objects of science, he writes, "There is a great difference between the Idols of the human mind and the Ideas of the divine mind." He immediately proceeds, however, to make clear that in his view "the Ideas of the divine mind" do not represent the nature and thoughts of God the Creator but are expressly limited to "the true signatures and stamps conferred upon creatures as they are found in nature."

"The singular advantage," says Bacon, "which the Christian religion hath [over pagan religions] towards the furtherance of true knowledge is that it excludeth and interdicteth human reason, whether by interpretation or anticipation, from examining or discussing of the mysteries and principles of faith." Indeed, so positive is this exclusion that it was through an overweening desire to penetrate divine mysteries by natural powers that man fell. The "angel of light" wanted power but not knowledge. The first man wanted knowledge and, "when he was tempted before he fell, had offered unto him the suggestion, *that he should be like unto God.*" "This approaching and intruding into God's secrets and mysteries was rewarded with a further removing and estranging from God's presence." "From desire of power the angels fell; from desire of knowledge man fell; but of charity there can be no excess, and never did angel or man ever come in danger by it."

"Let no man .... think or maintain that a man can search too far or be too well studied in the book of God's word or in the book of God's works; divinity or philosophy; but rather let men endeavor an endless progress or proficience in both; only let men beware that they apply both to charity, and not to swelling; to use, and not to ostentation; and again, that they do not unwisely mingle or confound these learnings together."

For while "all things are marked and stamped with this triple character of the power of God, the difference of nature, and the use of man," yet no interpreter of these created things may legitimately induce "out of the contemplation of nature, or grounds of human knowledge.... any verity of persuasion concerning the points of faith." "It is true," Bacon explains, "that the contemplation of the creatures of God hath for end (as to the natures of the creatures themselves) knowledge, but as to the nature of God, no knowledge, but wonder; which is nothing else but contemplation broken off, or losing itself..... There is no proceeding in invention of knowledge but by similitude; and God is only self-like, having nothing in common with any creature, otherwise than as in shadow and trope. Therefore attend his will as himself openeth it, and give unto faith that which unto faith belongeth; for more worthy is it to believe than to think or know, considering that in knowledge (as we are now capable of it) the mind suffereth from inferior natures; but in all belief it suffereth from a spirit which it holdeth superior and more authorized than itself" (*Works,* I, 209-10, 246; II, 105, 259; VI, 27-29, 75, 96-97, 207, 212; VIII, 36, 72, 471, 477).

The segregation of philosophy from theology and the extension of physics and its operative counterpart, mechanics, into the realm of metaphysics in the *Advancement of Learning* of 1605 explains to a considerable degree Bacon's inability to acquire assistance from those in high places for his philosophical endeavors. By 1608 he is gravely conscious of his "solitude" in the task of implementing a materialistic philosophy which is to culminate in works of "art" produced through a knowledge of generalized mechanics. He now finds three literary courses open to him. He may prepare for publication a vigorous assault on prevailing opinions and then present explicitly his own theories by way of alternative. He considers this possibility and actually proceeds with the writing of *Redargutio philosophiarum,* in which he discusses "scornfully" those who adhere to the opinions of the thinkers accepted in tradition. The piece, which he neither finishes nor publishes, significantly takes the form of a report on a conference in Paris in which a philosopher bent on reform addresses persons eminent in church and in state and reminds his hearers that contemporaneous theological speculations and political thinking require a common philosophy (*Works,* VII, 57–58, 62).

Or, again, he may write a "reasonable" account of a natural philosophy of the Democritean sort. He does compose such a document. This is the *Cogitationes de natura rerum* which, like the *Redargutio philosophiarum,* remains far from complete. Or, by way of alternative to both the foregoing, he can avoid a frontal attack upon received theories and undertake an indirect presentation of opposing doctrines. There is a method for stating philosophical truths which has had a long and impressive history from Plato onward, represented, as it has been, by Plutarch, by certain Stoics and Neo-Platonists, by Boccaccio, Macrobius, Comes, Machiavelli, and many others. It consists in the philosophical exposition of the parables contained within the ancient poets. Bacon himself has already employed this device to a degree in such pieces as the *Temporis partus masculus,* the *Valerius Terminus,* the *Advancement of Learning,* and the *Filum labyrinthi.* So far he has confined it mainly to figurative exposition and illustration of some doctrine which he has been expounding by other means. Yet, so interested has he been in the question of the parable as a source or vehicle of philosophic doctrine that he has raised the question—for example, after noting Machiavelli's interpretation of the fable of Achilles—whether "in many the like encounters.... the fable was first, and the exposition devised," or whether "the moral was first, and thereupon the fable framed." He has kept an open mind. "I find it," he has said, "an ancient vanity in Chrysippus, that troubled himself with great contention to fasten the assertions of the Stoics upon the fictions of the ancient poets. But yet that all the fables and fictions of the poets were but pleasure and not figure I interpose no opinion" (*Works,* VI, 35, 69, 135, 170, 188, 205–6, 214, 242, 419, 426; VII, 23).

Sometime between 1605 and 1609 Bacon reaches the conclusion that the fables of the poets have "inwardness" of "meaning"; and he determines to use their stories as the vehicle of his philosophy. Accordingly, in 1609 he publishes his materialism under the title *De sapientia veterum* ("Concerning the Wisdom of the Ancients"). He sends a copy of the work to Toby Matthew in February, 1610, along with a letter in which he states: "I make no haste to believe that the world should be grown to such an ecstacy as to reject truth in philosophy because the author dissenteth in religion." Four months before, he writes to the same correspondent: "Myself am like the miller of Huntingdon, that was wont to pray for peace amongst the willows; for while the winds blew, the wind-mills wrought, and the water mill was less customed. So I see that controversies of religion must hinder the advancement of science." And it would seem that the author hopes that the doctrine of the complete separation of theology from natural philosophy—a major thesis of the *De sapientia veterum*—may be the means by which the new science will escape the condemnation of the great and small among theologians. The book proves to be popular. It is translated into English and Italian. And its author deems it well to undertake an amplification and revision of it before his death. The work is unquestionably one of the most significant contributions to philosophy in the history of English thought. Its almost complete neglect by commentators is among the strangest phenomena in the history of philosophical exegesis. Why Bacon's editors, Spedding and Ellis, neglect to include the piece among his *philosophical* works is difficult to say.

The *De sapientia veterum* ("Concerning the Wisdom of the Ancients") contains interpretations of thirty-one fables. Four of these—"Metis, or Counsel"; "The Sister of the Giants, or Fame"; "Coelum, or the Origin of Things"; and "Proteus, or Matter"—are found in the collection of fragments, *Cogitationes de scientia humana*. Three of them—"Pan, or Nature"; "Perseus, or War"; and "Dionysus, or Desire"—appear in an enlarged form in the *De augmentis*. The late fragment *De principiis atque originibus* ("Concerning Principles and Origins"), contains a revision of the fable about Cupid. It is presumably the author's intention to provide in this piece further exposition of the concept matter through an amplified interpretation of the fables, "Cupid, or Eros" and "Coelum, or Uranus." The writing is broken off, however, before the treatment of the former of the two fables is concluded.

Bacon's interpretation of fables is thoroughly naturalistic. He hails the early poets as reflective materialists. Long before the corrupting of science by philosophical phantoms, even before the days of Homer and Hesiod, says Bacon, there were men who looked directly at nature. Their view was not yet obscured by abstract notions. They set forth in fables the things they saw; and like wise men in every age who would present new doctrines without "offence or harshness," they resorted to similitudes; the more especially because they lived in early times; for, even as in man's history hieroglyphics came before letters, so parables came before arguments (*Works,* VII, 121; XII, 431; XIII, 80).

The early poets, continues the author, whether great in their thoughts or lucky in their conclusions, fell upon matters of greatest import. And well may he so praise them; for these makers of fable, as he expounds them, think Bacon's own thoughts. For example, they separate things which belong to faith from those which are reached through human inquiry. They caution against the attempt to penetrate divine mysteries through the exercise of natural human faculties. They refuse to measure the Creator in terms which apply only to creatures. They divide wisdom into a revealed truth concerning divine things and a natural knowledge of matter, its forms, and its motions. And between these two divisions they interpose no natural theology which undertakes to scale the citadel of heaven either by doctrines of a First Cause lying beyond causes as understood in nature or by conclusions respecting the essence of the rational human soul which is the Image of the Creator himself. They find matter to be the oldest thing in creation. For them, the production of works through an understanding of motions and causes within formed—and not abstract or indeterminate—matter is the goal of scientific endeavor. And if they warn against the mere empiricism of the experimental chemists, they make art the end of science and operation the end of contemplation. They encourage continual investigation here and now and caution against lazy reliance upon the wits of a few historic persons who have merely begun to run the long course which is knowledge.

Let us look, then, at the fables themselves in order to discover the preliminary statement of Bacon's philosophy. We may begin appropriately with the story of Pentheus. This fable, according to Bacon, censures and condemns man's unnatural appetite to pry into secrets which he has no right to know. Pentheus, the fable runs, climbed a tree in order to behold the secret mysteries of Bacchus. For this iniquity he was struck with madness. His frenzy took the form of seeing all things double. He saw two Thebes, and, when he went toward one of these, he saw the other behind him and turned toward this, with the result that he spent his time and energy without rest going forward and backward.

The calamity of Pentheus informs us that perpetual inconstancy and a vacillating and perplexed judgment is the punishment of those who, with precipitate daring and unmindful of their mortality, aspire to perceive divine mysteries from the summits of nature and philosophy, as by climbing a tree. For, since the light of nature is one thing and the divine light another, these men are as those who see two suns. And because the decisions of the will depend upon the intellect, they are perplexed unto inconstancy in volition no less than in opinion; and they struggle to no purpose—Thebes, according to the parable, being Pentheus' home and place of refuge (*Works,* XIII 10–11, 108–9).

The lesson contained in the story of Pentheus is reinforced by the allegory of Prometheus' attempt on the chastity of Minerva and the consequent punishment of having his entrails continuously plucked by an eagle. This story represents the plight of those who, inflated with arts and much knowledge, undertake, as they frequently do, to subject divine wisdom to the dominion of sense and reason. It teaches men that, in order to escape the laceration of mind and endless torment which follow from such a course of action, they should with humble and sober mind distinguish between the oracles of sense and of faith—unless peradventure it is pleasing to them to have both a heretical religion and a fictional philosophy (*Works,* XIII, 51, 155).

From another deed of Prometheus we learn that the thinking part of man lies beyond the course of nature. Tradition teaches that Prometheus made man. He is thus representative of Providence, for the one thing which antiquity singles out from all others in the universe is man's creation. The reason seems to be that mind and intellect are in the nature of man as man, and to derive them from brutish, irrational sources is incredible (*Works,* XIII, 42–44, 144–47).

We gather, then, from the ancients that man, made as he is in the image of God, is the peculiar work of the Creator. Yet we are also instructed by them—this time in the story of Proteus—that it is not man, but matter, which is the most ancient of things. Proteus—so runs the story—was herdsman to Neptune, and it was his custom to count his flock in his cave every day at noon and then to go to sleep. He was also a prophet who knew the past, the present, and the future. And he gave his help only if he was secured with chains, when he would turn himself into all sorts of shapes, into fire, water, and wild beasts.

Proteus himself represents matter; and his flock, the ordinary species of animals, plants, minerals. In the production of these species, matter, as it were, diffuses and uses itself up and thereupon rests. This is what is meant in the parable by Proteus' counting his herd and going to sleep. Note, too, that these acts of Proteus are performed not in the morning or evening but at noon; that is to say, when the full, and as though legitimate, time has come for the separating and bringing-forth of matter already duly prepared and predisposed. He does these deeds when he is free. Proteus, however, may also be placed in chains. That is to say, matter may, by a skilful servant of nature, be forced through art to assume forms which lie beyond its ordinary species. Indeed, if a wise man, like the prophet Proteus himself, were to know the affections and processes of matter, its "sum and general issue," he could comprehend the general nature or essence of things—one would not include all the singularities, of things which have been, of those which are, and of those which in the future shall be (*Works,* XIII, 17–19, 116–18).

Another of the poets' fables construes the origin of things as the modification of matter. This is the story of Coelum. Coelum, according to the poetic tale, was the most ancient of the gods. His generative parts were removed with a scythe by his son, Saturn. The son was given to devouring his children, of whom only one, Jupiter, escaped. Jupiter overcame his father, cast him into Tartarus, and removed his generative parts. These he threw into the sea; and from them was born Venus. But before he was able to gain security for his domain, he had first to overcome violent opposition from titans and giants.

The teaching of this fable, explains Bacon, differs but little from the philosophy of Democritus, who asserts the eternity of matter, while he denies the eternity of the world. The doctrine of Democritus, incidentally, agrees with the divine narrative, where matter is represented as existing without form before the six days' works. Coelum signifies the concave or circumference which incloses matter. Saturn represents matter itself. As Saturn is said to have deprived his parent of all power of further generation, it may be inferred that the total of matter remains the same and the *quantum* of nature undergoes neither increase nor decrease. The devourings by Saturn and the actions of Jupiter represent the successive perturbations, transitions, and reshapings of the fabric of nature. Until Venus appears, Discord is stronger than Concord; afterward, Concord finally gains ascendancy, and thus the fabric of nature becomes entire, undisturbed, and harmonious. The conflict of Concord and Discord— which is described by a philosopher like Empedocles—represents no more than a phase of creation; for the world, in both its "matter and fabric," is in very truth the work of the Creator (*Works,* XIII, 15–17, 113–16).

The fable of Pan concerns nature or the universe or the universal frame of things. To Pan are ascribed horns—broad at the bottom, narrow at the top, reaching to heaven—and a biform figure, human in the upper part and brute in the lower. This representation of nature with tapering horns indicates that its structure rises to a point like a pyramid. Particulars are infinite and are collected into numerous species. Species, in turn, are gathered into genera; these genera again are brought under genera of a higher sort; and nature, contracting as it rises, ends finally in one point. Thus it is that Pan's horns may be said to touch heaven. The summits or universal forms of nature reach, in a manner, but only in a manner, up to God. The summits of things manifest not the real nature and inner will of God, however—these are reserved for the revealed Word—but only so much of God's goodness and design as he has chosen to make manifest in the laws and decrees of nature.

The biform nature of Pan is representative of the mixed character of natural species. Anyone who attempts to range things according to independent species finds the higher and the lower mixed. Indeed, there seems to be no species which can properly be regarded as simple. Each species seems to be compounded. Man, for instance, possesses something of the brute; the brute, something of the vegetable; and the vegetable, something of the inorganic.

It may be noted in passing that few amours are imputed to Pan over and beyond his marriage with Echo. The meaning of this is clear. To love is to want something; and Pan represents the universe of nature. The universe lacks nothing. Echo, whom Pan chooses for his wife, represents true philosophy and discourse. His spouse's function is to repeat and to echo and not to add anything of its own to nature (*Works*, XII, 441-45, 448-49; XIII, 92-96, 101).

We have learned from the story of Proteus that matter may be put under constraint and fashioned. And we are informed by two further fables that this is to be accomplished not through mere haphazard experiment but by a science based upon persistent trials. The first of these fables is the story of Vulcan's failure after his forced attentions upon Minerva. Here Vulcan represents art, which often employs fire in its attempts to subdue nature. Minerva, because of the wisdom of her works, represents nature. The fable shows how mere art, no matter how much it contrives with the artifices of experiment and however great and many the impostures it parades in triumph, can never reach its goal of commanding nature. The men of fire, the chemical experimenters, are intent upon immediate achievements. They prefer to contend precipitously with nature and will not wait to seek her embrace with due allegiance and care (*Works,* XIII, 31–32, 132–33).

The foolish practice of turning aside from the course of scientific investigation by experimental empiricists to seek immediate objects is well shown by the story of Atalanta. She it was who failed to reach her goal through a desire for golden apples which were tossed on the side of the course by Hippomenes. Atalanta represents art, and Hippomenes, nature. Art, like Atalanta, can, when it pursues the course of natural philosophy, be swifter in attaining ends than can nature itself. But if, like Atalanta, it stops short of its goal and turns aside to seek immediate profit and use, it then loses the race which is set before it (*Work,* XIII, 40–41, 142–44).

Art must be governed by science. And science it not only a course to be run but a riddle to be solved. Its latter role is represented by the Riddle of the Sphinx. The Sphinx propounded riddles. Persons who could not solve them were torn in pieces. Anyone who could was promised the reward of victory over the Sphinx. The Thebans, in desperation—for the Sphinx dwelt on a mountain near their city—finally offered their kingdom to anyone who could solve the monster's riddles and thus bring him under subjection. Oedipus, a man lame and slow of foot, finally succeeded. The riddles of the Sphinx contained questions of two sorts, one respecting human nature, the other respecting things. Persons who succeed in solving the first become rulers of men; those who can solve the second gain command over natural things, over bodies, medicine, and the mechanical arts and achieve "the proper and final end of natural philosophy."

The solution of the Sphinx's riddles by a lame man, when the others failed, is not without point. Men who approach, as most do, the riddle of nature with excessively rapid step and pace meet defeat. They obtain for their struggle nothing more than the rending of their minds through disputation (*Works,* XIII, 54–57, 159–62).

The course of science is set forth in yet another story—that concerning Prometheus. We are told that in his honor there were instituted contests in which the runners carried lighted torches. When a light went out, its bearer stood aside to leave the victory to those who came behind. These races represent investigation in the arts and sciences. They remind us that the perfecting of knowledge is not to be expected from the skill of one or a few but from the persistence of a succession of inquirers. It has unfortunately been the lot of mankind to have the races of the torch long intermitted. Aristotle, Euclid, and Ptolemy made lively beginnings; but their successors have done next to nothing. It behooves us, then, to revive the games of Prometheus. Men of inquiring minds must arouse themselves to try each his own strength and not leave all to the initiative and brains of a few who have begun that race which is knowledge (*Works,* XIII, 44, 51-52, 146, 155-56).

The deeds of Prometheus have still further meaning for us. Prometheus stole fire from heaven and gave it to mankind. But men, so far from being grateful to him for his daring, arraigned him and his invention before Jupiter. Jupiter, pleased by the human accusation against Prometheus, gave to man the gift of perpetual youth. Man, however, foolishly put the gift on the back of an ass. The ass became thirsty on his way home. He came to a spring and sought relief. The spring was guarded by a serpent who demanded what the ass was carrying on his back as payment for the water. The ass paid the serpent his price, and, as a consequence, mankind lost the gift of perpetual youth.

Here perpetual youth represents the achievement of man through his application of knowledge to medicine and the other arts. Jupiter's reception of man's seemingly ungrateful accusation against Prometheus for bringing him the gift of fire, which signifies art, means the arraignment by men of their nature; for Prometheus, we recall, represents the Creator. It also signifies the refusal by men to extol what they are and possess, and their striving to gain more than they have through the continual seeking of knowledge and art. Those of their number, therefore, who hold that human achievement in the arts is failing in nothing are both out of favor with the gods and wanting in usefulness to mankind. Some of them, and they not a few, have carried human indigence to the point of maintaining that all that is discoverable has already been found out by the Peripatetics. Indeed, so dominant is this belief of theirs that anyone who finds fault with that relatively small portion of Greek philosophy which they extol is regarded as useless if not well-nigh dangerous.

Others, however, in keeping with the accusers of our parable, are aware—as were Empedocles and Parmenides—of the hidden nature of things, and they not only charge inefficiency against the arts already possessed by man but drive the investigation of nature to new industry and new discoveries, thus seeking to draw down further bounties from the Divine Goodness. If it be said that these persons, having arraigned human achievements in the arts, risk their possessions on the back of a slow-paced ass, they might well reply, according to our fable, that they are but consigning their science and their arts to experience. For empirical discovery is slow-paced; and from its tardiness has arisen the adage, "Life is short, and art is long."

Experimental investigation—whose progress is represented by the tardy and slow experience of the ass—and the dogmatical—whose abstract notions move like a swift winged thing—have not thus far in the history of human invention been happily united and have continued to remain in opposition one to the other. Certainly this may be said in behalf of the ass; he would have done well enough except for his accident of thirst by the way. And, indeed, if investigation would submit itself to experience and proceed slowly by a proper rule and method and not let a thirst for experiments in the interests of immediate profit or ostentation distract it on the way, it would prove to be a bearer of new and increased measures of divine bounty to men (*Works,* XIII, 42–44, 46–48, 144–45, 149–51).

So far, the fables of the ancients have instructed us concerning the constraint of matter by art and by nature. We have yet to learn from them of matter's own activity and other of its native characteristics. These features, Bacon informs us, are made manifest in the fable, "Cupid, or the Atom." This fable he interprets in both the *De sapientia veterum* and the *De principiis atque originibus*. In the earlier work he includes the younger as well as the elder Cupid; in the latter only the elder.

The elder Cupid is represented in fable as the oldest of the gods, and the younger Cupid as the youngest. The former is said to be the most ancient of all things except Chaos. He is without parents. Some say he is the egg of Night. He is blind, naked, given to archery, and remains in perpetual infancy. These four attributes are also transferred to the younger Cupid, son of Venus. The infancy of Cupid, or Love, signifies "the appetite or instinct of primal matter; or to speak more plainly, *the natural motion of the atom*. This is indeed the original and unique thing that constitutes and fashions all things out of matter." Matter's inherent activity, so far as nature goes, is without cause, that is, without parent—cause being, as it were, the parent of effect. Of natural movement there can be no more primary cause than itself in nature. Neither efficient nor form can be before it. (Here we omit God, since as the producer of nature God exists outside its causal order.)

Philosophy can delineate the causes of phenomena, but a comprehension of the primary appetite or motion of matter, in which ultimately the things of nature and the products of art have their source, is hardly to be hoped for. "The summary law of nature, that virtue of Love given by God to the primary particles of matter, through which they unite, and by which through multiplication and repetition all varieties of things come forth and are brought together, is something which the thought of mortals may glance at but not take in." This law is well represented, therefore, as the egg of Night. The words of the sacred philosopher (Eccles. 3:11) describe it thus: "He hath made all things beautiful according to their seasons; also he hath submitted the world to man's inquiry, yet so that man cannot find out the work which God worketh from the beginning to the end."

The investigation hitherto made by philosophers of the principles of motion, in which all activity of operation lies, has been negligible and languid. Some thinkers, having taken a leap beyond nature, refer natural activity to God. The Peripatetics explain motion as the stimulus of indeterminate matter in its privation of form and, accordingly, do no more than state in their abstract terms a peculiar problem of their own to be solved. Democritus, who considers the question somewhat more deeply than they, first attributes to the primary atom dimension and shape and then assigns it two types of motion: a primary motion simply and a second by comparison. The first of these motions is to the center, where, according to Democritus, all things gravitate. The second is a motion of conflict engendered through the forcing from the center by what has more matter of that which has less. This interpretation of Democritus is much too limited in scope and, so far from explaining motion generally, fails to account even for planetary movements and the phenomena of contraction and expansion. As for the account of nature's processes by one of Democritus' disciples, Epicurus, in terms of "the declination and fortuitous agitation of the atom, this is a relapse to trifling and ignorance."

Others of Cupid's characteristics are said to be nakedness, blindness, and skill in archery. He is represented as naked because the primary particles of things, and they only, may be said to be so. Compounds are "masked and clothed." The significance of his blindness lies in the fact that active matter, which he represents, has a minimum of "providence" and directs its course like a blind man by whatever it finds adjacent. This procedure of created matter, comments Bacon, makes the Divine Providence the more to be admired because, out of things which are devoid of providence and, as one might say, blind, it brings by a fatal and sure decree all the order and beauty of the world. Here Bacon is instancing an observation which he introduces on occasions when he condemns the use of final causes in natural philosophy. In the *Advancement of Learning*, for example, he argues, "For as in civil actions, he is the greater and deeper politique, that can make others the instrument of his will and ends and yet never acquaint them with his purpose.... so is the wisdom of God more admirable, when nature intends one thing and providence draweth forth another."

Cupid's gift of archery signifies the fact that the virtue of the atom acts at a distance. Whoever believes in motion and the doctrine of the atom and the vacuum, even though he rejects a collected vacuum and accepts only a vacuum intermingled in space, necessarily recognizes the action of the virtue of the atom at a distance. Without this, bodies would remain immobile because of the interspersed vacuum.

So much for the elder Cupid, whose attributes are transferred also to the younger in fable. As for the younger Cupid, the son of Venus, he is, not without reason, called the youngest of the gods because, until the species of things are brought into existence, he cannot act. Venus stimulates the general appetite of conjunction and procreation; Cupid brings appetite to bear on an individual object. Venus, then, represents the general disposition; Cupid the restricted, the specific, and the exact sympathy. The more general disposition to conjunction is dependent upon the relatively more contiguous cause; the particular sympathy takes its derivation from principles more deeply decreed (*Works*, VI, 225; XIII, 22–25, 122–25, 225; *vide* II, 296–97; VIII, 511).

In the *De principiis atque originibus* only the elder Cupid is considered. This Cupid represents both the nature and the activity of matter, the oldest of all created things. Cupid is without parents or causal progenitor. This is to say, primary determined matter, with its ordered acts and forms, has no prior cause in the order of nature. It is the cause of causes in nature. It is to be taken positively for what it is. With it and through it the series of natural causes begins and ends. To argue from within natural causes to a First Cause which lies beyond nature is to be guilty of superficiality. Nothing corrupts natural philosophy more than the seeking for the parents of Cupid. Inquirers are not content to discover and then to stop with the elements of things themselves. They will go beyond these to first principles, mathematical infinities, or other of their fantastic creations beyond the limits of nature. These objects, curiously enough, they would fain present as more demonstrable and more causal than the solid principles which are discoverable through experiential observation of things which exist (*Works,* V, 289-92; X, 343-46).

Again, Cupid is said to come of an egg of Night. This part of the parable, stressing as it does the negation of positive light, represents the impossibility of knowing the summary law of nature. It instructs us that in contradistinction to things which are the offspring of light, and which may therefore be concluded by affirmations, there are also things which are "by negatives and exclusions elicited and brought forth as it were out of darkness and night." Democritus, the philosopher, speaks wisely when he says that the atoms or seeds of things and their virtue are not like anything perceived by the senses but are of a dark and concealed nature. They are not like sparks of fire, or drops of water, or bubbles of air, or grains of dust; nor do they have the power and form of such heavy or light, hot or cold, dense or rare, hard or soft, as appear in larger specific bodies. Nor, again, is the atom's natural motion one of descent, or expansion, or contraction, or impulse, or connection, or rotation, or any other motion of composite bodies; notwithstanding that in the body of the atom are contained the elements of all bodies and in its motion and virtue the origin of all motions and virtues. At this point, however, the wisdom of the early fable surpasses that of Democritus. Democritus here lapses into inconsistency, because from the motions of larger composite bodies he now chooses two, the descent of the heavy and the ascent of the light, and assigns them as primary motions to the atom; whereas he should, with his negative principles, attribute to the atom, as does the fable, a thoroughly *heterogeneous* motion, in keeping with the atom's thoroughly heterogeneous matter, that is to say, a motion which is not restricted to any of the specific types of motion to be found in composite bodies (*Works,* V, 292-94; X, 346-48).

So much for the negations of Night. The parable also hints that—since Night does not sit on the egg forever but only for a proper time of incubation—after exclusions and negations are to come affirmations. It thus cautions us that we are not to rely upon any purely indeterminate despoiled matter, devoid of form, meaning, and all else that is positive. For Cupid is not an abstraction but a person. The more ancient of the philosophers, it may be noted, attribute form and positive characteristics to the primary matter which Cupid in the parable represents and do not leave it merely abstract, unshapen, potential. The segregation of matter from form by such thinkers as Plato and Aristotle, who confound the theoretical separation of entities in disputation with inquiry into the most simple entities from which things are derived, ushers in the reign of pure forms, ideas, and essences in a fanciful world of abstractions. Once philosophers have denied all positive character to that matter out of which things come and through which they exist, it makes but little difference whether they believe that the world is made of what is indeterminate and inert, or of form and privation, or of any other fantastic nonreality.

The earlier philosophers, let it be repeated, no matter how greatly they disagree in other respects concerning the nature of the first reality, do "posit matter as active, as having some form, as dispensing that form, and as having the principle of motion within itself." And, indeed, any investigator who holds to experience and undertakes to account for the production and the movements of things, must be one with them in a refusal to separate matter, form, and motion. He will necessarily regard "the first matter as united to the first form, and likewise to the first principle of motion." Matter, motion, and form "are not to be separated, only distinguished. Matter (whatever it is) must be held to be so adorned, supplied, and formed, that all virtue, essence, action and natural motion, may be the consequence and emanation thereof" (*Works,* V, 294-99; X, 348-53).

Cupid is also said in the parable to be naked. Some philosophers, however, put a veil on him; some, a tunic; some, a mask; some, all three. One type of thinker will take as the explanation of nature a single principle and then argue that all the diversity which is found in things is due to the inconstant and variable character of the original unity. A second sort will see the principle of things as one in substance, and that fixed and invariable, and then derive the diversity of beings from the different magnitudes, figures, and positions which belong to this principle. A third will find two or more principles in nature and explain the diversity in things by the mixing of these principles and the tempering of one by others. A fourth will assert that the principles of nature are infinite, or at least greatly numerous and, since nature is found to be diversified from the beginning, give but little further explanation for the variety in things. Of these philosophers, the first type explain nothing. They merely throw a veil over Cupid. Thales, for example, with his principle of Water, Anaximenes with Air, and Heraclitus with Fire, either must assert an imaginary water, air, or fire—comparable in significance to the abstract "matter" of the Peripatetics—or must fall into the error, noted in Democritus' treatment of motion, of maintaining, as the primary factor in the explanation of all sorts of bodies, that which belongs specifically to certain kinds, and these of a composite nature. The third type, represented by Parmenides, with his two principles, Fire and Earth, and by his modern disciple Telesius, merely amplify the difficulty inherent in the theories of the first. They adorn Cupid not only with a veil but with a tunic as well. Those who hold the fourth view proceed even farther, and give, in addition to a cloak, a mask to the god who signifies the nature and virtue of the primary atom. Only the second type of philosophers represent him as he is—natural and naked (*Works,* V, 290–310 ff.; X, 353–64 ff.).

CHAPTER V

BACON'S MATERIALISM: ATOMS AND MOTION

THE first direct statement of the philosophical concepts by which Bacon would supplant Platonism and Aristotelianism is to be found in his *Cogitationes de natura rerum* ("Thoughts on the Nature of Things"). The exposition contained within this fragment which the author does not publish is far from complete—indeed, it is only a beginning; yet it serves to bring into sharp focus the presuppositions which determine the intense middle period of Bacon's philosophical thinking. Here he advances the theory of atoms as the explanation of things and their activities. The document opens with the observation that the doctrine of atoms which Democritus teaches is, if not adequate in all respects, a most useful explanation in philosophy. Indeed, says the author, it is not feasible to cope either in thought or in words with the subtlety of nature without the supposition of the atom. Eventually the question respecting the primary condition of atoms or seeds—here Bacon uses an alternative pre-Socratic term for the elements of things—turns out to be the most important question of philosophy; for it has to do with "the supreme rule of act and power, and the true moderation of hope and works."

The atom is defined in two ways: the first, by Democritus, as the smallest division of a body and the second, by Hero, as a body without vacuity. Democritus' interpretation involves two opinions: There are in things a division and a distribution of parts which escape the senses, and these parts are not perpetually or infinitely divisible. Hero, who attributes the second meaning to the atom, that is, a continuous body in opposition to a vacuum, denies the presence of a collected vacuum but acknowledges a vacuum interspersed in things. This thinker notes the constant nexus of bodies, and he finds no space where body is not. He also observes that bodies which are heavy will on occasion move upward and thus violate their own natures, so to speak, rather than endure separation from other bodies which are contiguous to them. As a consequence, he is convinced that nature abhors a collected vacuum. Again, he sees that the same body in expansion and contraction occupies unequal spaces, and he is unable to understand how the involved egress and ingress is possible unless by means of a vacuum interspersed through the body concerned.

In dealing with the last problem, Hero is faced with three alternatives. There may be, first, a reduction of an interspersed vacuum in proportion to the contraction; or, secondly, a forcing-out of a relatively finer body which is intermixed with the contracting body; or, thirdly, inherent condensation and rarefaction, as the Aristotelians would say, in the nature of the body concerned. Of these alternatives the last is certainly no explanation; it simply amounts to a pronouncement which relies, in turn, on something else which admits of no further explanation. To suppose, again, that in the contraction of a body a finer body which is intermixed with a coarser is squeezed out is to invite the further query whether, in the activity in question, there is squeezed out of this relatively finer body a still finer body and whether out of this, in turn, another, and so on *ad infinitum*. This second explanation would, moreover, run counter to the studied opinion that the finer the body the more capable it is of contraction. The third alternative, and this Hero chooses, is the hypothesis of a vacuum interspersed in bodies. If his explanation would seem incredible initially, it would be well to recall such examples as the coloring of a hogshead of water by a small amount of saffron which penetrates the whole body of liquid and the infecting of a body of air by an odor which diffuses itself everywhere.

Hero, having accepted an interspersed vacuum, and finding no evidence for another sort of vacuum in earthly things about him, is not content. He must go on to deny the existence of the collected vacuum anywhere. In so doing, he shows himself less a thinker than he should be— he is a mechanic rather than a philosopher. For he has not sufficient grounded observations to maintain that in the heavens, where there are doubtless greater expansions of body than in the earth, there cannot be a collected vacuum. In spite of this lapse, however, Hero is to be commended for his diligence in inquiry. And any infelicities which are to be found in his conclusions arise from the difficulties which inevitably pursue those who, refusing to take easy refuge in mere words and common theories, attempt to wrestle in dissection with experience, particulars, and the subtlety of nature.

In criticizing Hero, Bacon recognizes a difference in character between celestial and earthly bodies. But he takes pains to make clear, here and in the *Descriptio globi intellectualis* and in the *Thema coeli* as well, that he will not accept the traditional Aristotelian separation in *kind* between the natures of the two. Both, he says, have "common inclinations, passions, and motions."

But—to return to the question of the atoms or seeds of things—two accounts of these are generally entertained, one by Democritus who attributes to atoms inequality, configuration, and—through configuration—position; the other, probably by Pythagoras, which makes atoms equal and similar. We say probably by Pythagoras because this thinker explains all things according to numbers, and "he who assigns equality to atoms necessarily places all things in numbers." The question of choice between these two alternative accounts could probably be determined by the solution of a certain practical problem—one, it seems, which is broached by Democritus himself, who asks whether all things may be made out of all things. Democritus apparently believes that an answer in the affirmative is unreasonable and accepts diversity among atoms. Actually neither he nor any other philosopher has adequately stated the whole problem of the transmutation of bodies. The question is commonly construed in terms of immediate transmutation, to the neglect of the essential question whether all things may not pass through "circuits and intermediate changes." Certainly the similar seeds of things—we acknowledge them to be similar—when they are thrown together in certain groups and knots, take on the natures of dissimilar bodies; and these natures they retain until the groups or knots are dissolved. As a consequence, within any inquiry into transmutation the natures and "passions" of compound bodies become matters equally important with simple bodies themselves.

The question of the relation between separation and alteration in bodies is significant not only for the light it may shed on the character of the atom but in its own right in that, while its answer depends in the last analysis on the discovery of the nature of the atom, it itself approaches more immediately "to things and works." In handling this problem, a common error—and this has received considerable increase from the theories of the chemists—is that of attributing to the separation of parts of supposedly different sorts of body what is due to something else. For instance, it is said that in the case of the burning of wood the finer part of the body escapes in the flames, while the grosser remains in the ashes. How misleading this example is may be seen by taking others, say, the burning oil of lamps or burning tallow of candles. In these instances all the fat becomes volatile without a deposit of ashes, and soot is generated after the burning and not before. Soot is the carcass, so to speak, of the flame, and not a remaining sediment of that oil or tallow which is consumed. Such illustrations need not be pursued further, however; they are introduced merely to prepare the way for our overthrow of Democritus' doctrine of diversity within the nature of atoms. What we are anxious to deny is the notion that the alterations in things are caused by the separation of different sorts of bodies, because we believe that the matter which constitutes things is composed of similar parts and is "invested with such a nature, of which it may be truly said that one body contains more of it, and another (though filling the same measure) less" (*Works*, V, 204–9, 213–14, 215, 228; VII, 316, 355; X, 287–93, 298, 300, 313, 434, 474–75).

The next major question concerns motion. This is a subject which has been handled in a most unsatisfactory way by philosophers, notwithstanding the fact that motion is universal in all bodies. "Simple and absolute rest.... there is none; but in fact what is thought to be rest is the product of hindrances, restrainings, and equilibriums of motions." For example, when the stronger wrestler holds the other down, the motion of the weaker is present nonetheless, even if it does not prevail. Through the motions of nature matter is composed, decomposed, and composed again. Through the motions of art matter is brought under constraint to the production of works. But no efficient, either in production or destruction, adds to or subtracts from matter. Its sum remains the same. Only God can create or destroy. In order that matter should become less, the Creator would have to intervene.

Philosophers, in treating of motion, have been preoccupied in the main with theoretical distinctions which lend themselves to disputation but leave no issue in works. Investigators look for inert principles and overlook the virtues of matter. They inspect the corpse of Nature after her work has been effected and forget her active faculties. In seeking to know the components of things, they remain ignorant of the powers and the processes which bring bodies and their elements into being and operation. Look for a moment at the alternate account of motion given in a parade of philosophers, Aristotelians, Platonists, Anaxagoreans, Democriteans, Empedocleans, Parmenideans, Pythagoreans, Paracelsans, chemists. "The stimulus of matter by privation, of the forming of matter according to an idea, of the aggregation of similar particles, of the fortuitous agitation of atoms in a vacuum, of strife and friendship, of reciprocal impressions of heaven and earth, of alliance of the elements by symbolizing qualities, of the influence of celestial bodies, of the sympathy and antipathy of things, of occult and specific virtues and properties, of fate, fortune, necessity..... Such generalities are mere spectres and shadows on the surface of things." They may serve to fill the imagination of the learned, but they provide neither understanding of nature's way nor direction for the mutation of bodies and the production of works. And of what greater use are the accepted divisions between "motion from without" and "motion from within," between "natural" and "violent" motion —Aristotelians, when they contribute a set of verbal distinctions, think that they have solved a problem!

The philosopher's duty is, of course, to make inquiry into the actual motions of bodies. Enough verbal defining has been done. The time has come to proceed to an investigation which is based on observation and experiment of those "appetites and inclinations by which all that variety of effects and changes which we see in the works of nature and art is made and brought about." Bodies can be transformed through an understanding of the effect of increase or decrease in specific types of natural motion. The true knowledge of motion, its kinds and their efficacies, is the real means to the constraint of Proteus. Traditional accounts of motion are of little help in the understanding and control of nature. They are logical and popular. At best, they indicate only effects and not the means of operation. Generation, corruption, augmentation, diminution, alteration, carriage to place—such terms mark in an obvious manner nothing more than the end of operation after it has taken place. They indicate what has been done but manifest nothing of the manner of its accomplishment. The motions which they signify are not simple but are the results of other motions in combination.

What philosophy requires, then, or rather what is required of philosophy, is not learned disputes about accepted terms, not an increase of verbal distinctions, but a solid investigation into "the principles, sources, causes, and forms of motions, that is, the appetites and passions of every kind of matter . . . . and in turn the impressions or impulses of motions, the restraints and reluctations, the passages and obstructions, the alterations and mixtures, the circuits and series; in a word, the universal process of motions." When the philosopher knows these, he will be able "to excite, restrain, increase, remit, multiply, calm and stop any motion whatever in matter susceptible of it; and thereby to preserve, change, and transform bodies." He will no longer be restricted in the production of works by occasional observation, mere chance, and local materials specially prepared. He will have nature's resources at his disposal, for he will have acquired the knowledge of the simple motions common to natural bodies, out of which compound motions are composed, decomposed, and again composed. Even as the words of a language are made up of relatively few simple letters, so are the actions and powers of things constituted of relatively few natures and primary simple motions. And therefore a shame it is that men should have studied with care the tinklings of their own voices and be ignorant of the voice of nature—just as in the primitive days of the world, before the invention of letters, only composite sounds were discerned, and the elements of these were left unrecognized (*Works,* V, 209-18, 222; X, 293-302, 307; *vide* I, 462; IV, 29-30; VI, 74; VIII, 278; X, 179-80).

Bacon's thinking in his *Cogitationes de natura rerum* is obviously dominated, as it is in the middle period of his writing generally, by the problem of motion. Motion is the subject of his first attempt, announced in the *Commentarius solutus* of 1608, to provide a "table" of discovered knowledge. As much of this inquiry as he is able to pursue—it is scarcely more than a list of types of motion—he sets down under the title *Filum labyrinthi; sive inquisitio legitima de motu.* Apparently he hopes at the time this investigation is entertained that a solution of the problem of motion will reveal the thread of the labyrinth of nature and furnish a key to the interpretation of bodies. The later *Descriptio globi intellectualis* and *Thema coeli* of 1612 give prominence to the same problem. In the first of these the author classifies the activities of nature under generations in her regular course, pretergenerations of "monsters" in her erring, and the production of arts when under constraint. He lists five topics within generations: celestial bodies, meteors, earth and sea, "major colleges" or elementary masses, and "minor colleges" or species. And he names a sixth, the primary virtues of bodies, which he says here, as also in the *Novum organum* and *Parasceve,* is to be reserved for special treatment. Of these six he selects for philosophical consideration celestial bodies and then resolves the problems of their disposition into problems respecting their motions.

Initially he asks five questions: Is there a celestial system? If there is, what is its center? Is there a depth between its parts? What is their connection? And what are their respective positions or order? He assumes that of these several inquiries the first depends on another, whether the earth stands still or revolves, and the second and third on the respective movements of the planets concerned. The fourth resolves itself into a preference for a vacuum, contiguity, or continuity. If a vacuum amounting to a "solution of continuity" in the system is rejected, the problem comes to this: "whether the differences in the tract of pure air insinuate themselves gradually and with a continuous flow; or whether they are constituted and distributed at certain distinguishable limits." The answer to the fifth question respecting the positions and the order of the several parts depends on whether there are in the system "many centres and so to speak many dances" (*Works,* VII, 287–89, 292–94, 298–313; X, 406–7, 411–13, 418–31).

At the beginning of the *Thema coeli* the author announces his intention to discuss the nature of "the universe." He will proceed to do this, he says, by propounding "some things respecting the matter of the heavenly bodies, whereby their motion and construction may be the better understood; and then bring forward.... views concerning the motion itself, which is now the principal question." He divides the motions of the heavens into two sorts: first, cosmical motions, which celestial bodies get through the co-operation of the heavens and of the universe as well; and, secondly, reciprocal motions in which celestial bodies depend on other celestial bodies. And having prepared the way by an attack on astronomers, mainly on the Aristotelians, he concludes the fragment with a listing and brief examination of four sorts of greater motions in the heavens, "motion through the depth of heaven, upward and downward; motion through the latitude of the zodiac, deviating to south and north; motion in the direction of the zodiac, rapid, slow, progressive, retrograde, and stationary; and motion of elongation from the sun" (*Works,* VII, 344, 348–50, 357–58; X, 463, 468–69, 478; cf. IV, 262; V, 213; X, 262, 298).

We have already seen enough of Bacon's doctrine concerning nature to discern the pre-eminence in his philosophic scheme of a certain sort of motion. This is local motion. In taking this as the philosophical explanation of activity and change, the author is, of course, no more and no less than a disciple of Democritus. He is consistent in his thought when he casts away the doctrines of change and motion which the Platonists and Peripatetics entertain. For the Platonists, discernible change is the relinquishing of one disembodied form and the participation in another disembodied form. Motion according to the Peripatetics includes several sorts: generation and decay, increase and decrease, change in character, and carriage to place; and each kind, even carriage to place, involves the merging of form with indeterminate matter, the passing from potency to act, the supplanting of privation by an actualized form in matter through the attainment of a *telos* which, as "final" cause, is the explanation of the process. According to Bacon all activity is to be explained as the local juxtaposition of parts of matter.

This interpretation of motion has already been instanced in his treatment of the atom, the vacuum, condensation, and rarefaction. He says, also, in his early *Valerius Terminus* that the colors of things are said to be caused by "the position of the solid portions .... of some magnitude." In the fragmentary *Historia soni et auditus* of 1608 he poses for "diligent inquiry" the question of "the relation and correspondence which sound has to the local motion of air." Heat, the subject of his *Inquisitio legitima de calore et frigore* of the same year, is explained in his *Novum organum* of 1620 as an "expansive motion" acting in the contact of strife upon matter. And, while arguing in the *Descriptio globi intellectualis* of 1612 against the Peripatetic separation of nature and art, Bacon claims "that things artificial differ from things natural, not in form or essence, but only in the efficient; that man has in truth no power over things, except that of motion—the power plainly of putting natural bodies together or separating them. Wherever it is becoming *to move natural bodies towards one another or away from one another,* man and art can do everything; where it is not appropriate they can do nothing." And in the Preface to *Historia gravis et levis* within the *Historia naturalis et experimentalis* (1623) having stated "it is quite certain that a body is affected only by a body," he adds "there is no local motion which is not instigated either by the parts of the body moved, or by the adjacent bodies, or by those contiguous or proximate to it, or at least by those which lie within the orbit of its activity" (*Works,* I, 397; III, 300; VI, 56; VII, 220, 289; VIII, 217; IX, 468; X, 408).

When Bacon writes his *Inquisitio de motu,* he expects, apparently, that a knowledge of motion will provide the clue to the "labyrinth" of nature. In the earlier *Advancement of Learning,* in which he stresses, as he does in the *Valerius Terminus,* abstract natures, he teaches that knowledge is to culminate in the summary law of nature. This law is construed in the *De sapientia veterum* as the primary motion of matter. In the *Cogitationes de natura rerum* the author begins with simple natures and then proceeds to simple motions; and here too he hopes to find in the simple motions of bodies that alphabet of nature by which investigators may be enabled to decipher "all the actions and powers of things" (V, 213; VI, 62–63, 220; X, 297).

However, sometime between the writing of the *De sapientia veterum* and the preparation of works for the Instauration, at least as early as the *Descriptio globi intellectualis* and the *Thema coeli,* the earlier emphasis on motion undergoes modification; and, finally, in the works of the Instauration proper the activities of bodies take a subsidiary place in explanation to their component natures and forms. The change in stress, and the change is not without relapse, becomes noticeable when one compares the earlier treatment of the fable of "Cupid, or the Atom" in the *De sapientia veterum* with the later treatment in *De principiis atque originibus.* In the former work emphasis is all upon movement. Cupid represents the appetite, motion, or instinct of primal matter. As an egg of Night he signifies "the impulse of desire given to the primary particles of matter." In the latter fragment, however, Cupid is said to represent the nature of atoms or first elements as well as their virtues. "Primary matter, together with its properties" is distinguished in treatment from matter's motion. Matter is prior, "self-subsisting," "adorned, furnished, and formed"; "virtue.... action, and natural motion" are its "consequence and emanation." Again, in the later work Cupid's origin in the egg of Night signifies not only the lack of ability in the human mind to comprehend the summary law of nature, but also the procedure of knowledge by "exclusions and negatives," in contradistinction to "affirmatives." And the latter is significantly an integral part of the method which Bacon is to use in the *Novum organum* when he searches for the forms of things as distinct from their mere motions. And it is noteworthy that, in illustrating this part of his method in the *De principiis et originibus,* he separates the nature of atoms or seeds from their powers and virtues.

In the *Descriptio globi intellectualis* and the *Thema coeli* the author deals largely with the heavenly bodies by way of their motions; yet he does segregate doctrines concerning "the matter of heavenly bodies, whereby their motion and construction may be the better understood" from "views respecting the motion itself"; and he seems definitely to recognize the celestial system as in some sense prior in nature and character to its activities. In his mature *Novum organum* and the *De augmentis* in 1623, while Bacon lists the simple motions which make up the complex motions—he includes some nineteen in the former piece and some fifteen in the latter—he places by far a greater stress on forms. It is these forms, and not simple motions, which are now said by him to constitute the alphabet of nature. Not that he intends in the late writings to supplant the earlier doctrine which stresses motion by one of fixed formal abstractions—for this would mean a capitulation to Platonism or Aristotelianism—but rather because he finally comes, as we shall see, to regard forms both as the constituents of things and as the laws of their activity (*Works,* I, 488 ff.; II, 282-83; V, 293-94, 296-99; VII, 344-45; VIII, 315 ff., 344 ff.; X, 346-47, 351-53, 463-64).

CHAPTER VI

THE EARLIER FORMULARY OF INTERPRETATION

A FURTHER project which dominates Bacon's thought from his first dissatisfaction with the practices of the Aristotelians is the provision of a new method of investigation. In his early "Praise of Knowledge" he describes the conclusions reached through the method employed by the Schools as purely theoretical and altogether inoperative when put to the test of utility. These consist merely of "common notions" knit together by a refined discourse. The logic in vogue permits the human understanding to range at will and then suddenly to fly up to the most highly abstract "first principles," which, when once enunciated, dominate all further conceptions. This art encourages the mind of man to regard itself as the measure of things, when, actually, "the mind itself is but an accident to knowledge, for knowledge is a double of that which is." A crying need of learning, then, is for a new sort of method, an inductive logic, which will control the understanding and bring it into functional relation with the universe.

Bacon in several writings describes the new logic under various names. He calls it a "clear and radiant light" which will supplant the "feeble and pale lamps" of the past, "the formulary of interpretation," "the art of discovery and invention," "the thread of the labyrinth," "the key of interpretation," and a "machine" constructed to control and to aid the capacities of man. It is a new organon which will render the antiquated method of Aristotle obsolete (*Works*, I, 206, 536; II, 362; V, 177, 452; VI, 69, 261, 416; VII, 16, 93, 142; VIII, 33, 347, 354; IX, 64).

The title itself of the early *Temporis partus masculus* ("The Masculine—or Fertilizing—Birth of Time"), we are informed by a statement in the *Cogitata et visa,* refers to this new method of science. The former piece lists at the beginning, as one of three books to be completed, "The Light of Nature, or Rule of Interpretation." In the second "chapter" of the extant fragment this rule is described as "one clear and radiant light of truth" and hailed as the lamp of learning which when placed in the midst of knowledge will "illumine all, and in an instant dispel all errors." The *De interpretatione naturae prooemium* of 1603 merely mentions a "machine" for the interpretation of nature. In the *Valerius Terminus* of the same year Bacon stresses several errors which have been made by those of the past and present who "have descended and applied themselves to experience, and attempted to induce knowledge upon particulars." First, he says, they have not had sufficient resolution and strength of mind to free themselves from theoretical "anticipations" of nature, either from those received in tradition or from those which present themselves to the mind after a short period of observation and experiment, "but have from particulars and history flown up to principles without the mean degrees, and so framed all the middle generalities or axioms, not by way of scale or ascension from particulars, but by way of derivation from principles; whence hath issued the infinite chaos of shadows.... wherewith both books and minds have been hitherto, and may be hereafter much more pestered." When in the course of this derivation "any light of new instance appeared" they have chosen "rather to reconcile the instance, than to amend the rule." Again, those who have been "conversant in experience and observation" have fixed their "consideration" on an immediate effect in immediate circumstances. They have not broken things according to the "natures" of which these are compounded; have concluded "upon inductions in gross, which empirical course is no less vain than the scholastical"; have sought "action and work.... for present use," and have not set as the object of inquiry the discovery of axioms. Through their refusal to be inhibited in the beginning, they have attained no profitable rule for invention in the end. Their collecting of "natural history" has been "weak" without sufficiency in its quantity, variety, subtlety, and "without those advantages and discretions in the entry and sorting which are requisite." Lastly, they have had "no knowledge of the formulary of interpretation." This is the method which, bringing, as it does, aids and control to human faculties, will "abridge experience and.... make things as certainly found out by Axiom in short time, as by infinite experience in ages" (*Works*, VI, 66–69; VII, 29, 89, 128).

The end and the test of the new method is operation. "All knowledge.... is to be referred to use and action." "In deciding and determining the truth of knowledge.... the discovery of new works and active directions not known before, is the only trial to be accepted of . . . . where particulars induce an axiom or observation, which axiom found out discovereth and designeth new particulars." Moreover, "the nature of this trial is not only upon the point, whether the knowledge be profitable or no, but even upon the point, whether the knowledge be true or no; not because you may always conclude that the axiom which discovereth new instances is true, but contrariwise you may safely conclude that if it discover not any new instance it is vain and untrue." Yet, while the aim of science is the production of works, the object of its "search" is not the "causes and productions of things concrete, which are infinite and transitory," but "abstract natures, which are few and permanent." In the search for these, particulars are to be reduced "by exclusions and inclusions to a definite point."

To discern only the causes of concrete things is to be limited in operation by local efficients governed by particular circumstances. To know abstract natures is to possess both "certainty and liberty" in direction "to work and produce effects." Operation through knowledge is possible when the direction satisfies the two conditions, "certainty and liberty." "Certainty is when the direction is not only true for the most part, but infallible. Liberty is when the direction is not restrained to some definite means, but comprehendeth all the means and ways possible." That is to say, if the "direction be certain, it must refer you and point you to somewhat which, if it be present, the effect you seek will of necessity follow, else may you perform and not obtain. If it be free, then must it refer you to somewhat which if it be absent the effect you seek will of necessity withdraw, else may you have power and not attempt" (*Works*, VI, 51–53, 62–63; cf. VII, 131).

The foregoing doctrine, observes Bacon, Aristotle had "in light though not in use." His rules, according to which the axioms of science are made convertible and named by the "latter men" (the Ramists) the "rule of truth" and the "rule of prudence," "are the same thing in speculation and affirmation which we now observe." Bacon is referring here to the distinction which Aristotle makes between two sorts of predication. In the former of these the predicate may be asserted of all the examples of the subject, and in the latter the predicate may be both so asserted and also affirmed of the subject as that which the subject may be said to be. In the latter case the proposition is convertible; one may say, for example, both that a triangle is a three-sided figure whose angles are equal to two right angles and that a three-sided figure whose angles are equal to two right angles is a triangle. Aristotle, however, does not by any means regard the demonstrable assertions generally of science as convertible propositions. (Because one can say that all crows are black things, one cannot necessarily say that all black things are crows). The followers of Ramus criticize Aristotle for his failure to do so. Apparently Bacon is, to a point, in agreement with them, although he generally condemns their attempts to provide a substitute for Aristotle's logic. He seems to adopt two of their rules of proof: first, that the established proposition must in all instances be true—the Ramist rule of "truth"; and secondly, that the converse of a true axiom must also be in a sense true—the Ramist rule of "prudence." Bacon regards the first purpose of investigation as the discovery of a "nature," which is what in an "axiom" of truth the object may be said to be. That is to say, the "nature" of the affirmed object is in knowledge and in operation convertible with that object. Operation follows when the "nature" is present and is absent when the "nature" is absent. This is why for him the engendering of a work in practice can be made the test of the truth of the proposition which in knowledge asserts the presence in the object of the engendering "nature" concerned (*Works*, VI, 51, 62-63).

Bacon undertakes to provide an illustration of what he means by "certainty" and "liberty" in direction for the production of an infallible and universal effect, that is to say, for an effect which is not restricted to local means but which comprehends "all the means and ways possible." Let whiteness, he says, be the effect desired. And let the first "direction" be the intermingling of water and air, as in foam or snow. From this intermingling, whiteness will ensue. Here the direction is certain but without liberty, since it is particular and restrained, being tied to air and water. This first direction may, however, be freed from water if left tied to air by a second direction, namely, the pounding to a white powder of an uncolored transparent body "more grossly transparent than air itself," such as glass or crystal. By a third direction the restraint of the uncolored body may be removed, as in the use of amber and sapphires, for instance, which, when beaten, have whiteness, as have also the froth of wine and beer. A fourth direction will "exclude the restraint of a body more grossly transparent than air" by using flame, which "were it not for the smoke.... would be more perfect white." In all these four directions air has a part; yet, by a fifth direction this restraint also may be removed, by the combining of oil and water in an ointment, for instance, or by the placing of powdered glass in water.

So far, the direction in the production of whiteness is freed from air, but it is still tied to transparents. Having noted this fact, the author refuses to give further directions. "To ascend further by scale," he says, "I do forbear, partly because it would draw on the example to an over-great length, but chiefly because it would open that which in this work I determine to reserve..... Our purpose is now to give an example of a free direction, thereby to distinguish and describe it; and not to set down a form of interpretation how to recover and attain it." Later, however, he mentions, but does not describe, a sixth sort of "direction." He also distinguishes between whiteness as something inherent in an object and as appearance to the senses. With this latter complication of the problem he decides not to deal and reserves an explanation which, he tells the reader, would "open that which I think good to withdraw" (*Works,* VI, 54-58).

Having set down this much of the working of his formulary of interpretation, Bacon goes on to acknowledge that his method, "as far as a swimming anticipation could take hold" is to be found in the philosophies of Plato and Aristotle. These writers employ it, however, merely in a "wandering" manner. Plato seeks to "divide and define" things according to their *"true forms and differences";* but he relies in his attempts, as examples in his writings show, on nothing more substantial than mere "anticipations." The School of Aristotle confess that there is "no true knowledge but by causes, no true cause but the form, no true form known except one." Thus far their contention is correct; but the means of demonstration which they employ in their efforts to reach causes carry them merely from one more general notional abstraction to a less general. They end with nothing but shadows. Their science is verbal and not operative. It becomes necessary, then, the Aristotelian dominance of contemporary science considered, to set down a general rule and three notes of caution. The rule is as follows: "Though your direction seem to be certain and true by pointing you to a nature that is unseparable from the nature you inquire upon, yet if it do not carry you on to a degree or remove nearer to action, operation, or light to make or produce, it is but superficial and counterfeit." The first note of caution is "that the nature discovered be more original than the nature supposed." That is to say, the explanation of the "nature" under investigation is to be sought, not in "properties, effects, circumstances, concurrences, or what else you shall like to call them," but in "radical and formative natures." The second is "that the nature inquired be collected by division before composition, or to speak more properly, by composition subaltern before you ascend to composition absolute." By this Bacon means—if we may interpret his earlier formulary through his later exposition of induction in the *Novum organum*—that, even as the more general nature stands to the less in the relation of genus to species, inquiry is to be made into less general natures before a more general nature, which eventually is to explain this and other lesser natures, is sought. The third note of caution is not given; and the discussion is brought to an abrupt conclusion (*Works,* VI, 58–61).

Bacon's next attempt to furnish an inductive method is recorded in his *Partis instaurationis secundae delineatio et argumentum* ("Outline and Argument of the Second Part of the Instauration") of 1607. Here he sets forth in considerable detail the groundwork of a new sort of logic which, he says, is different from the accepted Aristotelian analytic in three respects: in the point of departure, the order of demonstration, and the end or purpose served. This new method of discovery brings into question, he explains, things which the older discipline takes for granted, namely, general principles and the information of the senses. Secondly, its order of demonstration is not downward from more general principles through middle propositions to less general principles but upward in a continuous scale from particulars to less general axioms and then to more general and more inclusive axioms. Thirdly, its end is a knowledge of things and the operation of works and not mere argument and discourse (*Works,* VII, 41–43).

To begin scientific investigation with the inquisition of individual facts will, the author continues, undoubtedly appear to many philosophers as the plunging of the mind into a Tartarus of confusion or the consigning of the understanding to the interminable waves of infinite particulars. Yet, actually, the submitting of the mind to empirical experience is not nearly so dangerous as is the subjecting of it to the whirl, gyration, and agitation of abstract speculation and meditation. In fact, when we say that investigation begins and ends with particulars, we do not mean mere particulars but particulars as understood in notions and axioms. For knowledge begins with the introduction into indiscriminate particulars of significant determination. Yet, while this is so, investigation must start from individuals and go forward from these to notions and intermediate axioms. Somewhere between high generality and indeterminate particularity knowledge lies.

Of the two alternate ways of philosophizing, the new logic chooses the harder. To begin, as the old analytic does, with most general axioms, and from these to deduce less general propositions is easy. To control the understanding when it would soar to first principles, to keep it conversant with actual particulars, and from these to lead it gradually to solid axioms is difficult. The former procedure ends, we repeat, in idle speculation, while the latter attains an understanding of things and issues in the operation of works (*Works,* VII, 44–46).

So much by way of introduction. The rules or directions which aid and control the human mind in its ascending interpretation of nature are of three sorts: aids to sense, aids to memory, and aids to reason. The first provide the sense with material for their function, with assistance where they are deficient, and with direction where they err. The purpose of these helps is threefold. First, they serve in the elicitation of a good notion. Knowledge, while constituted of axioms, is based on good notions properly elicited from sense; and to obtain these the testimony of sense, which is ever after the analogy of man, must, through direction, be brought into relation with the universe of things. In the search for good notions no great weight is to be attached to the mere unaided senses beyond the direct evidence they provide of motion or change in the things perceived. Secondly, aids to sense provide for the bringing-under-observation of objects which—because of the minuteness of their parts, their remoteness in distance, extreme slowness or swiftness of motion, subtlety, or familiarity—escape ordinary sight. To this end are required artificial instruments and directions for watching such things as gradations of speed from very slow or very fast to moderate and for drawing analogies between those characteristics of bodies immediately available to the senses and those which are hidden from them. The third sort of aids to sense are rules for the observation of experiments and the recording of the data of natural history generally in such a manner that the more pertinent materials of science may be apprehended by the mind (*Works,* VII, 48).

Aids to memory serve for the extracting, out of the relative disorder of a heap of natural history, of a particular history so arranged that the judgment can act upon it. Among the weaknesses of the human mind are an incapability of containing the infinity of things and a lack of skill, when left to itself, for making a selection of things which may properly be assigned to any definite area of inquiry. The first of these deficiencies may be treated by the prescription that no inquiry or discovery is to be entertained unless it is submitted in writing. If accounts which require a daybook cannot be kept by rote, much less can the data of experience and the various stages of inquiry which enter into their interpretation.

With the second deficiency of the memory greater pains are to be taken. This can be remedied by three sorts of aid, first, by topics or points (*loci*); secondly, by tabulation; and thirdly, by the renewal and repetition of inquiry. In the first instance, on the mind's running over natural history with the subject given or proposed in view, certain topics will be found to be proper objects of inquiry. Next, these topics should be set forth in an orderly way in separate tables. At the beginning, of course, the subject matter of inquiry will hardly be arranged according to the structure of things investigated. Yet the dividing of data into significant parts is necessary, even if initially the divisions are rather of appearance than of reality: for truth emerges the sooner from falsehood than from confusion, and reason can the more easily rectify false divisions than penetrate a chaotic meaningless mass of things. And, finally, provision should be made for a moving-forward of tables or charts to new charts along with a repetition of investigation. The first series of charts resultant upon inquiry are to be regarded as movable ends of axes, that is, as trials and attempts at proof, since obviously the mind cannot be expected to obtain its lawful right over nature without repetition of suit (*Works*, VII, 49-50).

Aids to sense and to memory are both subsidiary to the office of reason. Knowledge consists in axioms. Unless, then, reason acts, no truth can be known. Preceding the axioms of science come simple notions and a natural history which is founded in sense and disposed by memory for the operation of reason. The office of this third faculty, although one in nature, is twofold in aim. The end of man is either to know and contemplate or to act and make. First, he understands the causes of a given nature or effect; and, secondly, on a given basis of matter he imposes or superinduces an effect or nature within the limits of possibility. These two procedures, when closely inspected and properly estimated, are seen to meet in one, because what in contemplation is taken as cause may in operation be taken as means. Man knows through causes and operates by means.

Aids to the reason further, then, its contemplative and operative offices. The former office is the forming of a true axiom, which in turn is the connecting of ideas. A simple independent notion is only the surface of that truth of which the axiom is the solid portion. The axiom can be elicited and formed only by a legitimate induction which breaks experience into parts and, by means of apt exclusions and rejections, arrives at necessary conclusions. In this ministration of rejection the new logic differs from that of the Schools by the stress it lays upon exclusions or negative instances. The Scholastic induction operates only by the examination of positive instances of phenomena, and its conclusions are, therefore, upset by single contradictory instances (*Works,* VII, 50–51).

Knowledge begins with particulars, moves by ways of notions to slightly general propositions, and from these in turn progresses by unbroken scale of ascent to higher and more general axioms. Toward its assistance in this proceeding three rules may be given, namely, the Continuation, the Variation, and the Contraction of Inquiry. In the Continuation of Inquiry, lesser axioms are employed for the searching-out of those of a higher and more general sort (granting that the former have already been established through the Rule of Interpretation), so that by an unbroken succession of true steps in ascent the unity of nature may be reached.

Variation of Inquiry brings the causes of things under reckoning. In the inquiry of causes forms come first—not final causes, the search for which has thoroughly corrupted natural philosophy. After forms come efficients and matters. By efficient is meant an efficient special and immediate to the operation concerned and not a remote efficient. By a matter is meant matter present, available, and equipped with definite character —not that unascertainable, indeterminate matter about which the Schools dispute. Next follow latent processes in the ordered series of change which is induced through the agency of efficients and the movement in matter which results from this agency. So far as things themselves are concerned, Variation of Inquiry is determined by the relative simplicity or complexity of the subject matter under consideration as well as the relative abundance or scarcity of the history prepared and made available for the inquiry. One sort of investigation is adapted to things simple, another to things intricate, another to things in composition or in decomposition. In each of these cases, when the history is plentiful, the inquiry proceeds freely and expeditiously; when it is thin and scant, the inquirer labors within straits.

Contraction of Inquiry both makes a way through pathless areas and also cuts a direct road, as it were, across windings and turnings. It is definitely an abridging of investigation and, like every abridging, proceeds mainly through the selecting of objects. The special objects which enable it to operate are such as carry the prerogative of sovereignty. This prerogative is to be found in the Prerogative of the Instance and the Prerogative of That Inquired Into. Therefore, in the act of investigation attention is to be directed to certain instances of things or experiments which may illuminate the subject under investigation more than would a multitude of others, and thus serve to obviate much labor of running to and fro in the amassing of natural history; and emphasis is to be placed also on those objects which, because of their great certainty, their universality, and their indispensability in mechanical trials, serve to dominate others (*Works,* VII, 51–54).

So far, we have been concerned with the ministration to the contemplative reason. Directions for reason in its active or operative function include two warnings and three positive doctrines. The first of the warnings is this: The active part of reason must have a continuous intercommunication with the contemplative part, that is, with a truth established according to the rules already indicated. Such a truth consists of axioms obtained through an examination of existent things. Any attempt to apply to particulars and works truths derived from general axioms obtained initially by logical argumentation from theoretical principles will prove uncertain and fantastic.

The second warning is to this effect: The inquirer should bear in mind that, while the contemplative function of reason proceeds by way of ascent from particulars to lesser axioms and then to axioms of a more general sort, the operative office is exercised through a scale of descent. Operation takes place in individual things, and these in knowledge are at the bottom of all. Hence, for operation, the steps which lie between general axioms and particulars must be descended. Moreover, descent is not to be made from single axioms, because every work, as well as the manner of performing it, is resolved upon, and designed through, the connecting of more axioms than one.

The doctrines of aid for active reason are three. The first includes a distinct and appropriate form of inquiry in which the end in view is not the establishing of axioms but the effecting of operation. The second exhibits a method of compiling tables for practice, from which designs for all sorts of works may the more quickly and easily be obtained. While the third shows a way to the discovery and invention of new works from observations of extant works. It will be found that there is a means of operation which moves from one experiment to another without proceeding meanwhile to the establishing of axioms. By this passing from experiment to experiment without an initial ascent to axiom and then a descent to particulars there is opened up a way which, however unsteady and hazardous it may be, is not to be passed over in silence. "And," states Bacon, "this to this point is a plain and brief sketch of the Second Book" (*Works,* VII, 54–55).

The exposition of method in the *Delineatio* goes considerably beyond that of the *Valerius Terminus.* In the earlier piece the Rule of Interpretation operates in the discovery of convertible propositions; and the validity of a proposition is attested, as it is also according to the later *Cogitata et visa,* purely and simply by the pragmatic test of effective operation in works. The *Delineatio* separates, however, the contemplative function of knowledge from the operative. In the *Valerius Terminus* the search for an axiom is presented through an elementary attempt at an exemplary segregation of a notion. The *Delineatio* indicates several means for the control of sense, memory, and reason in the establishment of axioms, which are connected with particulars in a scale of both ascent and descent. It avowedly makes knowledge a matter of definition, in which the first stage is the proper "determination," somewhere between general axioms and infinite particulars, of the notion. Bacon's stress on this gathering from particulars of a good notion as a major task in scientific proof marks, as we shall have occasion to note later, a departure from the Aristotelian logic. For Aristotle, proof is the deduction within the framework of the syllogism of a less general proposition from a more general through the agency of a middle term which is used in a universal manner in one, at least, of the propositions. Yet Aristotle provides no directions in his organon for the eliciting from the experience of particulars the notion represented by this middle term. Bacon is aware of the problem of making good what he considers this fundamental deficiency in Aristotle's logic—not that he believes that an independent notion by itself constitutes scientific knowledge, for such an isolated notion is, he says, no more than a "surface" in comparison with the solid body which is truth.

CHAPTER VII

THE VANITIES AND ERRORS OF LEARNING

THERE still remains another project of Bacon which is preparatory to his Great Instauration, namely, the refutation of past and prevailing "learning." Bacon's refutation of this is varied and complex. For purposes of exposition it may be divided into three parts. First, he gives an account of the "errors and vanities which have intervened amongst the studies themselves of the learned"; secondly, an analysis of the prepossessions of the learned mind which have "distorted and tinged its notions and impressions"; and thirdly, an assessment of the methods and the concepts of historical philosophers.

The major "distempers" of learning, says the author, are three: "the first, fantastical learning; the second, contentious learning; and the last, delicate learning; vain imaginations, vain altercations, and vain affectations." The first of these is found where men concern themselves with words and not matter, that is to say, predominantly with texts, language, style, and correct reading and annotation of authors. In modern times, argues Bacon, this distemper has been increased by the eager return on the part of Reformers to ancient authors, pagan and Christian, in order to discover therein means for attack on Scholastic doctrine. Learning, with this revival of the ancients, becomes characterized by "the admiration of ancient authors, the hate of the Schoolmen, the exact study of languages," and an insistence upon the "efficacy of preaching"—this last "because the great labour" is "with the people." The concurring of these four causes often makes scholars "hunt more after words than matter, and more after the choiceness of the phrase . . . . than after the weight of matter"; with the consequence that learning in many instances becomes "delicate"—"rather towards copy than weight." Erasmus can claim ten years' devotion to Cicero, and Ascham and Car of Cambridge come almost to deify Cicero and Demosthenes. Scholars take great pains to know the ancient rhetoricians. Every quirk of ancient style is noted. Speakers undertake to be persuasive by means of the vanities of eloquence; and the multiplication of trope, figure, and coinage of speech generally takes ascendancy over the "lawfulness of the phrase or word" (*Works*, VI, 118 ff.).

The second distemper of learning is worse than the first, even as "vain matter is worse than vain words." It consists in the construing of wisdom as traditional opinion and of proof as the assumption of fixed "positions" for defense in contentious argumentation. The third, which is the worst of all three, consists in the imposture of authors and the credulity of readers and listeners. It is because of this weakness of the learned that Aristotle is accepted at his own valuation as the dictator of the sciences (*Works*, II, 124–25; VI, 117–129).

Along with the three major diseases or vices of learning go several "peccant humours," not so "intrinsic" as these, not "formed diseases," yet nevertheless real distempers. Chief among these minor vices are "the two extreme humours of admiration of antiquity, and love of novelty." "Antiquity envieth there should be new additions, and novelty cannot be content to add but it must deface." Certain contemporaries accept the modern fantasies of empirical chemists; but, for the greater part, those who look for knowledge look only backwards and undertake no "reexamination and profession" (*Works*, II, 136–37; VI, 129–30).

Closely allied with, and resultant in part from, this turning to the past are several other vices. There is, first, the manner of the delivery of knowledge, which is not presented ingenuously, as something to be accepted or rejected on evidence, but peremptorily and magistrally, as something to be believed (*Works*, II, 141; VI, 133).

Secondly, everywhere there abounds a prevalent "distrust that anything should now be found out, which the world should have missed and passed over so long time" (*Works*, I, 303; II, 139; VI, 130; VII, 111; VIII, 128).

Thirdly, a common belief prevails that those truths, methods, and divisions of the sciences which have been accepted in common tradition as the most authoritative are the most valid; that the philosophic systems which have dominated school-learning are the soundest. Preference is given, for instance, to an inflated Aristotelianism before the more solid atomism propounded by Democritus (*Works*, I, 282–83, 288; II, 138; VI, 131; VII, 70; VIII, 108, 114).

Fourthly, the dominance of Aristotelianism in traditional learning serves to perpetuate a certain hard and fast division of the sciences and a separation of these from a common and inclusive primary philosophy experimentally established. Yet it is only the latter that can save from shallowness and error the several independent disciplines which treat of nature's motions in respectively narrow fields (*Works,* I, 285, 286-87; II, 139, 310; VI, 131-32; VIII, 110, 112; IX, 14).

Fifthly, men are prone to take satisfaction in the discoveries and inventions which have already been attained. The admiration of learned possessions, simple and childish as it is, has been increased by the artifices of those who have practiced and transmitted the sciences. The sciences have been so skilfully set forth in display by logic that their divisions appear to include and conclude everything, when, in truth, these parts are no better furnished than so many empty cases (*Works,* I, 291-92, 295; VIII, 117-18, 120).

In addition to those errors, which spring mainly from a reliance upon a specific tradition of learning, there are others which seem to be inherent in the practice of investigation itself, when pursued in any age, ancient or modern. There is, for instance, the persistent substitution of "anticipations" for "interpretations" of nature. The former are mere collections of ideas, gathered from a few instances of familiar occurrence, which serve to fill the imagination; while the latter are established truths, garnered methodically from varied and widely dispersed facts. These latter, because they do not readily penetrate the common understanding, "appear harsh and out of tune." The former serve "to negotiate between man and man (because of the conformity and participation of men's minds in like errors)," and are useful for gaining a common assent, to which end they work more powerfully than do true interpretations. And indeed one is disposed to reflect that, "if men went mad at the same time together and in the same manner, they might agree among themselves well enough" (*Works,* I, 247-48; VI, 64-66; VIII, 73-74).

Again, thinkers pursue their conclusions by detaching themselves from "the contemplations of nature and the observations of experience" and then tumbling "up and down in their own reason and conceits." Having become intrigued with some theory or other or by some topic of investigation, each thinker proceeds to weave a whole philosophy out of a preoccupation. The cause of this practice is conceit and a failure to collect particular observations of sufficient number, variety, and certainty to inform and enlighten the understanding. High-sounding generalities are impressive; their solemnity and dignity serve to captivate the mind of the speaker and of the hearer. They feed the affection of pride which holds it a diminution of the intellect to be "much conversant in experiences and particulars subject to sense and bound in matter, which are laborious to search, ignoble to meditate, harsh to deliver, illiberal to practise, infinite as is supposed in number, and no ways accommodate to the glory of the arts" (*Works,* I, 306–8, 289–90; V, 450–52; VI, 68, 74, 132, 427; VII, 114, 118–19; VIII, 115–16, 128, 132–33).

Inquirers in general and system builders in particular are not disposed to struggle with particulars. Having made a few observations on some subject or other, they proceed to embroider these by means of "solemn and formal art," through which the gaps in their knowledge are filled in. Then they become satisfied and secure in their opinions, as if no more inquiry were ever again necessary. And, if they are confronted with any questions which are not readily assimilated or solved by their dogmas, they lay the fault to the charge of nature. They maintain that what their logic cannot perform cannot be done by any method of investigation. Thus they confound hope, engender despair, and cut the sinews of human industry, circumscribing human power in order to have their art thought perfect and to make men believe that what has not been hitherto discovered or comprehended by them or their predecessors may not in the future be discovered or comprehended by anyone else (*Works,* I, 288–89, 297–98; V, 104, 123; VI, 70, 418–19; VIII, 114, 122–23).

Here we are brought face to face with one of the most considerable maladies of human learning—despair. Intelligent and serious men, considering how obscure nature is, how brief is life, how deceitful the senses, how infirm human judgment, how difficult observation and experiment, come to the conclusion that, because the sciences have reached a certain grade and place, knowledge can advance no farther. And so it is that if anyone entertains a belief, and a promise, that inquiry can be advanced by a new and adequate direction for observation and experiment, this belief is assigned to an uncontrolled and unripened mind and prediction is made that the project, even if seemingly prosperous in the beginning, will terminate in failure and confusion (*Works,* I, 303; VI, 72; VII, 111; VIII, 128).

Knowledge has been brought to a standstill, then, because men unaware of their own strength have flown to foolish conceits or taken refuge in inert despair of further discovery. There are sober and grave wits who are content to rely on the opinions furnished by authors and traditions. Others of a "more vain and credulous sort" resort to "revelation and intelligence with spirits and higher natures." Theirs is a "religion that is jealous of the variety of learning, discourse, opinions, and sects, (as misdoubting it may shake the foundation,) or that cherisheth devotion upon simplicity and ignorance, as ascribing ordinary effects to the immediate working of God." This abuse of faith, practiced in the name of the Christian religion, is really a revival of the opinion of the heathen. It exemplifies in a striking manner the truth that in every period of its history natural philosophy has had a troublesome opponent in the unenlightened superstitions and immoderate zeal of the representatives of religion. Those among the Greeks who proposed explanations of nature's activities in terms of natural causes were held guilty of impiety. The early Christian Fathers showed no forbearance with men who maintained, on grounds that no one in his senses would now think of questioning, the opinion that the earth was round. And any discoursing of nature which might go beyond accepted views has been rendered perilous, even up to recent times, by the merging of philosophy and theology —and the more especially by the incorporating of pagan Aristotelianism into the Christian religion (*Works,* I, 299-301; VI, 72, 75, 420-21, 424; VII, 108-9; VIII, 124-26).

The office of human science, which is pursued by natural human faculties, is to know not the essence and will of God but the works which he has created. Natural philosophy, when so practiced and so limited, becomes after the Word of God the most effective means against superstition and the best help of faith. Heresy may be said to have two sources: ignorance of the will of God revealed in the Scriptures and ignorance of the power of God in his works, discoverable by intelligence in his creatures. Scientific knowledge, accordingly, while it should be limited by religion, is not to be exterminated by divines. Its employment for the relief of man's estate is not least among the examples set by the founder of Christianity Himself (*Works,* I, 209-10, 301; VI, 28-33, 75, 423-24; VII, 109-10; VIII, 36, 126).

We come now to the final error of learning, "the mistaking, or misplacing of the last or furthest end of knowledge. For men have entered into a desire of learning and knowledge, sometimes upon a natural curiosity and inquisitive appetite; sometimes to entertain their minds with variety and delight; sometimes for ornament and reputation; and sometimes to enable them to victory of wit and contradiction; and most times for lucre and profession; and seldom sincerely to give a true account of their gift of reason to the benefit and use of men: as if there were sought in knowledge a couch, whereupon to rest a searching and restless spirit; or a terrace, for a wandering and variable mind to walk up and down with a fair prospect; or a tower of state for a proud mind to raise itself upon; or a fort or commanding ground, for strife and contention; or a shop for profit and sale; and not a rich storehouse, for the glory of the Creator, and the relief of man's estate. But this is that which will indeed dignify and exalt knowledge, if contemplation and action may be more nearly and straitly conjoined and united together than they have been; a conjunction like unto that of the two highest planets, Saturn, the planet of rest and contemplation, and Jupiter the planet of civil society and action. Howbeit, I do not mean, when I speak of use and action, that end before-mentioned of the applying of knowledge to lucre and profession: for I am not ignorant how much that diverteth and interrupteth the prosecution and advancement of knowledge; like unto the golden ball thrown before Atalanta, which while she goeth aside and stoopeth to take up, the race is hindred..... Neither is my meaning, as was spoken of Socrates, to call philosophy down from heaven to converse upon the earth; that is, to leave natural philosophy aside, and to apply knowledge only to manners and policy. But as both heaven and earth do conspire and contribute to the use and benefit of man, so the end ought to be, from both philosophies to separate and reject vain speculations and whatsoever is empty and void, and to preserve and augment whatsoever is solid and fruitful....."

"Lastly," concludes the author, "I would give one general admonition to all; that they consider the true ends of knowledge, and not to seek it either for the gratification of the mind, or for contention, or that they may despise others, or for emolument or fame, or power, or such low things; but for the benefit and use of life; and that they perfect and govern it in charity" (*Works,* I, 209–10; II, 141–42; VI, 134–35; VII, 105–6; VIII, 36; cf. VI, 34).

CHAPTER VIII

IDOLS OR FALSE PHANTOMS

SO MUCH, then, for the main vices of human learning. Next for consideration comes the infirmity of the human mind by which these vices are engendered and perpetuated. The mind of man "is not sincere, but of an ill and corrupt tincture." It mixes its own nature with what it beholds; tinges and distorts objects, and substitutes false images or "Idols" for the intelligible marks set upon creation by the Maker of the world. "Far from the nature of a clear and equal glass, wherein the beams of things should reflect according to their true incidence, it is rather like an enchanted glass, full of superstition and imposture, if it be not delivered and reduced."

The cure for the mind's waywardness will be found in the disciplinary rules of a true inductive method of inquiry. Yet warnings against its propensity to entertain and communicate false imaginings are not to be overlooked. The caution of these Idols "(for all elenches.... are but cautions) doth," says Bacon, "extremely import the true conduct of human judgment." As a means of discovering and eliminating error "the doctrine of Idols is to the interpretation of nature what the doctrine of the refutation of sophisms is to the common logic" (*Works*, I, 219, 250-51; II, 400; VI, 66, 276, 279-80; VII, 123; VIII, 45, 76-77; IX, 98).

Of Idols or "false opinions," "dogmas," "errors," "superstitions," the author lists four sorts; and for purposes of presentation he assigns to them the titles, "Idols of the Tribe," "Idols of the Cave," "Idols of the Market-Place," and "Idols of the Theatre." The doctrine of Idols takes shape early in his writing. It appears in the *Temporis partus masculus* and persists with increasing emphasis, and some modification, throughout the different periods of his thought. It is given considerable prominence in the *De augmentis scientiarum* and receives a relatively full exposition in the *Novum organum*. In the *Temporis partus masculus* three Idols are mentioned by name, those of the Theatre, Market-Place, and Cave. In the *Advancement of Learning* are instanced, without assigning them specific names, three "profound kinds of fallacies in the mind of man" which correspond to what are called elsewhere the Idols of the Tribe, Market-Place, and Cave. In the *Delineatio* the general treatment of the errors of learning is again brought under three Idols. And in the *Novum organum,* and the *De augmentis* as well, four Idols—of the Tribe, Cave, Market-Place, and Theatre—are expounded. The *Valerius Terminus* lists and names four Idols in an order different from that which appears in the two late works. It would seem that at the stage of Bacon's thought which the *Valerius Terminus* represents the author intends to add to their number. His words are, "four Idols or false appearances of several and distinct sorts, every sort comprehending many subdivisions: the first sort I call idols of the *Nation* or *Tribe;* the second, idols of the *Palace;* the third, idols of the *Cave;* and the fourth, idols of the *Theatre,* &c." It will be noted that what both before and afterward are called the Idols of the Market-Place are here named Idols of the Palace. The word "palace," however, may well be the result of a slip of the scribe's pen, "palace" being written or transcribed instead of "place" (*Works,* I, 219, 250; II, 397–403; VI, 62, 274–80; VII, 28; VIII, 45, 76; IX, 98).

From his brief reference to Idols in the *Partis secundae delineatio et argumentum* it would appear that in 1607 Bacon intends to include the whole of the *pars destruens* of his philosophy within the treatment of three Idols broadly conceived. Here he calls them the "Idol of the Mind," the "Idol of Demonstration," and the "Idol of Philosophies." In projecting their reduction, he apparently hopes to achieve a "refutation" of (1) the human mind itself, (2) the methods of traditional demonstration, and (3) prevailing philosophies. But it would seem that, having discerned the ramifications of the several systems to be refuted, and having begun to list the many disorders and errors of learning, and having entered into a comparison of traditional doctrines and methods with those which he himself proposes, he abandons the plan as unworkable (*Works,* VII, 41–43).

The account of Idols which is to be found within two of the late writings, the *Novum organum* and the *De augmentis,* may be taken as authoritative because of its relative completeness—and the more especially because the author himself states in the latter of the two works that the regulative statement of the "Great Elenches," or "detection of fallacies," or "Idols of the Human Mind" is to be found in the *Novum organum*. Bacon includes in these two works an exposition "of the particular kinds of these four Idols, with some chosen examples of the opinions they have begot, such of them as have supplanted the state of knowledge most." The four, he explains, have to do respectively with human nature as such, the individual nature of each person, words and means of communicating ideas, and, finally, with erroneous systems of philosophy. The last of the four sorts is adventitious and may be expelled by a solid natural philosophy reached through the control of the inquiring mind by a proper method of induction. The others can never be quite eradicated. Once recognized, they can, however, be avoided or at least subordinated and governed (*Works,* I, 258, 264; II, 397, 399-403; VI, 67; VIII, 79, 89; IX, 95, 98-102).

The first class of Idols, those of the Tribe, have their foundation in human nature as such; in the senses, intellect, will, and passions; in the mind's manner of receiving impressions from objects; and in its preoccupation with accepted opinions. The senses are indispensable in scientific investigation; but by themselves they are not competent. The impressions which strike them the most vividly are often of least use for gaining a knowledge of things. Their powers in observation are greatly limited, even when assisted with instruments devised for their sharpening and enlarging. The springs of action in tangible bodies, for example, are not accessible to them, nor is the nature of such things as air and less dense bodies, nor is the change of form produced in the parts of substances by local motion through exceedingly small spaces (*Works,* I, 217, 258; VI, 66, 267; VIII, 43-44, 82-83).

As for the intellect, it is no dry light but receives an infusion from the will and the passions and proceeds to produce sciences as it would have them. What a man prefers to be true, that he the more readily believes. He rejects difficult things from lack of patience in inquiry; serious things because they limit immediate hope; the deeper things of nature because of superstitions; the light of experimental knowledge from arrogance and pride, lest he should seem to be occupied with the transitory and the vulgar; and difficult things, which turn out contrary to expectation, because of deference to common opinion. Numberless, indeed, are the ways in which the passions saturate and corrupt the human understanding (*Works,* I, 257-58; VIII, 82).

In the reception of knowledge the mind is moved by those things which impress it simultaneously. It presumes that all things are similar to these by which it happens to be surrounded. Once it has adopted an opinion agreeable to itself, it draws all things to the support of this opinion. Contrary examples, no matter how many, it overlooks, sets aside, and forgets. A few instances of presence will serve to countervail many absences. It was Diagoras, was it not, who said, on being shown the pictures in Neptune's temple of those who after an escape from shipwreck had paid their vows, "Yea, but.... where are they painted that were drowned?" The practice of drawing affirmative conclusions from a number of positive examples both in unlearned experience and in traditional scientific induction is a source of much error. In the proving of axioms the negative instance must be reckoned with no less than the positive, and often more so; especially because one contrary instance will serve to disestablish a hypothesis (*Works,* I, 254-55; VI, 576-77; VIII, 79-80).

Again, the human understanding is in its peculiar nature given to the practice of assigning constancy to things which are fleeting. It supposes also more order in the world than it finds—and more similarity, too; for it is always devising and bestowing conjugates, parallels, and relatives, which do not exist, upon its objects: hence the fiction of the Aristotelians that all celestial bodies move in perfect circles and hence their introduction of fire to make up a quaternion with the other three elements, earth, air, and water (*Works,* I, 253-54; II, 400-401; VI, 297; VIII, 79; IX, 99).

Finally, the human mind is unjust; it cannot limit its conclusions to what is borne by evidence received through the observation of things. It refuses, for example, to conceive of any limit to the world or to time or to the divisibility of lines and proceeds to manufacture its own paradoxes respecting the relation of time to eternity and the finite to the infinite. It affirms a First Cause which it places beyond causes and effects; and, then, having in its concern with causes gone beyond what is warranted, it turns to what is nearest at hand, namely, human nature, and ends with a doctrine of final causes wherein it asserts that the activities of physical nature are comparable to those of man. It thus succeeds in making man the *communis mensura* of nature and, in its identification of a First Cause— illegitimately manufactured by its own imaginings—with the God of revelation, affirms a doctrine "not much better than the heresy of the Anthropomorphites.... who supposed the gods to be of human shape" (*Works,* I, 256-57; II, 401; VI, 61, 277-78; VIII, 81; IX, 99).

The second sort of Idols, the Idols of the Cave, have their origin in the peculiar constitution, education, habits, and accidental circumstances of the individual concerned. The title of these Idols, Bacon tells us, is taken from a Platonic allegory. Plato reflects that a child reared in a dark grot or cave under the earth until his maturity would, on his emerging, observe the heavens to be filled with absurd imaginings. It is so with men, thinks Bacon. Although all behold things that are, each one is shut within the cave of his own nature with the customs which arise from his peculiar training, the impressions he receives according to the predisposition of his constitution, the books he reads, the authorities he esteems, and the preoccupation of his mind. Indeed, so varied is human nature in its individual manifestations that there would seem to be good ground for maintaining that each example of it is determined by something akin to chance (*Works,* I, 251-52; II, 402; VI, 278; VIII, 77; IX, 100-101).

The Idols of the Cave which occasion individual peculiarities are many. Four sorts, which may be distinguished according to their sources, will serve for the present purpose. These arise respectively from (*a*) an attachment to a predominant subject, (*b*) an excessive tendency either to unite or to differentiate, (*c*) a partiality for a particular age in history, and (*d*) a desire to contemplate larger or lesser objects (*Works,* I, 259-60, 261; VIII, 84, 86).

In cases of the first sort men become attached to certain subjects of which they sometimes fancy they are inventors or discoverers, or of which through long preoccupation they have made a habit of mind. Obsessed with certain methods, concepts, and presuppositions, they proceed to compose a supposedly complete knowledge of things. Aristotle, for example, constructs a whole philosophy by deductive demonstration out of logical distinctions, Proclus one out of mathematical notions and definitions, and Gilbert yet another on his theory of the loadstone.

In the second place, thinkers fall into two groups: those who seek differences and those who seek resemblances. The former, often with much subtlety, multiply distinctions. The latter put things together under one complete unity of principle, in which ultimately all differentiations disappear. Against the extravagancies of these two extremes Plato gives warning when he says that it is in the middle propositions, somewhere between absolute unity and endless multiplicity, that the truths of knowledge lie. Scientists in their theorizing would do well to shun, on the one hand, the fault of Antoninus Pius and not be "splitters of cummin seeds," and, on the other, to avoid those excessive generalities which give no tractable information about things and are about as useful in practice as is an Ortelius' universal map to direct the way between London and York.

In the third place, men are given over to the admiration of some period or other in history and are prone to accept its findings as wise or sufficient and to despise everything that is affirmed by thinkers of other periods. Yet certain it is that "truth is to be obtained not by the good fortune of any age, which is an inconstant thing, but by the light of nature and experience, which is eternal."

And, fourthly, among investigators there are those who consider nature as a totality and those who, on the other hand, ceaselessly break bodies up into minute particles. In the case of the former the mind is overpowered by its object and rendered ineffective, while the latter's understanding is distracted and rendered fragmentary. Most of the traditional sects have been so thoroughly given over to the admiration of the general structure of the world that they have failed to notice its lesser portions. On the other hand, the atomists, led by Leucippus and Democritus, have been so busy with their particles that they have rarely considered the structure of nature. Whereas, in fruitful scientific procedure two sorts of object, one a totality and the other partial, should alternate, so that observation may penetrate to the details of nature while the understanding brings wide and varied discoveries within comprehensive axioms (*Works,* I, 259-61; II, 435-36; VIII, 84-86; IX, 129).

The third general class of Idols is the most troublesome. It consists of words which are common to men and are suited to and sustained by a common understanding of common notions. The Idols in question are, therefore, not inappropriately described as "of the Market-Place" because of the human dealings which by means of common coin there prevail. Words are the instruments by which men hold commerce one with the other in education, in discovery, and in the acceptance and the perpetuation of science and learning. Linguistic symbols are, therefore, good and necessary. This fact notwithstanding, words in their origin and sustenance have an inherent frailty; and because of their infirmity they may indeed serve to weaken the knowledge which presumably they should uphold and perpetuate. For they are usually framed and employed according to the capacity of the common man and made to mark those divisions of things which are obvious to the vulgar understanding. Usually, when men call things by a name, they are disposed to think that they know them; indeed, this practice is so universal that even the serious discussions of the learned are often about terms and their meanings and not about things. Words once coined and defined are greatly esteemed by both the learned and the unlearned; and the result is that when any man would alter the meanings of accepted terms or employ new ones to suit newly discovered divisions, motions, and structures in nature, he is straightway met with a general opposition founded in common acceptance and buttressed by common tradition.

Men, because they make words, believe that they can control them; "yet certain it is that words, as a Tartar's bow, do shoot back upon the understanding of the wisest, and mightily entangle and pervert the judgment." It is true that mathematicians take the precaution to set down at the beginning of their science the exact definitions of the terms they are about to employ; and those who engage in formal disputations do the same at the beginning of their exercises; while the traditional "distribution of things into certain tribes, which we call categories or predicaments," is employed as a caution "against the confusions of definitions and divisions." And so far, so good. In natural philosophy, however, where it is not enough for a word to represent a notion, but where the notion must represent things and the combinations of words must contain and convey true axioms inductively established, mere exactitude of definition is not sufficient. The fact is that science in the learned tradition has been encompassed by words, founded in logical definitions of words which in turn have begotten more words, and defended by disputes about words. As a consequence, demonstration has not reverted sufficiently to particulars in their orders and connections and has been no match for nature's subtlety—for the workings of nature are more subtle than the logical definitions of the learned (*Works,* I, 215, 243–44, 252–53, 261–62; II, 402–3; VI, 275, 279; VII, 112, 113; VIII, 41, 69–70, 78, 86–87; IX, 101).

The Idols imposed by words are of two main sorts: (*a*) names for objects which have no existence except in the imagination of the learned and (*b*) names for vague, ill-determined abstractions inadequately devised from existent things. Of the first kind are such terms as "Fortune,"

"Prime Mover," "Element of Fire." Such Idols as these can, of course, be expelled by rendering obsolete that scientific demonstration which proceeds by means of "notional" and verbal deduction. The second sort are more difficult to uproot because they have some relation to things and hence appear to be more true and solid than they are. These are the fruits of faulty and unskilled abstraction. They manifest several degrees of error and distortion. The least erroneous among them are terms which represent so-called "elementary species of substance," such as "chalk" and "mud." The term "earth" is badly used when the Aristotelians elevate it to a primary element, with fantastic properties, of terrestrial things. A more faulty sort of term is that which represents types of action within the Peripatetic scheme under "generation," "corruption," and "alteration." And yet more misleading are the accepted names of qualities, "heavy," "light," "rare," "dense" (these "qualities" are not, of course, to be confused with those of the same names which are the immediate objects of sense) (*Works*, I, 262–63; VIII, 87–88).

So far, three sorts of Idols have been considered, those of the Tribe, of the Cave, and of the Market-Place. All three are inherent in human nature. They can be controlled even if they cannot be eradicated. There is a fourth sort, the Idols of the Theatre, which are not inherent in the nature of man as such. These can be expelled, and their entrance into the mind can be prevented. They are to be found in the theatrical pieces and play-books of those who have composed philosophical systems. The historical systems of philosophy are mere inventions, some with greater, some with lesser, subtlety, through an imaginary representation of selected happenings in nature; and, like the plays of poets, they present things more compactly, more elegantly, and more as one would have them to be than do true narratives of fact.

The theatrical creations of the philosophers are many; and no doubt there would be more were it not that the inventive mind has busied itself for many ages with religion and theology and had not civil governments frowned upon—even exposed to contempt, envy, and decrease of fortune —those who would have introduced novelties into settled speculation. In their construction of philosophic pieces some romancers have taken much out of a few things; others, a little out of many things; all have based elaborate representations of nature on a minimum foundation of observation, experiment, and natural history. The rationalistic or "Sophistical" school, which Aristotle in both his metaphysics and physics most adequately exemplifies, "snatches hurriedly from experience a variety of common instances and leaves all the rest to meditation and agitation of wit"; while the empiricists, of whom the alchemists are typical, produce a monstrous and deformed body of doctrine out of the darkness of a few experiments (*Works,* I, 265–69, 272, 274; II, 400; VI, 29, 37; VII, 74, 80–81, 118, 139; VIII, 90–94, 97, 99; IX, 98).

CHAPTER IX

FIRST REVIEW OF EXTANT PHILOSOPHIES

WE NOW turn from the errors of learning and the false phantoms of the human mind to the "refutation" of historic and prevailing philosophies. Bacon's first considerable attack on the philosophers of tradition is to be found in his *Temporis partus masculus* ("The Masculine—or Fertilizing—Birth of Time"). This fragment, as we have noted, is, with occasional exception, mere invective. It stands apart from its author's subsequent reviews of past and present systems of thought by its lack of information, perspective, and proportion. The piece should therefore be considered by itself and may be given in free translation and paraphrase, if only to show Bacon's early attitude toward the philosophers and schools with which he finds himself confronted.

The piece opens with the calling of all philosophers, past and present, "phrenetics," the leaders and the followers of an insane band. The leaders are philosophasters, defilers of minds, falsifiers of things, more given to fables than the poets; their attendant satellites and parasites make up a professorial and hireling multitude. Of the former, demands the author in juristic fashion, let Aristotle first be summoned for indictment, because he is the worst of the Sophists, confounded with useless subtlety, a laughingstock of words. This Aristotle is the person who, when man's understanding, carried as by chance, had arrived at some truth, did put the human mind under duress by an insane art of logic and then delivered it over to verbiage. He produced and nourished those artful babblers who, on their retirement from Peripatetic ramblings, have tendered, from the material of his precepts and propositions and by the agitation of their own wit, the innumerable trash of the Schools. Aristotle himself, their dictator, is more deserving of accusation than they, especially because, after familiarizing himself with the clear and open facts of nature, he put into his record the most obscure Idols, like shadows of some subterranean cave, and wove constructions on history of particulars like the webs of spiders, which he would have appear as actual causes—such makeshifts even as Hieronymus Cardan in our age has fabricated, at variance with things and unsuited to his own capacity.

We condemn Aristotle; but do not divine, my son (the author addresses his remarks to an imaginary disciple), that we are in accord with that modern rebel against his teachings, namely, Peter Ramus. We have no traffic with this modern lurking-hole of ignorance, with this insect destructive of letters, the progenitor of handbooks, who constricts things with the fetters of his method and compendium. Ramus binds together empty and arid trifles. The more ancient Aquinas, Scotus, and their associates have fashioned a variety of things when their matter has been nonexistent; but this man produces the nonexistent out of existent subjects. He is indeed worse than the Sophists.

Let Plato be called next—Plato the cultivated scoffer, the elated poet, the theologian out of his senses. This Plato, when he refined and merged in a system popular philosophic opinions and at the same time stirred and loosened men's minds by means of vague inductions, might well have been content with supplying grace and charm to conversation and discourses for the feasts of literary and civilized men. Instead, he undertook to disguise facts. He turned the human mind, which is the proper habitation of truth, away from the observation of things and in upon itself and instructed it to ponder, under the name of contemplation, blind Idols. He reached the apotheosis of simple folly when he called upon religion to secure his poorest meditations. Plato is the man who interpreted learning as letters. Led by his guidance in many directions and satisfied with accrued fame and the pleasantness of contemplating mild notions, his literary disciples have brought to ruin and waste the severer investigation of truth. Among such followers are Marcus Cicero, Annaeus Seneca, Plutarch of Chaeronea, and many others unequal in stature to these (*Works*, VII, 18–20).

Let us now proceed to examine the physicians. There is Galen, a man most narrow of mind, the deserter of experience and the vainest of pretenders. He is the one who banishes ignorance and slothfulness from medicine! He puts its practitioners into a place of security and then brings to an end by inactivity their art and their office. Are you not he, Galen, who, in pronouncing so many diseases incurable, dooms by your prescription so many of the ill and cuts off the hope of patients and the industry of physicians? O sinister, baleful star (*O canicula*)! O infectious plague! who craftily degrade human capacity and guard perpetually your ignorance with despair!

Away with Galen and with the triflers associated with him, the Arabians, who substitute promises for cures! with Fernelius who surpasses the rest in forming enunciations for those who esteem orderly and elegant delivery an all-comprehending art! with Arnoldus de Villa Nova and others like him whose more varied observations and experiments are lost in the silliest pretexts!

Over there is a troop of chemists, among whom Paracelsus vaunts himself and merits, because of his audacity, correction separately from the rest. We shall address Paracelsus. O mad joiner of false images! You, Paracelsus, have turned man into a mummer. We can more easily endure Galen weighing his elements than you embellishing your fancies. By mixing the divine with the natural, the profane with the sacred, the heretical with the fabulous, you, O sacrilegious impostor! have polluted truth, both human and divine. The light of nature, whose sacred name you ofttimes appropriate to your impure speech, you have not concealed, as have the Sophists, but have quenched. They have been the deserters of experience, you the betrayer. Among your adherents I grudge you one Peter Severinus, a man not deserving to spend himself on absurdities. Surely you are greatly indebted to him; for he has made things, which you, Paracelsus—O adopted of asses—have been accustomed to bray, pleasing and harmonious by a certain melody and modulation and most happy diversity of speech, and he has transmuted the hatefulness of falsehood into the delightfulness of fable.

So much for Paracelsus and his ingratiating disciple. As for the rest of the chemists, those arrogant persons, while they accept Paracelsus, they do occasionally in their chance ramblings hit upon useful things. But, like the spoiled youth who when he found a tholepin on the seashore aspired to build a ship, these burners of charcoal attempt out of a few experiments of distillation to construct a whole philosophy. To be sure, they are not all of one type. Some of them are not too solicitous of theory and do manage by a mechanical skill to arrive at contriving inventions. Such a one is Roger Bacon. Others again, from all sides, are of a pernicious and detestable sort, whose only aim is to obtain applause and commendation for their wild experiments and ridiculous theories. This end they pursue through appeals to religion, in absurd promises of things hoped for, and by imposture generally.

But let us not forget Hippocrates; for to his authority both Galen and Paracelsus eagerly betake themselves as to the shadow of an ass! This Hippocrates is the produce of antiquity and the vendor of the years. Take a look at him. He seems to direct his gaze continually to experience. But actually his eyes are not active and inquiring; they are inattentive and uncontrolled. His vision now collects itself a little, and he takes in certain false images or Idols, not the immense Idols of theory but the neater sort which beset the surface of history. And at length, under the protection of brevity—according to the fashion of his age, half a Sophist and puffed up after having quaffed these Idols—he delivers himself of those oracular sayings of which Galen and Paracelsus would be esteemed interpreters. His wise words, however, prove to be mere sophistical, disconnected, and suspended utterances or rustic remarks arrogantly set forth (*Works,* VII, 20–26).

We have now reviewed the cases of several persons; and what we have said of them is correct. But perhaps you will ask whether, among all who have thought and written in mankind's long past, there are those who have discovered some truth. Is it not possible that while Time, like a river, has brought down the light and inflated things we have mentioned, it has also carried in its course some solid and weighty things which have been forgotten because they have sunk beneath its surface? What of those ancient inquirers, Heraclitus, Democritus, Anaxagoras, Empedocles, and others of like kind, whose writings have disappeared and who are known through the records of others? To this we reply that there is in the surviving fragments of these thinkers (they have left no books) some evidence of diligence and ingenuity in contradistinction to scientific knowledge. We must caution you at this point, however, that the person who is concerned with benefits for the future of mankind will seek truth from the light of nature and not from the darkness of antiquity. What has been done in the past does not matter so much as what may be achieved in the future. Knowledge must look forward and not backward. In observing the flowings and courses of learning, you may be gratified with your observation of what has gone by, but it is far more important that you find satisfaction in the foreseeings of things to come.

An immense sea flows around the island of truth, and the scatterings and the injuries from the winds of Idols still abound. Just now, for example, Bernardinus Telesius mounts the stage and presents a new philosophic piece, with no great applause, and properly so, for it has no sound argument. In astronomy both the contrivers of eccentrics and epicycles and the wagoners who move the earth about use the same evidence to support mutually contradictory theories. Quarrels among investigators of nature are evidence of the error that prevails in science. Diversity belongs to error, unity to truth.

It is the way with scientists to perceive a few significant things in natural history; next, to introduce their own particular Idols—I refer not to Idols of the Theatre but to Idols of the Market-Place or Den—into their thoughts; and then, seizing upon those things which agree with their prepossessions, to construct a whole philosophy. They are like an orator who, knowing only his vernacular tongue, undertakes to compose a speech in an unknown language. He notices that a certain few words of the latter are similar in letters and sound to those of his own speech, he confidently assumes that the meanings of the two are the same, and then he proceeds with much labor and wit to divine after his own idioms the content of a whole oration.

We have brought indictments against past and present thinkers and their several species of sect, particularly the tallest scions of these species. We have made the charges less than their guilt warrants. In condemning them we would not act like Velleius, the rhetorician and literary person, for instance, who touches hastily on the opinions of Cicero merely to cast them from him and not to break them down, nor like the modern Agrippa, that trivial buffoon, who in reviewing the opinions of others distorts every idea in order to give it over to ridicule. O miserable me! who, because I have taken to condemning the follies of the past, am compelled to compare myself with irrational animals (*Works*, VII, 26–29)!

But you are still wondering whether absolutely all the teachings of all the philosophers which we have mentioned are empty and false. We are prepared to answer that there is no man, however learned or unlearned, who does not at some time or other hit upon something which is true. When Heraclitus, for instance, contends that men seek knowledge in their private worlds and not in the common world, his philosophy has an auspicious beginning. Democritus, when he opposes the slaves of custom and ascribes immense variety and infinite succession to nature, does not philosophize unhappily. The number theory of Pythagoras is of good omen. And Dindamus the Indian is to be commended for calling custom "antiphysis" (the opposite of nature). To Epicurus' disputing against natural causation through purposes and ends, though he is a childish, literal man, we are not unwilling to listen. To Pyrrho, also, and the vacillating Academics who conduct themselves against Idols like capricious lovers, always reproaching their loves but never deserting them, we turn for pleasure of the mind. Finally, we desire greatly to have Paracelsus and Severinus for public criers. With their din they will summon men to attend to the suggestion of experience!

Are we to say, then, that these several philosophers have been partakers of knowledge? Nothing less! for indeed are not some adages of rustics apposite of truth? Yet, were a swineherd's charge to impress with its snout the letter *A* upon the ground, we should not expect the animal to compose a whole tragedy! We contend that a single item of experience hit upon by chance is not informed knowledge, because the former is sterile and solitary, while the latter is germinous and involves relations among things. To illustrate what we mean: Gunpowder, for example, had it been discovered by an ordered design and not, as it was, according to accident, would have issued forth in conjunction with other excellent works and not by itself, as it did. And thus it is with all scientific propositions and consequent operations (*Works,* VII, 29-31).

CHAPTER X

BACON ON THE PRE-PLATONISTS

THE early *Temporis partus masculus* bears evidence of only the slightest acquaintance with the history of philosophy and science. The author's awareness of the need for a knowledge of past human reflection becomes evident in the *Advancement of Learning* of 1605. "No man," he says in this treatise, "hath propounded to himself the general state of learning to be described and represented from age to age, as many have done the works of nature and the state, civil and ecclesiastical; without which the history of the world seemeth to me to be as the statua of Polyphemus with his eye out; that part being wanting which doth most shew the spirit and life of the person." There are available, he continues, some poor accounts of the inventions of arts and practices, occasional memorials of authors, books, schools, law, mathematics, rhetoric, and philosophy; "but a just story of learning, containing the antiquities and originals of knowledge, and their sects; their inventions, their traditions; their diverse administrations and managings; their flourishings, their oppositions, decays, depressions, oblivions, removes; with their causes and occasions of them, and all other events concerning learning throughout the ages of the world; I may truly affirm to be wanting."

That Bacon remains impressed to the end by the importance of this history of learning is clear from his re-writing and enlarging directions for its compilation during his preparation for publication of the *De augmentis*. According to this late work the history is to include accounts of conditions in the ages and regions in which the sciences have flourished, the educational practices by which knowledge has been transmitted, and the means provided in institutions for its acquirement and use. The history is to bring under review the natures of peoples, whether apt and disposed to disciplines of learning; the accidents of times, whether adverse or propitious to the sciences; the jealousy of divines; the ill-disposition or partiality of laws; the effectiveness of men with eminent virtues in the promotion of learning; and the controversies in which the learned have taken part.

This inclusive account of the state of learning from age to age and from place to place will serve to make men wise in both the use and the administration of knowledge. It will indicate what should be undertaken by showing what has, and what has not, been attempted and performed. And it will help to emancipate the human understanding from the thraldom of any particular tradition, and rouse it to discovery of its own. Bacon is insistent throughout his works, from the first to the last, on the need for arousing the human mind to act freely in its own right. This need motivates overtly or by implication his own historical observations, criticisms of past and present learning, discussions of alternate method of investigation, and demands for operative knowledge. Here and there it appears in the form of a direct call to men to use their native powers. In the *Cogitata et visa,* in which he maintains that the present, and not the ancient, time marks the adulthood of the race, he says, "If we knew our own powers and would try and put them forth, we should hope for more than from former times." The speaker in the *Redargutio philosophiarum,* which takes the form of an address given in Paris to an imaginary audience, admonishes his hearers as follows: You behold all your fortunes and hopes placed in the brains of some six men—Aristotle, Plato, Hippocrates, Galen, Euclid, Ptolemy. But surely God has allotted you the information of sense not to contemplate the works of these persons but rather to observe the works of God himself, his heaven and his earth. And while you raise your hymns in celebration of your Creator's praises, you may admit, if you will—since there is no reason why you should refuse—these men beside you in the worshiping choir. And in the *De sapientia veterum,* in which Aristotle, Galen, Euclid, and Ptolemy are instanced as inquirers who have begun to seek the goal of science and in which their successors are berated as persons who have added nothing to their efforts, Bacon appeals to men "to rouse themselves, and to try each his own strength and the chance of his own turn, and not to stake the whole venture upon the spirits and brains of a few persons" (*Works,* II, 198–201; VI, 180–84; VII, 60–61, 73, 132; VIII, 418–21; XIII, 52, 156).

Actually, Bacon contends, in mankind's civilized history only a very few persons, and these for a relatively short period of time, have been active and original in scientific pursuits. Certainly not more than six centuries in all—two of these among the Greeks, two among the Romans, and two among the Western nations of Europe—have seen men's energies devoted to the observation of nature. Antiquity's Seven Wise Men, as they were called, Thales alone excepted, applied themselves to morals and politics. When Socrates brought philosophy down from heaven to earth, he occupied himself mainly with ethical questions. The thought of the Romans was mainly taken up with matters of custom and politics, because by the magnitude of their empire these people were forced to devote their wits to affairs of state. As Christianity developed and grew strong, its best thinkers turned to theological studies and its literature became in large measure critical of scientific dogmas. With the Arabs and the Schoolmen natural philosophy became a matter of book learning; and to this day it has so continued in the Scholastic tradition.

The heaviness of libraries has been greatly increased by commentaries, but no weight has been added to scientific matter. Contemporary science is, to all intents and purposes, traditional learning. Knowledge is the content of books; and a few authors, with Aristotle as their chief, are dictators. The books are many, and every new one is a repetition of the old. The stock of learning which seems great proves on examination to be scant. In natural philosophy, then, there is no increment; "for as water will not ascend higher than the level of the first springhead from whence it descendeth, so knowledge derived from Aristotle, and exempted from liberty of examination, will not rise higher than the knowledge of Aristotle."

The sciences have been torn from their empirical roots. Had they remained attached to the womb of Nature, they would not have shriveled and died. Whatever strength a dogma may have possessed originally is lost in its weakened repetition. More often than not the lively ideas of an Aristotle or a Plato or a Hippocrates have been reduced to the mere instruments of formal debate. Thus it is that while "in arts mechanical the first deviser comes shortest and time addeth and perfecteth.... in sciences the first author goeth furthest, and time leeseth and corrupteth."

Philosophers parrot the dogmas of the ancients and of each other. They aspire to second prizes. They would be embellishers of texts, skilful commentators, profound interpreters, sharp champions and defenders of a learned opinion. They overrate the accumulated store of knowledge while they underrate their own natural capabilities. The strong confidence of a few original teachers and the slothful indolence of many successors who have put their judgment into others' keeping have convinced the learned world that knowledge in its form and content is complete and finished. The sciences stand like statues to be worshiped and not to be moved. And the belief that whatsoever has not already been comprehended or discovered cannot be comprehended or discovered has produced a paralyzing circumscription of human power and invention (*Works*, I, 199–201, 285–86, 297–98; II, 134–35; VI, 40, 128, 418; VII, 60–61, 83, 86, 106–7, 108, 115, 119–20, 131, 133, 136; VIII, 25–27, 110–11, 123).

While our description of contemporary learning is in the main just, it must be admitted, continues Bacon, that the present age is not totally devoid of discoveries. There are moderns who have greeted the *ne plus ultra* inscribed as by fate on the pillars of Hercules with a *plus ultra* and have gone on voyages of discovery over seas unknown to the ancients and have brought back printing, gunpowder, and the magnet. These three discoveries, one in literature, the second in warfare, the third in navigation, have changed the whole face of the world, so much so that no sect, empire, or planet has exerted more influence on the affairs of men. Modern men, when compared with the ancients, need not be ashamed of their discoveries. The ancients gained a knowledge of but a small portion of the world. The travels of Pythagoras, Democritus, and Plato were suburban jaunts rather than journeys afar. The ancients knew nothing of Africa beyond Ethiopia or of Asia beyond the Ganges; they gave the title, Scythians to all peoples of the north, and called all the peoples of the west Celts. Of the New World they were completely ignorant. Many places and climates which they described as uninhabitable have been found to be populated with people of varied customs and lives. They sailed by the stars about the Mediterranean and became dogmatic about the rest of the world. But modern men, by means of the mariner's needle, have found out through their distant travels much about the sea and the earth and, by means of the telescope, have, as it were, travelled to the stars. They need not, then, accept any longer the restrictions imposed by traditional dogmatists who would put the rights of ancient authors before the rights of Time which is the "author of authors" (*Works,* I, 205–6, 291, 336; V, 452; VI, 39; VII, 65, 93, 128, 132; VIII, 32–33, 117, 162).

We say that Time is the author of authors. We are not impressed by those who ascribe seniority to the ancients in the judgment of Time. We believe that antiquity marks not the maturity of the race but its childhood. "These [present] times," says Bacon, "are the ancient times, when the world is ancient, and not those which we account ancient *ordine retrogrado*, by a computation backward from ourselves." Certainly the scientists of antiquity have this characteristic of the young: they can prattle, but they cannot generate. Greek science consists of talk. It has not produced a single experimental truth—beyond an occasional medical doctrine hit upon by chance—for the improvement of man and the relief of his estate (*Works,* I, 200–202, 278, 290–91; II, 136–37; VI, 49, 130; VII, 64; VIII, 26–28, 103, 116–17; XIII, 403–4).

Bacon's own review of the philosophers, schools, and dogmas of the past is scattered throughout his several works. It is intended mainly to be a "refutation" of all and sundry thinkers of past and present. There is no evidence that he has undertaken on his own a compilation of materials for a disinterested history of learning. Not all his statements concerning ancient philosophers are accurate; and not many of them are unprejudiced, for, generally speaking, he assesses the methods and conclusions of all thinkers in terms of philosophic naturalism. Aristotle he often interprets through the amplifications of the Schoolmen. The opinions of the Platonists, such as Philo Judaeus and the Church Fathers, are sometimes instanced when his intended criticism is obviously directed against Plato himself. He tends to confuse the doctrines of Democritus with those of his followers, Epicurus and Lucretius. Rarely does he separate the teachings of Pythagoras from those of the "mystery" school of the later Pythagoreans. A good deal of his history is undoubtedly taken from the paraphrases and quotations of commentators. The question of learned sources in the case of seventeenth-century writers in general and of Bacon in particular is a difficult one and need not be undertaken here. With these cautions, then, let us proceed to Bacon's account of the history of philosophy.

There is and has been in the learned tradition, says the author, a widespread belief that all considerable philosophy originates and ceases with one Greek, namely, Aristotle; and a common opinion prevails that most, if not all, thinkers since the publication of Aristotle's writings have agreed with him. In philosophic tradition the works of the Stagirite are presumed to mark a culmination of thought. Since he wrote, it is thought, nothing better has been invented. These opinions, says Bacon, indicate a false reading of history; for, long after Aristotle's philosophy was promulgated, down to the times of Cicero and also in subsequent ages, the works of earlier thinkers still held. With the inundation of barbarians into the Roman Empire human learning suffered shipwreck, as it were; and then, and not before, the systems of Aristotle and Plato, like pieces of light and inflated material, floated on the waves of time and consequently were preserved, while the more solid sections of thought such as the philosophies of the pre-Socratics and Democritus were lost from view.

Take the case of Democritus. His philosophy "respecting atoms, ... because it penetrated somewhat more acutely and deeply into nature and was more remote from common notions, was regarded as childish by the vulgar, and was, moreover, by the disputes of other philosophies, which were adapted to the capacity of the multitude, tossed about and almost extinguished. And yet this man was distinguished and much admired in his day, and was called *Pentathlus* from the variety of his knowledge, and by general consent was esteemed the greatest physical philosopher. .... And neither could the battles and rivalries of Aristotle .... nor the majesty and solemnity of Plato so far prevail—the one by violence, the other by reverence—as to annihilate this philosophy of Democritus." While the doctrines of Aristotle and Plato were noised abroad and celebrated in the Schools with professorial clatter and pomp, those of Democritus were held in great honor by the wiser sort and with those who kept themselves closely to silent and difficult sorts of reflection. Certainly in the age of Roman learning, the philosophy of Democritus still endured and was well received. Cicero especially mentions him everywhere with terms of the highest praise (*Works,* I, 102, 283; V, 295–96; VII, 70; VIII, 29, 108; X, 349–50).

The reputation of the early Greek philosophers, notwithstanding the wisdom of their thoughts, has been obscured because they left behind them no considerable writings, and their opinions have been preserved mainly through the works of later authors. While the system of Plato is vitiated by a doctrine of abstract forms, and that of Aristotle, even his physics, is inflated by a logic of abstraction, the *Homoeomerae* of Anaxagoras, the Fire of Heraclitus, the Heaven and Earth of Parmenides, the Strife and Friendship of Empedocles, the Atoms of Leucippus and Democritus, these "have the discernment of the natural philosopher, and a savour of the nature of things, and experience, and bodies." The early Greek physicists, with less affectation and ostentation than Plato and Aristotle, submitted themselves to things and simply and severely betook themselves to the investigation of the first and oldest of existing things, namely matter. And almost all of them, however much they may differ in other respects, agree in assigning to matter activity, form, dispensation of form, and the principle of motion.

These pre-Socratics are not, however, immune from the vice of their race. They are ambitious to gain public favor with their speech, and each to found a sect of his own. They cannot resist the Greek temptation to follow words and are led captive by verbal equivocation. They explain things by the terms, "fire" and "earth" and "water." But their terms may not be predicated either of natural fire or air or water but only of fantastical and notional fire or air or water which "retains the name, but denies the definition." Historically speaking, they suffer from the fact that, when they labor, the Predicaments of the Aristotelians have not yet begun their reign and hence they cannot give their principle of matter any shelter within the abstract predicament, substance, and have, therefore, to propose "a principle according to sense."

The matter which they posit—unlike the Aristotelian matter—is actual with respect to itself and is yet—like the Aristotelian matter—potential with respect to all else. As a principle of explanation it is therefore deficient, since "it deserts and lays aside its nature in compositions." Moreover, its "dispensation" is obscure, for its exponents "do not discover, nay, do not even invent an explanation, by what appetite or stimulus, or by what reason, way, or inducement, this principle .... degenerates from, and again recovers its nature. And seeing there are such a multitude of contraries in the world, dense and rare, hot and cold, light and darkness, animate and inanimate, and many others, which oppose, deprive, and destroy one another in turn; to suppose that all these emanate from some one source of a material thing, and yet not exhibit any manner in which the thing can be, seems but a confused speculation and abandonment of inquiry" (*Works,* I, 102, 267, 276–77, 283, 332; II, 228–29; V, 301–9; VII, 67, 112; VIII, 29, 91–92, 102–3, 108, 157–58, 446–47; X, 355–64).

The philosophy of Democritus is more successful. It is so good that it should be revived; and for many reasons. To begin with, Democritus' doctrine penetrates further into things than all other historic philosophies. Its author recognizes that the constituent parts of nature are imperceptible by the senses, yet he does not use abstract reason glibly to abstract from things and then to build a system on their surface, as does Aristotle, but proceeds to solve and dissect nature to the quick. Indeed, the procedure of probing and dissecting nature may be called the Democritean method (*Works,* I, 258, 272, 472; IV, 220-21; V, 204; VIII, 83, 97, 288; X, 287).

Democritus' account of the "beginnings of things" as "solid, void, and motion to the centre," surpasses Aristotle's "matter, form, and shift" and Plato's "mind, motion, and matter"; so greatly so that "no man shall enter into the inquisition of nature, but shall pass by that opinion of Democritus, whereas he shall never come near the other two opinions, but leave them aloof for the schools and table talk." For the matter of Democritus is not the indeterminate and inert stuff of the other two; it is not unintelligible; it is a positive reality, furnished and active, the oldest thing created, prior to species and motion, prior to whatever specific form it assumes in the composition of objects. Such a real matter, with the actions and laws of actions—for forms, unless we mean by them the laws of matter's action, are mere abstractions of the human mind—are the true objects of philosophy (*Works,* I, 258; V, 295; VI, 42; VIII, 83; X, 349).

In treating of matter's motions, Democritus avoids reading into nature something akin to human motives, namely, final causes. "The handling of final causes.... in physical inquiries hath intercepted the severe and diligent inquiry of all real and physical causes, and given men the occasion to stay upon these satisfactory and specious causes, to the great arrest and prejudice of further discovery. For this," says Bacon, "I find done not only by Plato, who ever anchoreth upon that shore, but by Aristotle, Galen, and others, who do usually likewise fall upon these flats of *discoursing causes.* For to say that *the hairs of the eye-lids are for a quickset and fence about the sight;* .... *or that the leaves of trees are for the protecting of the fruit; or that the clouds are for watering the earth*.... and the like.... are indeed but remoras and hindrances to stay and slug the ship from further sailing, and have brought this to pass, that the search of the Physical Causes hath been neglected and passed in silence."

When teleologists find the acts of a Supreme Final Cause in the operations of nature and thus turn their natural philosophy into a theology, they inevitably reduce God to nature and elevate nature to God. Democritus, on the contrary, aptly magnifies the Divine Creator by removing the Divine Nature from the natural operations of his creatures and keeps human inquiry into the virtues and motions of created things within its proper bounds.

The philosophy of Democritus is not, however, free from defects. While a good dissector of nature, he, like Leucippus, from whom he takes the notion of atoms, is so preoccupied with nature's minute parts that he rarely considers its structure. Also his account of the motion of matter is not satisfactory, depending as it does on his assignment of two primary motions, one upward and the other downward, by reason of lightness and heaviness, to the atom. He erroneously maintains that there is variety and not homogeneity in atoms, because it seems to him contrary to reason that all things can be made out of all things. And his doctrine of atoms presupposes a void or vacuum in nature.

On the question of the vacuum, Bacon, both in his criticisms of Democritus and elsewhere, finds it extremely difficult to make up his mind. In the *Cogitationes de natura rerum* he seems to hold with Gilbert, and against Hero, that there is a collected vacuum in the heavens. In the *Descriptio globi intellectualis* he observes that Democritus, along with Hero and Telesius, admits a vacuum interspersed; and he apparently favors their opinion. While in the *De principiis atque originibus* he seems uncertain whether he should accept the doctrine of a collected vacuum, which, he now says, Democritus and Telesius assert. In the *Novum organum* he states expressly, "We cannot say for certain whether there be a vacuum collected or interspersed." Yet of one thing he is sure, both here and in the *Cogitationes de natura rerum*: the problem which for Hero, Leucippus, and Democritus occasions the theory of the vacuum —the filling by the same body of sometimes smaller and sometimes larger spaces—may be solved by the doctrine of condensation and rarefaction. And, finally, in the *canones mobiles* of the *Historia densi et rari* the author puts himself on record, provisionally, at least, that "there is no vacuum in nature either collected or interspersed" (*Works,* I, 352, 513; II, 294–97; IV, 114; V, 203–9, 215; VI, 223–25; VII, 308–9; VIII, 177, 326; X, 262, 288–93, 300, 427, 508–11).

Of the remaining early Greek thinkers, Hippocrates, Pythagoras, and Socrates are treated with respect by Bacon. The Sophists he regards as victims, more or less deservedly, of the calumny of the two arch-Sophists, Plato and Aristotle. Hippocrates he quotes deferentially both by name and anonymously on the treatment of diseases and regrets "the discontinuance of the ancient and serious diligence of Hippocrates which used to set down a narrative of the special cases of his patients, and how they proceeded, and how they were judged by recovery or death" (*Works,* IV, 174, 193, 200, 345; VI, 246).

He instances Pythagoras' distinction among the three types of person who attend the Olympic games: the buyers and sellers of wares, the competitors for honors, and the contemplators of wisdom; and he remarks, after Augustine, on Pythagoras' choice of the contemplative life, "Men ought to know that in the theatre of human life it is fitting only for God and the angels to be lookers-on." He notes the Pythagoreans' rule of asceticism and their faith in the efficacy of numbers. While he thinks that, on the whole, "their inventions and beliefs . . . . were mostly of such a nature as were rather suited to found an order in religion than to open a school in philosophy," he recognizes that their opinion that things consist in numbers may be found "to penetrate to the principles of nature," in that "quantity . . . . when applied to matter is as it were the dose of nature, as causative of very many effects in natural things, and therefore is to be reckoned as one of the Essential Forms of things." With them, however, the theory of numbers, like the logical principles of the Aristotelians, has been allowed to go out of control, and "it has come to pass," he says, "I know not by what bad fortune, that mathematics and logic, whose place is that of handmaidens to physic, presume nevertheless because of the certainty they boast to exercise dominion over it" (*Works*, II, 306; III, 14; V, 207; VI, 226, 314; VII, 30, 117; VIII, 518–19; IX, 198; X, 291).

In his discussion of Socrates, Bacon instances the former's placing virtuous felicity in a "tranquil and constant peace of mind," while the Sophists find it in the enjoyment of appetite. The Sophists maintain that Socrates' felicity is that of a log or stone, and Socrates contends—as in Plato's *Gorgias*—that theirs is merely that of those who continually itch and scratch and itch again. Anytus accuses Socrates of seducing the young by "discourses and disputation . . . . from due reverence to the laws and customs of their country"; while, in fact, the words of Socrates are "sovereign medicines of mind and manners, and so have been received ever since till this day." They serve as an "answer to politiques, which in their humorous severity or in their feigned gravity have presumed to throw imputations upon learning."

Socrates separates philosophy from rhetoric. Before his time the same professors of wisdom have professed to teach "an universal Sapience and knowledge both of matter and words." Socrates, however, divorces the knowledge of words from the knowledge of matter and leaves "rhetoric to itself, which by that destitution [becomes] but a barren and unnoble science." And having cast rhetoric forth and using his own peculiar wandering method of induction, he makes truth the object of discourse; while the Sophists, such as Isocrates, Gorgias, and Protagoras, busy themselves "rather about light of speech than the darkness of things."

In pursuing his investigations, Socrates assumes that he knows nothing. The oracle of Delphi declares him to be the wisest man in Greece. Socrates himself is accustomed to say ironically: *"There could be nothing in him to verify the Oracle, except this; that he was not wise, and knew it; and others were not wise and knew it not."* The Sophists, on the other hand, are continually in dread "of nothing else so much as of seeming to doubt about anything." Socrates is that dramatis persona in the Platonic dialogues who disposes of "sophistical fallacies" most excellently by example and who, in association with the Sophists, Hippias, Protagoras, Euthydemus, and the rest, wittily handles all form of objection and redargution, by infirming what is affirmed by another (*Works*, I, 273; II, 369, 397–98; III, 24; IV, 14; VI, 43, 98, 105, 186, 274–75, 321; VIII, 98; IX, 70, 96, 205–6; XIII, 377).

It is the destiny of Socrates to be immortalized by his pupil Plato and to have his thoughts pass into the received tradition of Western philosophy. The Sophists, on the contrary, are ridiculed by Plato, Aristotle, and later thinkers too, as disputatious hirelings utterly opposed to the inquisition of truth. There is an unfairness about this calumny against them, which appears even in the very connotation of their name—"clever" persons, in that actually the whole troupe of Greek philosophers, not to mention their disciples in succeeding centuries, forsake as well as they the strict investigation of truth and give themselves over to disputation about words. Indeed, the title "Sophist," so far from being restricted to the rhetoricians, like Gorgias, Protagoras, Hippias, and Polus, may be appropriately applied to the entire class of Greek philosophers, to Plato, Aristotle, Zeno, Epicurus, Theophrastus, as well as their successors, Chrysippus, Carneades, and the rest. The only difference between the two species of talkers is that the former were wandering and mercenary, while the latter gave their knowledge gratis and were dignified and impressive as the founders of schools with settled habitations. Both sorts were professorial; both turned philosophy into disputation; and both were jealous founders of battling sects with declared dogmas and defined heresies. The teachings of one and all are for the most part, to quote Dionysius' reflection on Plato, the talk of idle men to ignorant youths (*Works*, I, 276–78; VII, 67; VIII, 102–3).

Plato would condemn rhetoric by placing it among the voluptuary arts as a species of cookery and forget that, while cooking sometimes spoils and disguises wholesome meats, it can also by variety of sauces make unpleasant foods more palatable and acceptable. Aristotle reduces rhetoric and then places logic in control; thus he substitutes a pair of shears, so to speak, for a rich wardrobe. Aristotle is nevertheless correct when he distinguishes the office of logic from that of rhetoric. "Logic handleth reason exact and in truth, and rhetoric handleth its as it is planted in the popular opinions and manners." And wisely does he place rhetoric somewhere between logic and moral or civil knowledge and make it participate in both. He properly observes that demonstrations should not be required from orators, or persuasions from mathematicians, because logic works upon the reason, while rhetoric moves the affections through the imagination. If the affections were obedient to reason, there would be no need of "persuasions and insinuations to the will" beyond naked propositions and proof. The affections are given over to "continual mutinies and seditions," and reflection would easily become their captive and slave if the eloquence of persuasion did not make a confederacy between the reason and the imagination to keep them in place. Take the case of moving men to virtue. Was it not Plato who maintained that, since Virtue cannot be made manifest to sense by corporeal shape, she should be shown to the imagination "in lively representation." To represent her to reason merely by subtlety of argument is useless; for Virtue cannot be thrust upon men "by sharp disputations and conclusions, which have no sympathy with the will of man."

Rhetoric, then, serves a worthy end. It can no more be properly charged "with the colouring of the worse part, than Logic with Sophistry, or Morality with Vice..... Logic differeth from Rhetoric not only as the fist from the palm, the one close, the other at large; but much more in this that Logic handleth reason exact and in truth, and Rhetoric handleth it as it is implanted in popular opinions and manners." Therefore, among "helps for the intellectual powers"—Bacon is not thinking here of the exact interpretation of nature but of "popular" knowledge and communication in manners, law, religion, and morals—rhetoric is to be included along with logic; and the study of the Sophists, of Protagoras and Gorgias, is to be added to the reading of Plato, Aristotle, and Cicero (*Works,* I, 334; II, 440–42; VI, 298–300; VIII, 160; IX, 132–34; XIII, 302).

CHAPTER XI

BACON AND PLATO

OF BACON'S reflections upon thinkers of the past, none are more striking than those which have to do with Plato. It would appear that Bacon, after his revolt from Aristotelianism and historic systems of philosophy, generally goes to an opposite extreme and finds the proper approach to truth—or at least the beginning of this—in the theories of the pre-Platonists who identify natural science and philosophy. And later, when he begins to discover the need for a methodology of knowledge, he turns to Plato. Plato, he says, in his *Cogitata et visa* of 1607-9 "was without doubt a man of higher capacity" than Aristotle because of his concern with forms and his use of induction. In any event the Baconian philosophy, materialistic as it is in its presuppositions and conclusions, exhibits in its methodology many Platonic principles.

Bacon's writings contain many more or less incidental references to Platonic statements and doctrines. They instance, for example, Plato's observation in the *Phaedrus* "*That virtue, if she could be seen, would move great love and affection;*" the comparison, in the *Gorgias*, of rhetoric to the voluptuary art of cooking; the thesis from the *Republic*, "*Then should people and estates be happy, when either kings were philosophers, or philosophers kings.*" The author credits Plato with the authorship of the "parable of exquisite subtlety," the Idol of the Cave. He treats with detachment Plato's placing, as in the *Timaeus*, of the seat of the understanding in the brain, "animosity" in the heart, and sensuality in the liver: "it deserves," he says, "neither to be altogether despised nor to be eagerly revived." And he rejects the theory allegedly based by the School of Plato on another passage in the *Timaeus*, where Plato assigns mind, soul, and life to the cosmos, namely, that of "spiritus mundi," the spirit or soul of the world, by which, interprets Bacon, "they did not intend God (for they did admit of a deity besides), but only the soul or essential form of the universe. This foundation being laid, ... they did insinuate that no distance of place, nor want or indisposition of matter, could hinder magical operations; but that (for example) we might here in Europe have sense and feeling of that which was done in China, and likewise we might work any effect without and against matter .... by the unity and harmony of nature" (*Works*, II, 154, 319, 402, 440-41; V, 177; VI, 146, 240, 274-75, 298; IX, 22, 100, 132-33; cf. VII, 120).

Bacon's assessment of the respective pleasures of the life of sense, the life of honor, and the life of knowledge, is apparently a summary, derived from the original or a secondary source, of passages in Plato's *Symposium* and *Republic*. The value of learning, says Bacon, may be rated in terms of pleasure and also in terms of permanence of achievement. "The pleasure and delight of knowledge and learning, it far surpasseth all other in nature." Human pleasures belong, respectively, to the pursuits of the senses, to honor, and to the intellect. Pleasures of sense and honor are transitory, unstable, deceptive; *"but it is a pleasure incomparable, for the mind of man to be settled, landed, and fortified in the certainty of truth."* Man seeks the permanence of "immortality or continuance." For this he begets, builds, thinks, discourses, writes, and leaves foundations and monuments. The monuments of learning and discovery are durable beyond those "of power or of the hands." The verses of Homer remain, while innumerable cities, temples, and palaces have decayed. Even "philosophers which were least divine and most immersed in the senses and denied generally the immortality of the soul, yet came to this point, that whatsoever motions the spirit of man could act and perform without the organs of the body they thought might remain after death; which were only those of the understanding, and not of the affection; so immortal and incorruptible a thing did knowledge seem unto them to be" (*Works*, VI, 167-69).

Again, Bacon finds an ally in Plato when he undertakes to assail the prevalent opinion that it is dishonoring and degrading for men of science to examine the natures of common and mechanical things "except they be such as may be thought secrets, rarities, and special subtleties." Plato, he finds, notices and condemns a similar attitude in an earlier age, when he portrays, in his *Hippias major*, Socrates—"after his wandering manner of inductions"—entertaining as examples of Beauty a fair virgin, a fair horse, a fair pot well-glazed. The other character of the dialogue, the "learned" Hippias, takes offense at the mention of such "base and sordid instances" and is thereupon exposed to the

Platonic irony (*Works*, II, 193-94; VI, 186; VIII, 413-14; see I, 290; VI, 68, 74, 427; VIII, 115-16).

Bacon accuses Plato and his School of bringing into philosophy the doctrine of "acatalepsia," the disability of the mind to know. Acatalepsia, he recounts, was introduced by Plato and his early followers merely in jest, irony, and disdain of the pretensions of the older Sophists like Protagoras and Hippias. Afterward members of the New Academy raised the practice into a positive dogma. This at first the Academicians employed against arbitrary conclusions; and probably they did not intend that it should be used to deny all knowledge, as did Pyrrho and his followers. But it came to pass that philosophers, having begun to raise questions about knowledge itself and not about things to be known, turned to doubt and disputation about doubt and deserted the more difficult course of the strict and severe inquisition of nature (*Works*, I, 272-73, 281, 333; VI, 65-66; VII, 88; VIII, 98, 107, 158).

The author's severest criticism of Plato is reserved for those occasions on which he treats of him in conjunction with Aristotle. Plato, he says, uses the thoughts of many predecessors, dramatis personae in his dialogues, to construct one philosophy; Aristotle impresses the thoughts of one philosopher upon many successors; and both make the breadth and inclusiveness of discourse their primary concern. Either begins with a few inquiries and reaches conclusions which severally belong to relatively narrow parts of science; but neither remains content with such limitations; he would—like many an investigator since—build an all-inclusive structure on a few findings which apply properly to a corner of human knowledge. "Plato made over the world to thoughts; and Aristotle made over thoughts to words." Discourse is enabled by both to supplant observation, and the building of fantastic systems out of theoretically consistent opinions is substituted for the statement of modest principles established through exact observation. The logically coherent propositions which come down from these philosophers belong, therefore, to discourse and to discourse alone and are to be condemned as a class rather than refuted one by one; "for they are the opinions of those who wish to talk much and know little" (*Works*, I, 265-66, 268, 276-78, 331-32; V, 298; VI, 62, 132; VII, 68, 117-18; VIII, 90-91, 93-94, 102-3, 157-58; X, 352).

Plato and Aristotle are both teleologists. With their doctrine of final causes they read purposes, comparable to the mental acts of men, into nature, to the arrest of solid knowledge. Their disquietude of mind will not readily permit them to accept the most universal principles of physical matter for what these are; and they must soar from physics into theology. In the Platonic system the crowning point of explanation is the Good. This Good, which is said to be the cause of all knowledge and all existence, is identified with God. Aristotle finds the ultimate explanation of all things in the supreme Final Cause. This he equates with God. But he has already identified this Cause so thoroughly with the processes of nature that God becomes with him either the movement of things themselves or a mere superfluity. Plato, on the contrary, does assign his independent God a real function; he is, therefore, more consistent at least than Aristotle in his theological theorizing. Yet the fact remains that Plato's philosophy is dominated by a man-made, and therefore fantastic and superstitious, theology (*Works*, I, 256-57; II, 288-90, 294-97; VI, 61, 223-24; VIII, 81, 504-6, 509-11; IX, 99-100).

Having thus criticized several of the Platonic teachings, Bacon acknowledges the originality and importance of Plato's main methodological presuppositions. In the *Filum labyrinthi, sive formula inquisitionis* and the *Cogitata et visa* Bacon notes the fact that the philosophy of "the schoolmen, Aristotle's succession, which were utterly ignorant of history resteth only upon agitation of wit; whereas Plato giveth good example of inquiry by induction and view of particulars; though in such a wandering manner as is of no force or fruit." In the later *Novum organum* he less grudgingly acknowledges that his own "true induction," which proceeds by "proper rejections and exclusions" and reaches conclusions regarding affirmative instances only after the examining of negative instances, "has not yet been done or even attempted, save only by Plato, who does indeed employ this form of induction .... for the purpose of discussing definitions and ideas" (*Works*, I, 312-13; VI, 427; VII, 116; VIII, 138-39).

The immediate purpose of the inductive method is, for both Bacon and Plato, to discover through the agency of sense and reason the forms which constitute things. The form of a thing, according to both thinkers, is "the very thing itself," the particular as cognized in relation to the universe and not according to the senses of man; it is constitutive of reality as distinct from appearance. Bacon acknowledges that it was Plato, the man of "sublime wit," who descried that these forms are the true object of knowledge, yet he finds that Plato who "had a wit of elevation situate as upon a cliff.... lost the real fruit of his opinion, by considering of forms as absolutely abstracted from matter and not confined and determined by matter" (*Works,* I, 342-43, 371; II, 288-89; VI, 219; VII, 116; VIII, 168, 193, 504-5).

Bacon agrees with Plato that the form is known by reason and not by the senses, for it is a universal and not a particular; and indeed he goes so far as to call the senses, after the Platonist Augustine, "mere reporters." He holds with Plato also that the rational spirit of man is "inclosed in a body of earth" and must therefore be sharply separated from the creature of physical sensories which is brought forth in the natural process of reproduction. And while it would be a bold observation upon his writings to discern in them a positive acceptance of the Platonic doctrine of Reminiscence—"that particulars rather revived the motions.... of the mind than merely informed"—yet we are not surprised to see this doctrine instanced on more than one occasion. For example, in addressing his *Advancement of Learning* to his learned sovereign, when he is not likely to speak in careless vein, Bacon instances "Plato's opinion that all knowledge is but a remembrance, and that the mind of man by nature knoweth all things, and hath but her own nature and original notions (which by the strangeness and darkness of this tabernacle of the body are sequestered) again revived and restored." And on another occasion in the same work Bacon takes from Plato's dialogue the *Meno, locus classicus* of the doctrine of Reminiscence—where an untutored slave-boy, on seeing a succession of diagrams, enunciates the general proposition that the square on the diagonal of a square is double the original figure—Plato's answer to the question of how one can inquire respecting that which he does not know: "*Whosoever seeketh, knoweth that which he seeketh for in a general notion; else how else shall he know it when he hath found it?*" However, in the *Cogitata et visa* he expressly calls the doctrine which asserts that "the senses rather excite than inform the understanding" a "wild and unfounded opinion." And even as in Plato's later dialogues the doctrine of Reminiscence becomes one of re-cognition, so with Bacon the preknowledge mentioned in the early *Advancement* is superseded in the late *De augmentis* by Prenotion or "the cutting off of infinity of inquiry" (*Works,* I, 245, 249, 311-12; II, 97-98, 187, 407; VI, 27, 271, 427; VII, 115; VIII, 71, 137-38, 408; IX, 48-51, 105).

This last doctrine, "the cutting off of infinity"—that is, definition and determination by inquiry—occupies a position so central in Bacon's theory of knowledge that it may be regarded as the basic principle of his methodology. It is thoroughly Platonic, and would seem to be taken, whether directly or indirectly, from the Platonic dialogues. Plato finds the solution, as does Bacon, of the problem of combining unity with multiplicity in the act of definition which merges the "finite" or "limited" with the "infinite" or "undelimited" by a process of determination. Plato, in the *Philebus* and *Timaeus,* interprets this definition by means of the example of language, of music, and of mathematics. Mere undelimited sound, he explains, is chaotic until brought within discernible limits through the agency of word, syllable, and letter; or through the agency of tone, part-tone, and modal sequence; when it becomes intelligible, respectively, in language and music. In the *Timaeus* he regards space as a sheer indeterminate until there is introduced into it the "limits" of point, line, angle, triangle, circle, and quantity, when it becomes mathematically significant.

Bacon's account of "the cutting off of infinity," or the delimitation of objects from the indeterminateness of chaotic multiplicity is, to quote his own summary, this: "The nearer investigation approaches to simple natures the clearer and more intelligible will everything become; the business being transferred from the multiple to the uncompounded, from the incommensurable to the commensurable, from surds to rational things, from the infinite and vague to the limited and certain; as in the case of letters of the alphabet and the notes of musical harmony. And investigation yields the best results when physics is mathematically determined" (*Works,* I, 352; VIII, 177).

For both Plato and Bacon the process of knowing is the combining of multiplicity with the unity of form and axiom. Particulars are "infinite" and if entertained by themselves will plunge the mind into great confusion. Yet, on the other hand, if one begins with mere abstract unity—with such a proposition, for instance, as "Being is"—and undertakes to deduce from this a science of reality, he will never reach a knowledge of particulars. Somehow, then, multiplicity must be merged with unity. The solution of the difficulty Bacon instances in the early *Delineatio,* when he claims that his method of investigation proceeds by marking off, by limitation or unity of definition, an area of intelligibility from the endless immensity of particulars. And this solution, he tells us in the earlier *Valerius Terminus* and *Advancement of Learning,* as well as in the late *Novum organum* and *De augmentis*, is originally given by Plato when "Plato casteth his burden and saith *that he will revere him as a God, that can truly divide and define.*" "Plato noteth well.... *that particulars are infinite, and the higher generalities give no sufficient direction; and that the pith of all sciences, which maketh the arts-man differ from the inexpert, is in the middle propositions.*"

The lowest axioms of reflection, Bacon explains, "differ but little from bare experience" and furnish no knowledge. Yet, on the other hand, if we turn to the prevailing method of proof in philosophic tradition, where the mind is encouraged to fly to the most remote propositions and investigation proceeds according to syllogistic deduction of the lesser axiom from the greater, we find that both the more and the less general propositions are "notional and abstract, and have no solidity." Sound knowledge becomes possible only when a way is found through which progression is made by "a proper ladder of ascent, continuously, step by step, without lapse or hiatus from particulars to lesser axioms; and then to middle axioms, one above the other; and lastly to the most general..... The middle are the true and solid and living axioms on which depend the affairs and fortunes of men; and beyond these are those that are really the most general, such as are not abstract, but which are limited by the middle."

"And therefore the speculation was excellent in Parmenides and Plato, although but a speculation in them, That all things by scale did ascend to unity. So then always that knowledge is worthiest which is charged with the least multiplicity.... as that which considereth the Simple Forms or Differences of things, which are few in number, and the degrees and co-ordinations whereof make all this variety."

For Bacon, as for Plato, unified metaphysical knowledge is attained by a scale or ladder of ascent, that is, by traversing earlier stages of less authoritative and less inclusive knowledge. For Aristotle, on the contrary, metaphysics—the most general, abstract, and certain of the sciences—can be entertained immediately on the awareness that what is perceived has, or is, being. Its practice does not follow upon an ascent through knowledge contained within the other theoretical sciences, physics and mathematics. Even as with Plato the ascent to dialectic is made through three subsidiary stages of perception—elementary sense awareness, operative knowledge of particulars in use, and cognition of universals in the less comprehensive sciences—so with Bacon metaphysical doctrines are attained only on the reaching of the apex of the pyramid of knowledge after having passed through the lower sections or divisions, natural history and physics (*Works,* I, 311–12, 352, 413; II, 292–93, 363; VI, 58, 222, 262; II, 33–35, 41; VIII, 137–38, 177, 231, 507–8; IX, 65).

The historic philosophy against which Bacon wages his main polemic is that of Aristotle and his followers. And this is not surprising, since theirs is the philosophy which largely dominates the sort of learning which Bacon is undertaking to supplant. With Aristotle he finds himself in almost complete disagreement. And so consistently does he press his attack from many sides against Peripatetic doctrines that the account of his anti-Aristotelian polemic implicates the major tenets of his whole philosophy. We shall therefore postpone the statement of the issues involved in his attack until we have entered into a review of certain of the teachings of his Instauration.

CHAPTER XII

OF THE POST-ARISTOTELIANS

BACON'S treatment of post-Aristotelian thinkers is in the main sketchy. His writings contain but few specific references either to Neo-Platonic or to Scholastic thinkers. He does, however, pass in review the opinions of the Epicureans; the Stoics; the Skeptics; the Schoolmen; the two "reformers" of logic, Lully and Ramus; writers of natural history; the alchemists; Telesius; Copernicus; Galileo; Gilbert; and the "modern" chemists. He notes that Epicurus and his followers are revivers of the atomic theory of Democritus. They assert that the universe has "come together through a fortuitous concourse of the atoms," and thus they scandalize the consciences of men, who are thereupon driven to look beyond physical theory for a theology. So little, he reflects, does the expulsion of theological doctrines from natural philosophy militate against religion! The earlier Epicureans find their good in pleasure, and make virtue a servant of pleasure, after the manner of certain comedies of errors, "wherein the mistress and the maid change habits." Their "reformed" school places felicity in the sereneness of a mind free from perturbation. The sect, as a whole, subjects natural philosophy to moral ends thus understood and makes the aim of its science the expulsion or prevention of such opinions as may depress and disturb the mind. In accordance with this end they undertake to reject the necessity of Fate as well as the fear of the gods (*Works,* II, 230, 296–97; III, 16, 24; VI, 225, 315; VIII, 448–49, 511; IX, 199, 206).

In the ethical teaching of the Stoics, Bacon finds views not dissimilar to those of the Epicureans. Epicurus places felicity "in those things which are in our power, lest we be liable to fortune and disturbance"; he and his contemporaries thus convert philosophy into an "occupation or profession," whose business is "to fly and avoid" rather than "to resist and extinguish" things which produce mental perturbations. This sort of thinking, Bacon comments, is for persons who can abstain from, but cannot sustain themselves in, the affairs of life. Its devotee is like a man who refrains from all activity except attendance upon his health. The fact escapes him that even as the healthiest body is one which is "ablest to endure all alterations and extremities," so that mind is soundest which "can go through the greatest temptations and perturbations" (*Works*, III, 16–18; VI, 316; IX, 200–201).

The Skeptics profess acatalepsia, or the denial of the capacity of the mind to know. This is a doctrine which Plato and his school have originated by way of negative irony. With Pyrrho and the later Academy it becomes a positive tenet of belief and passes permanently into philosophy as a dogma whose consequence is the disabling of the human mind. Skepticism marks a misinterpretation and misuse of philosophy. It is based on futile argument about the possibility of knowledge. It disregards the discovery and invention of such means as are available for knowing. As a development in history it signalizes two faults in human reflection. In the first instance, while its exponents oppose with their arguments the traducers of knowledge, the wholesale dogmatists, they fail to return to the tenable position maintained by the more ancient of the Greeks between a boastful pronouncing on everything and a despair of knowing anything. It is bad for men to think their knowledge perfect and yet know nothing which they ought; it is good, and well concluded, that men should think their knowledge imperfect and yet have discovered and invented the means to know what is necessary. In the second place, the Skeptics commit their chief error in charging deceit to the senses, which despite their "cavillations .... are very sufficient to certify and report truth .... by help of instrument," when they should blame the intellect with its futile attempts at theoretical demonstration and its refusal "to submit itself to the nature of things." In any event, they pull the sciences up by the roots through an argumentative attack on false methods of demonstration which nobody should ever have accepted or practiced (*Works,* I, 233–34, 273, 281–82, 333; II, 369–70; VI, 65–66, 267–68; VIII, 59–60, 98, 107, 158; IX, 70–71).

The teaching of the Schoolmen Bacon interprets merely as a "degenerate" version of Aristotle's doctrines and method. Many of the Peripatetics, he says, were undoubtedly men of "sharp and strong wits" with abundancy of leisure; and they might, except for the circumstances of their living, reading, and contemplation, "have proved excellent lights, to the great advancement of all learning and knowledge." Even as their bodies were shut up in the cells of monasteries, so were their minds confined to a few authors. Their reading was limited and without variety. They possessed but "little history, either of nature or time." And it became their endeavor to spin "out of no great quantity of matter, and infinite agitation of wit.... laborious webs of learning which are extant in their books." The wit of men, if it work upon matter, works according to the structures and motions of nature; "but if it work upon itself, as the spider worketh his web, then it is endless, and brings forth indeed cobwebs of learning, admirable for the fineness of thread and work, but of no substance or profit."

The procedure of the Schoolmen was "upon every particular position or assertion to frame objections, and to these objections, solutions; which solutions were for the most part not confutations, but distinctions." And so far did they stress these distinctions that they "broke up the solidity and coherency of the sciences by the minuteness of their questions." Their method of inquiry engendered many questions as soon as it solved one. They refused to set up, so to speak, one great light in the habitation of knowledge; and when they carried their candle into one remote corner, the rest was darkened. An apt "image" of their philosophy is the fable of Scylla. Scylla was transformed into a comely virgin in the upper parts but had barking monsters about her loins. For when philosophical doctrines descend from certain "good and proportionable" generalities to subtle distinctions, "instead of a fruitful womb for the use and benefit of man's life, they end in monstrous altercations and barking questions" (*Works,* I, 200; II, 128–30; V, 441; VI, 122–24, 427; VIII, 83, 119, 120; VIII, 26–27).

Bacon notes two attempts to improve upon the Peripatetic method of discovery and demonstration, one by Lully, the other by Ramus. And, while he would have these "reformers" included in the curricula of schools of the traditional sort along with Plato, Aristotle, and Cicero, he nevertheless finds no satisfaction in their teachings. Lully undertakes to symbolize subjects and predicates of propositions by letters. He then sets down rules which are to govern the possible combinations among these symbols. Their several conjunctions he would represent by arrangements of mathematical figures and colors; so that, by a manipulation of the latter, the meanings of the original symbols having been made definite, an answer to any question might be given representation. This sort of demonstration, Bacon comments, is even more "verbal" than that of Aristotle himself and pushes nominalism to sheer futility.

It is nothing more or less than "a method of imposture .... to give men countenance that those which use the terms might be thought to understand the art" (*Works,* II, 436; VI, 296; IX, 129-30; XIII, 302).

Lully would reform logic by a manipulation of symbols, Ramus merely by the conversion of statements. Ramus will have the predicate belong to the subject in such a manner that the predicate is what the subject is and the subject is what the predicate is. That is to say, he would make all knowledge a matter of convertible propositions.

Bacon recognizes a meritorious intention in this opinion of Ramus, for he himself maintains in a special way, as we have had occasion to note, that what is ultimately affirmed of an object in scientific knowledge is its very identical nature. He finds, however, that Ramus' interpretation of the proposition is rendered nugatory by the formal character of his logic. Ramus is still thinking in terms of demonstration from abstract notion and principle to abstract notion and principle and not from observed data through successive stages of graded axioms. Bacon is reminded "that according to the ancient fables, *the most precious things have the most pernicious keepers";* and is given to reflect, "He had need to be well conducted that should design to make Axioms *convertible,* if he makes them not withal *circular,* and *non-promovent,* or *incurring into themselves"* (*Works,* II, 434-35; VI, 294-95; IX, 128).

Turning from the method of demonstration to the compilation and use of natural history, Bacon finds that in the gathering of historical data "there hath not been that choice and judgment used as ought to have been." The books on natural history are filled with "fabulous experiments, fabricated secrets, and frivolous impostures." None of their compilers, with the notable exception of Pliny, have brought together the data of nature in her three manifestations, that is to say, in her natural course, in her constraint by art, and in her production of monstrosities by her "errors." Most of the extant histories, including works by Pliny, Cardan, Albertus Magnus, and divers of the Arabians, are loaded with fabulous matter, much of it untried and untrue, "to the derogation of the credit of natural philosophy with the grave and sober kind of wits." Aristotle shows integrity in his refusing to mingle the history of living creatures, except sparingly, with "vain" and "feigned" matter, and in his placing of "all prodigious matter which he thought worthy the recording into one book"; yet neither he nor Theophrastus, Dioscorides, Pliny, nor the modern naturalist, has set before him the task of collecting history as the primary material and stuff of an inductive philosophy (*Works,* II, 48, 133; VI, 126; VII, 290; VIII, 358, 412; X, 409).

Bacon, having noted these deficiencies in the design and the performance of the original compilers, finds it necessary nevertheless to turn to their work in order to obtain matter for his topics when he undertakes to bring together data for the demonstration of the working of his new scientific method. He draws on Albertus Magnus to a degree, through a secondary source, Porta; from Theophrastus rarely, and through Porta or Pliny; from Cardan considerably; and much from Pliny, Porta, and Aristotle—especially from the pseudo-works (see *Works,* III, 239, 263, 290, 355, 467; IV, 160, 161, 165, 175, 187, 250, 256, 290, 293, 360 ff., 393, 399, 446, 452; VII, 388; IX, 405, 430, 458; X, 34, 129).

If Bacon has but little respect for those attempts which are made to reform the Aristotelian logic by Lully and Ramus, he does pay tribute to certain amendments to the Aristotelian physics which are advanced by such "moderns" as Gilbert, Copernicus, Galileo, and Telesius. He notes Gilbert's just derision of the theories of traditional astronomy—for instance, of the doctrine that the motions of the heavens are performed in perfect circles and of a theory of eccentrics and epicycles which makes nature so strange in her workings that she has devised wheels a couple of miles in circuit to carry a ball the size of a palm! Gilbert has to his credit, also, the conception of that selenography which now has been nearly attained through the labors of Galileo and others. He has also properly ridiculed the Peripatetic definition of heat as "that which separates heterogeneous parts" with the comment that this is a definition "simple by effects, and those particular"—as if man were to be defined as that which sows wheat and plants vines.

Bacon acknowledges Gilbert's skilful and sustained observations of the loadstone and his conclusion that the "flight" of iron from one pole of the magnet is not, strictly speaking, a flight at all but a "conformity and meeting in a more convenient situation." His work on the theory of magnetic force has not been unscientific. The fact remains, however, that he ascribes too much to that force: this recorder of nature, like many a predecessor, after he makes his laborious observations in one field—in his case the loadstone—will proceed to construct an entire system out of narrow observations. He accordingly builds a ship out of a shell and becomes a philosophical dogmatist (*Works,* I, 260, 444, 496,

501; II, 140; III, 300; VI, 132; VII, 75, 118–19, 332, 356; VIII, 84, 261, 301, 315; IX, 469; X, 449, 476).

The astronomical theory of Copernicus, Bacon neither accepts nor rejects. He notes that the same phenomena may be explained both by the traditional geocentric astronomy, with its epicycles and eccentrics, and by the doctrine of Copernicus, which assumes that the earth moves. Such astronomical facts as have so far been brought under consideration are indifferently agreeable to either theory; and it may be assumed that other constructions may be similarly brought forth to satisfy the phenomena in question. To find the real truth a new and untried severity of investigation is required. This will involve two things: first, a natural history and, secondly, a philosophy of nature, especially of matter. The history should include records of astronomers of past and present, including Ptolemy, Copernicus, and other writers on celestial bodies; also observations made by the naked eye, with the help of calculations, and especially through the use of optical instruments which are now available and by which there has been opened up "a new commerce with the phenomena of the heavens."

The only philosophy capable of correcting the opinions of the ancients and of the Copernicans, both of which are, in opposite ways, designed to adjust certain observations and to save appearances, is one which rests on an understanding of the "common passions and desires of matter" in both the terrestrial and the celestial worlds. The divorce of ethereal and sublunary bodies has been superstitious and rash: for certain it is that there are many effects, such as expansion, contraction, impression, cession, collection into masses, and attraction, which occur on the surface of the earth, in its inner parts, and at the summits of the heaven as well. Without natural history properly compiled and without a philosophy of matter, it is not possible to establish or to refute any major hypothesis of scientific astronomy. Let there be arranged, then, between philosophy and astronomy, as by a convenient and legitimate alliance, that the latter shall prefer those hypotheses which are most convenient for compendious calculation, and the former those which approach nearest the truth of nature, and that the hypotheses of astronomy shall not prejudice the truth of the thing, while the decisions of philosophy shall be such as are explicable by the phenomena of earth and the heavens (*Works,* II, 310–11, 386; V, 294–96, 303–4; VI, 234; VIII, 502–3; IX, 14; X, 413–15, 422–23).

In Galileo's observations of the heavens Bacon finds much that is commendable. He rejects the former's theory of the tides, based as it is on the inability of water to keep up with those varied velocities of different parts of the earth which are produced through a combination of two types of motion—the motion of the earth in its orbit and its motion about its axis. Bacon hails the ingenious constructing and use of telescopes by Galileo as one of the greatest events in the whole history of astronomy. A new intercourse, he says, like that by boats or vessels, can now be carried on with the heavens. These glasses make it evident, for intance, that the Milky Way is a collection of small stars—a fact no more than suspected by the ancients. They enable observers to descry the dances of smaller stars about the planet Jupiter, to see spots on the sun, and to practice selenography. And they provide grounds for new hypotheses about centers of motion among the stars. These fruits of inquiry mark an eminent advance in astronomy (*Works*, I, 456-57, 484-85; VII, 297, 333-34, 346, 348; VIII, 272-73, 299; X, 416, 450, 465).

Of the "moderns" the thinker whom Bacon admires most is Telesius, who, he says in his later works, has propounded a philosophy widely received and honored. While he calls Telesius an indifferent observer and a thinker who becomes entangled in his own theories, he hails him as one who "loves truth," a man useful to the sciences, and altogether the "best of the novellists." Immediate reasons for his praise are not difficult to see. In the first place, Bacon finds in the teachings of Telesius and his pupil Donius a fundamental doctrine of his own, and one without which his separation of physics and theology could not be made complete, namely, that the sensible soul is purely physical. Secondly, Telesius, schooled as he is in the thoughts of the Peripatetics, turns their own reasonings against them. Thirdly, Telesius, having rejected Aristotle, returns, like Bacon himself, to pre-Socratic philosophy. And, fourthly, Telesius is preoccupied with problems respecting heat and cold; and these are factors which for Bacon constitute the "great instrument of operation" in both nature and art (*Works,* I, 522; II, 347-48; IV, 204; V, 310, 339, 342; VIII, 334; IX, 50-51; X, 364-65, 391, 394).

Bacon discerns in the writings of Telesius a revival of the opinion of Parmenides to the effect that there are in things two principles, heaven and earth or fire and earth. And he understands the School of Telesius to assert that the primary things to be reckoned with in an understanding of nature's structures and motions are heat, with its light and motion, and cold, with its darkness and inertness. The two entities, heat and cold, have no body but follow a passive and potential matter which renders possible corporeal bulk and is indifferently susceptible to either nature. Light is a shooting-forth of heat; heat is dominant in all motion; darkness is a destitution radiating from cold. Rarity and density are textures made by heat and cold; what is produced is rendered dense and thick by cold and separated and extended by heat. From these textures a disposition toward motion is given to bodies; promptness and aptness to rare bodies, and torpidity and aversion to dense. Heat, through tenuity, excites motion; cold, through density, subdues and checks it. Such being the case, then, there may be posited two sets of conjugates: one including heat, lucidity, rarity, mobility, and another including cold, darkness, density, and immobility. The seats and regions of the former are to be found in the heaven, and especially in the sun; those of the second, in the earth. The heaven, with its unimpaired heat and its tenuous matter and lucidity, is the most mobile; while the earth, on the contrary, with its unreduced cold and most contracted matter, is the coldest, darkest, densest. The earth by itself, apart from the activity of the heaven, is not only averse to motion but immobile as well.

In the heaven some of the stars are hotter, more tenuous, and more vivid than others. The celestial region admits, then, of *diversity* of nature. But it does not countenance *contrariety,* for cold cannot have a part in it. The stars, because of differences in their heats and rarities, are subject to differences in motion and velocity. While celestial motion is circular in the main, there are certain stars in which a spiral motion is manifest. The latter motion is of a rotary sort, not returning to the point from which it begins, and is compounded of a straight line and a circle.

Telesius does not definitely determine the exact area within which cold is bounded. But he does maintain that there is a part of the earth in which coldness remains undisturbed and inviolate, completely removed from the heat of celestial things. This is an area in which absolute and undiminished coldness, opacity, density, and rest prevail. Between this and the heaven there exists a middle region of things which is the recipient of some heat, radiation, tenuity, and mobility, and which is composed through the impact of hot sun upon the cold earth. Throughout the spaces between the regions of the heaven and the innermost parts of the earth cold and heat compete, the latter seeking to subdue the former. The two principles come together for contribution in no third primary nature but only in *hyle* or indeterminate matter (*Works*, V, 310–18, 336; X, 364–71, 388).

Bacon, in reviewing the philosophy of Telesius, finds it contemplative and "pastoral," written by a man who is careful to balance a system but not prepared to come to grips with nature's free activities and her "vexations" in the works of art. He is not surprised to find that Telesius, when he undertakes to give an accounting—according to his principles—of the specific processes in the courses of nature and art, is driven to take refuge in despair. Telesius intimates that, while the strength and quantity of heat and the disposition of matter may be determined grossly and in sum, the measuring of the manners of their behavior and their exact proportions in specific instances lies beyond his reach. He confesses, with more honesty than is to be found in many of his more dogmatic adversaries, that the question of the amount of heat required to turn this or that earth into this or that entity presents him with an insoluble difficulty. And in desperation he consigns the problem to those who may have the leisure and wit to solve it.

The basic difficulty within his system arises, says Bacon, from two sources: first, the functions which he assigns to heat and, secondly, his conception of matter as something purely passive and, apart from quantity in gross, altogether indeterminate. His doctrine respecting heat is nullified by four considerations: First, there are actions and effects—some of these great and widely diffused—which cannot be referred to the operations of heat and cold. Secondly, there are "natures" which are not produced by these operations. Thirdly, among things which derive their origin from heat and cold are many which proceed from these two factors as from an "efficient and instrument" and not as from a "proper and intimate" cause. Fourthly, on his being driven to acknowledge that there are mobile, bright, and rare things which are also cold and hot things which are also dark and dense, Telesius finds that his doctrine of the combination of four connaturals—mobility, light, rarity, and heat—and of their opposites becomes mixed up and confused. Here he reaps the reward of those who, like the Peripatetics before him, form their opinions of nature before they examine and record her ways!

To the Parmenidean doctrine of fire Telesius adds a doctrine of indeterminate matter which he borrows from Aristotle and then modifies. He considers matter as something passive, without decrease or increase, and finds the property by which it preserves itself merely quantitative and not belonging to either its form or its action. Here he commits the gravest of errors, for he fails to recognize that matter, even the most minute, possesses in itself active virtue, first, to the preserving of resistance to annihilation and, secondly, in refusing to undergo separation from its kind. This active virtue is not the result of any quantity; nor can it be the effect of mere passivity; nor does it come from an absurd Peripatetic potentiality through which that which is arises from that which is not. Once more by the failure of Telesius' explanation are we driven from theories about indeterminate matter to the doctrine of a determinate atom, of a "true being, materiate, formed, dimensional, and spatially located, possessing resistance, appetite, motion, and emanation" (*Works,* V, 329-31, 334-36, 338-42; X, 381-83, 385-88, 390-95).

There remain for consideration a number of writers and "experimenters." These include the Paracelsans, the magicians, alchemists, and chemists. Some of them share certain common opinions. Most of their number are dogmatists who, having destroyed to their own satisfaction ancient philosophic systems, would provide equally fantastic alternatives. Generally they compound a mixture of fact, superstition, and fable. A few of them record honest, if inadequate, observations of nature. And, unfortunately, not the simple, patient seeker of truth but the vain, frivolous impostor captivates the imagination of the public. Boastful talkers make preposterous promises. They announce and offer such extravagant boons as the retardation of old age, the alleviation of pain, remedies for natural defects, the transmutation of substances, the multiplication of natural motions at will, the illumination and exaltation of the intellectual faculties, the inhibiting and excitation of the passions, the revelation of the occult, the bringing-down and directing of celestial influences, the divination of future events—not to mention other of their absurdities (*Works,* I, 203, 267-68, 289-90, 295-96; II, 350-51; VI, 241, 256, 426; VII, 102-3, 113; VIII, 30, 92-93, 115, 120-21; IX, 53).

The School of Paracelsus pretend to find natural philosophy in the Scriptures and reject as profane all scientific teaching which lies beyond their interpretation of these. And, so far from honoring, as they think, the Scriptures, they depress what is divine to the mortal realm. "For to seek heaven and earth in the word of God.... is to seek temporary things among the eternal." It is not surprising, then, that their scientific observations are superstitious, fabulous, and inept. Their theory of the "imagination" is a good example of their philosophizing. This faculty, they teach, is, in its operation upon the bodies other than those of the imaginant, similar to "miracle-working faith." They strain the ancient representation of man as a microcosm, an "abstract or model of the world," to maintain that in the human body are to be found correspondences and parallels to all varieties of things, ranging from terrestrial minerals to the heavenly stars and planets (*Works,* I, 501, 525–26; II, 350–51; III, 182; IV, 223; VI, 241, 256, 405; VIII, 316, 338; IX, 53, 241, 353).

Close in practice and theory to the Paracelsans are the alchemists and magicians. These "light, idle, ignorant, credulous, and fantastical" people have brought great hurt and discredit upon natural science, the more especially upon its operative part which issues in works. The magicians have abused the name they bear; for natural magic in its true and ancient acceptance means "natural wisdom.... purged from vanity and superstition." The would-be miracle-worker, who bears in later times the name "magician," performs nothing that is permanent and profitable. Any works which he produces are aimed rather at "admiration and novelty than at utility and fruit." His procedure is to seek something "above nature affected" and, having found what he considers a breach in nature, to pretend to the performing of all things great and small. He is like a man who would till the ground and eat his bread without the sweat of his brow, for he relies upon hope and discards diligence. Hope works upon him like a soporific drug. First, it puts his understanding to sleep; next, it causes him to prattle about sympathies, antipathies, hidden properties, and heaven-sent virtues; and, finally, it leaves him in the repose of innumerable fancies (*Works,* I, 294–95; II, 301–2; III, 301–2; VI, 35, 214–15, 230, 241, 416–17, 426; VIII, 120, 514–15; IX, 470–71).

The alchemists profess to be experimenters and not workers of miracles. They have made some discoveries and inventions. Their practice is aptly illustrated by the fable of the old man who bequeathed to his sons gold presumably buried in a vineyard. The heirs applied themselves to digging everywhere, and, although the expected gold was not found, the vintage was made the more abundant by the tillage. The alchemist has great deference for the prescriptions given by his authors and in auricular tradition. When these directions fail him he lays the blame on himself, thinking that he has wrongly varied the rigidly prescribed experiment by a scruple of ingredient or a moment of time. The result is that he continues to experiment endlessly. If perchance he hits upon some conclusions which he regards as significant and useful, "he feedeth upon them, and magnifieth them to the most" (*Works,* I, 294; VI, 417; VII, 121; VIII, 119–20).

The chemists are experimenters and not traditionalists. They make a few discoveries. Some of their number turn out to be theorists; others remain pure empirics. Certain of them maintain that there are four elements present in nature—earth, water, air, and ether—these being the "womb" wherein the specific "seeds" of things are generated. And beyond these they find, instead of the despoiled and indifferent matter of the Peripatetics, "sulphur, mercury, and salt." Their terms are good but indeterminately construed.

The empirics among them rely on variety and variation of experiment. They acknowledge neither rule for discovery nor axiom of interpretation. They commit themselves to the waves of experience and pursue a wandering course without purpose, organization, or skill. They assign themselves single, often petty, works for accomplishment, and are content with premature conclusions. They conduct fruit-bearing experiments and disregard light-bearing experiments. Like Atalanta they turn from the course of investigation to seize the golden apple of immediate results and let the victory over nature escape them.

Natural philosophers, chemists, and others are, generally speaking, either empirics or dogmatists. "The empirics like the ant only collect and use; the dogmatists like spiders make cobwebs out of themselves." But the bee holds to a middle course. It gathers its materials in the field, and these it digests and transforms by an ability appropriate to itself. Not unlike to the bee, says Bacon, is the true investigator of nature. He refuses merely to collect and to put away in his memory history and experiment; nor does he manufacture his dogmas by the mere power of his mind. Rather, through a union between the experimental and the rational in the exercise of his powers of discovery, he produces enlightened conclusions from those materials which he has received from his senses and assimilated by his understanding (*Works,* I, 275–76, 280, 306; III, 303–4; VII, 92, 137; VIII, 100–101, 105, 131–32; IX, 472–73; XIII, 404).

CHAPTER XIII

CLASSIFICATION OF THE SCIENCES RESPECTING GOD AND NATURE

HAVING set forth his "refutation" of past and present philosophies, the accepted methods of demonstration, and the prevailing errors of the human mind, Bacon proceeds to reconstruct human thought and learning in accordance with a new design. His positive undertaking is an ambitious one, nothing less than a complete reconstruction of the sciences through the use of a new method. It is such, he says, that those who are made acquainted with it will wonder why it has not occurred to them. The undertaking he describes as something accidental to its author and the age in which he lives, "the offspring of time rather than of wit." He is aware that many will read and condemn, because they are satisfied that the ways of science can be neither changed nor improved. To these he makes answer: It is not good to contend that what has never been done cannot be successfully brought to pass by means which have never been tried. Certainly there is no comparison between the loss by not trying and the failure by not succeeding. In the former case the chance of a great good is thrown away; in the latter only a small amount of labor is lost. Certainly the time has come for men to betake themselves from the mists of tradition and the whirl and eddy of "learned" argument and to enter upon a course which may eventually lead to the goal of real discovery and useful invention. In undertaking this way, solitary as it is, we are not, says Bacon, seeking the role of combatant against other scientists. We would be a trumpeter who, as Homer says, moves freely among the bitterest enemies. We would summon and rouse to activity our fellows, not that by contentions they should cut one another to pieces but that, united in concord and having made peace among themselves, they may storm and capture the heights and strongholds of nature and extend the boundaries of human empire "so far as God Almighty in his goodness may allow."

While we are innovators we are not mere empirics groping in darkness; we have a direction to show us the way. Nor are we precipitate. We do not believe that the task which we set ourselves can be performed by one man or by many men in any one generation. We are proposing a plan for the future. We have cleared the ground of the scientific mind and are undertaking to lay a new groundwork. Our foundation is an inductive method which can be challenged neither by wit nor by theoretical presuppositions but only by works.

We are not seeking luster for our name but light for the human mind through the use of a new means of inquiry. We do not rely on any historical school of philosophy for support—after the fashion of persons of no family who devise for themselves genealogies of descent from an ancient line. We shall be content with the increase of human dignity, power, and happiness through the discovery of nature's ways by directed observation of humble facts (*Works,* I, 195–96, 204–8, 221, 227, 237–38, 248, 287–88, 320–22, 328; II, 307–8, 310–11; III, 185; VIII, 18–19, 30–34, 47, 53, 64, 75, 113, 146–48, 154, 520; IX, 13–14, 356).

In such statements as these Bacon introduces his Great Instauration, which is formally announced to the learned world in his *Novum organum* of 1620. Under this title are included a proem, a dedicatory epistle to King James, a preface to the "Instauration," the "Plan of the Work," an explanatory page; and the "Second Part of the Work Which Is Called the New Organon" or "True Directions concerning the Interpretation of Nature." The last includes a preface and two books of aphorisms. In the initial proem the author explains that he is attempting "a total reconstruction of sciences, arts, and all human knowledge, raised upon the proper foundations."

Bacon has resolved upon publishing as much of the undertaking as he has been able to complete, because of a solicitude that in case of his death "some design and specification" of what his mind has compassed should remain. The "Plan of the Work" includes a list of the six parts of the Instauration: (I) "The Divisions of the Sciences"; (II) "The New Organon, or Directions respecting the Interpretation of Nature"; (III) "The Phenomena of the Universe, or Natural and Experimental History for the Foundation of Philosophy"; (IV) "The Ladder of the Understanding," (V) "The Forerunners or Anticipations of the New Philosophy"; (VI) "The New Philosophy, or Active Science." The explanatory page contains two announcements: The new organon which comprises the six parts of the Instauration is not yet set down in treatise form but only summarily in aphorisms, and the first part of the Instauration is wanting, although it may be found in some measure in the Second Book of the *Proficience and Advancement of Learning, Divine and Human* (*Works*, I, 195-96, 212; VIII, 18-19, 38).

Published in the same volume with the *Novum organum* is a brief work, *Parasceve ad historiam naturalem et experimentalem*. By way of preface to this, Bacon explains that even as he publishes the *Novum organum* to put his new method "out of peril," he would now for the same reason give permanent character to the delineation of the sort of natural and experimental history which is appropriate for the constructing of the new philosophy, lest, he says, for want of proper suggestion men should direct themselves according to the examples of natural histories now employed and stray from "our usage."

By 1620 Bacon is undertaking to make public something of each of the first three parts of his sixfold Instauration. Scarcely anything beyond prefaces survive in his written works of the three remaining parts of the projected scheme. The first part is to be represented by the *Advancement of Learning*, abridged in certain parts and amplified in others and put into Latin under the title, *De dignitate et augmentis scientiarum;* and the second only by the *Novum organum*, deplorably incomplete and in summary form; while the third is to be set forth in such "histories" as the author—working against time and physical weakness—is able to amass before his death.

An entry in the *Commentarius solutus* under the date, July 26, 1608, reads: "Proceeding with the translation of my book of Advancement of Learning—hearkening to some other if Playfer should fail." In the dedicatory letter to Bishop Andrews which is prefixed to his *Advertisement touching an Holy War* of 1622, Bacon also writes, "That my book of Advancement of Learning may be some preparative or key for the better opening of the Instauration, because it exhibits a mixture of new conceits and old, whereas the Instauration gives the new unmixed, otherwise than with some aspersion of the old for taste's sake, I have thought good to procure a translation of that book into the general language, not without great and ample additions and enrichments thereof, especially in the second book, which handleth the partition of sciences; in such sort as I hold it may serve in lieu of the first part of the Instauration, and acquit my promise in that part" (*Works*, XIII, 186).

When asking Dr. Playfer to put the work into Latin, Bacon offers the reason: "Wherefore since I have only taken upon me to ring a bell to call other wits together, ... it cannot but be consonant to my desire to have that bell heard as far as can be." Dr. Playfer dies early in 1609. The Latin translation, made "by the help of some good pens" and under the supervision of Bacon himself, is not sent to the press until 1622. It appears in the "general language" Latin in 1623 under the title *De dignitate et augmentis scientiarum*. The piece published in 1623 is both an amplification and an abridgment of the original of 1605. Uncomplimentary references to the Roman church are deleted, passages which concern English history are removed or shortened, and expressions which might offend Continental traditionalists softened or changed. Rawley explains in the Preface that the author finding "the part relating to the Partitions of the Sciences already executed, though less solidly than the dignity of the argument demanded .... thought the best thing he could do would be to go over again what he had written, and to bring it to the state of a satisfactory and completed work. And in this way he considers that he fulfils the promises which he has given respecting the first part of the Instauration." In a letter sent with a presentation copy of the work Bacon tells King James "I have been .... mine own *Index Expurgatorius*, that it may be read in all places. For since my end of putting it into Latin was to have it read everywhere, it had been an absurd contradiction to free it in the language and to pen it up in the matter."

Of these statements two, at least, contain an obvious note of apology for a work which quite fails to measure up to the requirements of the first part of the Great Instauration. And there are other indications that Bacon is forced by circumstances to republish the early work in representation of the first part of a sixfold scheme which takes definite shape at a period much later than that of the original work's preparation. There is, for instance, no summary or listing in the *De augmentis* of the matter of the first book of the *Advancement* under *Argumenta singulorum capitum:* this begins with chapter i of Book II. And it is not without meaning, as Spedding has remarked, that the late work is not even assigned the name *Partitiones scientiarum*. Nor has the work a title which covers or even suggests the first part of the Instauration. Again, in the "Plan of the Work," included within the *Novum organum*, where the respective designs of the six parts of the Instauration are set forth, the author says that in the first part he will proceed not as an augur who takes auspices but "as a general who intends to take possession." He will also, he says, on observing a difficult and obscure deficiency in learning "subjoin either directions for the accomplishment of such work, or else a portion of the work executed by ourselves in exemplification of the whole that we may aid in individual cases either by works or by counsel." But there is no such occupation, direction, or execution in either the early *Advancement of Learning* or the later *De augmentis*. And without these Bacon's review of extant sciences becomes, indeed, after its announcement in 1620, an anticlimax. For in the *Novum organum* he has rejected "all sciences and all authors," has granted the prevailing sciences no further function than "to supply matter for disputation and ornaments for discourses," and has maintained consistently and proved to his own satisfaction that no scientific doctrine is acceptable which has not been tried by the true method of induction, heretofore unknown, of the Instauration. And so thorough is Bacon's refutation in 1620 of the learning of the past that any later attempts of his to give recognition to its achievements bear witness to the retrenchment of a man who finds himself without the available means to uproot the old philosophy and plant his reformed science (*Works*, I, 213–14, 328; VIII, 39–40, 153).

It should be remembered that Bacon is no longer young or robust. In 1623 he is sixty-three years of age. He has scarcely any natural history collected. His new method is not written out with any completeness. Unless the method is provided, the history cannot be interpreted. And without an interpretation of natural history any philosophical synthesis is out of the question. Time is short. A version of the *Advancement of Learning*, with such amendments as may be possible, must suffice.

The *De augmentis* contains a general description of the knowledge possessed to date by the human race. Yet it is no detached history or summary of learning, the author informs us, but rather a coasting voyage past the sciences by a critical traveler who is intent upon discovering what regions may be improved and what waste areas may be brought under cultivation. It exhibits no regard for the accepted boundaries and methods of cultivation which have been heretofore observed in the recognized sciences, and the classification of the parts of knowledge which the work contains marks a definite and consequential departure from the Aristotelian tradition and is destined to have most far-reaching effects in determining the course of future philosophy.

For Bacon the principle of division among the sciences is determined, first, by the absolute chasm which exists between the truths given in revelation through the Word of God and axioms discovered by the powers of man and, secondly, through distinctions among the human faculties. Bacon ranges the varieties of truth according to the varied mental dispositions of the human subject. From the "three faculties of the rational soul," memory, imagination, and reason, proceed respectively the three major divisions of knowledge, history, poetry, and philosophy. These knowledges are attained by man through his own powers. The same threefold division of knowledge applies also to that theology which is given through revelation. While the information received through revelation is unique in its object and conveyance, profane and sacred knowledges are nevertheless only different liquids poured through different funnels into the same vessel. Revealed theology consists of sacred history—including prophecy, which is history "before the event"; parable, which is "divine poesy"; and doctrines and precepts, which are, so to speak, a perennial philosophy.

The parts of knowledge—namely, history, poetry, and philosophy—are not, however, completely separable. The lowest stage of history and remembered experience are the same thing. Three sorts of poetry—narrative, dramatic, and parabolic—may be brought under history and philosophy. Narrative poetry is an "imitation" of history, dramatic is "visible" history, and parabolic is intellectual history appealing to sense and imagination. All three may be regarded as an illustration and communication of philosophical truths. Parabolic poetry is an instrument in revealed theology for conveying truths from the Divine Being to the human mind (*Works,* II, 186–88, 221–25; VI, 186–87, 203–5; VII, 285–87; VIII, 407–9, 440–43; X, 403–5).

This intermixture of knowledges is due mainly to the predominance of the cogitative faculty of the rational soul. The rational soul is bestowed by God when he makes man in his own image. All the faculties which man uses in knowledge are its instruments. Once reason is given to man as a part of his nature, it acts as a general faculty in all his perceptions, even if reason cannot understand the nature of the inspired soul to which it belongs. "He who remembers or recollects, thinks (*cogitat*); similarly he who imagines, thinks; just as he who reasons, thinks; in fine the spirit whether prompted by sense or left to itself, whether in the functions of the intellect, or of the will and affections, dances to the measure of thoughts (*cogitationum*)" (*Works,* II, 186–87, 221, 235–36, 344–48; VII, 286–87; VIII, 407–8, 440, 453–54; IX, 48–51; X, 404–5).

While thought thus dominates experience, sense plays a major part in perception. The senses are the door to both the imagination and the intellect. The sense is affected only by individuals, whose images "fix themselves in the memory, and pass into it in the first instance entire, as it were, just as they come. These the human mind proceeds to review and ruminate; and thereupon either simply rehearses them, or makes fanciful imitations of them, or analyzes and classifies them. Wherefore from these three fountains flow these three emanations, History, Poesy, and Philosophy." Philosophy, having discarded individuals, proceeds through general notions. In the "composition and division of these according to the law of nature and of things themselves perspicuity lies. And this in fact is the office and work of reason." Poetry is concerned with "invented" individuals which exceed those of actuality, while history has to do with individuals "circumscribed by time and place." One should not assume, however, that history is characterized by the mere particularity of sense-experience. Knowledge, even at the level of history, involves a degree of classification. In both sense and memory the universalizing reason is active. The object of history is the species which is recognized by resemblances of things through common factors. Memory contains "prenotion." Prenotion is the means of delimiting experience from the indeterminateness of mere empiricism by applying fruitful inquiry to nature by "topics" which are special questions. Wise interrogation is the beginning of knowledge. Plato rightly says, "Whosoever seeks a thing knows that which he seeks for in a general notion; else how shall he know it when he has found it?" (*Works,* II, 59, 187, 388, 407; VIII, 371, 407; IX, 86, 105).

History is of two sorts, natural and civil. The latter, which includes ecclesiastical and literary histories, deals with the deeds of men; the former with the works of nature. The subject mater of natural history includes three states of nature: nature "free" in her usual course; in "error" when she produces monsters and "wonders"; and in bonds when restrained, molded, and made new, as it were, by the hand of man. The history of nature may be said, then, to include a record of generations, of pretergenerations, and of arts—the last of these in "mechanical and experimental history." The history of pretergenerations is of great import, since it provides "an unimpeded transit from the wonders of nature .... to the wonders of art." The pursuit of nature in her wanderings enables man "to lead and drive her afterwards to the same place again."

The history of "nature wrought or mechanical" in the various arts is "most radical and fundamental" for the construction of an operative natural philosophy; for, even as Proteus does not exhibit his many shapes until held in chains, so nature reveals her latent character and possibilities when subjected to the trials and vexations of art.

Bacon is aware that in his including an account of the arts within natural history he is running counter to traditional opinion; and he takes pains to insist that in both natural and artificial things the "form and essence" are of the same kind. He maintains, moreover, that it is not the function of art to augment nature or to bring to completion what nature has begun, much less to correct nature when degenerate or to move her fundamentally in any respect. While man as artisan has the power of "motion" over matter, in that he can unite and separate natural bodies according to their relative activities and passivities, the fact remains that whatever effects are produced by nature in her own workings, or by man in conjunction with nature by art, are all natural, the works of God's creatures.

Natural history may also be classified under two sorts, according to its end. These are narrative history and inductive history. The former is common and found in considerable abundance. It consists mainly of antiquities, citations from authors, fables, controversies, philology, and other pleasing adornments which are "more fitted for table-talk and *noctes* of learned men than for the instauration of philosophy." Of inductive history, however, there is practically nothing yet to be found. Yet this is "the primary matter" of solid knowledge and indeed may be called "the nursing-mother (*mammam*) of philosophy" (*Works,* II, 44-45, 48, 49, 188-96; VIII, 354-55, 358, 360, 409-15).

Civil history is of three sorts: ecclesiastical, civil in the narrow sense, and history of learning and the arts. The first and second are well represented; the last, important as it is for the emancipation of the human mind from traditional errors, is wanting. Ecclesiastical history contains three parts. The first is ecclesiastical history in its restricted sense; this has to do with the times and states of the church militant. The second is the history of prophecy, where each prediction of Scripture is set against the event in its fulfilment; and the third is the history of Providence. The last has for its task the recording of "that divine correspondence, which sometimes exists, between God's revealed will and secret will. For though the judgments and counsels of God are so obscure that to the natural man they are altogether illegible, yea, many times hidden from the eyes of those that behold them from the tabernacle, yet at some times it pleases the Divine Wisdom, for the better establishment of his people and the confusion of those who are without God in the world, to write it . . . . in such capital letters that (as the Prophet saith) 'He that runneth by may read it.' "

Civil history may be divided also into "antiquities" or "remnants" of the past, "memorials" which are the first rough drafts of history, and "perfect history" which "represents a portion of time, or a person worthy of mention, or an action or deed performed of the more distinguished sort." It may also be divided into pure civil history and mixed civil history. An example of the latter is cosmography. This is a mixture of natural history in respect to regions with their sites and products, of civil history in respect to the habitations, government, and manners of the people, and of mathematical calculations in respect to climate and to the configurations of the heavens beneath which the regions of the earth lie. It is a kind of knowledge in which the contemporary age excels. The world of late has been "wonderfully open and thorough-lighted." Men have traveled. A small vessel, emulating the heaven itself, has encompassed the tortuous course in encirclement of the terrestrial globe. The present age may put on its motto *plus ultra* (farther yet) in defiance of the *non ultra* (no farther) of the ancients and substitute for their "inimitable thunder" the challenging "imitable thunder." Modern navigation and the new discoveries it portends may well be according to divine plan. "For so the Prophet Daniel, in speaking of the latter times, foretells 'Many shall go to and fro on the earth, and knowledge shall be increased,' as if the opening and thorough passage of the world, and the increase of knowledge, were appointed to be in the same age" (*Works,* II, 203-18; VIII, 422-37).

The second primary division of knowledge is poetry. This contains three parts: narrative, dramatic, and parabolic. The third of these, as we have already seen, is much employed in the teaching of antiquity, where "fables, parables, enigmas, and similitudes abound" and bring "to the sense by images and examples" philosophical doctrines (*Works,* II, 220-25; VIII, 439-43).

The third and highest of the general divisions of human knowledge is philosophy. Poetry is, so to speak, "the dream of learning," history "walks upon the earth" and performs the office of a guide, whereas philosophy is the "palace of the mind" and is to be aproached with fitting reverence. Philosophy is natural knowledge. Human knowledge is "as the waters." Some waters descend from above, some spring from the earth. Philosophy arises initially from the natural senses. Inspired divinity is let down to man by divine revelation. Philosophical knowledge is resultant from "three kinds of ray—direct, refracted, and reflected. For nature strikes the understanding with a ray direct; God, by reason of the unequal medium of His creatures, with a ray refracted; man as shown and exhibited to himself, with a ray reflected." Philosophy, then, is a natural knowledge of God, man, and nature. It includes natural theology. This science may appropriately be called "divine philosophy" since, while natural in respect to its knowledge, it is divine in respect to its object.

Bacon is emphatic in his statement that natural theology is not to be confused with what the Aristotelians call by the same name, or with metaphysics—which for Bacon is no more than generalized physics. Natural theology, according to him, admits no doctrine of being, as such, nor does it permit an intellectual commerce between secondary causes in nature and a supranatural First Cause, between materiate beings and a Pure Form, between natural motions and a Prime Mover. What it discovers of its object, God, is only a "refracted" light through the observation of his creatures. Its doctrines may serve to refute atheism; they cannot establish religion. The latter is the office of revelation. No natural light is adequate to discover the nature and will of God. "For us all works show the power and skill of the workman, and not his image; so it is of the works of God, which show his omnipotency and wisdom, but do not partake of the image of the Maker." Any attempt to educe out of the contemplation of nature, through the natural processes of human knowledge, a persuasion or conclusion concerning the mysteries of faith is superstitious and ends in error and futility (*Works*, II, 250-51, 259-61, 264, 266, 357; VI, 217; VIII, 470-71, 477-79, 482, 484; IX, 59).

The different divisions of natural knowledge are to be regarded not so much like the lines of angles which meet at a single point but rather as the offshoots of a common nourishing stem which remains one and continuous before a division into branches. The main trunk from which the less general sciences derive their strength and vigor is First Philosophy or Sapience. First Philosophy includes axioms which are common to the several sciences and Transcendentals or Adventitious Conditions of

Beings, such as much and little, like and unlike, possible and impossible, being and not being. These transcend the lesser classifications of things and apply to all objects of science.

Natural knowledge may be arranged as a pyramid. The base is natural history; the stage next to the base is physics; the vertical point is metaphysics. "As for the cone and vertical point ('the work which God worketh from the beginning to the end,' namely, the summary law of nature), we are justly at a loss to say whether human inquiry can attain to it. But these three are the true stages of knowledge; which are to men inflated by their own knowledge and rebellious against God as the giants' three hills [Pelion, Ossa, and Olympus] .... but to those who emptying themselves refer all things to the glory of God, they are as the threefold acclamation: Holy, Holy, Holy. For God is holy in the multitude of His works, holy in the ordered connection of them, and holy in the union of them" (*Works,* II, 269, 291-93; VIII, 486, 507-8).

The philosophy of nature contains two main divisions, the speculative and the operative. The former of these has to do with the mine, so to speak, the latter with the furnace; the former with the inquisition of causes, the latter with the production of effects; the one searching into the bowels of nature, the other shaping nature as on an anvil. Speculative science includes two sorts, physics and metaphysics. Operative knowledge which has to do with the application of the axioms gained in the speculative sciences to matter, includes mechanics and magic. Metaphysics is the ultimate science of nature. The term "physics," which literally means the science of nature, is here used in a special sense to denote that part of speculative natural science which is subordinate to metaphysics. Physics is concerned with three subjects: the principles of things, the fabric of the world, and the varieties shown in the "lesser" parts of nature—for nature in her many parts manifests specific activities, fire, for example, producing hardness in respect to clay, softness in respect to wax. Physics investigates the Latent Schematisms and Latent Processes in matter.

Physics may be divided into physics of concretes and physics of abstracts. The first of these has to do with "creatures"; the second with "natures." In the latter instance, gravity or heat, to take an example or two, is examined as a "nature" inherent in many substances. In the physics of concretes an oak, or a lion, is investigated in order to record its many attributes. The physics of concretes approaches somewhat closely to natural history. Certain subjects belong to both, for instance, the heavens, the earth and sea, the greater colleges (or elements), the lesser colleges (or species), pretergenerations, and mechanical arts. In its records of these, natural history relates the facts, while physics indicates the causes (*Works,* II, 264, 267–69, 357; VIII, 482, 484–87; IX, 59).

Abstract physics has two parts; one deals with the schematisms of matter and the other with matter's appetites and motions. In order to show "some shadow of the true physic of abstracts" several of the topics which fall within its two divisions may be indicated. To the schematisms of matter are to be assigned the following: dense, rare; heavy, light; hot, cold; tangible, pneumatic; volatile, fixed; determinate, fluid; moist, dry; fat, crude; hard, soft; fragile, tensile; porous, close; spirituous, jejune; simple, compound; absolutely, imperfectly mixed; fibrous and venous, simple of structure or equal; similar, dissimilar; specific, nonspecific; organic, inorganic; animate, inanimate. "Further," the author says, "we do not go. For Sensible and Insensible, Rational and Irrational, we refer to the doctrine concerning Man."

As for the appetites and motions of matter, they are either simple or compound. The task of physics is to discover the former, for out of these the latter and indeed all natural actions—subject, of course, to the conditions imposed by the schematisms of matter—are produced. Chief among simple motions are motion of *resistance,* which is commonly called motion to prevent penetration of dimensions; motion of *connection,* commonly called avoidance of vacuum; motion of *liberty,* to prevent preternatural compression or extension; motion into a *new sphere,* or to rarefaction or condensation; motion of the *second connection,* or to prevent solution of continuity; motion of the *greater congregation,* or toward masses of connatural bodies, commonly called "natural motion"; motion of *lesser congregation,* commonly called "motion of sympathy and antipathy"; motion of *disposition,* that is, for the ordering of parts with reference to the whole; motion of *assimilation,* or multiplication of its own nature upon another body; motion of *excitation,* where the superior agent excites a motion dormant and latent in another; motion of *signature* or *impression,* that is, operation without communication of substance; *royal* motion, or restraint of other motions by the motion predominant; motion *without limit,* or spontaneous rotation; motion of *trepidation,* or systole and diastole, of bodies, that is, between what are agreeable and what are not agreeable; and, last, motion of *repose,* or abhorrence of motion, which is causative of very many things. From these simple motions, by complication, repetition, continuation, restraint, alternation, and other sorts of combination, proceed those compound motions or sums of motion which are commonly recognized under such names as "generation and corruption," "augmentation and diminution," "alteration," "local motion," "mixture," "separation and conversion" (*Works,* II, 282-83; VIII, 498-500).

Having indicated the topics of abstract physics, Bacon adds by way of appendix "the measurements of motion" in respect to the "dose" or the "how much" in nature. These furnish answers to questions concerning the distance through which virtue or activity acts, its rapidity or slowness; the length of delay in operation; the strength or weakness of the object; the amount of stimulus from surrounding things; and like matters. Such calculations fall within the ancillary science, mathematics; they are nevertheless an integral part of the physics of abstracts (*Works,* II, 281-83; VIII, 498-500).

The next natural science, metaphysics, must be distinguished both from first philosophy and from natural theology. To first philosophy has been assigned the "axioms common and promiscuous" to the sciences, as well as Transcendentals or Adventitious Conditions of Beings. "The inquiry concerning God, Unity, the Good, angels and spirits .... we have referred to natural theology." What then, Bacon asks, "is left remaining for metaphysic?" "Certainly nothing beyond nature; but of nature itself much the most pre-eminent part" for this "branch or descendant of natural science." The subject matter of metaphysics is the forms, the "natures," the laws, the causes, of natural things in motion.

Of the four causes named in tradition, the material and the efficient are to be assigned to physics, the formal and final to metaphysics. So says Bacon, and confounds his readers with an example of his use of traditional terms changed in "their sense and definitions." And, unless the commentator is on his guard on this occasion, he will be led astray, as he will on others, by the author's use of Aristotelian terms. Bacon's preservation of such terms as "metaphysics," "first philosophy," and "final cause" has proved too great a temptation for many an expositor, who finds in his philosophy a belated or a modified Aristotelianism. Bacon's own statement of the case is not too informative, for it does far less than justice to his practice. "Our custom in using terms," he says, "is of this sort. Both in the term metaphysic, as well as in other cases where our conceptions and notions are new and deviate from those received, we retain most religiously the ancient expressions. Because we hope that the ordering itself and the evident exposition of things which we are attempting will free the words we use from misapprehension, we desire earnestly—so far as may be without loss to truth and the sciences—to deviate as little as possible from antiquity, either in speech or opinions. And herein we cannot a little marvel at Aristotle who not only exercised unrestrained liberty of coining new words of science at pleasure but who also made an effort to extinguish and obliterate all venerable wisdom..... But to us for the other part (who desire, as much as lies in our pen to ground an alliance and commerce between the old and the new in learning) the principle holds.... to retain the ancient terms, though we oftentimes alter their sense and definitions; following that moderate approved mode in civil matters, by which when the status of things is changed, yet the forms of words endure: as Tacitus notes, 'The names of the magistrates are the same.' "

Proceeding with this mild caution of the author's in mind, we discover that doctrinally there is nothing in common between Bacon's four causes and those which Aristotle calls by the same names. Bacon's material cause is not a nonsignificant indeterminate but something with configuration of its own; it can in itself be discerned; it has a "nature." Again, for Bacon, matter is an actual existential thing; it is not an unknowable substrate which provides continuity in the actualization, potency, and individuation of substance in conjunction with a form which inheres in it. His efficient cause is not conceived as something which acts within a process of agency, to overcome privation and bring potency into act. Form for him is not to be interpreted teleologically, either as an end achieved in activity or as a *terminus* marking a significant stage in process but as a real existential thing, efficient in action, and self-sustaining. Of final causes, different from, or lying beyond, forms, Bacon makes no use in his account of the objects and methods of scientific observation in either the late *De augmentis* or the *Novum organum*. In the early *Advancement of Learning* he describes the fourfold classification of causes as "the received and sound division." In the *De augmentis* of 1623 he prefaces the fourfold division of causes with the comment that he is able without loss of truth to be in accord with, or to re-echo, the ancient way of thinking. This observation is intended, of course, to placate an audience whose philosophic ideas are clothed in the terms of tradition. Yet almost immediately he introduces a new statement of the designation of causes which discards final causes. "As physic," he says, "and the inquisition of efficient and material causes produces mechanic, so metaphysic and the inquisition of Forms produces magic. For the inquisition of final causes is sterile and, like a virgin consecrated to God, produces nothing." A similar omission of final causes is to be found in that section of the *Novum organum* in which he assigns tasks to the four sciences which investigate nature. "Let the investigation of Forms," he writes, "which (according to reason at least and after their own law) are eternal and immutable, constitute *Metaphysics:* and let the investigation of the Efficient Cause, and of Matter, and of the Latent Process, and the Latent Schematism (all of which have reference to the common and ordinary course of nature, not to its fundamental and eternal laws), constitute *Physics*. And to these similarly let there be subordinate two practical divisions; to *Physics, Mechanics;* to *Metaphysics, Magic* (in a purified sense of the word), on account of its broad ways, and its greater command over nature" (*Works,* I, 352-53; II, 264-68, 288, 298, 357; VI, 218-19; VIII, 177-78, 482-85, 504, 512; IX, 59).

But to return to the sciences which have to do with nature: the subject-matter of metaphysics, as well as of physics, is the constituents of material things. Investigation of things begins with an elementary observation of bodies and ends with a knowledge of the eminent natures in matter. First, the investigator gathers a mass of historical data; this is necessarily diffuse and relatively disorganized, although in it, if collected properly, rudimentary causes and structures are to a degree foreshadowed. The next stage in discovery is the inductive observation in physics of local efficients, for example, friction and sunshine, in the case of heat; of types of matter, such as clay and wax, which are differently affected by heat; and of such processes and schematisms of matter as are involved, for example, in the heating of earth, air, water. Finally, the discovery is made in metaphysics of the nature of heat as such.

Or to take another example, suppose the cause of whiteness is investigated in physics and in metaphysics. In the former case the inquiry will be limited to the cause of whiteness in snow, in froth, and the like. The solution will be the intermixing of air and water, thus showing an efficient cause working within specific sorts of matter, but providing no account of the nature of whiteness as such. A metaphysical account of the cause of whiteness would run something like this: "Two transparent bodies intermixed, with their optical portions arranged in a simple or uniform order, constitute whiteness." In the latter case the nature of whiteness is described independently of any restricting reference to a special sort of matter, special sort of schematism, or narrow agency in production (*Works*, II, 264–69, 288–91; VI, 217; VIII, 482–86, 504–6).

The search in metaphysics is for the forms of natures and, finally, for the most eminent of these, the "Forms of the First Class." Forms are "the true object of knowledge" and the real constituents of things. They are not infinite, like particulars, or very many, like types of material things, of processes, configurations, and local efficients; but are definitely limited. Even as relatively few letters make up a language, so forms constitute the parts and plan of nature. He who would know substances of manifold sorts will seek, then, these simple and limited forms, whose conjunctions and concatenations produce all things, even as he who would search for the composition of words must turn to combinations of letters. To discover the nature of gold, for example, or of water, or air, or an oak, or a lion (man must be excluded because the nature of the endowed soul, the image of God, is not a subject for science but rather for revealed theology), one will investigate such natures or essences as dense, rare, hot, cold, heavy, light, tangible, pneumatic, volatile, fixed, and the like.

It will be noted that the objects which are here assigned to metaphysics are also included within physics. Physics examines the natures of things in a narrow context of action, metaphysics in a wider. Physics considers bodies in relation to local efficiencies and specific types of matter, provides light for direction of work in matters of a limited sort, and sends the human laborer into "narrow defiles, imitating the ordinary flexuous courses of nature." Metaphysics, on the other hand, approaches a knowledge of the "summary law of nature." It abridges "the circumlocutions and long courses of experience" and liberates, enfranchises, and leads to the "widest and most open field of operation," the power of man. Discerning the form, the metaphysician "knows also the utmost possibility of superinducing that nature upon every sort of matter," and in operation escapes restraint "either to the basis of the matter or to the condition of the efficient" (*Works*, II, 288–93, 357; VIII, 504–8; IX, 59).

The form with which metaphysics deals may be variously described. It is constant, "eternal," and universal, both in essence and in operation, and is "the foundation as well of knowledge as of operation." It is also the "fixed law" of the operation of body; that is to say, granted nothing really exists as the object of natural science except individual bodies, performing individual acts according to law, yet this law, its investigation, discovery, and explication, is the basis of speculation and of works. And it is this law and its sections (*paragraphos*) we mean, says Bacon, when we use the word "Forms"—a term we employ because it is of familiar occurrence and generally prevails.

The form does not give existence; the form exists. "The Form of a thing is the very thing itself.... the existential." We would not, explains Bacon, "be understood to speak of abstract Forms and ideas, either not determined in matter at all, or ill defined. For when we speak of Forms we mean nothing more than those laws and determinations of pure actuality, which order and constitute any simple nature as heat, light, weight, in every kind of matter and subject that is susceptible of them. Thus the Form of Heat or the Form of Light is the same thing as the Law of Heat or the Law of Light. Nor indeed do we ever cut ourselves off or retreat from things themselves and the operative part. Wherefore when we say (for instance) in the investigation of the Form of Heat, 'Reject rarity,' or 'Rarity does not belong to the Form of Heat,' it is the same as if we said, 'One can superinduce heat on a dense body' or 'One can take away or keep out heat from a rare body.'"

The form of a nature is such that, given the form, the nature infallibly follows. The form is always present when the nature is present; it universally attests its presence and is inherent in the whole of it. If the form be removed, the nature necessarily vanishes and so is always absent when the corresponding nature is absent. Finally, the form "deduces the given nature from some source of being which is inherent in more natures," and which is "more known to nature" than the form itself. Hence a "true and perfect" axiom of knowledge is this: "that *another nature be discovered which is convertible with the given nature, and yet is a limitation of a more general nature, as of a true and real genus.*" For example, suppose we determine that "heat is a motion expansive, restrained and putting forth exertion upon the smaller particles" of bodies, we then conclude that motion is a genus of which heat is a species, with "specific differences" which serve to set it apart from other species within the large class. And when we say that heat is a species of motion, we mean "not that heat generates motion or that motion generates heat.... but that Heat itself, its *quid ipsum,* is Motion and nothing else" (*Works,* I, 343, 345–46, 371, 385–86, 391, 397; VIII, 168, 170–71, 193, 205–6, 211, 217).

Those sciences which are the operative counterparts of physics and metaphysics, namely, mechanics and magic, are not to be confused with practices traditionally and currently designated by the same, or similar, names. By mechanics we mean the application of causes discovered in physics to the production of works. Here works are not to be confounded with such inventions as have been hit upon by chance and without scientific knowledge, nor with mere empirical operations which result from a few preliminary experiments—these belong to natural history—nor yet with such operations as are brought about by extending, transferring, or combining earlier inventions. These last are works of ingenuity rather than philosophy, of "learned experience" rather than true inductive demonstration (*Works,* II, 298-300; VIII, 512-13).

It is time that magic in its ancient meaning was restored to its high and rightful place among the sciences. For it is nothing other than "the knowledge of the universal consents of things" which enables the natural philosopher to introduce radical alterations and innovations into nature through a knowledge of her primary forms. Its truths should not be confounded with the bookish, frivolous, and superstitious "principles" which are called "magic" by certain contemporaries. In bygone days this science was both useful and sound. It was regarded among the early Persians as "sublime wisdom." Its name should be rescued from the discredit it bears and re-established in its proper meaning as "the knowledge which applies the cognition of hidden Forms to the production of works, and by uniting—as it is the custom to say—actives with passives, makes manifest the wondrous works of nature" (*Works,* II, 300-302; VIII, 513-16).

Actually the active and contemplative parts of knowledge, however necessary it may be to separate them for purposes of analysis, "are the same things: what in operation is most useful, that in knowledge is most true." "Upon a given body to generate and superinduce a new nature or new natures, is the work and aim of human Power. Of a given nature to discover the Form, or true difference, or nature-engendering nature (*naturam naturantem*), or source of its emanation (for these are the available terms which come nearest to a description of the thing), is the work and aim of human Knowledge." Power over and knowledge of forms are the respective ends of magic and metaphysics. Subordinate to these two ends are two corresponding tasks of secondary and of inferior mark: first, the transformation of concrete bodies from one to another, within the limits of possibility, and, secondly, the discovery of the Latent Schematisms of bodies at rest and in motion and of the Latent Processes through generation and motion which proceed without break in bodies from the manifest efficient and the manifest material to the given form.

According to the axioms of metaphysics, bodies are to be regarded as "a troop or collection of simple natures." In gold, for example, are found conjoined the natures yellowness, heaviness, malleableness or ductility, fluidity, solubility, and others. The metaphysician who knows the forms of yellowness, weight, ductility, fixity, fluidity, and so on, knows gold from "the Forms of simple natures." The operative metaphysician or magician who discovers how to join these forms together in one body will know how to produce gold. "For if a man can make a metal that hath all these properties, let men dispute whether it be gold or no" (*Works,* I, 341–2, 346–48, 352–53; IV, 318–19; VIII, 167, 171–73, 177–78; *vide* VII, 375–77).

Physics in its final reaches discovers natures and forms and universal laws of operation. Its more immediate and expeditious, if subordinate, task, however, is the discovery of the "special usages of nature," in preparation for the superinduction in mechanics of a specific nature upon a specific sort of body whose respective schematisms and processes have already been ascertained. Physics assesses processes and structures of things in their more concrete, more specific, and more restricted happenings. In seeking, for example, the Latent Processes which are involved in the generation of a metal or stone the physicist endeavors to trace the course of production in either case from its first menstruums or rudiments up to the perfect mineral. Similarly, in tracing the action of nutrition, he follows the process from the first reception of food to complete assimilation. The production of voluntary motion in animals is detailed by him from the first impression of the imagination to the movements of the limbs. The Latent Schematism of bodies he seeks by anatomizing the parts concerned.

Anatomy has hitherto been applied with restraint and some success to the bodies of men and animals. Its use can be extended with effect to the structures of plants as well as animals, to their roots, leaves, flowers, flesh, blood, and bones, as the case may be. Attempts are sometimes made with experiments "by fire" to probe into what is not obvious to sense or on the surface of things. Care should be exercised in such cases lest the characteristics segregated do not belong to the bodies concerned but are the result of those agencies which are employed in their examination. And here the caution should be registered, with the practices of the empirical chemists in mind, that "the separation and solution" of bodies is not to be achieved "by fire, but by reason and true induction. .... And certainly we must pass from Vulcan to Minerva, if it be in our mind to bring to light the true textures and schematism of bodies, on which every occult and, as they call them, specific property and virtue in things depend" (*Works,* I, 342, 348–52; VIII, 168, 173–76).

In the earlier stages of physics examination is made of specific types of vehicle which sustain and convey the form. But when physics approaches metaphysics it undertakes the discovery of forms as such and "embraces the unity in nature in materials the most unlike; and is able therefore to lay bare and produce things not hitherto done, and such as neither the vicissitudes of nature, nor industry in experimenting, nor chance itself would ever have brought into act." It is metaphysics, however, with its primary forms that alone can give direction "which is certain, free, and disposing or leading to action." The "primary and catholic axioms" of this science, which treat of the most general natures that are, make manifest the deep, fixed boundaries of things. And because its knowledge is removed from the accidents of particular times, places, processes, and structures and because its operation proceeds from what is constant and eternal and universal in nature, metaphysics opens up for magic the ways to human power "such as (in the present state of things) human thought can hardly comprehend or anticipate" (*Works,* I, 343–44, 345, 347, 348–49; VIII, 169, 170, 172, 173–74).

Before leaving the discussion of the sciences which deal with nature, Bacon pauses to consider a discipline which, in his opinion, is an auxiliary to all four of them, namely, mathematics—an auxiliary to these sciences, note, and not their master; for it has come to pass, he comments, that mathematics, which, like logic, should be but a handmaid in the investigation of nature, has, in its pride, like logic, presumed to dominate natural philosophy. In the Aristotelian classification mathematics is listed as one of the theoretical sciences, physics and metaphysics being the others. Bacon, however, refuses to consider it a science in its own right. It may, perhaps, he says, be assigned a certain independence but only as a branch of metaphysics; "because Quantity (which is the subject of mathematics), when applied to Matter, is, as it were, the dose of nature, and is causative of very many effects in things natural, and therefore it must be reckoned as one of the Essential Forms of things."

Mathematics is either pure or mixed. Quantity is of all forms the most abstract. The principles of pure mathematics are entertained in complete severance from matter and things. This part of the discipline has been well cultivated since the days of Pythagoras, and not surprisingly so, since the human mind prefers the "open plains" of generalities to the "woods and enclosures of particulars." Mixed mathematics has for its subject the axioms of natural philosophy and has to do with quantity in so far as it enters into the explanation, demonstration, and operation of things. Among the sciences which mixed mathematics aids are music, "perspective," astronomy, cosmography, the knowledge of machinery, and architecture (*Works,* II, 304–7; VIII, 517–20).

CHAPTER XIV

CLASSIFICATION OF THE SCIENCES RESPECTING MAN

THE next major division of natural knowledge concerns man. This consists of two parts, one dealing with man segregate, the other with man congregate in society. The first is the Philosophy of Humanity, the second Civil Philosophy. The latter of the two may be divided into three sections: "the knowledge of conversation, the knowledge of negotiation, and the knowledge of empire or government," these corresponding to the three sorts of good "which men seek in society, comfort against solitude, assistance in business, and protection against injuries." Civil knowledge is, says Bacon, "conversant about a subject which of all others is.... with most difficulty reduced to axioms." The fact that the author finds it "difficult" is attested by his tentative and, on the whole, nonphilosophic treatment in a series of biblical proverbs with commentary, prudent aphorisms, and shrewd pieces of advice for guidance on occasions of immediate practice (*Works,* II, 309, 311; III, 52-54, 54 ff., *passim;* IX, 13, 15, 231-33, 233 ff., *passim*).

The Philosophy of Humanity has two parts; these concern, respectively, the body and the mind. It contains subjects, however, which require considerations of both mind and body and accordingly cut across the main division. One of these has to do with the person of man, his miseries, his prerogatives, and his excellencies. It includes the "peaks" of his behavior, in such matters as speech, for instance, and endurance through pain. Philosophers and theologians have treated human misery; but no one as yet has set down a record of the ultimates (as the Schoolmen might say) or the summits (as Pindar would have it) to which human nature per se may and might attain through its several endowments of body and mind. The second subject in question is the League of Common Bond which holds between soul and body. This includes that commerce between body and mind which manifests itself in such things as effects of narcotics and stimulants, dreams, diseased conditions, and in correspondences between physical lineaments and mental dispositions (*Works*, II, 307, 311–19; IX, 13, 15–23).

As for the studies which concern man's body specifically, these are of four sorts: medical, cosmetic, athletic, and voluptuary. Cosmetic may be divided into two parts, one civil, the other "effeminate." The latter lends itself to artificial decoration. The former has to do with cleanliness of body which proceeds from a reverence for God, for society, and for a man's self. Athletic concerns such matters as conduce to any ability of which the human body is capable, whether of activity or of endurance—to strength and swiftness, on the one hand, for example, and to hardness against want and extremity and patience and fortitude in torment, on the other. Voluptuary or "arts of pleasure sensual" are to be divided according to the several senses. Pleasure is given to the eye by the art of painting and by a number of other arts which have to do with houses, gardens, vestments, vases, gems, and the like. The delight of the ear is furnished in music, by voices, wind instruments, and strings. Arts which belong to the eye and ear are esteemed the most liberal, attending as they do the purest senses—purest in that they are the instruments of those most enlightened sciences which have mathematics as a handmaid. The arts which relate to the other senses, such as those of perfumes and pleasures of the table, are less highly esteemed. Generally speaking, it may be said that military arts flourish when the state is in growth, liberal arts when a state is at its height, and voluptuary when it is moving toward declination and ruin (*Works*, II, 319, 341–44; IX, 23, 44–47).

Medical doctrine has three offices: the preservation of health, the cure of diseases, and the prolongation of life. Medicine is a science difficult to know and arduous to practice. It is more professed than labored and yet more labored than advanced. Its inquiry has been rather "in a circle than in progression." Its literature is a mass of iterations with few additions. As a profession it suffers peculiar disabilities because of the complexity and variability of its subject matter, the unpleasantness of its task, and the manner in which it is esteemed by the public. The difficulties inherent in its subject matter have made the study conjectural and, as a consequence, left room for imposture and error. And while the practitioners of almost every other art are judged by rules applied and not by the event—the lawyer, for instance, by his pleading and not by the ultimate decision in the case; the sea-captain by his skill in navigation and not by the fortune of the voyages—the physician is too often esteemed, and quite unfairly, according to his effecting or not effecting a cure. As a result, the lucky impostor often wins acclaim, while the sound physician is ridiculed and condemned; and the mountebank comes to be preferred to the learned practitioner. Members of the profession thereupon, noting the credulity of the public, will say with Solomon: "If it befall to me as befalleth to the fool, why should I labour to be more wise?" Or weary in an unequal contest, and not merely because—as some then say—they have so many sad and disgusting matters to deal with, they turn to other pursuits more agreeable and rewarding than their own. Hence we see among their numbers divines, poets, statesmen, rhetoricians, antiquaries, who care and know more about their respective avocations than about the art which they professedly practice.

Like every experimental science, medicine suffers at the hands of dogmatists and empiricists. Many of its practitioners look down upon nature as from a lofty tower and occupy themselves with high generalities. They entertain fixed principles and prescribe standard remedies. Occasionally these medical magistrates quit the precedents of tradition and compound recipes of their own by the simple device of adding and subtracting *quid pro quo* among accepted ingredients. Their command over nature accordingly becomes inversely proportionate to their authority over medication. Those of their remedies which are available in the shops serve mainly for the immediate comforting or purgation or other alteration of the body. The observation made by a distinguished practitioner on contemporary medicine is therefore not altogether inept: "Our physicians, like bishops, have the power of the keys, to bind and loose, and nothing more!"

The empiricists, which include chemical experimenters, do occasionally chance upon a remedy for a disease; but the effect of their discovery is commonly lost because the cure in a specific case is not joined with any general principle which prevails through variable circumstances. The chemists, in their eagerness to impress the public prematurely with their successes, promise alleviation of pain, the retardation of age, and the prolongation of life—the most important office of medicine, and fail to find those remedies which patient investigation in their science would undoubtedly produce. Some of their number are of the Paracelsan School. These, having accepted the opinion that man is a microcosm, find in the human body fantastic correspondences and parallels to all varieties of things in the greater cosmos, from the heavenly planets to nonassimilated minerals of the earth.

Taken as a whole, medicine suffers from three defects: first, the divorce of "learning" from experience; secondly, the severing of general principles of art from experiment; and, thirdly and greatest of the three —which contains the first and the second—the failure to succor doctrine by a sustaining philosophy of nature. Medicine, therefore, should initially undertake certain things. It should, in the first instance, cease to rely on summary histories already prepared and settled. It must return to the ancient procedure of Hippocrates, whose method was to set down specific histories of examples of diseases, their manifestations, their treatments, and their issues. This, of course, does not require the recording of every case of disease, for the mere compiling of infinite particulars would be absurd and to no purpose. But it does involve a departure from the commonly accepted and ineffectual course of confining new observation and comment to so-called wonders and prodigies. Physicians would be well advised to review diligently the history of examples of those diseases which are commonly called "incurable" and to record anew examples of cases which are not inordinately new in type or in derivation from type.

Furthermore, in addition to describing the minute particulars of bodies, a practice now observed by a considerable number, physicians should undertake the equally important task of noting in comparative anatomy variations of structure which are to be found among different bodies—for the hearts and livers of men differ as much as their noses and ears. Inquiry should be instituted of each cavity and receptacle of the "humors" of the body which are usually passed over under the subject of "purgaments," and their natures studied without setting too much store in the accepted divisions among them. Records should be made of the footsteps of diseases and of their devastations upon the interior parts of the body, as well as of the natures and effects upon the body of such things as imposthumations, ulcers, discontinuities, putrefactions, obstructions, dislocations, tumors, stones, carnosities, excrescences, worms—some of which are indeed to be found in the notebooks of observant physicians. Such records as these and many more having been compiled and inductively examined, medical science may then, and not before, begin to contribute to and relate its own discoveries to a comprehensive science of bodies without whose support it must forever remain feeble and infirm (*Works,* II, 310-11, 319-41; III, 331; VI, 241-51; IX, 14-15, 23-44; X, 11; cf. XIII, 396).

So much for the sciences which relate to the human body. The doctrine of man's soul is to be divided initially into two parts because of the soul's inherent dualism, and then again into two further parts in order to differentiate questions concerning the soul's substance and faculties from those which concern the use and objects of these faculties. The human soul is dualistic; one of its parts is rational, the other sensible. The former springs from the "Breath of God, the other from the Wombs of the Elements" in natural generation. The rational soul differs from the soul possessed by brutes not only in degree but in kind as well. The refusal by philosophers to separate the two sorts of soul has been the source of opinions which are superstitious, corrupt, and out of keeping with the worth and greatness of man. The human soul has, for instance, been contemned by such teachings as those of metempsychosis which imply a congenital agreement between the spirit of man and the souls of brutes.

Because the rational soul is breathed into man by God himself, questions concerning its substance, whether it is separable or inseparable from matter, mortal or immortal, how bound by, or free from, the laws of matter, must be "transferred to religion for determination and definition." Conclusions respecting its nature are finally to be "derived from the same divine inspiration from which the substance of the soul has proceeded." The nature of the rational soul must be sought, then, in revealed theology. The "sensible or produced" soul is, however, a proper subject for human investigation. This, which is the principal soul in brutes, and in man the instrument of the rational soul, will be found after due examination to be a "corporeal substance, attenuated and made invisible by heat; a breath .... compounded of the natures of flame and air, having the softness of air to receive impressions, and the vigour of fire to engender action; nourished partly by oily and partly by watery natures; enveloped by body, and in perfect animals located principally in the head, running along the nerves, and repaired and renewed by the spiritous blood of the arteries; as Bernardinus Telesius and his pupil, Augustus Donius, have in part not altogether unprofitably maintained."

The sensible or naturally produced soul is a physical thing in motion. Yet its functions are not to be confused with those of insensible bodies. There is a great difference between the "sense" of sensible bodies and what may be called the "perception" or mutual taking-hold which prevails among insensible things. All natural bodies possess "a manifest power of perception as it were, and also a kind of choice in embracing what is agreeable and avoiding what is hostile and foreign." The magnet, for instance, attracts iron, flame leaps toward naphtha, one bubble unites with another, the sponge absorbs water, the animal body assimilates food and expels what is not food. It may well be that all changing of, and being changed by, bodies should be described as perception. If so, we could justly say that a body perceives the force of a body to which it gives way or the removal of a body which holds it, that a body—witness the air—perceives heat and cold even more acutely than does the human touch.

The mutual adjustment of bodies which is everywhere prevalent, and is here called perception, has never been adequately investigated. It has been either completely neglected or its interpretation pushed to such an extreme that the adjustment has been identified with sensation. Indeed, some of the ancients have gone so far as to suppose that because of the relations which prevail among certain bodies a soul of some sort is infused indiscriminately into all of them. This confusion of perception, such as we have described it, with sensation—a function of soul—is not an explanation of the nature of either. There still remains the necessity then—because the matter is not a mere dispute about words but a problem of ascertaining the nature of things—for an investigation into the differences between the activities of the two different sorts of material body, sensible and insensible. The inquiry will involve, among other things, a consideration of such a question, for instance, as why many actions in sensible body, such as digestion and the beating of the heart, are performed without sensation at all. It will be furthered by observing "what sort of body, what length of interval, or what repetition of impression" is required to produce a sensation, such as that of pleasure or of pain (*Works,* II, 344–48, 353–55; IX, 48–51, 55–57).

The doctrine concerning the use and objects of the faculties of the soul is partly logical and partly ethical. Logic treats of the understanding and reason; ethic of the will, appetite, and affections. Reason produces decrees, the will actions. In both spheres imagination plays the role of agent and messenger. Sense sends all sorts of impressions to the imagination, and, out of these, reason makes its judgments. Reason, before putting its decrees into operation, having made its choice and demon-

CLASSIFICATION OF THE SCIENCES RESPECTING MAN 171

stration, returns these impressions to the imagination, with the result that voluntary motion is both preceded and incited by the imagination. Imagination is a Janus with two faces. The face that beholds reason has the image of truth; the face that looks toward action has the print of goodness.

Nor is the imagination merely a messenger. There is that in its nature to receive and to usurp no small authority. Indeed, in matters of faith and religion this faculty sometimes climbs and elevates itself above reason. Not that divine illumination has for its station the imagination —for its dwelling is rather within the rational citadel of the mind—but that divine grace, even as it employs the motions of the will as the instrument of virtue, so it uses the actions of the imagination as the means of illumination. This is why religion has always sought access to the human mind through parables, similitudes, visions, and dreams (*Works*, II, 359-60; IX, 61-62).

Ethics concerns the will of man. It includes the Exemplar or Platform of Good and the Regiment or Culture or Georgics of the Mind. In the case of both these the final word, however, is to be found in the revelation of religion—and, more specifically, for Bacon, of the Christian religion. No philosophy, pagan or otherwise, says Bacon, can by itself determine the final good of man or prescribe a cure for his vagaries. This is the office of sacred divinity. Not that moral philosophy is useless; indeed, it can well perform the service of a wise handmaid and faithful servant to theology, provided it remain willing to attend upon her. As the Psalmist says, "the eyes of the handmaid look perpetually to the hands of her mistress," nevertheless not a few things are left to the care and judgment of the servant. Ethics would do well to give allegiance to the doctrines of theology and comply with its precepts, yet in such a manner that it retains of itself within its own limits "many sound and useful lessons."

Moral knowledge must wait upon theology because, first, man's rational soul is made after the image of God and, secondly, the prerogative of God comprehends the whole of man. And, for the same reasons, revealed truth is so to govern both the human reason and the human will that man must deny himself entirely and give assent to God's will. He is to obey the Divine Law even when he has a reluctation in his will; he is to believe the Word of God even when he finds a reluctation in his reason.

Sacred theology is derived from the Word of God and not from natural knowledge, even as the breath of life is breathed into man by God and does not arise in natural generation. It is written that "'the heavens declare the glory of God'" but not that they declare his will. Yet by "the light and law of nature" man can have some notions of virtue and vice, justice and injustice, good and evil. The term "light of nature" has two meanings: one, that which "springs from sense, induction, reason, argument, according to the laws of heaven and earth"; and the other, that which "flashes upon the mind (*anima*) of man by an inward instinct according to the law of conscience." The latter is a spark and trace of man's original purity. Through it his soul participates in some light to discern in a manner what is moral. The light, however, is not clear and suffices only to denounce the vice and not to enlighten the duty.

This is not to say, however, that the employment of reason is to be proscribed in those matters, moral and otherwise, which have to do with revealed theology; for among the offices of reason is the cognition of the divine mystery and derivation of inferences from it. God descends to man's apprehension, in unfolding his mysteries, by the grafting of his revelations upon the notions and conceptions of human reason and by the application of his inspirations to open man's understanding "as the form of the key to the ward of the lock." And on these occasions man himself should not be found wanting but should direct his reason—just how, Bacon does not explain—in such a way that he may be the more capable of receiving and taking in God's mysteries, his mind being enlarged to the grandeur of the mysteries and not the mysteries contracted to the narrowness of human mind. As for the inferences to be drawn by reason from the mysteries of revelation, these are "secondary and respective.... not original and absolute." Divinity is grounded in the "Placets of God." The principles given in revelation are fixed. All judgments affirmed in the human realm over which they have jurisdiction must be brought into conformity with them. After, and not before, the articles and principles of religion have been set in their place, exempt from the examination of reason, is it permissible to deduce conclusions from them. Here the derivation of inferences is not comparable, obviously, to the reaching of conclusions in the natural sciences. In the latter case the procedure is the empirical examination of particulars, then the assertion, in turn, of a relatively less general proposition, a middle proposition, and a most highly general proposition, in such a manner that the lesser and the "first" or final principles are determined in the same inductive way and the more general proposition is made to depend upon the less and, in the last analysis, ultimately on particular instances. But in matters of revealed theology it is otherwise; here the "first" propositions are the original propositions, self-subsistent and self-supporting and quite independent of the lesser principles which may be derived from them and of the particulars to which they may be applied. Principles comparable to those of theology are to be found in several fields of human practice in which the basic propositions are more or less arbitrary. Law, for example, has placets or maxims "positive upon authority and not reason" which leave a wide area for interpretation of, and disputation over, questions thereon depending. In the game of chess, to take another instance, the moves are made in accordance with rules already determined and declared (*Works,* III, 10–19, 35, 174–80; VI, 394–97; IX, 194–201, 215, 345–51).

But to return to ethics itself, to whose care and direction, despite theology's domination, many things remain. The science, as has been said, contains two parts: the Exemplar or Platform of Good and the Regiment or Culture of the Mind. The former part contains two sorts of good: first, "self-good" or "private" or "particular" or "individual" good and, secondly, "good of communion." The good of communion, which is the greater good, since it tends to a general, and not a particular, conservation of man, respects society and concerns duty. (The term "duty" is properly used in describing a mind well disposed toward others, while "virtue" is to be applied to a mind rightly formed and composed within itself.) The good of communion has to do with the duty of man as a member of society and belongs to ethics rather than to politics. It includes the respective and special duties which are man's as a member of a profession or vocation and as a person with status, rank, or degree. It enjoins the "laws of friendship and gratitude," and the respective bonds and obligations and special duties which belong to husband, wife, parents, children, companies, colleges, neighborhoods, and the like.

Private good or self-good has two divisions: passive good and active good. Passive good, in turn, includes conservative good and perfective good. Every creature possesses a triple desire or appetite for the good of itself as an individual, first, to conserve itself; secondly, to perfect itself;

and, thirdly, in active good, to multiply and extend itself. Active good in certain cases may have an effect on society with incidence to social good, but it is not to be confused with the latter. The motives in the two cases are different. What is called "private" active good is not primarily for the benefit and happiness of others but for the increase of power and happiness in the agent concerned. Sometimes, indeed, this sort of good, when impelled by individual motive, may run counter to the good of society, as it does when pursued by those greater and lesser "troublers of the world" who would shape all things according to their own humors.

Of the two passive goods, the good of conservation may be described as "the reception and fruition of that which is agreeable to our own nature." This sounds like the most innocent and natural activity, yet actually it is the "softest and lowest." For not the consistency and sincerity of human fruition but its "vigor" makes man truly virtuous. To preserve a thing in a state or condition is the lesser activity; to raise it to a higher nature is the greater. Philosophers forget these truths and tend to restrict man's achievement by making his life a mere preparation for death; or by representing his nature as "uniform and harmonical" and not filled, as it is, by "contrary motions and extremes"; or by finding his virtue in "a serenity which cancels progression through trial and vicissitude." The poet Virgil has been wiser and has assigned to man "a fiery vigor and a heavenly origin." Others have said that "the assumption or approach to the Divine or Angelical nature is the perfection of his form." The angels, aspiring to be like God in power, and man, aspiring to be like him in knowledge, transgressed and fell; but neither angel nor man by aspiring to a similitude of God in charity ever did or shall transgress (*Works,* III, 19-26, 49; IX, 201-7, 228).

Thus far the Exemplar of the Good, the fruit of life, so to speak, has been considered. There remains the culture of the mind or the husbandry of life. Aristotle well maintains in precept, if not in example, that it is almost useless to know what virtue is if, at the same time, one is ignorant of the ways of acquiring it. Cicero, it will be remembered, praises Cato the Younger for his application of himself to philosophy "not for the sake of disputing.... but for living accordingly." And we may not inappropriately apply the words of Hippocrates to an age when men take but slight care for the cultivating and framing of their lives, "They that are sick and feel no pain are sick in their minds." Writers on ethics are for the most part, however, like men who would undertake to teach the art of writing by providing examples of fair copies of letters and then omit directions for the movement of the hand and the framing of the characters. It is their common practice to set down "draughts and portraitures" of good, virtue, duty, and felicity; but the method by which the mind may be trained and the will confirmed in these they either treat slightly and unprofitably or completely disregard. To be sure, the dominant Aristotle observes that moral virtues are fixed in the mind by habit and not by nature, that better men are convinced by doctrinal persuasions and the vulgar by rewards and punishment, that the mind may be straightened by bending it in an opposite direction, like a crooked stick. Such observations as these, however, are only "scattered glances and touches," and fall short of what is required for a directive ethic.

The moral cultivation of the mind cannot be undertaken until an accounting has been made of the dispositions of the mind. These must be understood before directions for practice can be given. It becomes necessary to discover what is and what is not within human power. The husbandman cannot control the earth or the weather according to the seasons; he can only adjust his actions according to what nature gives him. The physician cannot alter the constitution of the patient or the variety of human accidents; medical cure may be within his power, but not so the complexion or constitution of the ill man's body or the incidence of disease; yet, to effect the cure, he must have a knowledge of the rest. So it is in the moral realm. The appropriate remedy for vice cannot be prescribed until human dispositions and human affections with their accompanying perturbations are understood. By dispositions here we do not mean "common inclinations to virtues and vices," but something more radical, namely constitutive characters which in their concurrences are the source of all that follow as characteristics.

Consideration of such dispositions as these has been, for the most part, omitted from works on morals and politics. The poets, heroic, satiric, tragic, comic, have interspersed in their writings some representations of the constituents of man's character. There are certain classifications in tradition of the natures of persons according to the predominance of respective planets, some for contemplation, others for civil business, or war, or love, or arts, or a varied sort of life. But the best extant source of material for the study of human dispositions is the writings of the wiser historians who combine characterization with narrative and, in describing the actions of their subjects, present evidence concerning their natures.

The treatment of dispositions in ethics should not, of course, consist of a series of individual pictures, but must rather include the common lineaments and features through whose combinations and arrangements all portraits are composed. It will begin with a dissection of natural aptitudes and go on to assess the hidden springs of conduct. It will show how many dispositions or characters enter into the compositions of minds, and in what way, and in what relative subordinations one to the other. Nor will it treat merely of characters which are planted commonly by nature; it will include also those which are occasioned by variable circumstances. Among the latter are sex, age, locality, health, sickness, beauty, deformity, and the like, as well as those caused by human fortune, such as sovereignty, nobility, obscure birth, riches, want, adversity, prosperity, magistracy, and privateness. Some such factors, it will be remembered, are mentioned occasionally by Aristotle in his *Rhetoric,* and here and there in the writings of others. But they have never been incorporated into the structure of works on moral philosophy where they obviously belong. Nor have they consistent and ordered records comparable to the accounts of molds and earths in agriculture and of complexions and constitutions of bodies in medicine. Yet, until such time as they are investigated with thoroughness and understanding, moral philosophy will continue to practice the indiscretions of empiricists who, to take an analogy from medicine, administer the same indiscriminate remedies to all patients.

The nature of the mind having been determined, the next topic for inquiry is the affections whose perturbations and distempers constitute the mind's vices. Here again it would appear strange that Aristotle, who has written voluminously on ethics, has failed to undertake a considerable and consistent treatment of this subject. To be sure, he discusses the affections—and well, at that—in his *Rhetoric,* but only in a collateral sort of way, as something to be moved by spoken words. The Stoics have mentioned them briefly and only to illustrate subtlety of definition. In books on philosophy there are occasional references to anger, tenderness of countenance, and some few adjacent subjects. Actually, the poets, and not the philosophers, have proved to be the best "doctors" of the affections; they have dissected them and have portrayed in lifelike manner their performances. They have shown, for example, how they are kindled and incited; how pacified and restrained; in what manner they disclose themselves when repressed; how they operate, vary, are involved within one another; and how they contend one with the other. These matters of which the poets treat are readily seen to be of the greatest consequence to the moral agent, both as individual and as citizen. Take as an example the case of conflict among the affections. Commonwealths rest upon reward and punishment; these in turn are dependent upon hope and fear which, as predominating affections, suppress and bridle all the others. And as in affairs of state it is sometimes wise to set one faction against another, so in the internal organization of the mind it is sometimes necessary to set one affection against others and to use its aid in mastering them.

The dispositions and affections of moral agents are inherent in human beings; their nature and influence are not within our control. There are other factors in conduct, however, which are under our command. These too can move the will and the appetites and can alter manners. They include custom, exercise, habit, education, imitation, emulation, company, friendship, praise, reproof, exhortation, fame, laws, books, studies, and the like. And out of them as ingredients, through proper selection and choice, may be compounded recipes for preserving and recovering under direction the good estate of the mind.

Of the several means to moral remedy only one or two can now be considered. Custom and habit will serve for a brief discussion. The assertion that custom has no power over natural actions seems to be the narrow and negligent opinion of Aristotle. His examples are these: If a stone is thrown up a thousand times, it will not learn to ascend of itself; by often seeing or hearing, we do not learn to see or hear the better. The principle which Aristotle attempts to derive from such examples as these is true only in those cases in which nature is "peremptory." It has no bearing on the areas in which nature admits a certain latitude and "remission." A tight glove, for example, will go on more easily after use; a twig can be trained into a position contrary to its natural growth; by exercise the voice becomes louder; and by accustoming themselves, men can the better withstand heat or cold.

There are precepts which may be prescribed for the ordering of nature by custom and habit. A few must suffice on this occasion: "The first shall be, that we beware lest we undertake at the first either a more difficult or lighter load than the case requires." If the load is too light, progress will be retarded; if too heavy, a diffident nature will be discouraged and a confident nature will become opinionated and promise itself more than it can perform, and both in the end will become confounded. "The second precept shall be, to exercise any faculty by which a habit may be acquired, two several times shall be observed; the one, when the mind is best disposed to the matter, the other when it is worst disposed; that by the one, you may gain a great step, by the other you may through strenuous exertion work out the knots and obstacles of the mind, and so make the middle times the more easy and pleasant."

"The third precept shall be that which Aristotle mentions by the way. 'To bear ever with all our strength (so it be without vice) towards the contrary extreme of that whereunto we are by nature inclined,' as when we row against the stream, or straighten a wand by bending it contrary to its natural crookedness."

"The fourth precept depends on that axiom, which is most true; that the mind is brought to anything with more sweetness and happiness, if that whereunto you pretend be not first in the intention, but be obtained as it were by the way while you are attending to something else; because of the natural hatred of the mind against necessity and constraint."

Of the many other precepts touching the regulation of custom for the provision of a "second nature" which might be mentioned there is one which seems "more accurate and elaborate than the rest"; it is to the effect that "the minds of all men are at some times in a state more perfect, and at other times in a state more depraved." By way of inference from this, another direction instructs men "to fix and cherish the good hours of the mind, and to obliterate and take forth the evil out of the calendar." The former may be performed by "vows or constant resolutions" and "observations or exercises" to keep the mind continually in duty and obedience. The latter may be achieved by "expiation" of what is past and the inception of a new sort of life. But this part of reform seems clearly to belong to religion, to which, indeed, all sincere and true moral philosophy is the handmaid. In conclusion, one further rule may be prescribed. This is "most compendious and summary" and yet a "most effectual" means for bringing the human mind to virtue. It is this: Let a man choose and place before him such right purposes as may be found reasonably within his compass to attain (*Works,* III, 7–8, 33–47; IX, 191–92, 214–26).

The second division of knowledge which has to do with the use and objects of the human faculties is logic. This includes the arts of discovery, of judging, of retaining, and of transmitting. Under the art of transmitting fall such topics as writing, grammar, poetical meters, rhetoric, words, gestures, hieroglyphics, and "real characters." The last of these are symbols which are not confined to any specific language and are used by men of different tongues to communicate with one another. They might, says Bacon, be put to good use in the provision of a common currency for intellectual commerce among the nations of the earth. And as a matter of history this suggestion of Bacon's is not without effect, for it is to encourage the members of the Royal Society to designate a committee for the preparation of a universal "real" language of science, which is calculated to supplant Latin, the general language of Western learning. The terms of Latin, these "virtuosi" are convinced, carry in their denotations and connotations concepts and principles which inevitably contain the implications of traditional science and are therefore not appropriate for "experimental" learning. The issue of the designation is John Wilkins' *Philosophical Language* (*Works,* II, 359, 409-13; VI, 284; IX, 60, 107-10).

The art of retaining consists mainly of aids for the memory. That of judging includes induction and deduction by syllogism. The latter has been dealt with exhaustively by the Schools and requires no further elaboration. Judgment by induction will be treated in the *New Organon* (*Works,* II, 395, 404; IX, 93-94, 103).

The art of discovery or invention consists of two parts, one having to do with the discovery of arts, the other with the invention of arguments. The former, says Bacon, is utterly deficient. It is still the custom to discover art by chance and, when an "invention" has merely "happened," to undertake its "demonstration" by science. Untrained men—whose ingenuity is comparable to the strategy of birds and beasts—have done more for the arts than have the trained logicians!

The office of the discovery of argument is the enabling of the mind to draw opportunely from the mass of knowledge which it has already accumulated that which is pertinent to a thing or question which is under consideration. There are two ways of using this stored knowledge: one by marking and indexing, as it were, the places—called "Topics"—where the thing is to be looked for; the other by preparing a repository of arguments—called the "Promptuary"—concerning things which frequently come under discussion. The Promptuary hardly deserves to be labeled knowledge. It is exemplified by those commonplaces which the ancient rhetoricians use in defending either side of a question. Cicero instances it when he cautions the orator to have ready premeditated matter for all causes on which he may speak. Demosthenes employs it to good effect in prefaces to his speeches. Aristotle ridicules it when he compares its user to one who professes the art of shoemaking and who, instead of teaching how to make shoes, exhibits a lot of them in all fashions and sizes! In any case, the question belongs more properly to the subject of rhetoric than to logic.

Topics, the other division of the discovery of argument, fall within knowledge proper and play no small part in the interrogation of persons, of books, and of things. Topics may be divided into "general" and "particular." The former are especially useful in argumentation, meditation, and reading. They quicken investigation, make available accumulated knowledge within the mind, and set the form for interrogation of matters without. Particular Topics are of the greatest moment, determining, as they do, specific objects for investigation. "We attribute," says Bacon, "such importance to Particular Topics that we have in mind, in the more important and obscure subjects of nature, the production of a special work concerning them." This work is never written; and what can be learned of the author's opinions on the subject must be gathered from the brief treatment in the *De augmentis* and briefer mention in other pieces, notably the *Parasceve* and the *Historia naturalis*.

Particular Topics arise in the mind by "prenotions" which belong to memory. Without prenotions questions cannot be asked nor answers recognized. They are the questions to be put to nature respecting varied subjects in varied sciences. As inquiries, they determine answers and are, in turn, subject to modification by the responses received from nature in observation and experiment; for scientific investigation is like a journey through an open country—the farther the traveler has proceeded, the better he can see what is to follow. Topics are to be the objects of search in natural history, which falls within the third part of the Instauration. They are also to be the subjects which are to be submitted to the specific induction of the second part and to be produced as exemplary Tables in the fourth part (*Works,* II, 59, 362–66, 385–90, 405; III, 213; IV, 140; VII, 298; VIII, 371; IX, 64–67, 83–88, 103, 377; X, 282, 418).

The art of discovery of arts consists of Learned Experience and the Interpretation of Nature. The former is the subject of the fifth part of the Instauration and may appropriately be treated there. The latter is the subject of the second part (*Works,* II, 362, 395; IX, 64, 94).

CHAPTER XV

THE NEW METHOD OF SCIENCE
INTRODUCTION

BACON in the first part of his Instauration has "coasted by the ancient sciences." This having been done, his next undertaking, he says, "is to equip the human intellect for passing beyond." He accordingly assigns to the second part "doctrine concerning the better and more perfect use of human reason in the inquisition of things, and the true aids of the understanding." This doctrine, which consists of a method of inquiry, is contained within the *Novum organum.* Despite the author's efforts through many years to bring this work to a state of completion, only the initial stages of the method are set down. Rawley tells us that he has seen "at least twelve copies" of the work "revised year by year, one after another, and every year altered and amended in the frame thereof, till at last it came to that Model in which it was committed to the press; as many living creatures do lick their young ones till they bring them to their strength of limbs."

Bacon calls his new method for the interpretation of nature "the most important thing of all (*res omnium maxima*)." It is to mark "the end and termination of infinite error." Nothing in science can be properly known except through its use. Upon its success all the rest of the Instauration depends. Its issue is nothing or everything. It is, he insists, a new way both unknown and untried and not a superinducing of a new procedure upon an old. Indeed, it has no commerce whatever with proofs formerly employed (*Works,* I, 196, 197, 210, 214, 236, 248; II, 385; VIII, 19, 23, 37, 40, 62, 74; IX, 83).

The ancient art or method of discovery in the sciences is so utterly deficient that, if one were to take an inventory of scientific knowledge as of an estate, he would be required to record "there is no money." The analogy is doubly appropriate in that, even as money will fetch all other commodities, so by this art all the rest of science is acquired. To change the metaphor, the new method is comparable to the mariner's compass. It is obvious that the West Indies would never have been discovered if the invention of the mariner's needle had not gone before, and so it should not be found strange that no progress has been made in the discovery and advancement of the sciences when the art of induction, which makes discovery and invention possible, has remained unknown. The ancients sailed by the stars; and before men could leave the Mediterranean Sea, pass the Pillars of Hercules with their *ne plus ultra,* and voyage over the great ocean to discover a new world, a surer guide, the mariner's needle, had to be found out. Analogously the inventions which have thus far been made in the arts and sciences are such as might be obtained by empirical practice, meditation, observation, argumentation; and before men can hope to penetrate to the remoter and more hidden parts of nature, it will be necessary to provide a new means to the better discipline and application of the human faculties. Therefore, says the author, we shall set forth "our conjectures," even as Columbus did his before he made his voyage across the Atlantic, when he produced reasons why he believed that new lands and continents might be discovered. His opinions, though rejected at first, were afterward established by experiment and became the causes and the beginnings of the greatest events. "And surely it would be disgraceful to mankind if, while the regions of the material globe, that is to say of lands, seas, and stars, have been in our times laid vastly open and surveyed, the borders of the intellectual globe were confined within the discoveries and straits of the ancients."

Bacon will not have his new method confused with the old. With "one stroke" he will remove "all sciences and all authors." It is of no moment whether or not in the new investigation any truth of which the ancients were aware is brought to light, any more than it would matter if the New World should turn out to be the island which the ancients called Atlantis. The only thing that really matters is the founding, through controlled observation and experiments, of solid and usable knowledge (*Works,* I, 206, 291, 304, 328; II, 362; VIII, 33, 117, 129, 153–54; IX, 64).

The new method or interpretation of nature is such that men would naturally fall into it, were they able to "bind themselves to two rules— the first, to lay aside received opinions and notions; and the second, to restrain the mind for a time from the highest generalizations and those next to them." It is a kind of logic or dialectic. (Bacon, like other writers in the seventeenth century, uses these terms interchangeably. The term "dialectic" means, for Plato, the organization of forms and, for Aristotle, the method of arguing from an asserted premise, which may lie in the realm of probability, as distinct from true logical demonstration from premises properly established. The term "logic" seems to date from the Stoics, who use it to represent what Aristotle calls "analytic.") The purpose of the new *Organon* is to discover the nature of things and to produce arts and works. It will command nature in operation and provide the human race with new inventions. Its goal is the solid founding of human utility and power for the promotion of "the common good." As a method, it will be tested not by arguments but, like religion, by its fruits. Its works will be the pledge of its truths. For the office of knowledge is not contemplation but operation. To produce works, man must know causes; and these he can discover only through what he observes of nature's structures and ways. What in knowledge is the cause is in operation the rule. The chain of natural causes cannot be broken. Nature, therefore, to be commanded must first be obeyed. When this is done, human power and knowledge will meet in one (*Works,* I, 210, 214-15, 227, 241-42; VIII, 36, 40-42, 53, 68).

Science investigates causes and produces works. Two sorts of experiments are, therefore, to be noted: light-bearing experiments and fruit-bearing experiments. The one manifests the scientific principle, the other the operation of law in works. Either throws light on the other. The latter sort of experiment is not to be confused with the trials of pure empirics. These experimenters, in their anxiety to obtain the fruits of practice, spoil their chances of knowing natural causes and therefore of producing continually, through a knowledge of causes, considerable works. They would do well were they to take the Divine wisdom and order as their pattern. God on the first day created light. He gave a whole day to its creation and on that day created nothing else. The lesson to be learned from the divine example is that man should first seek out the discovery of causes and axioms by experiments of light and then, having found these, proceed to experiments of fruit. For the road of science does not lie on a level but "ascends and descends; first ascending to axioms, then descending to works" (*Works,* I, 204, 275-76, 309, 322-23, 326, 353; II, 385; VIII, 31, 101, 135, 148-49, 152, 178; IX, 83; see IV, 157).

The invention of works has in the past been well esteemed by men. Divine honors were conferred by the ancients upon their inventors and only heroic honors upon founders of cities and empires. The Egyptians, indeed, paid tribute to those useful inventions by brutes which had arisen merely from instinct. The arts are older, of course, than science and logic.

Inventions throughout human history have been made accidentally, when their discoverers, so far from seeking them, have been engaged in other pursuits. Surely, then, there will be occasion for praise and thanks, when God's creatures, men with eyes and reason, no longer relying on instinct, accident, and the like, turn with industry and application to observation and experiment according to the rules of a true induction and, having discovered nature's operations, are enabled to create manifold works for the relief of man's estate (*Works,* 279–80, 311, 335; II, 363–65; VIII, 105, 137, 161; IX, 65–67).

This interpretation of the end of science may meet with certain objections. It stresses inventions, and inventions can be perverted to base uses; it associates truth and utility; and it assesses human power in terms of useful arts. Now while it is true that the arts and sciences may be debased "to wickedness, luxury, and the like," the same may be said "of all earthly goods, of wit, courage, strength, beauty, wealth, light itself and the rest." And there is this sound principle through whose application knowledge in use, like other goods, may be kept from working evil: Let knowledge be "governed by right reason and sound religion."

The second objection is to the effect that "the contemplation of truth" is a thing worthier and "more heavenly" than magnitude of works and that the proposed scheme of knowledge drags down the mind "from the serenity and tranquility of abstract wisdom as from a more divine state" to the turmoil and confusion of common things. In a certain respect these observations are sound. Light, for example, is a most excellent thing; it makes possible human locomotion, reading, and the exercise of the arts. Yet the vision of light is more excellent than its uses. And the "contemplation of things, as they are, without superstition or imposture, error or confusion, is in itself more worthy than all the fruit of inventions." But, while the supremacy of knowledge over works must be acknowledged, we should beware lest we substitute mere contemplation for real knowledge. Man, with the faculties he possesses, cannot know and work upon created nature unless he first turns his mind under proper direction to the common particulars which are round about him. If he refuses to do this, his science is erroneous, imaginative, and superstitious. The objector, therefore, who, following philosophic tradition, begins with the "contemplation" of "first principles," unexamined and unproven, and then goes on to identify these, or the other Idols which result from these, with those Divine Ideas which are engraven upon things, let him be informed that it is only by a new method of induction that there can be built in human understanding "a true pattern of the world," such as it is actually found to be and not such as a man's own reason may have made it for him. This pattern, which cannot be discovered save after a most diligent dissection and anatomy of the world, contains none other than "the true seals (or signet—*signacula*) of the Creator upon creatures, impressed on and determined in matter by real and exquisite lines." In it wisdom and works cannot be separated; truth and utility are one.

The third objection concerns human power over things and the benefits which accrue therefrom. Now there are three kinds or grades of human ambition. The first is to extend one's power in one's own country; this is "vulgar and degenerate." The second is to increase the dominion of one's country; this is more dignified than the first but not less covetous. The third is "to reestablish and enlarge the power and dominion of the human race" over the universe of things; this is better and more magnificent than the other two. Dominion over nature belongs to man by divine bequest. It is a heritage that can be entered into only by a knowledge of natural causes and a benefit that can accrue only through the application of this knowledge to works. Its acceptance marks the difference between the barbarian and the civilized man. For the divergence between these two not the soil, or the climate, or communal organization but the development of the arts is responsible. Moreover, the fruits of informed art are not confined to any time, place, or people but extend to all men and all future ages of mankind (*Works*, I, 330–31, 335–38; VIII, 156–57, 161–63).

The new method of interpretation will make "the mind by an art a match for the nature of things." "Neither the naked hand nor the understanding left to itself can do much. It is by instruments and helps that the work is done, which are as much needed for the understanding as for the hand. And as the instruments of the hand either give motion or guide it, so the instruments of the mind supply either suggestions for the understanding or cautions." There is practically no one, for instance, who can draw a straight line or a true circle by the hand alone; yet both may be readily drawn by aid of a ruler and compass. Or suppose a vast obelisk were to be moved; if a few men were to undertake the task unaided by machines and instruments, using only their naked hands, a bystander would think them mad. Nor would they appear any less foolish, were they to call for more helpers of their own sort or to give the task over to other persons trained in the athletic arts. Yet in some such manner as this do the learned proceed to the tasks of demonstration. They engage in fruitless co-operation, consign their investigations to those persistently exercised in the logic of the Schools, and, when it comes to making a real discovery of nature, they prove by their failures that unaided human minds, like unaided human muscles, are not sufficient for the task.

To compensate, then, for human insufficiency is a major end of the new induction. The new logic is an instrument to aid the mind in discovery and not to exercise mental gymnasts. It places but slight emphasis, if any, on acuteness of wit, and it does not separate the "learned" from the unlearned, the subtle logician from the lowly observer. Indeed, it serves, in a manner, to reduce to a common level all who employ it. One who, because of greater steadiness of hand or acuteness of eye, draws a straighter line and a more exact circle can challenge comparison of abilities; but one who draws these with the help of a rule and compass makes no boast. So it is with those who employ the new instrument of investigation. The new logic "levels men's wits, for the most part, and leaves but little to their excellence; because it performs everything by the surest rules and demonstrations" (*Works*, I, 234-35, 241, 264-65, 329; II, 370; VIII, 60-62, 67, 89-90, 155; IX, 71).

This new art of induction is designed to direct the process of knowledge from the beginnings of sense-experience to the conclusions of reason. It commences with the collecting of natural history and gradually proceeds by the controlled observation of things to the formulation of general axioms. It does not hold in reverence the "first notions" of the mind; nor does it acquiesce in the immediate information of the senses. It advances into the several provinces of science without respect for the so-called "axioms" on which these sciences are traditionally said to rest. It divides experience and examines its parts, supports sense, controls the intellect, closes with nature, and by exclusions and rejections—not by the mere collecting of affirmative instances—leads to an inevitable conclusion intent upon works (*Works*, I, 215-17, 274; VIII, 42-43, 99-100).

The induction of tradition which proceeds by simple enumeration of positive instances is hazardous and useless. Its result is upset by a single contradictory instance. It contains no directions for probing nature. The other traditional proof by syllogism deduces a lesser proposition from a greater through the use of a middle term and rests on the supposition—a proposition of "mathematical certainty"—that things which agree in a

THE NEW METHOD OF SCIENCE

middle term agree with one another. Obviously, any conclusion which it establishes is purely verbal unless the middle term and the premises which this term unites are representative of notions well founded in the facts of nature. Unfortunately, the practice of the learned has been to depend on types of middle term—"the basis of the whole structure and fabric"—which are "badly and rashly abstracted from things, vague, not sufficiently determined and defined"; and also to fly immediately from sense and particulars up to the highest generalities, as certain fixtures about which disputation might turn, and from these to derive, stage by stage, lower. propositions. Contrariwise, the new logic leads knowledge from the particulars of sense to lesser axioms or propositions, then to "middle" axioms, and finally to those most general axioms which are those solid, properly defined propositions which nature herself "would acknowledge" (*Works,* I, 214–16, 243, 312–13; II, 368, 398–99, 404; VIII, 41–42, 70, 138–39; IX, 69, 97, 102).

The senses, through which the mind is in contact with particulars, are both infirm and given to error. Nor can mechanical aids like the microscope and telescope avail in overcoming their "dullness, incompetency, and deceptions." Sometimes the sensories give false information, sometimes they give no information. Always they provide an "uncertain light.... sometimes shining out, sometimes clouded over, through the woods of experience and particulars." What strikes them vividly outweighs what impresses them slightly, no matter how important for a knowledge of nature the latter may be. They are unable to penetrate to the inner structures, or register many significant movements, of bodies, such as local motions through exceedingly small spaces, very quick and very slow movements, even when they are well disposed and unobstructed.

Again, the particulars which impress the senses are "infinite." When not controlled by the inquirer, they provide a mere collection of impressions, like "a broom without its band." An endless series of "experiences" merely confounds investigation and ends in ignorance. The scientist in order to escape their domination will submit himself to a direction for observation and experiment which leads him from particulars to universals which are the proper aim of investigation (*Works,* I, 205, 217–18, 221, 249, 258, 289, 307–8, 310; VIII, 32, 43–44, 47, 75, 82–83, 115, 133, 136).

Scientific knowledge arises necessarily from particulars or individual things in contact with sense. Its content, however, does not consist of "impressions" immediately received from objects but only of "abstract notions derived from these impressions." "Only individuals strike the sense, which is the door to the intellect," and there can be "no investigation, not even a dream, of what is not first in sense." The individuals are fixed in the memory in the form or manner in which they occur and are, on review, analyzed and divided, classified, and compounded, in accordance with nature and things, by the reason. Knowledge as such "discards individuals." It begins with "whatever has been from the occurrence of individual objects collected and digested by the mind into general notions" (*Works,* II, 187; VII, 285–86; VIII, 408; X, 404–5).

The assumption of empiricists, then, that "the sense of man is the measure of things" must be rejected. At the same time, care must be taken lest one fall into the opposite error of supposing that whatsoever the reason concludes is true of natural objects. For, even as the sense deceives, so does the intellect distort. The human understanding is unquiet; it cannot rest. It makes its own difficulties. Having "but cast a glance or two upon facts and examples and experience," it precipitately leaps and flies from particulars given in sense to remote axioms of the greatest generality, abstraction, and emptiness—in other words, to "first principles, as they are called, of arts and things." And, taking its stand upon these, it engages in specious meditations and speculations to the point of "madness" and finally erects magnificent philosophical structures which have no foundation in nature.

The understanding, therefore, is not to be supplied with wings but rather is to be hung with weights. It must at every stage of its activities be brought "to the particulars themselves." It can be allowed to proceed but slowly and by gradual successive steps from particulars to lesser axioms, then to middle axioms—the most useful axioms, and last of all to most general axioms. As each axiom is being established, care should be taken to see whether the axiom in question applies only to those particulars from which it is originally derived or whether it be larger and wider. If it indicates new particulars, its greater inclusiveness may be confirmed; so that investigation may neither be confined to what is already known nor made to grasp at shadowy abstractions (*Works,* I, 195, 211, 219–21, 243, 247, 249, 251; VIII, 17, 37, 45–46, 69, 73, 75, 77).

The new method of demonstration "will not give much weight to the immediate object of sense," but it will accept the evidence of the senses, if assisted and corrected. Mental operations consequent to sense it will suspect and, for the most, reject. It will prepare a new and certain way for the mind to proceed to knowledge directly from the perceptions of sense. It will not disable the senses but supply them with aids. It will not overlook the understanding but control it. Its office will be to establish "a true and lawful marriage in perpetuity between the empirical and the rational faculty, the captious and unfortunate separations and divorces of which have thrown into confusion all the affairs of the human family." Its purpose will be to restore to mankind the "commerce between the mind and things," whose importance and gravity are surpassed by nothing on earth or of the earth (*Works,* I, 195, 206, 208, 218–21, 234, 245–46, 273, 288–89, 333; VIII, 17, 33, 34, 44–46, 60, 72, 98, 114–15, 158).

CHAPTER XVI

BACON CONTRA ARISTOTLE. I

WE HAVE reached a point at which the main pattern and design of Bacon's scheme of knowledge is becoming evident. We may now return to a historical question which we postponed after sketching our author's agreements and disagreements with Plato, namely, the respects in which he agrees with, and departs from, the philosophical tradition founded by Aristotle. The answer to this question will serve in a measure to complete Bacon's account of historical philosophies and also to give perspective to his search for forms through a method peculiarly his own.

Bacon considers Aristotle a clever man who came upon good fortune. His sojourn at the court of Macedon, while he was tutor of Alexander (destined to be known as "the Great"), gave him the opportunity to collect, through aid of hunters, fowlers, fishers, and the like, who were placed at his disposal, materials for natural history. Yet, of these materials, according to Bacon, he made but little use in his philosophy and set them aside to pursue "abstractions." Even as he gathered through contact with his ambitious pupil treasure for aid, he also developed a humor to subdue, with the consequence that the master became filled with ambition "to conquer all opinions, as the pupil to conquer all nations." Aristotle became a "challenger of all the world." Like an Ottoman despot who could not think himself secure unless he had first destroyed all his brothers, this philosopher was to proceed in "a spirit of difference and contradiction towards all antiquity; undertaking not only to frame new words of science at pleasure, but to confound and extinguish all ancient wisdom; insomuch as he never nameth or mentioneth an ancient author or opinion, but to confute and reprove; wherein for glory, and drawing followers and disciples, he took the right course."

"His success well fulfilled the observation of Him that said: *If a man come in his own name, him will you receive.*" For his word has become the law of learning; his judgments have been accepted as unalterable precedents; and over a period of centuries his obedient followers in the Schools have considered knowledge the work of this one man. Everywhere Aristotle "goeth for the best author," "towards whom envy is ceased, and reverence by time amortised." His doctrines have prevailed in both secular and religious learning (*Works,* I, 273, 299, 308; II, 180, 265, 285; V, 295; VI, 41, 177, 215–16, 424–25; VII, 66, 70, 117; VIII, 98, 124–25, 134, 401, 483, 502; X, 349; XIII, 264).

The Stagirite's followers have added but little to their master's teaching beyond specious meditations and glosses. They have been content to become editors, copyists, and discursive amplifiers, who after great and prolonged effort produce an occasional distinction within their author's argument. If by their verbal subtleties they have weakened Aristotle's original doctrine and deprived his teaching of whatever strength and vigor it originally possessed, they have done one thing at least to add to the authority of their master; they have, by their logical art, so exhibited and defended his system with sundry artifices that it carries a show of counterfeit perfection. This performance has been impressive. Successive generations of the learned have been captivated. Disciples have become masters, and, in the continuity of learning, successive masters and disciples have become of one mind, thinking the same thoughts, speaking the same words, and constituting the most "unfortunate succession of wits which the world hath yet had, whereby the patrimony of all knowledge goeth not on husbanded or improved, but wasted and decayed." Among them an erroneous and malignant opinion has long prevailed that the entertaining of common notions by many marks a true and unanimous consent in knowledge. "True unanimity proceeds from the coincidence of free judgment, after examination of fact; but by far the greater number of those who have assented to the philosophy of Aristotle have given themselves over to it from prejudgment and upon the authority of others; so that it is an obsequiousness and concurrence, rather than consent. And even if there were a real and widespread agreement, still so little ought consent to be taken for a true and solid authority, it would in fact occasion a strong presumption to the contrary. For the worst of all auguries is that derived from agreement in matters intellectual (divinity excepted, and politics where there is the right of suffrage). For nothing pleases the multitude unless it strikes the imagination or binds the understanding with the bands of common notions. . . . . So that the saying of Phocion may well be transferred from moral to intellectual matters, that when the multitude assent and applaud men ought straightaway to examine themselves as to what blunder or fault they may have committed" (*Works*, I, 202–3, 282–84; II, 128; V, 450; VI, 41, 128; VII, 19, 62, 71; VIII, 28–29, 108–9).

Bacon treats with considerable deference Aristotle's wit and certain of his minor opinions. He quotes with approval certain Aristotelian aphorisms—that *"words are the images of cogitations"; "that the hand is the Instrument of Instruments, and the mind is the Form of Forms"; "that the mind hath over the body that commandment which the lord hath over his bondman, but that reason hath over the imagination that commandment which a magistrate hath over a free citizen who may come also to rule in his turn."* He notes that Aristotle has skilfully handled by precept the fallacies of reason which have been the more excellently set, forth by Plato in example. In an epistle to Lord Mountjoy he humorously describes his *Colours of Good and Evil* as "the best book of Aristotle of Stagira" and confesses: "I .... do freely acknowledge that I had my light from him; for where he gave me not matter to perfect, at least he gave me the occasion to invent." Again, while he considers the Schoolmen "owls" where experimental observation is concerned, he recognizes in Aristotle a capacity for the accurate recording of plants and animals and the shrewd observation of human conduct. And when he finds himself forced by pressure of time and circumstances to compile, without aid from others, the historical and experimental material upon which his own induction may be put into operation, he turns on not a few occasions to the writings of the Stagirite both for topics and for observations (*Works*, I, 308; II, 360, 397; IV, 174, 181, 199, 256, 476; V, 23–129, *passim;* VI, 258, 260, 274, 283; VII, 60; VIII, 134; IX, 61, 96).

Apart from such infrequent instances as these, Bacon finds himself in entire disagreement with the opinions of Aristotle and his followers. He takes issue from the beginning with the divisions made by the Aristotelians among the parts of human knowledge. The sciences, according to them, are of three sorts—the theoretical, the practical, and the productive. The end of the first is contemplation; of the second, which includes ethics and politics, conduct; of the third the making of things by "art," as in poetry, rhetoric, and medicine. Of these three kinds, only the theoretical sciences are, strictly speaking, demonstrable and concerned with what cannot be other than it is. The demonstrable sciences lie in the realm of abstraction. Physics manifests a first grade of abstraction in that its concepts and principles are not particulars but universals; mathematics a second, since its objects consist of bodies under the aspect of quantity abstracted from matter and motion; and metaphysics (or first philosophy or natural theology) a third, in that its subject matter is being-as-such in abstraction from all lesser determinations.

Bacon rejects both the underlying principles and the parts of this classification and proceeds to divide human science into history, poetry, and philosophy, according to the respective predominance of one of the three human faculties of memory, imagination, and reason. The only verifiable human philosophy is, he maintains, natural philosophy or, specifically, less general and more general physics. This philosophy has three subjects, nature, man, and God—as known through his creatures. Man as a natural creature produced in animal reproduction is a fit subject for physics. Man as the image of God falls appropriately under revealed theology. Natural theology, in distinction from revealed theology, deals not with God's nature but only with that aspect of God's working which is revealed in the structures and actions of his creatures. Bacon refuses, accordingly, to pass, as does Aristotle, by way of a natural theology, from a physics of nature to a metaphysics of God. He rejects Aristotle's principle of abstraction as a basis for a classification of the sciences and maintains that "one who philosophizes rightly and orderly should dissect nature, and not abstract her" (*Works,* I, 258, 472, 536; III, 52 ff.; VI, 348 ff.; VIII, 83, 288, 347; IX, 231 ff.).

For Bacon, metaphysics is extended physics. He will not recognize the independence of mathematics among the sciences and considers it merely an instrument to be employed in the several parts of physics. His first philosophy includes such lesser principles as have application within the several areas of physical science. These principles are not, as they are with Aristotle, doctrines concerning being-as-such. Physics, in its narrow sense, treats, according to Bacon, of relatively restricted explanations of the configurations and functions of things, while metaphysics contains the more general laws of nature. Both these sciences lead through a knowledge of causes into practice and operation in the production of works. There can be no separation, then, between the theoretical, the practical, and the productive sciences. "Discourse" is not to be separated from works. What in physics and metaphysics is theoretical is also operative in mechanics and magic. Moreover, what is traditionally called "ethics" is not a human science at all, for its doctrines are finally to be dictated by the dogmas of revealed theology (*Works,* II, 297 ff.; III, 46, 176–77; VI, 228 ff., 342, 348 ff., 395; IX, 226, 231 ff., 347–481).

There is one art or science which Bacon classifies under "Use and Objects of the Faculty of the Soul," while Aristotle excludes it from his classification on the ground that it is presupposed in all scientific demonstration. This is logic, called by Aristotle "analytic" and by Bacon the "interpretation of nature." Aristotle's logic includes deduction and induction. The instrument of deduction is the syllogism. This may be described as a form of argument in which certain things being given, certain other things necessarily follow without recourse to anything outside the given. The syllogism contains three propositions; two of these are premises, and the third is the conclusion. Each proposition consists of a subject and a predicate united by a copula. The three propositions are composed, in all, of three terms. The two premises are related through the agency of a common middle term which is used in a universal sense in at least one of the premises. The two remaining terms, as a result of this relation, come to be related in the conclusion. To prove a scientific proposition is to join it syllogistically to other known statements. To show the cause or reason why a thing is so or not so is to relate the conclusion in which something is asserted or denied of this thing to the premises through the agency of a middle term which functions as cause or reason of that which is concluded.

Logical procedure rests upon three primary principles or laws of thought. The first of these is the Law of Identity: What is, is; the second the Law of Contradiction: The same thing cannot both be and not be what it is; and the third the Law of the Excluded Middle: A thing must be either this or that—there is no middle alternative. Logic has to do with the processes of orderly thought. In one respect it is a description of the habits of the rational mind. But it is more than this. It has to do with the arrangement of terms in proper sequence. It is characterized by formal consistency. Its end is the validity of thoughts and propositions in the representation of reality. The predicates which in logical demonstration set forth the attributes of subjects concerning which certain things are to be affirmed or denied in propositions are listed by Aristotle under the heading of "categories." These include being or substance—both in its primary sense of being as individuated and in its secondary sense of universal being, quantity, quality, relation, place, time, position, state or condition, activity, passivity. And of these, all but the first are attributes of substance in which, as accidents, they inhere. Since words are the symbols of thought, science makes true or valid propositions concerning substances. Substances exist as individuals. Scientific propositions make manifest the relations among universal natures or essences. The scientist discerns natures or essences which are common to many substances and, by so doing, is enabled to classify the substances concerned within their proper species and to relate these species to others within a larger genus.

Each substance treated in physics is a single entity. It has a substantial form of its own which is sustained existentially through the agency of matter. Nor is its substantiality a combination of multiple forms—a doctrine developed by certain of Aristotle's successors. In science substances appear as essences; yet essences can be regarded under the aspect of existence only in their actualization in constitutive matter. That which in existence is real is in knowledge an essence. And while the universal nature or essence, which in scientific proof is established as cause or reason, exists in fact through individuation in matter, this matter remains an indeterminate which is never known. Consequently, the actual substance as existent individual, composed as it is of matter and form, can never, for an Aristotelian, be completely intelligible, even if (according to the teachings of the Schools) it can be cognized by a supramundane intelligence.

Substances which are dependent upon matter for existence and activity are corruptible. The species, on the other hand, is not subject to generation, decay, and other vicissitudes of motion which beset the particulars of time and place. As a universal essence, species does not move or change; it is not corruptible. The individual substances which existentially manifest the species come and go; but the species remains, and in its preservation nature fulfills her natural ends. To know species is to perceive final causes in nature; for, while the end or final cause is the actualized perfection of the individual substance, this individual's parts are adapted to the ends of function within the limits of the species, or division of nature, to which it belongs. The hybrid, Aristotle says, is rarely produced in nature and, when it is, usually lacks—as in the case of the mule, for example—the capacity to reproduce its kind and thus to attain a true organic end appropriate to animal species. Monsters may, therefore, be regarded as deviations from nature.

Every science, according to Aristotle, is limited and determined by the axioms which are presupposed in its proofs. In establishing propositions within a science, some premises or axioms must be accepted as axiomatic, that is, as requiring no further proof; otherwise demonstration would go on ad infinitum. To ask for proof of axioms would be to invite a further proof of their proof, and so on without end. Axioms are severally determined according to the respective subject matter of each science. The axioms of one science are not deducible from those of another, nor yet from a more inclusive or general set of axioms which transcend those of all the sciences taken individually. The three demonstrable sciences thus remain distinct, even if they treat of the same existent things, under different grades of abstraction. Yet it would seem that, if Aristotle does on occasion regard metaphysics merely as *primus inter pares,* this science, when he construes it as natural theology, marks an apex, to which the consideration within physics of matter and form, potentiality and actuality, efficient and final causes is subsidiary. Certainly, with the later Aristotelians, metaphysics becomes a commanding and directive science, furnishing as it does general criteria for examination and demonstration within all theoretical science.

In each science which is amenable to logical demonstration there is to be found, according to Aristotle, a genus of substances and attributes which are to be demonstrated of these substances. By demonstration each substance concerned is assigned membership in a species and each species is defined *per genus et differentias.* Every science, in its dealing with substances, is thus bounded by the limit of its own special genus. And within this genus the *infima species* is understood through attributes which severally are wider in implication than the subject to be defined but which collectively are coextensive with it.

The demonstrations of science are, Aristotle maintains, to be pursued by means of logic. Yet he himself does not employ this method in the "proofs" of his metaphysic. Here he bases his doctrine of "being" on the Law of Identity; and in this case he interprets the law not as logical but as ontological. In founding metaphysics, he excludes the other logical principles of Excluded Middle and Contradiction (one cannot say, "Being is not"). His equation of the transcendentals—being, unity, and goodness—in universal and convertible propositions involves a departure from the use of the universal affirmative proposition in syllogistic logic where its subject and predicate cannot both be taken as distributed (one can say, "All crows are black things," but not conversely, "All black things are crows"). Generally speaking, Aristotle establishes his metaphysical truths by a dialectical argument which is designed to disestablish objections and reduce counterpositions.

In addition to deduction Aristotle recognizes another sort of scientific procedure which he calls "induction." This he describes as argument from particulars with a common nature to the universal. Yet in his exposition of demonstration or proof he never undertakes to show just how a general truth, representative of a common nature, may be derived from particular instances. His scientific demonstration proceeds through universals. He assumes that, in an inductive enumerating of particulars, positive agreement, which could establish a universal truth, would necessarily entail an examination of all possible members of a class under consideration—an impossible procedure. Actually, of course, for Aristotle, there is no "pure" induction, because, for him, in the cognition of the instance there is discerned an intelligible nature. At the stage of perception at which science begins, this nature is related as a species to other species and to a relatively more general species, the genus, within which several species lie. It is not surprising, then, that Aristotle undertakes to represent induction as a form of syllogistic proof through the agency of species. To exemplify, he explains: (C) Man, horse, mule (A) are long-lived. (C) Man, horse, mule (B) are without gall. Therefore (provided B is no wider than C) all animals without gall are long-lived.

The conclusion in this case depends, of course, on the condition that the second premise is convertible. Unless such be the case, no universal causal connection can be established. The argument, moreover, falls completely within the realm of species. In this instance induction has been made without an exhaustive examination of the particular men, horses, and mules in order to ascertain whether each and all possess, or do not possess, gall. It has proceeded on the assumption that gall-lessness is an attribute of the species concerned. Accordingly, in this type of induction the phenomena presented, no matter how many or how few, become significant only through their exemplification of defined types, which fall within an arrangement of species and genus. Failing this exemplification, any instances presented would remain mere irregularities beyond the pale of scientific classification.

Bacon finds nothing but futility in Aristotle's theory of induction. He notes that it receives but relatively scant attention from his followers in the Schools, who hasten on to elaborate their dogmaticals by means of syllogism. Certainly, he says, we are not surprised to find that those who pay much attention to it are regarded as men who have fallen into a second childhood.

Aristotle's induction is, in certain respects, incorporated within the syllogism and tied, as all syllogistic reasoning is, to "fixed poles." In others it draws inferences after an examination of a few positive instances and neglects negative examples. It is subject to the "peculiar and perpetual error of the human intellect to be more moved and excited by affirmatives than negatives." We say "error," because "to conclude *upon an enumeration of particulars without instance contradictory* is no conclusion, but a conjecture; for who can assure .... upon those particulars which appear of a side, that there are not others on the contrary side which appear not" (*Works,* I, 255-56, 274, 312-13; II, 367; IV, 69; VI, 265-66; VIII, 80, 99, 138-39; IX, 68).

As for deduction by syllogism, this is a useful instrument for expounding questions in politics, ethics, law, and similar fields in order to bring "popular" opinions into order and consistency. But where the task is not exposition but invention and discovery, where the aim is to produce arts and not arguments, where the end is not to overcome an adversary in disputation but to command nature in operation, the method turns out to be both useless and erroneous (*Works,* I, 215-17, 334; II, 368; VII, 115-16, 123-24; VIII, 41-43, 160; IX, 69).

The Aristotelians commit the initial error of mistaking consistent theorizing for proof in science. They assume that the human intellect is soundly "logical" in its nature and identify demonstration with rational argument, definition, and propositions. Logic, for Bacon, is not a method of consistent argument by means of a middle term; it is not a means to verbal definition; it is not primarily rational. It is an instrument among other instruments invented by man, in this case an instrument for governing his intellect, for binding it to particulars and sense, for controlling it by complex and rigorous means at each and every stage of its ascent from the lowest axiom—which differs but slightly from empirical history —to the next higher and then to the next until it reaches the highest and most general axiom or law of nature.

There can be only two ways, says Bacon, of making discovery. One is to take an intellectual leap from immediate experience to first principles, set these up as fixed and certain, and from them proceed to deduce lesser principles. This is the prevailing procedure in the Schools and has made for error and the destruction of science. Or one may rise from sense and particulars gradually in an unbroken ascent, step by step, under a proper direction, until one finally arrives at a first principle. This is as yet untried (*Works, I,* 214–16, 218, 221, 243, 273–75, 311–12; II, 370; VI, 265–66, 268; VII, 123–24, 139; VIII, 40–42, 44, 47, 69, 98–100, 137–38; IX, 71).

The Aristotelians begin with particulars; and, having acknowledged these in the beginning, they neglect them in perpetuity. The prepossessions of the intellect they initially claim to hold in suspicion; then they place them in complete authority. Their practice is to recognize sense-experience and, having done so, to fly immediately in metaphysics to a first principle which confirms their science of being; in logic to first principles of the mind which furnish the foundation for the demonstration of causes in nature; in the sciences to first axioms which set the boundaries of fields of investigation; and in knowledge generally to notions overhastily abstracted from things, which are construed as essences in the mind, as species in nature, and as terms in the syllogism. Vague and high notions and principles having been thus established, the proof of a scientific conclusion proceeds from the more general axiom to the less through the agency of a middle term which is assumed to be established. The whole practice "rather serves effectively for giving stability to and fixing errors (which are founded in common opinions) than for the investigation of truth..... The syllogism is not applied to the first principles of sciences, it is applied in vain to the middle axioms..... And so it constrains assent, not things" (*Works,* I, 243; II, 187, 368, 395; VI, 267, 273; VIII, 69–70, 408; IX, 69, 93).

We should not, Bacon cautions, be misled by Aristotle's professions about particulars or by his frequent dealings with facts in the compiling of his natural histories. The truth is that in the actual framing of the "decrees and axioms" of his science Aristotle, despite his professions, habitually deserts experience. Everywhere he makes division and distinctions by arbitrary definition and then proceeds to drag experience along as a captive tortured into conformity with his placets. He is, indeed, more open to indictment than his followers, the Schoolmen, "who have deserted experience altogether."

Aristotle is not alone in his overanxiety to take hold of "certainties." This is a common vice. It seems that "the nature of man doth extremely covet to have somewhat in his understanding fixed and immovable, and as a rest and support of the mind. And therefore as Aristotle endeavoreth to prove that in all motion there is some point quiescent; and as he very elegantly expoundeth the ancient fable of Atlas (that stood fixed and bore up the heaven from falling) to be meant of the poles or axle-tree of heaven, whereupon the conversion is accomplished; so assuredly men have a desire to have an Atlas, or axle-tree within to keep them from fluctuation, which is like to a perpetual peril of falling; therefore men did hasten to set down some Principles about which the variety of their disputations might turn" (*Works,* I, 215, 245, 267, 332; II, 396; V, 441-42; VI, 273, 427; VII, 90, 91; VIII, 42, 71, 92, 157-58; IX, 94).

Among the "certainties" which have dominated Aristotelian demonstration four sorts predominate. These are, in turn, the first principles or laws of thought, axioms, middle terms, and defined species. The first of these, the primary laws of thought—of Identity, Contradiction, and Excluded Middle—from which this syllogistic demonstration proceeds, are, according to Bacon, purely notional and abstract. In themselves they provide no knowledge of any observed object. Taken as the first axioms of science, they serve to divert the mind from the proper starting-point of knowledge and occasion much wasted labor. Solid investigation of fact begins with particulars and proceeds through the perception of agreements and disagreements among the characteristics of things. Only gradually, and after "all sorts of exclusion," does it arrive at principles.

The Aristotelian demonstration begins by accepting as certain and fixed those several sets of axioms which are said to belong respectively to independent sciences. If you ask for the proof of these axioms you are referred on faith to the particular science concerned, with the excuse that investigation has to stop somewhere. This, of course, amounts to saying that you must in the end establish knowledge on what is itself not tested or proven. Actually such a contingency could not arise in an induction which proceeded from the known lesser principle to a knowledge of the greater and more inclusive principle and which called every principle—axiomatic or otherwise—into account until properly established by an observation of nature.

The practice of basing scientific demonstration on the disparate axioms of the several sciences serves to give stability to the accepted divisions of knowledge and to prevent inauguration of new sciences. It keeps what natural philosophy there is in subjection to medicine, mathematics, and other narrow fields of inquiry. It serves to separate the parts of knowledge one from the others and from a common nourishing stem of general knowledge. As a consequence it renders the sciences more weak and barren than they should be. It prevents the increase of solid knowledge by the refusal to acknowledge the dependence on natural philosophy—experimentally demonstrated to be the mother of all sciences and arts—of such sciences as astronomy, optics, and music, such arts as medicine and those called mechanical, as well as such sciences and arts as may yet be established (*Works,* I, 217, 243, 286–87, 289, 314, 358, 383–84; II, 310, 362–63; VI, 236, 261; VIII, 43, 69, 112, 114–15, 139–40, 181–82, 204; IX, 14, 64).

Again, proof by means of the syllogism "is but the reduction of propositions to principles in a middle term." This term must be construed in one premise, at least, as an established universal. Its function is to connect as a "mean" the two premises—containing, in all, three terms—from whose conjunction a valid demonstration is to issue. Now if the terms involved in syllogistic "proof" were taken as purely verbal, demonstration would be regarded simply as a matter of connecting definitions through a middle term. But if the Aristotelians admit, as they must do, that to define the meaning of a word is not to know a class of things and to complete a syllogism is not to determine nature, then a primary task for them is the proving and the establishing of a middle term according to the facts of nature. At this point their logic completely fails. It makes no provision for the forging of the very link on which their demonstration depends. We are not surprised, then, to find as a result that, while the Aristotelians insist that a premise which contains the middle term in a universal sense must "be agreed by all and exempted from argument," they have never been able to prevent the practice according to which the middle term is "elected at the liberty of every man's invention." This election having taken place, all further stages of demonstration are inevitably without warrant. "The error lies, as the physicians say, in the *first digestion,* which is not rectified by subsequent functions" (*Works,* I, 215, 243, 313; II, 368, 395, 398; VI, 266, 272–73; VIII, 41–42, 70, 139; IX, 69, 93, 97).

Another fixation employed in Aristotelian demonstration is the species. When the human mind contemplates nature "at liberty" in her common and obvious course it is impressed with certain "species" of things, animals, plants, minerals; and it is led on to the thought "that there are in nature certain primary forms of things which nature strives to produce, and that the variety which is left over proceeds from impediments and aberrations of nature in completing her work, or from the collision of different species and transplanting one into another."

The peremptory acceptance of this opinion respecting fixed natural species has issued in several unfortunate results. It has caused collectors to exclude from natural histories such works of nature as have "a digression and deflection from the ordinary course of generations, productions, and motions" and to segregate them in collections of "marvels." But surely, counters Bacon, the unusual manifestations in nature have a place in a nature's history, and for "two reasons, both of great weight; the one to correct the partiality of axioms and opinions, which are commonly framed only upon common and familiar examples; the other because from the wonders of nature is the nearest intelligence and passage towards the wonders of art." By following nature in her wanderings and deviations and by discovering the causes for these in processes and schematisms of matter the operative scientist will be enabled to produce species of "wonders" comparable to her accidental and rare prodigious works.

The doctrine of natural species has also aided in producing the opinion "that art is something different from nature, and things artificial from things natural." The natural thing, such as a tree, is said to have a primary form, the artificial thing, such as a table made from the tree, a secondary form. In consequence of this separation most writers of natural history omit any mention of experiments in the arts. Art is assessed as a means to add to nature, or to improve, complete, or liberate nature when impeded, but not a method of nature's working. Bacon is opposed to this view and demands that it "be firmly settled within the minds of men, that the artificial does not differ from the natural either in form or in essence, but only in the efficient..... Nor matters it, provided things are put in the way to produce an effect, whether it be done by man or apart from man" (*Works,* I, 225, 269–70, 282, 420–22; II, 189–93; VI, 185; VII, 288–90; VIII, 80, 94–95, 107, 237–39, 410–13; X, 406–9).

All in all, the logic of the Aristotelians has provided poorly for human knowledge and not at all for the union of human knowledge with human power. It has contributed no means for the invention either of independent arts or of such specific useful works as may be founded in proven science. In the history of discovery "the mind of herself doth manage and act on induction much better than they describe it." Those inventions which are of the greatest use to mankind have been found out by "chance," and quite without logical direction. Medicine, for example, was first discovered, and afterward its reasons and causes were assigned. Prometheus came upon fire through no speculation; he had no expectation of the spark when he struck the flint. The flying-open of a pot led to the discovery of artillery; drops in condensation on a cover over boiling liquid to the discovery of distillation. So great a portent are the instances of chance that one may not unjustly conclude that where the rational and dogmatic sciences begin, there discovery of useful works ceases.

Inventions have accrued to man only "casually" with great gaps, often ages, between. There can be no doubt that very many more of nature's secrets—of excellent use, not cognate or parallel to those already discovered—would in the course of many ages come to light of themselves in the manner of the former. How much better and how much more worthy of human capacity it would be, if, through a new and adequate method for discovering nature's activities, secrets for the relief and benefit of mankind could be "speedily and suddenly and simultaneously hastened and anticipated" (*Works,* I, 242, 292–93, 316; II, 362–67, 378; VI, 261–63, 265; VII, 128–34; VIII, 68, 118, 142; IX, 64–68, 77).

CHAPTER XVII

BACON CONTRA ARISTOTLE. II

ARISTOTLE has left major treatises on physics and metaphysics. Of the former the subject consists of natural things in motion. Movement is the proceeding from potentiality to actuality. Potentiality marks the capacity in a thing to become that which it has in it to become; actuality is its attainment through becoming. The condition of a thing which has not undergone this movement or change from potency to act may be described as one of privation. In privation the thing concerned is as yet deprived of its form. The significant end of motion is the form which in movement is actualized. Form makes the thing to be what it becomes, determines its unity and its perfection according to its nature. It is therefore indispensable to the explanation of its being, its activity, and its significance. Matter, on the other hand, is an indeterminate through which what is not yet anything becomes something. By itself matter is completely inert and unreal; and yet in conjunction with the agency of form it is potential of activity and actuality. Activity is a passing from significant state to significant state, i.e., from form to form; matter is to provide continuity and to avoid a cleavage in the process. In the production of substances matter is the source of individuation. Without matter the form, according to the Aristotelians, remains a mere essence without existence. Yet apart from the form, which is actualized in it and marks the end of process in which matter plays its necessary role, matter remains negative and nondeterminate.

Motion may be considered also under the question of causation. In motion four sorts of cause are manifest. The first of these is the material cause, that out of which a thing is produced. This cause is an indeterminate relative to the actualized form and capable of significant determination by the form. The second sort of cause is the formal, the significant essence according to which a thing or state comes to be; the third, the efficient cause, that immediate agent by which the thing is produced; and the fourth, the final cause, the end or aim of production.

Four sorts of motion are discernible within the realm of nature. (Aristotle is not always consistent here; sometimes he omits generation from his list.) The first sort is generation and decay, on which depend the origination and destruction, respectively, of the substance concerned. This affects the substantial form of the individual—which in the case of other sorts of motion persists as an identical being throughout a considerable range of modification. The second type of motion is increase and decrease; the third that of qualitative change; and the fourth local motion. The last of these is analyzable into two sorts of primary or simple motion, namely, circular and rectilinear. Of these the circular sort belongs to the celestial bodies, and the rectilinear to terrestrial bodies.

In nature the simplest or first bodies are the four elements, fire, air, water, and earth—matter is, of course, no body at all. These four elements correspond to primary or fundamental qualities of bodies perceived in touch—the hot, the cold, the wet, and the dry. As elements, they are not actually found in isolation, for it is in their nature to enter into combinations one with another. Of their combinations six are theoretically possible; but actually, since the contraries, dry and wet, hot and cold, do not combine, only four groupings are possible. The hot and the dry are found combined in fire, the hot and the moist in water, the cold and the dry in earth. In each instance of combination one pair of elements concerned is found in predominance: in earth, the dry; in water, the cold; in air, the wet; in fire, the hot.

To the elements or first bodies which constitute the terrestrial and lower bodies in the *scala naturae* rectilinear motion is natural and appropriate. Each of the four, earth, air, fire, and water—considered in the abstract—when left to itself follows its appropriate rectilinear path and, when displaced or mixed with others, tends to take an appropriate natural position through upward or downward rectilinear movement. Its tendency to do this reveals its weight and discloses its nature generally, which in its tendency it seeks to achieve through appropriate activity. The natural position of earth, which is the heaviest of the four elements or first bodies, is the central region; of fire, which is the lightest, the upper and outer region; of water and air, regions in between these extremes. Water and air rise or sink through their relations to earth and fire. Air will rise above earth and sink below fire. Every natural body, composed as it is through a combination of elements, has its natural place. Its place is that which the natural body fills. There is no void or vacuum in nature. Space is that which is inhabited by one body and then in turn inhabited by another body which replaces a former inhabitant.

The four elements enter into further combination to produce homoeomerous bodies, such as minerals and the tissues of plants and animals. These bodies are not mere additions of elements but are chemical unities, their natures being determined by respective proportions among the constitutive elements. In the case of vital substances—whether vegetable, animal, or rational—bodily tissues receive a further determination through their being the organs of soul. A living thing, characterized as it is by soul, is not a mere sum or combination of a chemical entity and a psychic entity but is in each case a single unified substance to which soul contributes form, act, and end.

In the astral domain is found a special type of motion and a further body or element—the quintessence, or the ether. For the four terrestrial elements, rectilinear motion is appropriate; not so for the fifth element, or quintessence; its motion must be circular, because this is the only motion fitting for that which is the First Moved. Circular motion, Aristotle argues, has a priority to the rectilinear because the perfect is prior to the imperfect, and the circular figure is the most perfect, lacking, as it does, beginning, end, finitude, and irregularity.

The heaven consists of fifty-five concentric spheres with the earth at the center. Its motions are communicated from the motion of the outer sphere whose motion is initiated, as the First Moved, by the Prime Mover himself. Celestial motions may be interpreted, like the motions of lesser things as well, in terms of desire for the Prime Mover. The activities of the celestial intelligences are "imitations," by each according to his station, of the activity of God.

Bacon is especially concerned with Aristotle's physics because his own final philosophy is generalized physics. Bacon, as we have seen, acknowledges only one kind of motion, namely, local motion; only one kind of natural being, namely, that composed of formed matter determined by motion in space. He interprets the subjects of traditional metaphysics, such as being and nonbeing, permanence and change, unity and multiplicity, possibility and nonpossibility, in terms of his physics. His pyramid of knowledge, which begins with natural history and proceeds through physics to metaphysics, is in no sense comparable to the Aristotelian hierarchy of the sciences but marks only stages in the exactness and inclusiveness of a search within the physics of matter.

The physics of Aristotle is, says Bacon, purely theoretical. It issues, he maintains, from a logistic. It is motivated by a desire to produce a world through the device of categorization and definition. It contains no doctrine respecting actual matter. Its matter is completely indeterminate, and the classification and organization of its factors is derived from purely verbal definition. It turns out to be thoroughly nominalistic, composed as it is by a thinker who deals with terms and not facts and who is "always more solicitous.... to deliver something positive in words than about the inner truth of things" (*Works,* I, 266–67, 274, 306; II, 140; V, 298, 340; VI, 132; VII, 115; VIII, 91, 99, 132; X, 352, 393).

The explanation of nature in terms of matter, form, privation, passive potentiality, and actuality Bacon regards as "fantastical." Potentiality can mean but negation of what is found to be in the case of actuality. The opinion "that the lively and moving beginning of things should be shift or appetite of matter to privation" is but a "conceit." Potential, unshapen, despoiled, and passive matter "seems altogether a fiction of the human mind." It cannot be known and it cannot be described, except by negative definition. The Aristotelians, pretending to be rational scientists (with their feigned separations and distinctions far beyond what truth will bear) will persist in explaining what is in terms of what is not, the active in terms of the inert, and the significant in terms of what is indeterminate, unintelligible, unknowable. "Would," says Bacon, "that this were agreed upon once for all, that beings are not to be made out of beings that have no being." Existential matter—whatever it may or may not consist of—must, contends Bacon, be so "formed" and "equipped" that natural motion is the natural consequence and emanation of its positive nature (*Works,* I, 244, 266; V, 231, 296–99, 333, 335–40; VI, 64; VII, 115–16; VIII, 70, 91; X, 315, 350–53, 385, 387–92).

As for the concepts of the heavy, the light, the dense, the rare, the moist, the dry, and such like, these are purely "popular" and ill defined. Of the four "elements," fire has been introduced to "keep square" earth, air, and water, the hot being added to make, as by a quaternion, a theoretical balance among contraries. All four so-called "elements" have been chosen with an undue regard for sense. They are not available for or by experimentation. The earth of theory, for example, is not, according to its exponents, like common perceivable earth; nor, indeed, can it be found to be like anything except its own verbal definition. The theory that bodies move to their proper places is inept. The so-called "appropriate place" to which a body tends turns out to be no place at all; for space is explained by the Aristotelians in terms of body's occupancy. It transpires, then, that mere nothingness attracts bodies as their "end"! But "body is not acted upon save by body" (*Works,* I, 244, 253–54, 262–63, 429–36, 494; II, 401; IV, 37; VIII, 70, 79, 87–88, 247–53, 308–9; IX, 99; X, 187).

Bacon, as we have already seen, berates the Aristotelians for their search for final causes. The inquisition of these in natural philosophy is, he says, a barren undertaking and a hindrance to knowledge. The reading of nature's motions in terms of near and remote purposes is too easy; it provides an excuse for failure to make diligent inquiry into the inner workings of things. Indeed the whole interpretation of nature by the Aristotelians is "vulgar" and "popular." Their several types of motion—change in place, alteration in quality, augmentation and diminution, generation and corruption—indicate no more than such limits of motion as are grossly obvious after action has taken place. The names of the divisions represent in a manner what has been done but nothing involved in the doing of it. They mark that from which, but in no case that *by* which, the phenomenon is produced. They merely indicate effects and fail to penetrate to the operations of causes. The motion of resistance by which things refuse to be annihilated the Peripatetics—"who almost always define the thing rather by effects and by what the bodies lack than by inner causes"—either explain by the axiom, "Two bodies cannot be in one place," or simply call it "motion to prevent penetration of dimensions." The same philosophers draw a distinction between natural and violent motion as if nature's violence did not belong to her! The action whereby bodies strive to escape preternatural pressure or tension they describe as "motion in accordance with the Form of the Element," and "injudiciously enough," since this action is to be found not only in fire and water and the other so-called "elements" but also in wood, lead, cloth, and parchment (*Works,* I, 244, 270–72, 489; II, 295, 298; IV, 36–37; V, 211–12, 222–23; VI, 223–24; VIII, 70, 95–97, 304, 508, 512; X, 186–87, 295–96, 307).

Not least unfortunate among the Aristotelian assumptions is the segregation of rectilinear motion, which belongs to earthly elements, from the circular motion of a fictional heaven composed of a fifth essence or ether. There are, says Bacon, four "axioms or rather agreeable opinions" about the earth and the heavens, handed down by the "philosophers," which have served to "corrupt" science: that all things above the moon are incorruptible and invariable; that the heaven, composed as it is of a fifth essence, is moved by a Prime Mover and is not subject to the "turbulent actions of compression, relaxation, repulsion, submission, and the like"; that each natural body has its own inherent proper motion; and that all celestial motion proceeds in circles. All these statements serve to violate that unity of nature in which bodies of all sorts influence one another. They engender burdensome doctrines of cycles, epicycles, and eccentrics. They disregard the fact that in the course of nature natural bodies are moved by other natural bodies and by nothing else (for the Prime Mover is not a natural body); that types of motion are common to earth and heaven; that movements in terrestrial bodies are sometimes circular. The four propositions spring, as a matter of history, from a pagan regard for the supposed eternal character of the heaven. It is from this that the issue is the doctrine of the First Moved motivated by the Prime Mover (*Works,* I, 253-54; V, 228-29, 231, 340; VII, 318, 323-27, 340, 354-56; VIII, 79; X, 313, 315, 393, 436, 440-44, 457, 474-76).

In his criticism of the doctrine of the Prime Mover, Bacon assails Aristotle's natural theology. The latter is the science which Aristotle employs to bring his metaphysics into relation with his physics and also to identify the Prime Mover, Pure Being, Pure Form, and the Supreme Final Cause. The subject of metaphysics Aristotle defines as being qua being. Being, he finds, is attested by sense and known in rational reflection. Being is prior to such less general and less abstract subjects as fall within classifications according to species and genera and prior to all determinations of objects through the assignment of predicates to subjects by ordinary logical propositions in scientific demonstration. Being is affirmed in the first principle of knowledge, the Law of Identity: What is, is. From this principle there follows being and identity, which are convertible terms: being is unity, and unity is being. Aristotle further assigns to being goodness, by which he means perfection of an object in its actualization. He thus provides a basis for that doctrine of Transcendentals which is enunciated by later Aristotelians.

Having reached these conclusions respecting being, Aristotle is far from content. He will go on to equate being which is founded on the

Law of Identity with the Supreme Final Cause, the unmoved Prime Mover, Pure Form, and, as the highest point in the *scala universi,* God. God's activity, he says, consists of pure contemplation in which thinking is identical with the subject of thought. He thus adds to the original problem of being-as-such further questions, including those of knowledge and the relation of God as Prime Mover to the *scala naturae.*

The question of knowledge presents Aristotle and his followers with a considerable problem. To explain knowledge, Aristotle holds, two factors are required, a subject capable of knowing and an object capable of intelligibility. In the case of human organisms the process of knowing begins with sense-impressions. From these impressions "experience" is acquired. And from experiences, in turn, knowledge, which is a perception of objects of varied sorts—of a sense-quality, for instance, of a species of substance, of an axiom, of a relation between a species and a genus. We perceive that white is white, for example; that the object before us is a triangle or has triangularity; that things which are equal to the same thing are equal to one another; that the species triangularity lies within a more inclusive species or genus of figured things. Perception is the actuality of a potentially capable subject acting in conjunction with a potentially capable object. The potential capacity to know is present in the perceiving organism, or it is not; the organism which is not capable of cognizing such objects as those mentioned is without capacity for knowledge. Perception of attribute, species, axiom, is perception of what is universal. The existent object which causes the original impression is a particular substance; yet it can be known in scientific classification and demonstration only as that which contains a universal nature, form, or essence. As a particular immersed in matter it lies beyond the pale of human knowledge.

The process of knowing is initiated through the stimulation of a sense organ by an external object. In the sensation which results from this activity a sensible essence which is specified under some sensible quality or other becomes present to the subject. The sensible essence, having been received through the sense and retained in the imagination, is through the agency of the image made capable of determining the intellect to generalize and in its generalizing to know universal essences. The essence as a universal logical entity is in knowledge identified with the mind; it also can possess an existence in particular things through the individuating agency of matter.

In the reception of the known object the passive intellect functions, but for the final epistemological identification of subject and object an active intellect is also required. The former of these intellects is perishable and dependent upon matter, while the latter, as pure activity, is not so dependent and is immortal. As an intelligence it possesses, according to Aristotle's account, only such characteristics as are assigned to the Prime Mover. It is presumably, then, separate from the faculties and functions of natural organisms. Just how this immortal active intellect with divine attributes is to be brought into conjunction with the passive intellect Aristotle in his extant writings does not explain. He does not say, as do certain of his successors, for instance, that the passive intellect is made active by a kind of Divine Illumination imposed upon it from without, or that God is the thinker of all human thoughts.

The further problem of relating the being of Aristotle's metaphysics with the *scala naturae*, which culminates in God as Prime Mover, is rendered difficult by certain of the presuppositions which underlie his organization of the sciences. By definition he excludes from metaphysics that indeterminate matter which individuates and enters into the motion of natural substances. Yet having excluded this matter, along with privation, he goes on to regard metaphysically such concepts as Pure Form, Prime Mover, and Supreme Final Cause, all of which are understood through the negation of matter, natural movement, and limited final causes.

Again, in his classification of the sciences, physics, mathematics, and metaphysics or first philosophy are ranged according to grades of abstraction; yet it is not to be assumed that the quantity which is the subject of mathematics is a relatively higher genus with respect to which the subject matter of physics is properly regarded as species. Nor should one suppose that metaphysics includes, in the last synthesis, all the data and principles of the other two less abstract sciences. By definition metaphysics does not treat of things in motion through the agency of matter—which are the objects investigated in physics—nor with the quantitative determinations in mathematics of such things in abstraction from motion so produced. Each science is, by its very nature as a subject of demonstration, separated from the others according to its respective axioms. From the several axioms of the several sciences taken in conjunction no scientific demonstration can proceed. And there is no comprehensive science, with or without axioms, within whose framework all truths about reality are ultimately to be included.

Aristotle, however, surmounts the difficulties presented by his several definitions and presuppositions by the simple device of introducing a natural theology, which is neither physics nor first philosophy but a mixture of things which by definition are excluded from either one or the other, as the case may be. This device enables him to move in argument from physics into metaphysics and from metaphysics into physics at will, from form to Pure Form, from motion to Prime Mover, from final cause to Supreme Final Cause, from categorized substances to substance qua substance. It makes plausible his consideration in metaphysics, as well as in physics, of potency and act, privation, matter and form, material and efficient, formal and final cause, and substance. It brings the subjects of three separate sorts of science under a common *scala universi*. It provides a means of equating being with God, with the Prime Mover, and the Final Cause of all natural things. It enables Aristotle to pass from indeterminate matter through relatively more and more significant form to Pure Form and to argue from motion to a Supreme Final Cause, which initiates the causal activity prevailing in all lesser things and which is motivated by no further final cause.

Bacon's treatment of metaphysics and natural theology is, needless to say, thoroughly antithetical to that of Aristotle. For Bacon, metaphysics is general or summary physics. Its object is nature's bodily motions and structures. Its end is not contemplation but operation in works. Knowledge is a continuous pyramid, whose basis is natural history and whose apex is generalized phyics. Science proceeds continuously by a gradual unbroken scale of ascent from the simplest proposition to the "highest generality of motion, or summary law of nature," which, says Bacon, God reserves "within his own curtain."

Bacon accordingly will not accept a metaphysics which is segregated initially by a highest abstraction. He will not recognize in the results of an examination of the Law of Identity a knowledge either of being or of God. For him the so-called "first principles" come last in consideration. Scientific knowledge—as distinct from Divine Revelation—recognizes no highest generalizations except those which appear after the apex of the triangle of empirical knowledge has been reached through an ascent from natural history (*Works,* I, 272, 311–12; II, 290–92; VI, 32, 221–22; VIII, 97, 137–38, 506–7).

The Aristotelians initially separate by definition their metaphysics from their physics and then proceed in practice to confuse the two through what Bacon considers a false and pagan brand of natural theology. By this hybrid science they mix together questions relating to God's nature and activity—which belong properly to revelation—with problems which concern nature and belong to naturalistic metaphysics. They undertake to pass from the causes of nature to a First Cause which is God. Aristotle assigns divine attributes to the heavens, and his followers equate the doctrine of the Unmoved Mover with tenets of Christian theology. The Peripatetics generally argue from the motions of the earth and the celestial spheres to a Prime Mover and from secondary causes in the processes of nature to a First Cause and thus pass from nature to God. Their proceeding, Bacon contends, is completely unwarranted. "If any man shall think by view and inquiry into sensible and material things, to attain to any light for the revealing of the nature or will of God, he shall dangerously abuse himself," because men without revelation can in their limited capacities know only the nature of creatures and the powers vouchsafed to them and not the nature of the Divine Creator. To argue from the series of causes and effects in natural things to a Cause which is beyond this series, from things mutually moved to a Mover impelled by nothing outside himself, is to engage in "false and vain" theorizing. Any presumed knowledge of an Infinite God through an examination of finite natural things marks an attempt to bring God's nature within the orbit of attributes which belong to his creatures (*Works,* I, 262, 299–300; II, 105, 259, 344–47; V, 291; VI, 29, 75, 96, 207, 212, 254; VIII, 72, 87, 125, 477; IX, 48–50; X, 344–45; XIII, 10–11, 51, 108–9, 155).

According to Bacon the doctrine of the image of God in man, that is to say, the rational soul as distinct from the sensible and physical soul, belongs not to human science but to revelation. The Peripatetic names for it, "Ultimate Act" and "Form of the Body," are but "trifles of logic." The rational soul is not produced in natural generation as are the natures of lesser vital creatures but is created by God himself. And, although it is "breathed" into him by God, it is nevertheless a faculty of man qua man. Yet, its nature is not a proper subject for natural philosophy and can be discerned only through the truths of revelation. Whatever knowledge man can possess of the image of God, then, must "be bounded by religion, or else it will be subject to deceit and delusion; for as the substance of the soul in creation was not extracted out of the mass of heaven and earth by the benediction of a *producat,* but was immediately inspired by God, so it is not possible that it should be (otherwise than by accident) subject to *the laws of heaven and earth,* which are *the subject of philosophy;* and therefore the true knowledge of the nature and state of the soul, must come by the same inspiration that gave the substance" (*Works,* II, 344–47; VI, 254; IX, 48–50; X, 146).

Bacon, because of the theological presuppositions which underlie his philosophy, has no concern with an investigation of either the rational soul in general or its cognitive functions in particular. He agrees with the Aristotelians that knowledge begins with sense-experience of particulars and ends in the cognition by reason of universals conjoined in propositions. For him sensation is an activity of the physical soul only, that is to say, of material body. The rational mind and the logical mind are not identical in function. Logic is not a description of reason in act but rather an instrument to restrain and direct this faculty in a general "levelling" of men's wits. Accordingly, Bacon's epistemology—as distinct from the rules of induction—all but disappears before the triple demands of a revealed theology, a materialistic psychology, and a mechanical logic.

There is one set of doctrines within one division of Bacon's array of the sciences which call for a word of comment here, namely, those which belong to his "first philosophy." A temptation besets his readers to identify his first philosophy either (*a*) with Bacon's own metaphysics or (*b*) with the metaphysics of the Aristotelians. The confusion is occasioned by the term "first philosophy," another and ancient name for metaphysics; by Bacon's inclusion within his first philosophy of Transcendentals, a division of Peripatetic metaphysics; and by his description of the subject matter of primary philosophy as the "summits of things."

Bacon's first philosophy and his metaphysics are quite distinct in character. The former is far wider in its comprehension of subjects than is metaphysics; it is also less general and less comprehensive in its principles. Metaphysics, as a crowning science, admits only those truths which in their greater generality affirm the fundamental composition, order, and rule of all nature. The subjects of first philosophy are, on the other hand, of two sorts: first, the Transcendentals, or Adventitious Conditions of Beings, such as much, little, like, unlike, possible and impossible, being, not being and, secondly, "such axioms as are not peculiar to any of the particular sciences, but qualify for several of them in common."

A very brief comparison between these subjects and comparable topics and principles in the Peripatetic first philosophy will reveal also how widely divergent the two respective types of first philosophy are. The doctrine which develops into the later Peripatetic theory of Transcendentals appears with Aristotle, who assigns unity and the good to being in such a manner that all three are to be affirmed of one another in convertible propositions and placed beyond all lesser categorical determinations, such as quantity, quality, time, and place. The Schoolmen add further characteristics of being, *verum, res, aliquid,* and make these terms, along with being, subjects or predicates in convertible propositions: being is unity; unity is being; being is true, a thing, something. These Transcendentals for the Peripatetics are metaphysical objects and therefore part of a science based on abstraction from the motions of materiate bodies and from quantitative determinations of things.

Bacon's Transcendentals have neither the character, the status, nor the locus of those of the Peripatetics. They include, for example, not being, which is not conceivably convertible with being; and much and little, which, so far from transcending all categorical determinations, fall within the category "quantity." Bacon's Transcendentals are definitely located in the context of natural science. As an appropriate inquiry respecting much and little, Bacon poses, for example, the question as to "why some things in nature are and can be so numerous and plentiful, others so few and scanty." For example, gold and roses are relatively scarce, iron and grass plentiful. When discussing like and unlike, he regrets that there has been no investigation of such a question as "why iron does not attract iron, which the magnet does; . . . . why gold does not attract gold itself, though it does attract quicksilver."

His consideration of the axioms for which his first philosophy is said by him to be a "receptable" is informative. Here he employs several examples. "Things which are equal to the same thing are equal to one another." This is a rule of mathematics so potent, he says, that all syllogism is based upon it. "The nature of everything is best seen in its smallest portions" is an axiom used by Aristotle in his *Politics* when he commences his inquiry respecting the commonwealth with a discussion of the family; and in physics it becomes such an efficacious rule that it produces the atomic doctrine of Democritus. "Putrefaction is more contagious before than after maturity" is a "rule in physics; and the same is an eminently true principle in ethics." "Whatever is preservative of a greater form is more powerful in action" is an axiom manifest in physics, where no severance of the connection of things is to be found; in politics, where whatever makes for the preservation of the whole state is more efficacious than that which conduces to the benefit of its individual members; and also in theology, where it appears in the enjoining of charity, which is "the most communicative excellence and excels all the rest."

These axioms of first philosophy Bacon describes as "one and the same marks and footsteps of nature impressed upon different subjects and matters." They are not, he warns us, to be construed as "mere similitudes —as they may seem to men of insufficient acuteness." Certainly they are not the doctrines of a Peripatetic metaphysics which commences its inquiry after abstraction of subject matter from matter, motion, and quantity has taken place; they are not descriptions of being qua being. Nor are they the discoveries within a most general and highly synthesized empirical science, which for Bacon himself constitutes metaphysics. At best they are local principles applicable with varying degrees of aptness, exactness, and inclusiveness to different areas and divisions of investigation. In their several respects, they are sometimes directives of inquiry, sometimes analogous conclusions of investigation, and not always precise in their meaning (*Works,* II, 253-58, 264-67; VIII, 471-76, 482-84; cf. VI, 206-11).

CHAPTER XVIII

THE NEW LOGIC: THE FIRST VINTAGE OF DISCOVERY

AFTER a digression in which Bacon's doctrines have been placed in certain settings and perspectives by virtue of his opposition to the tenets of the prevailing Aristotelian philosophy, we return to his exposition of the new organon of knowledge. The directions prescribed by this new method, he tells us, are designed, first, to show "how to educe and form axioms from experience" and, secondly, "how to deduce and derive new experiments from axioms." To the former end are required three ministrations: one to sense, a second to memory, and a third to reason. The ministration to sense is given in such a basic, ordered, natural and experimental history as prevents confusion and distraction on the part of the mind; that to memory in Tables and "arrangements of instances," which assist the mind in reaching conclusions respecting the classes of things recorded in natural history; and the third to reason by induction, true and legitimate induction, which is the very key of interpretation. It is the third of these, Bacon tells us, that he is undertaking to expound in the *Novum organum*.

Inductive investigation begins with particulars and proceeds to definition. Particulars are "infinite" and cannot be dealt with in knowledge except as exemplifications of determined natures which are common to many instances. In the recognition of these natures a "cutting-off of infinity" from indeterminate multiplicity takes place through the segregation of natures. With the termination of infinity goes the recognition that the forms of things are not infinite like particulars but are limited; that the discovery of the structures and ways of infinite individuals is possible only because particulars partake of a limited number of forms which produce by their conjunctions natural things in infinite variety.

One form is found in different things: heat, for example, in heavenly bodies and in fire; redness in roses, rainbows, and diamonds. The investigation of forms in such cases as these brings together things which are heterogeneous and alien from each other yet which agree in the form or law which governs heat or redness, as the case may be. Substances, or bodies, are "concrete natures" and contain in themselves many forms of natures in conjunction. Analysis of these bodies proceeds by their reduction according to possible forms. The forms of substance, which are unions (*conjugia*) of simple natures according to the course of the universe, are not to be sought until simpler natures have been investigated and segregated. "To inquire the form of a lion, or of an oak, of gold," says Bacon, "nay even of water or air would be to turn serious business into a game; but to inquire the form of dense, rare, hot, cold, heavy, light, tangible, pneumatic, volatile, fixed, and of similar things; and of schematisms as well as motions, which .... are not many and yet make up and sustain the beings (*essentias*) and Forms of all substances; this, I say, it is which we are attempting, and it constitutes and defines" the metaphysic of forms (*Works,* I, 223, 327, 351-52, 385-86, 411, 413; II, 289-90; III, 207; VIII, 49, 152, 176-77, 205-6, 228, 231, 505-6; IX, 371; cf. VI, 63).

The method of induction, by which the search for forms is carried out, includes eleven "directions." The first of these is called the "Presentation of Instances to the Understanding" and the second, the "Indulgence (*Permissionem*) of the Understanding, or the Commencement of Interpretation, or the First Vintage." These two procedures Bacon illustrates with an inquiry respecting the nature of heat, in which he reaches a definition. Just what status is to be assigned to this definition in a philosophy of nature he does not make clear. And he fails also to say whether heat is one of the forms which enter into the ultimate character of nature.

Having reached by way of illustration the First Vintage or the Commencement of Inquiry the author goes on to list "the other helps of the understanding in the Interpretation of Nature and true and perfect induction." These aids are nine in number: first, Prerogative Instances; secondly, the Supports of Induction; thirdly, the Rectification of Induction; fourthly, the Variation of Inquiry according to the Nature of the Subject; fifthly, Natures Prerogative with respect to Investigation— what should be inquired of first, what afterwards; sixthly, the Limits of Investigation or the Synopsis of all Natures in the Universe; seventhly, the Bringing Down to Practice; eighthly, the Preparations for Investigation; and ninthly and lastly, the Ascending and Descending Scale of Axioms.

Of these nine aids, only the first—exemplified in twenty-seven types of cases—is expounded by Bacon. The remaining eight subjects, which include matters essential to the Great Instauration such as "the synopsis of all natures in the universe," and "the ascending and descending scale of axioms," are left without exposition. That is to say, there is no extant account, either by way of precept or example, beyond the Commencement of Interpretation and directions for use of Prerogative Instances, of Bacon's method for the reform of the sciences. This being understood, we shall turn to these rather meager, if somewhat detailed, portions of the new scheme of induction which the author is able to set on record. (*Works,* I, 383, 390, 397–400; VIII, 204, 210, 217–19).

"The investigation of Forms," he says, "proceeds thus: in the case of a given nature we must first make a muster before the understanding of all known instances which agree in the same nature, though in matters the most unlike." Initially, then, induction is not, for Bacon, so-called "pure" induction; that is to say, it is not an indiscriminate amassing of "mere" facts but is rather the collecting of the instances of a nature which is presumed to be present in the several examples assembled. Induction rests on the foundation of sorted natural history. Bacon, in drawing examples from the natural history which he finds available, cautions the reader that this "is not so copious or verified as to satisfy or serve legitimate interpretation." Indeed, so poor is extant science in its store of accumulated observation and experimentation, he is sometimes forced to take the examples he employs from mere "traditions and reports (always however noting doubtful credit and authority)"; and he is "very often compelled to use such language as 'Let experiment be made,' or 'Let further inquiry be made.'"

The first form which he will investigate is that of heat. To inquire into the nature of heat, let there be prepared, he says, three tables, whose office is the Presentation of Instances to the Understanding. The first of these three is the Table of Essence and Presence. This will consist of a compilation of diversified sorts of instances in which the nature in question is present. He now lists in the case of heat some twenty-seven instances to which others are to be added. Among these are the rays of the sun, especially at noon in summer; the rays of the sun reflected and condensed, as on walls, in burning glasses, and between mountains; eruptions of flames from cavities of the earth; ignited solids; warm natural baths; boiling liquids; substances rubbed violently; quicklime sprinkled with water; the bodies of animals (*Works,* I, 354-58, 383; VIII, 179-81, 204).

The second table is to contain instances in which the nature under investigation is found wanting, since the form must be both present when the nature is present and absent when the nature is absent. These negative instances, from which the nature in question is excluded, are of the greatest moment. The mind, if presented with affirmative cases only, will—"as when left to itself it is always wont to do"—arrive at "fancies and guesses and notions ill determined and axioms that must be mended daily." Men are too prone to conclude from such affirmative instances as fall their way. It belongs only "to God the giver and maker of Forms, and it may be to the angels and [pure disembodied] intelligences to have an affirmative knowledge of Forms immediately, and from the beginning of contemplation. But this assuredly is beyond man; to whom it is granted only to proceed at first by negatives, and at last to end in affirmatives, after all sorts of exclusion."

The attempt to note anything like all the sorts of instance available from which the nature under invetigation is wanting would be a futile undertaking; therefore the negative cases which are to be instanced should be those which may be subjoined to the affirmative. These will permit the recording of the absence of the nature in question from subjects which are most akin to those in which it is to be found. Among examples of instances in such proximity from which the nature of heat is excluded are these (Bacon lists some thirty-two): the rays of the moon; the rays of the sun in the middle air; unheated liquids; oil mixed with quicklime; experiments—these to be tried—to catch the rays of the moon in a powerful burning-glass, and those of the sun in a glass fashioned in a manner contrary to the structure of this sort of glass, in order to see in the former case whether there is any heat and in the latter whether the heat of the sun is diminished; observations to see whether cold flames may be found. The table thus compiled is to be called the "Table of Deviation, or of Absence in Proximity" (*Works,* I, 358, 383-84; VIII, 181-82, 204).

Thirdly, a muster should be made before the understanding of instances in which the form under inquiry is found in different degrees more and less. "For since the Form of a thing is the very thing itself, and the thing differs from its Form no otherwise than as the apparent differs from the real (*existens*), or the external from the internal, or the thing in relation to man from the thing in relation to the universe; it certainly follows that no nature is to be taken as a true Form, unless it always decrease when the nature in question decreases, and in like manner always increase when the nature in question increases."

A third table, accordingly, should be prepared after the recording of observations of the increase or the decrease of heat in the same subjects and of its respective amounts in different subjects under comparison one with another. Examples are as follows (Bacon lists some forty-one): the increase of heat in animals by motion and exercise; persons seized with intermittent fevers, who at first become cold to shivering and then grow exceedingly hot; animals in winter, when they become colder externally and warmer internally; the sun's greater heat as it approaches the zenith; fires making way against a strong wind; anvils growing hot under repeated blows; air in process of losing heat. The table thus compiled is to be called the "Table of Degrees" or the "Table of Comparison" (*Works*, I, 371-82; VIII, 193-203).

These three tables having been prepared, the next task is to exclude or reject the several natures which are not found in those instances where the nature of heat is present and those which are found in instances from which heat is absent and those which are found to decrease where heat increases. When this is done, we may proceed to affirmation.

Employing the observations recorded in the foregoing tables, we may reject, says Bacon, the nature or natures of the "elements" from the form of heat, because heat is found in the rays of the sun. Also, because heat is present in common fire, we may reject the heavenly bodies. Since bodies when heated lose no weight, the explanation of heat as the communication of one body to another or as the admixture of one body with another is to be rejected. Because the rays of the moon are bright and cold and heated bodies are often dark, light or brightness is to be rejected. Since ignited metals as well as air may both be hot, rarity is to be rejected. Because of the dilation of air in calendar glasses locally without manifest increase of heat, merely expansive motion of body may be rejected; and so on. We exclude, therefore, certain factors from the explanation of heat, rarity, elements, motion, brightness, heavenly bodies. This we do, let it be noted, without first gaining any accurate determinations respecting the natures of what we exclude. And here we are brought face to face with a considerable difficulty in the first attempt to employ the method of negation in inductive inquiry: for how can we use for purposes of determination by definition the exclusion of things which themselves are vague and ill defined? We must, accordingly, go on from this point to devise more powerful guards than we have yet exemplified for the understanding, even in its preliminary attempt at an interpretation of nature (*Works*, I, 383–84, 386–89; VIII, 204–5, 207–10).

Meanwhile, we may proceed to make an affirmative essay in interpretation on the basis of our three tables. This essay Bacon calls the "Indulgence of the Understanding, or the Commencement of Interpretation, or the First Vintage." From a survey of instances, each and all, which are recorded in the three tables, the inference may be drawn that the nature of heat is a species of motion. And he cautions us that when he concludes that motion is a genus of which heat is a species, he is not maintaining that heat generates motion or that motion generates heat (though both may be true in certain cases), but is affirming that "heat itself, or its quiddity (*quid ipsum*) is motion and nothing else; limited however by [specific] differences." Nor, again, is he confusing with the form of heat the communication of heat or the "transitive nature" of heat by which a body when applied to a hot body becomes hot. Heat is one thing; heating quite another. The production of heat in a body through the proximity of a hot body is brought about not by the form of heat, but "depends entirely on a higher and more general nature, viz: on the nature of assimilation or self-multiplication—a subject which requires a separate inquiry." Nor yet again is the heat which is at present under inquiry "sensible" heat. The latter exists in "relation to man, not to the universe" and varies with the disposition of sense: the same body may produce a sensation of heat and a sensation of cold; for example, tepid water appears hot if one's hand is cold and cold if one's hand is hot.

After removing these possible ambiguities and misunderstandings, Bacon proceeds "to the true [specific] differences which limit Motion and make it into the Form of Heat." The first "difference," he finds, is this. "Heat is an expansive motion, whereby a body strives to dilate and to acquire a larger sphere or dimension than it had previously occupied." This sort of motion is pronounced in flames, and in such examples as heated air, liquids, woods, metals, stones. (For the many items of the tables, some one hundred in number, in which these "differences" are exemplified, the reader may consult the *Novum organum*) (*Works*, VIII, 179 ff.)

The second specific difference is a modification of the first, to the effect that "heat is a motion expansive, or towards the circumference, but with this condition, that the body has at the same time a motion upwards." This difference is manifest, for example, in the relatively less heating power of a fire placed above a body in comparison with that of a fire placed beneath a body. The third difference is as follows: "Heat is a motion of expansion, not uniformly of the whole body together, but in the small parts of it; and at the same time checked, repelled, and beaten back, so that the body acquires a motion alternative, always agitated, striving and struggling, and irritated by repercussion." The distinctive motion specified here is readily discerned in the fury of fire and in boiling liquids which are agitated, swelling in small portions and then subsiding. The fourth difference, which is a modification of the third, is to the effect that "the motion of stimulation or penetration should be somewhat rapid and not at all sluggish, and proceed by particles which, though minute, yet are not of extreme fineness but, so to speak, a trifle larger." For instance, the heat of fire acts through the larger particles of body and destroys rapidly, while time and age without heat reduce things slowly through acting on the more minute particles of body.

Taking into consideration, then, those differences which serve to segregate heat as a species within the genus motion, we have as the First Vintage, or Commencement of Interpretation, the definition: Heat is a motion, expansive, restrained, and acting in its strife upon the smaller particles of bodies. But the expansion of motion is modified thus, while it expands all ways, yet it is turned somewhat upward. And the struggle through the parts is thus modified also; it is not at all sluggish but rapid and with some violence.

This Vintage is, so far, theoretical. If we wish to make it operative we must go on to extract from the definition before us a direction for superinducing heat upon bodies. In seeking this direction, no account, it should be noted, is to be taken as to whether the body concerned be "elementary," or subject to celestial influence, or dense or rare, luminous or opaque, dissolving or remaining in its original state, or whether it be animal, vegetable, mineral; it is to be treated merely as something susceptible to a certain type of motion given within the definition. The direction accordingly becomes this: "If in any natural body you can excite a self-dilating or expanding motion, and can so repress this motion and turn it upon itself, that the dilation shall not proceed equably, but shall prevail in one part and be repulsed in another, you will undoubtedly generate heat" (*Works,* I, 390-97; VIII, 211-17).

CHAPTER XIX

THE NEW LOGIC: AIDS TO THE SENSES

IN GATHERING the First Vintage of discovery, Bacon cautions us, we are only at the commencement of inductive interpretation. He now proceeds to list the nine "remaining helps of the understanding" which are yet to follow. The first of these consists of Prerogative Instances, twenty-seven in number. They excel "common instances" in serving both the theoretical and operative parts of knowledge. They comprise, as we have said, the only one of the nine "remaining helps" which the author succeeds in discussing either within his *Novum organum* or elsewhere. His literary arrangement of the instances is more or less haphazard. He indicates, however, that he has designed them according to a plan—in keeping with the nature of his logic—to bring aid, respectively, (*i*) to the senses, (*ii*) to the intellect, and (*iii*) toward the furthering of works. Prerogative instances may accordingly be classified as follows: (I) Those helping the senses, namely Instances of the Lamp which are five in number. (II) Those which assist the understanding (*a*) by hastening the Exclusion of the form, Solitary Instances; (*b*) by indicating more narrowly and clearly the Affirmative of the form, Migratory, Striking Instances, Instances of Companionship, and Subjunctive Instances; (*c*) by "exalting" the intellect and leading it the more immediately to genera and common natures, Clandestine, Singular, Constitutive, Conformable Instances, Instances of Alliance, and Bordering Instances; (*d*) by correcting the understanding when led astray by habit, Deviating Instances; and (*e*) by guarding it against false forms and causes, Instances of the Fingerpost and of Divorce. (III) Those furthering the operative part of science which consist of three groups: (*a*) Intimating Instances and Instances of Power, which serve, respectively, to indicate the end to be sought in practice, provided means are given, and what should be undertaken in practice to avoid the retreading of ground already covered;

(b) four Mathematical Instances, which measure practice; and (c) Polychrest and Magical Instances, which facilitate practice generally.

Of Prerogative Instances, then, those of the Lamp or of First Information aid the senses. The interpretation of nature begins with the senses and goes on to the discernments of the understanding, which are its "true notions and axioms." The more numerous and exact the presentations to the sense, the more satisfactory will be the cognitions of the intellect. The first of the Instances of the Lamp are the Instances of the Door or Gate. Their office is to "strengthen, enlarge, and rectify" the immediate actions of the senses by enabling them to see such objects as are invisible to the naked eye, to discern things far away, and to perceive objects more distinctly and exactly. By microscopes are made manifest minutiae in the colors, motions, and configurations of bodies. And if the use of these instruments were extended to the examination of gems, liquors, urine, blood, wounds, and comparable things, undoubtedly more knowledge would accrue to science. The telescope enables sense to perceive at a great distance; by this device the heavens are seen to be full of stars, spots are discerned on the sun, and selenography is made possible. Other aids which make perception the more exact are measuring-rods, astrolabes, and the like; these not to increase, but to rectify and direct, vision (*Works*, I, 454–58; VIII, 270–73).

The second division of Instances of the Lamp are Summoning Instances—to borrow a term from the courts of law—or Evoking Instances. They serve to reduce the nonsensible to the sensible, that is, to make manifest to the senses things which are not directly perceptible by things which are. Objects escape the senses in one or other of several ways: (1) the distance between the object and the sense is too great for observation, (2) another body intervenes between it and the sensory, (3) because of its character a body is not fitted to make an impression on the sense, (4) it is too small in quantity to be perceived by sense, (5) there is insufficiency of time in its contact with the sensory, (6) the sensory is overwhelmed by the impression from the object, (7) the sense is filled with another object. In the first instance, when an object is found to be imperceptible by reason of distance, a third thing must be resorted to for challenging and striking the sense, such as a beacon or bell or like device. In the second case, when an object cannot be observed from any position because it is "internal" and cannot be uncovered, its condition must be inferred from the structure and activity of the surface or from things that make their way to the surface. The condition of the human body is discerned, for example, from the state of the pulse and of the urine. Cases of the third and fourth sorts, which are common, can be made available only by experiment. Heat and cold in low degrees, for instance, are not easily distinguished by touch; yet they can be brought under observation by means of a calendar glass. The "spirit" of body, that is to say, the source and process of function in body—such as expansion and contraction in inanimate things and assimilation in vegetables and animals—is not directly available to the senses; nor are the minute parts and constituents of bodies—such as water, ash, and salt, to mention but a few—and resort in their case must be had repeatedly to experiment. In the fifth instance, motion, which takes place in time, may be either too slow or too fast to permit of sensory perception, as, for example, in the hand of a clock or in the flight of a musket-ball. While a motion too slow for perception can be made manifest to the senses by aggregates of motion, no means have as yet been devised for apprehending a motion which is too fast; and in certain cases adequate investigation requires this. The sixth case is that in which the sense is hindered by the imposing character of the object, for example, by an extreme brilliance close at hand. Here the object may be removed to a greater distance from the sensory; or a medium may be introduced which weakens the effect of the object upon sense and does not at the same time annihilate the object; or the object may be observed, as in the case of the sun, through its reflection in some such medium as a basin of water. The seventh case is that in which the sense is so filled with one object that it cannot admit another. Examples of this are almost wholly restricted to the sense of smell. This sort of case has little to do, however, with most experiments, which to a marked degree depend primarily on sight and secondarily on touch.

In all the instances mentioned the reduction of the nonsensible to the sensible is accomplished by inventions for aiding the human senses. There are cases, however, in which this reduction can the better be made through the observation of the relatively keener sense of animals. A dog, for example, becomes aware of certain scents which escape man; and the light latent in unilluminated air is available to the eyes of the cat and the owl, which see in the dark (*Works,* I, 458–67; VIII, 273–83).

The third division of Instances of the Lamp are Instances of the Road, or Traveling Instances, or Articulate Instances. These serve to indicate the motions of nature gradually, as in continuous action, and not abruptly, as from stage to stage. Many motions escape notice because of our practice of observing in desultory manner the behavior of bodies at intervals and seeking the explanation of this behavior after its completion and not in the course of its process. If one purposed to study the abilities and the industry of an artificer, he would not be content to look initially at the rude materials of his art and then leave, only to return when the structure was completed. Rather he would wish to be present while the artificer was carrying on his work. And so it is with the man who would discern nature's ways. If he would investigate the vegetation of plants, for instance, he must begin with the sowing of the seed. After that he will watch continuously the development of the seed from the beginning of its swelling, through the bursting of its skin and its putting forth of fibers, some as roots, some as stalk. To understand the hatching of an egg, one must follow closely the process of vivification and organization, see what proceeds out of the yolk, what out of the white, and so forth. The problem of the expansion of liquid can be solved only by incessant observation of the continuous process in varied modes of expansion of different substances, of water, for example, of wine, vinegar, oil, milk. Such matters, however, will be treated at length when we consider the problem of the discovery of Latent Processes of things (*Works*, I, 467-69; VIII, 283-85).

The fourth sort of Instances of the Lamp are Supplementary Instances, or Instances of Substitution, or Instances of Refuge. These are described as a "refuge" because they supply succor when the senses completely fail. They provide a substitute, as it were, for observable objects; and in two ways, by gradual approximation and by analogy. In exemplification of the former, experiment may be made respecting the magnet's attraction of iron. There is no known medium through whose interposition this activity may be entirely prevented. Gold does not stop it, nor does silver, stone, glass, wood, water, oil, cloth, fibrous bodies, air, nor flame. And yet by careful tests some medium might be found which would deaden the magnet's power more than would any other. One might try, for instance, whether the magnet will attract iron equally as well through a thickness of gold as through an equal space of air, or through silver that is heated as well as through silver that is cold, and so on in other experiments.

Substitution by analogy, while useful, is none too certain and requires careful judgment. It may be employed when the things examined are cognate through characteristics or activities other than those under investigation. One might undertake by analogy to investigate, for example, whether there are winds and exhalations or other pneumatic things which fail to mix with common air and, unobserved by sense, either remain suspended in globules or are broken up by air rather than incorporated within it. One could do this by drawing an analogy from the case of liquids like quicksilver, oil, and water, among which no incorporation takes place. The usefulness of the procedure would depend in large part upon the discovery of a heterogeneity in pneumatic bodies comparable to that of these liquids. However, says Bacon, proper Supplementary Instances and their uses for investigating such a phenomenon as this will be discussed when we treat of Supports of Induction (*Works,* I, 470–72; VIII, 285–88).

The fifth and last Instances of the Lamp are Dissecting Instances of Awakening, or Democritean Instances. "We call them Awakening," says Bacon, "because they awaken the understanding; Dissecting, because they dissect nature; for which reason also we sometimes name them Instances of Democritus." These instances, while perceived by the senses, remind the understanding of the "exquisite" subtlety of nature and arouse it to attention, observation, and apt inquiry. They may be instanced by such facts as these: a silver gilt stretches to a length of gilt wire; a little saffron tinges a whole hogshead of water; a small amount of musk scents a great expanse of air; sounds like words are carried through wood or water; light passes through glass and water speedily; the magnet attracts through bodies of all sorts.

To Dissecting Instances should be subjoined a subsidiary sort of instance which marks the Limits of Dissection. In the cases cited above the action concerned is not impeded or extinguished by one of another sort. There are comparable cases, however, in which it is. These may be called "Instances of the Limits of Dissection." They are illustrated by such examples as the extinction of the light of a glowworm by the light of the sun, the drowning of the sound of the voice by the report of a cannon, the destruction of a mild scent by a stronger one, and so on. But this subject, says Bacon, will receive further treatment in its proper place among the Supports of Induction—a division of the *Novum organum* which, like several others promised by its author, is not to be expounded in his writings (*Works,* I, 472–74; VIII, 288–89).

CHAPTER XX

THE NEW LOGIC: AIDS TO THE INTELLECT

OF INSTANCES designed to aid the understanding, the first sort assist in the segregating of the form which is being sought. These are called "Solitary Instances" or—to borrow a term from the astronomers—"Ferine Instances." They are "instances which exhibit the nature under investigation in such subjects as have nothing in common with other subjects except that nature itself; or, again, those which do not exhibit the nature under investigation in such subjects as are similar in all respects to other subjects except in that nature itself." Certain colored objects, for example, dews, prisms, and crystalline gems, which yield colors not only in themselves but externally on a wall, are Solitary Instances of Resemblance. Colors in the cases mentioned have nothing in common with colors in flowers, metals, woods, and the like, except the color itself. It may be readily gathered, then, that color is "nothing more than a modification of the image of light projected and received, resulting in the former case from different degrees of incidence, in the latter case from various textures and schematisms of body."

To continue with color, the distinct veins of white and black in streaked marble and the variegation of color in flowers of the same species, when the subjects agree in all respects except color, are Solitary Instances of Difference. From these we gather that color has little to do with the "intrinsic natures of body, but depends upon the grosser and, as it were, mechanical dispositions of the parts" (*Works,* I, 400–402, 537; VIII, 219–20, 348).

The next main division of instances which assist the intellect are those which serve to inclose the Affirmative of the form within a narrow compass. It includes four kinds: Migratory Instances, Striking, of Companionship, and Subjunctive. The first of these exhibit the nature under investigation in the process of migrating to generation, or to corruption, or to increase, or to decrease. For example, if the nature under investigation be whiteness, it will be found that transparent water becomes white when agitated into froth. Glass is transparent and becomes white when pounded. Obviously, then, the form of whiteness is communicated and conveyed by the pounding of glass and agitation of water. And, since it is evident that nothing has been added to the glass or the water except the breaking of it into small parts and the introduction of air, we may conclude that "two bodies, both transparent in themselves but in a greater or less degree (viz: air and water, or air and glass), do, when put together in small portions exhibit whiteness through the unequal refraction of rays of light." In reaching this result considerable advance has been made toward the discovery of the form of whiteness. There is need of caution here, however, for at this point the understanding might hastily be led astray by a doctrine of "efficients" (actually the efficient is nothing more in any instance than the "vehicle" of the form) and conclude that air is always required for the generation of whiteness as such, or that whiteness is produced by transparent bodies only—notions entirely false.

Examples of Migratory Instances in which the nature is passing toward increase or toward decrease have already been noted in the case of the Table of Degrees, one of three Tables of Presentation (*Works*, I, 402-5; VIII, 220-22).

Striking Instances (or Shining Instances, or Instances Freed and Predominant) exhibit the nature in question "naked and standing by itself, and also in its exaltation or the height of its power; that is, emancipated and free from impediments." Concrete bodies admit of many forms. These forms in their conjunctions depress and enthrall one another. Sometimes a constitutive nature appears in great vigor either through the absence of impediments or through the predominance of its own strength, and then we have a Striking Instance of a nature. An example is weight in quicksilver or, in the case of motion of expansion (which, as we have said above, is the principal part of heat), heated air in a calendar glass. There is need for much caution in the use of Striking Instances, however, for these instances, by thrusting the form or nature into prominence, may lead the understanding to conclude too rapidly. It may be set down as a salutary rule, then, that whatever displays the form too conspicuously is to be held in suspicion until submitted to severe and careful examination for the purpose of its segregation (*Works*, I, 405-6; VIII, 222-24).

Instances of Companionship and of Enmity or Instances of Fixed Propositions exhibit a body or substance in which a nature is constantly found or from which it is constantly excluded. These serve to narrow the range of the Affirmative of the form, since the form of the thing must be something which either enters or refuses to enter as an ingredient into a concretion of body. An instance of Companionship in the case of heat is flame. Heat in water, in air, stone, metal, is movable; it comes and goes. But all flame is hot. An instance of Enmity in the case of consistency is air. Metal and glass, for intance, can be fluid and also consistent. The same is true of water, which can be either liquid or frozen. Air, on the contrary, can never put off its fluidity.

Bacon calls Instances of Companionship and of Enmity "Instances of Fixed Propositions" because their discernment leads to universal affirmative and universal negative propositions. For example, in the propositions "All flame is hot" and "No air is consistent" the subject is a body concrete, and the predicate indicates the nature in question. And he proceeds to offer certain admonitions concerning the status and use of these propositions. In inductive procedure it is not necessary, he says, to have absolute affirmation or negation in universal propositions. Here the proposition which admits of a "singular or rare" exception is sufficient for the purpose in hand. Here also particular propositions which have no considerable prerogative, except in the case of Instances of Migration, can be of great use when collated with those of a universal character. (How this is so, Bacon promises to show "in the proper place"—which is not, unfortunately, to be found in his unfinished *Novum organum*.) Here again, he admonishes, notation should be made of cases in which a universal proposition is wanting. If the nature under investigation should be eternity or incorruptibility, for instance, neither could be made a predicate of a universal affirmative proposition respecting bodies which lie at least "below the heavens and above the bowels of the earth." And, finally, he advises that to affirmative and negative universal propositions concerning any type of concrete body there should be subjoined those concretes which most nearly approach to cases of what the body is not; in the case of hot body for example, the gentlest flame. Concretes of this sort will serve to indicate "the limits of nature between being and nonbeing, and help to circumscribe Forms, lest they spread and wander beyond the conditions of matter" (*Works,* I, 426–29; VIII, 244–46).

With this last admonition in mind the author goes on to mention, among aids to the intellect in its limiting the compass of a nature, Subjective Instances, or Instances of Ultimity or Limit. These manifest the lowest and the highest extremes of a nature in question. Examples of the highest extremes are gold in the case of weight, the whale in animal bulk, and the combustion of gunpowder in rapid expansion; examples of the lowest are spirit of wine in weight, tiny worms in animal bulk. Such instances as these are to be used in conjunction with universal propositions; yet they may also be employed by themselves both to indicate the divisions of nature and to demonstrate how far in certain respects things act or are acted upon (*Works,* I, 429; VIII, 246–47).

The next section within the Prerogative Instances which assist the understanding includes those whose purpose is to "exalt" in varied degrees this faculty toward the pursuit of common natures, genera, and the Fabric of the Universe. Conformable Instances elevate the intellect in the least of three degrees; Constitutive Instances in a second degree; and Instances Clandestine, Singular, of Alliance, and Bordering Instances, in a third degree.

The instances which show forth "the resemblances and connections of things .... in the concrete, and so are as the first and lowest steps towards the union of nature" are the Conformable Instances or Analogous Instances. They may also be called "Parallels" or "Physical Resemblances." These indicate agreements among bodies, agreements, however, which do not as yet fall within axioms which manifest critically the union of natural bodies. By themselves they can effect but little toward the discovery of forms; yet they manifest the structures of nature's parts and exemplify something akin to the anatomy of its members and consequently lead the investigator—by the hand, as it were— to lofty and excellent axioms, chiefly to those which have to do with the schematism of the world rather than with simple natures and forms.

Examples of Conformable Instances are the looking-glass and the eye, the construction of the ear and of the place which yields an echo. From conformities such as these manifest it is easy to reach the conclusion that "the organs of the senses and bodies which beget reflections to the senses are of like nature." The intellect, urged on by this observation, will readily be led to another observation, namely, "there is no difference between the consents or sympathies of bodies possessed of senses and those of inanimate bodies which are without sense, except that in the former an animal spirit is added to body so disposed, but is wanting in the latter." There are, for example, many kinds of pain in animals, such as pain of burning, pain of intense cold, of pricking, of squeezing, of stretching, and so on; and it is most certain that *so far as motion is concerned* all these are present in inanimate bodies. In the case of the latter they are not classified as sensuous pain simply because of the absence of the animal spirit. That is to say, inanimate bodies and animate bodies have activities in common except that the former lack the distinctive process, structure, and organization which permit of sensitive functioning.

Further Conformable Instances are the roots and the branches of plants, the hairs of animals and the feathers of birds, the fins of fish and the feet of quadrupeds, the bills of birds and the teeth of fish, wideness at the top and narrowness at the bottom of the southern continents of both Eastern and Western Hemispheres. The careful examination of instances of similitude and analogy, of which the foregoing are but a few examples, should do much both to make manifest the character of nature's unity and to assist in the establishment of new sciences. It would also help to overcome a deficiency in natural history which serves to divide knowledge by recording the differences, and not the agreements, among animals, herbs, and fossils. Incidentally it should include the conformity between such things as the mathematical postulate: "Things which are equal to the same thing are equal to one another" and the device of the logical syllogism which unites propositions which agree in a middle term (*Works,* I, 413-19; VIII, 231-36).

Constitutive or Manipular Instances "are those which constitute one species of nature in question as a sort of Lesser Form." They do not exemplify, that is, the genuine forms "which are always convertible with the proposed natures"; nevertheless their segregation is important, for "whatever unites nature, though in inadequate measures, paves the way to the discovery of Forms." "The Prerogative of Constitutive Instances is," says Bacon, "very great; for they do much towards the forming of definitions (especially particular definitions), and towards divisions or partitions of natures; respecting which it was not ill said by Plato, That he is to be held as a God who knows well how to define and to divide." Great care, however, must be observed in the use of Constitutive Instances. They manifest only the "Lesser Forms." And the human intellect, having found these, is liable to take them for real divisions of nature, conclude that nature in its "roots" is divided, reject any notion of the union of things as a matter of useless subtlety verging on mere abstraction, and fail to proceed to the legitimate discovery of the Great Form or Fabric of the Universe.

Constitutive Instances may be exemplified in an inquiry respecting "memory or that which excites and aids memory." In this case they are seen to include order, locus, and verse. Verse is learned and recollected more readily than prose. Order clearly aids the memory, as do loci or points of reference, such as persons, animals, words, letters, symbols, historical personages, a door, perhaps, or a window. From these three, then—order, place, and verse—one species of aid to the memory becomes manifest. This species may with propriety be called "the cutting off of infinity."

Other instances will give a second species: "whatever brings the intellectual to that which strikes the sense—which indeed is the rule which is esteemed in mnemonics (*memoria artificiali*)—aids memory." And still other instances provide a third species, namely, those which impress by way of strong feeling, such as that of fear, admiration, shame, delight. Further instances of impression, when the mind is clear and free and not preoccupied before or after, manifest a fourth species—things learned in childhood, happenings for the first time, what is thought over before going to sleep; such stick longest in memory. A fifth species is revealed in instances with many circumstances or points on which one may take hold, such as writing whose continuity is broken with divisions. And, lastly, still further instances will give a sixth species: what is awaited with desire and arouses attention is more fixed in memory than that which flits by. "So there are, it seems," says Bacon, "six Lesser Forms of those things which aid the memory; viz: the cutting off of infinity; the leading of the intellectual to the sensible; impression on a strong feeling; impression made on a clear or free mind; multitude of points to take hold of; expectation beforehand."

To consider another example, let the nature in question be taste or tasting. The following instances are Constitutive. Agents without a natural sense of smell cannot perceive or distinguish by taste things which are rancid, putrid, flavored with garlic or roses. Nor can those whose nostrils are accidentally stuffed up by a cold distinguish by taste what is rancid, putrid, or sprinkled with rose water; while those who are so affected by a cold have a clear perception of the taste of these immediately on violently blowing the nose. "These instances then will give and constitute (*constituent*) this species, or rather division of taste; that the sensation of tasting is nothing but an internal smelling which passes and descends from the higher passages of the nostrils to the mouth and palate." Again, those whose capacity for smelling is wanting or is obstructed temporarily can sense as well as any one else what is salt, sweet, pungent, acid, rough, bitter, and the like. It is manifest, then, that the sense of taste is a compound of internal smell and some kind of exquisite touch.

And to take yet another example, let the nature in question be "the communication of quality without admixture of substance." The instance of light gives or constitutes one species of communication, that of heat and magnetic power, another. The communication of the first occurs momentaneously and ceases on the removal of the original light; that of heat and magnetic power occurs after excitation in another body, and the communicated presence remains after the removal of the first motive power (*Works*, I, 409-13; VIII, 227-31).

Those Prerogative Instances which serve especially to exalt the intellect by leading it "to genera, that is, to those common natures, whereof the natures in question are nothing more than limitations," are Clandestine Instances, or Instances of the Twilight; Singular Instances; and Instances of Alliance. The first of these, Clandestine Instances, exhibit the nature under investigation in its lowest degree of power. They are not to be confused in character and use with Subjunctive Instances, which exhibit both the lowest and the highest power in the nature concerned and whose examples of diminished power are to be subjoined to those general propositions which fall within Instances of Companionship and of Enmity. Clandestine Instances are to be employed independently by themselves for the guidance of the intellect to genera, even as Striking Instances are to be used to lead it to specific differences. If, for example, the nature in question be consistency, then those are Clandestine Instances which exhibit a feeble and low degree of consistency in fluids, such as is the case of bubbles and streams of water. Water dropping downward lengthens itself out into a thin thread to avoid discontinuity. If, however, there is but little of it forthcoming, it falls in drops; that is, it assumes a figure which best sustains it against discontinuity. Children take water made slightly more tenacious by soap and expand it into bubbles, which are given so much consistency by the interposition of air that they may be thrown some distance without breaking. Through frost so great a degree of consistency is acquired by liquid things that they can almost be cut through. Instances like these instruct us that the consistent and the fluid are nothing more than "vulgar notions," determined merely by what is manifest to sense. Actually the question of consistency and liquidity in bodies resolves itself into one of degrees of avoidance of discontinuity. All bodies strive to avoid discontinuity, weakly and infirmly in the case of homogeneous bodies like liquids, vigorously and strongly in the case of bodies compounded of heterogeneous parts.

Another example of the use of Clandestine Instances is to be seen in the examination of the nature of the attraction or coition of bodies. The most prominent instance in the investigation of attraction is given by the magnet; the least prominent is found in the case of like substances. Iron does not attract iron; lead, lead; wood, wood; or water, water. Yet the iron in an armed magnet does attract iron, sustaining as it does a far greater weight of iron than one that is not armed. In this case the attraction is altogether clandestine, even to its being latent in the iron before the magnet is applied. The instance serves to lead the understanding from attraction or coition in iron and attraction or coition in the magnet to the more general question of attraction or coition (*Works*, I, 407-9; VIII, 224-27).

Singular Instances, or Irregular, or Heteroclite—to take a term from grammarians—exhibit those bodies in the concrete which seem to be "extravagant and as it were abrupt in nature," and which appear not to agree with other things of a same kind and hence seem not—initially, at least—to be members of species. While Conformable Instances are like one another, Singular Instances are like themselves. Among Singular Instances are the sun and the moon among stars; the magnet among stones; quicksilver among metals; the elephant among quadrupeds; the scent of hounds among kinds of smell; *S* among letters, because of its ready combination with consonants, sometimes with two, sometimes with three. Such instances correct the intellect which, when depraved by "custom and by the common course of things," tends to regard them as "causeless," as "secrets," as exceptions to nature's rules. For the mind should not desist from inquiry until the properties of singular things which are assessed as "miracles" of nature are "reduced and comprehended under some Form or fixed Law; so that all the irregularity or singularity be found to depend upon some common Form, and the miracle to lie in fact only in exact specific differences, and degree, and the rare concurrence, and not in the species itself" (*Works,* I, 419–20; VIII, 236–37).

Instances of Alliance or Union are those "which join and unite natures thought to be heterogeneous, and denoted and marked off as such in the received divisions." They show that those operations and effects which are attributed to a so-called heterogeneous nature, as peculiarly its own, belong to other natures; so that a supposed heterogeneity among natures is not actual or essential and is nothing else than a modification of a common nature. Consequently, Instances of Alliance are of very great use for elevating and advancing the intellect beyond differences to genera. To illustrate: Suppose the nature in question be heat. There seems to be a thoroughly settled and authorized division of heat into three kinds: heat of heavenly bodies, animal heat, and heat of fire. These three heats, so it is said, are in very essence, or in species, or in specific nature, different and quite heterogeneous: especially is one of them distinguished from the other two—since the heat of celestial and animal bodies "generates and cherishes," while the heat of fire "corrupts and destroys." Yet a simple experiment or two will show that this is not so, that the three heats partake of a common nature. If, for instance, a branch of a vine still attached to a limb is brought indoors where a fire is constantly burning, its fruit ripens much more rapidly than if it were left out of doors exposed to the sun and atmosphere. And eggs may be hatched by the heat of fire, which performs sufficiently for generation the function of a supposedly different sort of heat, animal heat.

Take also the questions of motion and weight. Aristotle, in order to retain his opinion that the motion of the heavenly bodies is circular and altogether even and regular and that of the sublunary bodies otherwise, ties the comet to, or makes it follow, some star which moves in circular fashion. This fiction of his has long since been exploded, not merely theoreticaly but experimentally, by the manifest fact that the motion of comets is not circular but wandering and irregular. An instance which would help disestablish this philosopher's doctrine respecting weight, which rests on a theory of motion to appropriate place, would be one in which a solid and dense body does not fall to the earth. The phenomenon of the waterspout perhaps comes nearest to what is required.

The common division of "thinking" into human reason on the one hand and the ingenuity of brutes on the other seems to be correct. Yet Instances of Alliance might appear which showed that brutes in their actions even syllogize. Again, in the case of visibility there is a division which seems true and certain. Light is said to be primarily visible and to confer the power of seeing, and color to be visible secondarily, not discernible without light, and but an image or modification of light. Yet snow in great quantity and the flame of sulphur are Instances of Alliance in which there seems to be color primarily giving light and light verging toward color (*Works,* I, 429-36; VIII, 247-53).

For bringing the intellect to discern the actual and possible species of things, Bordering Instances, or Participles, are of great use. These, because of their relatively rare and extraordinary occurrence, might with propriety be included among instances called "Singular" or "Heteroclite"; yet because of their worth they are to be treated apart. Bordering Instances suggest the causes for the number and character of the ordinary species in the universe. They also conduct the intellect from that which is to that which can be, as in the case of new species. They exhibit such species of bodies as seem to be compounded of two species or to be rudiments between one species and another. Examples are the bats, between birds and quadrupeds; the apes, between men and beasts; the comets, between stars and fiery meteors; the flying fish, between birds and fish; biformed births of animals; and the like (*Works,* I, 421-22; VIII, 238-39).

The two remaining types of instances which belong to the informative section of Prerogative Instances serve, respectively, to guard the human intellect against the slavery of habit and the enticement of false "Forms and causes." The first of these are Deviating Instances, that is, examples of "errors, vagaries, and prodigies: wherein nature digresses and turns aside from her usual course." They are not to be confused with Singular Instances. The latter are prodigies of species; the former are, so to speak, prodigies of individuals and are not assumed to possess such singularity as do instances like the sun and the magnet. Inquiry into the former will not lead one to forms but will rather indicate those Latent Processes which lead to forms. He who knows the ways of nature will the more readily observe her deviations, and he who knows her deviations will describe her ways with greater accuracy. Deviating Instances differ from Singular Instances also in their greater assistance to practice and operation. To generate new species would be a very arduous matter; but to vary known species, and thus to produce many rare and unusual things, would not be so difficult. Once nature is detected in her variation and the reason for this made evident, it will be easy by art to lead her where she has wandered by accident and thus to make a transition from the "miracles" of nature to the wonders of art.

Examples of Deviating Instances are abundant and need not be given here. There are available books filled with all sorts of wonders and prodigies (*Works,* I, 420–21; VIII, 237–38).

The second sort of instances which "guard" the intellect includes those of the Fingerpost and of Divorce. Instances of the Fingerpost—to borrow a name for signs set up where roads meet—may also be called "Decisive and Judicial Instances" and in some cases "Oracular and Commanding Instances." Their role is this: "When in the investigation of any nature the intellect is in such equilibrium that it is uncertain to which of two or sometimes more natures the cause of the nature in question should be attributed or assigned, because of the frequent and ordinary concurrence of many natures, Instances of the Fingerpost show that the union of one of the natures with the nature investigated is faithful and indissoluble; that of the other is variable and separable: whence the question is determined, and the former nature is admitted as the cause, and the latter dismissed and rejected." These instances are of great light and authority. In them the course of interpretation sometimes comes to a close and through them is perfected. Occasionally they are met with accidentally, sometimes being found among those instances already noted; but, for the most part, they are independent, are designedly thought out and applied and are unearthed through persistent and keen diligence. To illustrate: In the problem of weight or heaviness we confront a place, so to speak, at which roads meet. Heavy and weighty bodies either must tend in their own nature, by reason of their peculiar schematism, to the center of the earth or must be hurried there by the corporeal mass of the earth, as by a sympathetic congregation of kindred bodies. If the latter of these interpretations be the proper one, it follows that the nearer heavy bodies approach the earth, the more strongly and more rapidly will they be carried to it; the farther they are from it, the more feebly and slowly, as is the case with magnetic attraction; and that this activity of theirs is confined within certain spatial limits, so that if these bodies were removed to so great a distance from the earth that the latter's virtue could not act, then the bodies would remain suspended, like the earth itself, and not fall at all. For solving this problem, an Instance of the Fingerpost is as follows: Take one clock which operates by leaden weights and another which is moved by a spring, and let the two be so exactly adjusted that one does not go any faster or any slower than the other. Then let the clock with the leaden weights be placed on top of the steeple of a very high church, while the other is kept below, and note carefully whether the clock on the steeple goes more slowly than it did because of the diminished virtue of its weights. Next, take the clock from the tower and place it in a deep mine below the earth's surface and see whether it goes faster than it did because of the increased virtue of its weights. If the weight be lessened on the steeple and increased in the mine, then attraction of the corporeal mass of the earth may be taken as the cause of weight. (*Works*, I, 436–52; VIII, 253–68).

Instances of Divorce serve to indicate "separations between natures of very frequent occurrence." These instances are not to be confused, however, with those of Enmity. The latter serve to dissociate the nature in question from some concrete with which it is usually conjoined; those of Divorce serve to separate natures; and, unlike instances of the Fingerpost, while they separate, they determine nothing but the separation. Their use is primarily to expose false forms and to dissipate foolish reflections which follow observation of the obvious. They add, so to speak, leaden weights to the intellect. By way of example, let the natures considered be those which Telesius regards as messmates and chamberfellows, heat, brightness, rarity, and mobility. Many Instances of Divorce are to be found among the four. We find, for instance, that air, while rare and mobile, is not hot or bright; that the moon is bright but not hot; boiling water is hot but without light; that there can be quick motion in a cold, dense, and opaque needle on a pivot.

Again, let the natures in question be corporeal nature and natural action. The latter seems not to be found except as it subsists in some body or other. Yet this may be a false conclusion. The action of the magnet, for example, may prove to be an Instance of Divorce in which natural body and natural action are separate. Suppose, then, we agree that by magnetic action iron is drawn to the magnet, heavy bodies are drawn to the earth, and operations are performed at a distance. These acts take place, first, in time—that is, through moments of time and not instantaneously—and, secondly, in space, passing through positions and distances. Since space, through which the virtue concerned operates in time, lies between the two bodies concerned in an action, there is some period of time and a distance of space in which the virtue or action hangs in the interval between these two bodies. Our problem, therefore, becomes a matter of two alternate questions. Do those bodies which are the termini of action dispose or alter intermediate bodies, so that by a succession of actual contacts virtue, while it passes from terminus to terminus, subsists in the intervening body or bodies? Or is anything required for the action in question except the terminal bodies, the virtue, and the intervening space or spaces? In operation at a distance of many things such as rays of light, sounds, and heat, it is probable that intermediate bodies are disposed and altered. But in magnetic action it would seem that this is not the case. If it should transpire, then, that magnetic action or virtue has nothing to do with intermediate bodies, it would follow that natural action or virtue can subsist for a certain time and in a certain place without body. And magnetic action would prove to be an Instance of Divorce between corporeal nature and natural action (*Works,* I, 452-54; VIII, 268-70).

CHAPTER XXI

THE NEW LOGIC: AIDS TO THE FURTHERING OF OPERATION

SO MUCH, then, for the Informative section of Prerogative Instances; let us now turn to the Operative or Practical. These two sections cannot be legitimately separated, of course, except for purposes of classification and analysis, because, even as information is the beginning of investigation, so are practice and operation its end. Practical instances are of three sorts and have three respective functions—the indication, the measurement, and the encouragement of operation. The first sort includes Instances of Power. These serve to indicate any works which should be attempted by making manifest what has already been done. The second are Mathematical Instances or Instances of Measure, and the third are Propitious or Benevolent Instances. The office of the second and third is the overcoming of two respective factors which contribute to the failure of operation: first, the inexact determination of the strength and action of bodies with respect to space, time, quantity, and predominance of virtue and, secondly, the laboriousness of practice because of the admixture of useless things with the useful, the multiplication of instruments, and the mass, both of matter and of bodies, which may be required for the particular work in hand (*Works*, I, 474, 537–38; VIII, 290, 349).

Instances of Power or of the Fasces—to borrow a term from the insignia of empire—or Instances of the Wit or of the Hands of Man indicate, then, what works may be undertaken by showing what have been performed. They also serve to rouse and elevate the intellect to the discovery of forms, even as do Singular Instances, like the sun, the moon, and the magnet. They are in a manner Singular Instances, in this case, of "art," and include products of great impressiveness and perfection, such as paper, silk, wool, linen, brick, earthenware, glass, enamel, porcelain, and so on. In their use the investigator must be cautioned against the bewitchment of his mind by extant works already available. These, generally hit upon by chance, are poor things indeed in comparison with discoveries that are possible through inductive knowledge. Let him remember that operation for the future "depends upon and is in due order derived from the sources of Forms, of which not one has as yet been discovered.... and nothing.... anticipates chance (whose custom is to act at long intervals of ages) except the discovery of Forms" (*Works,* I, 422-26; VIII, 239-43).

The first sort of Mathematical Instances are Instances of the Rod or Rule, or Instances of Range or of Limitation (*de non ultra*). These have to do with the calculation of the distances or spaces involved in the operations of things and their virtues. Some bodies and powers act by contact, such as medicines on bodily organs and the objects of touch and taste on the senses. Others act at a distance, as objects upon sight, especially among the elderly; amber or jet upon straw; the magnet upon iron; heat and cold upon bodies; and light and sound upon the senses. And there are varied extents of increase in expanding bodies and of decrease in contracting bodies of all sorts in their several circumstances. Now the spaces involved in these operations are not indefinite and incidental but determinate and regular, and, if recorded with exactitude, they will prove of the greatest service both in preventing the failure of practice and in increasing its range. Among examples for record are the distances required for seeing, in the case of the aged; whether or not an eye can see a small object pressed close, and at what distance from the pupil; the calculation of the location of icebergs by the cold which makes the senses aware of their proximity; the short range at which the magnet acts upon iron and the great range at which the earth acts upon the needle of the compass; the limit of compression of water when inclosed in a lead ball subject to pressure in a mill (*Works,* I, 475-81; VIII, 291-96).

The second kind of instances which lie within the Mathematical division are Instances of the Course or Instances of the Water—to borrow a term from the hourglass of the ancients, which contained water and not sand. These instances show the necessity of calculating processes by periods of time. All natural action is performed in time, some more quickly, some more slowly. Even things which are done, as we say, in the twinkling of an eye are found to admit of a degree of duration. The revolutions of the heavenly bodies take place in calculable times; likewise the tidal ebb and flow of the seas; also the falling of bodies to the earth, in accordance with the nature of the body moved and the medium in which it moves; the sailing of ships; the transmission of missiles; distillation; the compressing and expanding of bodies. Jugglers by quick movements turn vessels full of liquid upside down without spilling. An eye fails to see a fast-moving projectile which passes within its range. The earlier effect of an infusion of rhubarb upon the bodily organs is purgative, and the later effect is astringent. Is there, because of a delayed seeing of heavenly bodies, an apparent and a real time? One sees the flash of a gun at a distance before hearing the report. There is an apparent simultaneity in the striking of strings on a musical instrument which are actually plucked in succession. These and many like matters can be brought within the range and use of practice only by a mathematical investigation of the temporal sequences, the priorities, and the posteriorities within the processes involved (*Works,* I, 481-86; VIII, 296-301).

Mathematical Instances include, thirdly, those of Quantity or Doses of Nature—to borrow a term from Medicine. They enable the inquirer to measure virtues according to the quantities of the bodies concerned in operation. Certain virtues, it seems, are found only where bodies exist in "cosmical" quantity. The earth, for example, stands; its parts fall. The water of the seas ebbs and flows, but not the water of the rivers. In other cases virtues seem to depend on less tremendous quantities of body. A considerable body of water, for instance, does not become putrid so quickly as a small body. If an herb is put into a large quantity of water, there is infusion rather than impregnation. A piece of a magnet does not attract so much iron as the whole magnet. And then, again, there are virtues in which the smallness of the quantity makes for greater effectiveness; for example, a sharp object pierces another more quickly than a blunt one; a pointed diamond cuts glass.

We should not be disposed to believe, therefore, that the quantity of a body and the mode of its virtue are in direct proportion—that, for example, a leaden ball weighing two ounces would fall twice as rapidly as one weighing one ounce—for this is not so. Reliance is not to be placed on any general principle of proportion; rather, strict measurements of the ratios which hold between virtue and quantity in specific sorts of body in specific circumstances should be recorded. And everywhere cautions must be scattered about respecting *too much* and *too little* (*Works,* I, 486-88; VIII, 301-2).

The fourth and last sort of Mathematical Instances are those of Strife

THE NEW LOGIC: AIDS TO FURTHERING OF OPERATION 245

or of Predominance. The purpose of examining these, says Bacon, is to measure comparatively the relative strengths among predominant virtues and subject virtues in bodies. He thereupon proceeds to mention some nineteen sorts of motion, which correspond to a large extent, but not entirely, with those included within the subject matter of physics as set forth in his *De augmentis*. Having done so, he adds in conclusion: "And so we have now set forth the species or simple elements of motions, appetites, and active virtues, which are in nature the most universal. Nor is it a small part of natural science which has been sketched out under these divisions. And yet we do not deny other species may perchance be added, that these divisions themselves may not be changed in accordance with the more actual inmost nature or veins of things, and finally that they may be reduced to a smaller number."

The nineteen species of simple motion are Motion of Resistance (*antitypiae*), of Connection, Liberty, Matter (*hyles*), Continuity, Motion for Gain or of Want, Motion of Greater Congregation, of Lesser Congregation, Magnetic Motion, Motion of Flight, Assimilation, Excitation, Impression, Configuration or Position, Transition or according to the Passages, Royal or Political Motion, Spontaneous Motion of Rotation, Motion of Trepidation, and Motion of Repose or Abhorrence of Motion.

Motion of Resistance exists in each and every portion of matter, and by it each portion refuses to be annihilated. Burning, weight, pressure, violence, time, cannot reduce this motion to nothing. No matter how matter changes its place or its form under necessity, always it occupies some space and will not be annihilated. No particular examples of this motion are called for, since it is found within all bodies. "This motion the Schoolmen .... either denote by the Axiom that 'Two bodies cannot be in one place,' or call it a motion 'to prevent penetration of dimensions'" (*Works*, I, 488-89, 512; VIII, 302-3, 325).

The second motion, of Connection, is what prevents the separation of one body from another. Examples of this are attraction by suction in water pipes and cupping glasses and the failure of water to run from perforated jars unless the mouth of the jar is opened to admit air. This kind of motion the Schoolmen call "motion to prevent a vacuum" (*Works*, I, 489; VIII, 303).

Motion of Liberty is the activity by which bodies strive to free themselves from any preternatural pressure or tension and to return to their appropriate dimensions. Examples are springs in clocks; water in row-ing; air in flying; the rebounding after tension of strings, leather, and cloth. This motion the Schoolmen call motion "in accordance with the Form of the Element" (*Works,* I, 489–91; VIII, 303–6).

The fourth sort of motion, Motion of Matter, is in a manner the converse of Motion of Liberty. By the latter, bodies avoid a new dimension; by the former, they desire a new sphere, or a new dimension, or a new expansion or contraction (these are all names for the same thing). The most common, though certainly not the only, instruments of this motion are heat and cold. Air, if expanded by tension, as when drawn by suction from a glass egg, labors under a strong appetite to recover itself; yet, on the application of heat it desires to expand and to possess a new sphere into which it passes and migrates, as into a new form (so it is commonly phrased). Nor does it care to return to the old unless it is invited to do so by the application of cold; and when it does, the change is not a mere return but a new and second transmutation. Similarly, water when compressed resists and would become what it was; but, if there intervene intense and continued cold, it accepts change and acquires the density of ice (*Works,* I, 491–92; VIII, 306).

The Motion of Continuity is not to be confused with that of Connection. The latter involves a primary continuity of one body with others; the former is the motion within a body itself by which it abhors a solution of its own continuity. All bodies dread discontinuity, some more, some less. In hard bodies, like steel and glass, the resistance is strong. In liquids, where Motion of Continuity seems to be inactive, or at all events to be feeble, it is actually not absent, but exists in its lowest degree of power. This Motion of Continuity exhibits itself obviously in many instances, in bubbles, for example, in the roundness of drops, in the thin threads of drips of water from roofs, in the cohesion of glutinous bodies (*Works,* I, 492–93; VIII, 306–7).

"Motion for Gain or of Want .... is that by which bodies, when placed among other bodies quite heterogeneous and as it were hostile, if perchance they encounter means or convenient opportunity of avoiding them and of attaching themselves to more cognate bodies (even though these cognate bodies be such as have no close agreement with them), do nevertheless straightway embrace the latter, and choose them as preferable." For example, gold or other metal in the leaf is not attracted by the surrounding air; yet, if it meets with a tangible and dense body (as a finger, paper, or what you will), it immediately adheres to it and is not easily torn away. Paper, too, cloth, and the like, do not get on well with air which is introduced into their pores; and so they readily imbibe water or other fluids and drive out the air. Sugar or a sponge partially dipped in water or wine gradually attracts the wine or water to all its parts. If we disregard for the time being, then, corrosive and strong liquids, which open a way for themselves into things, we may formulate an excellent rule: If there can be found a body proportioned and better disposed to another solid body than to that with which it is as of necessity mixed, the body straightway relaxes itself and takes unto itself the body with which it is in friendly agreement and excludes the other which it finds less agreeable (*Works,* I, 493–94; VIII, 307–8).

The seventh species is Motion of the Greater Congregation. By this, bodies are carried toward masses which are connatural with them; that is, heavy bodies toward the earth, light bodies toward the heavens. This the Schoolmen have distinguished by the term "Natural Motion." In so doing they have manifested no considerable reflection; for they have called it by this name either because they have observed that the motion never ceases or because they have discerned nothing externally visible which could produce the motion and therefore have been content to regard it as innate and inherent within things themselves. This motion, although it has so filled the minds of thinkers that it has all but obscured every other kind, still remains without investigation and continues to be the subject of many erroneous notions (*Works,* I, 494; VIII, 308–9).

The eighth sort of motion is that of the Lesser Congregation. This is a motion, first, by which the homogeneous parts of a body separate themselves from the heterogeneous and unite together and, secondly, by which whole bodies through similarity of substance cling to and support one another and are sometimes congregated, attracted, and assembled from a considerable distance, as when cream in milk after a while rises to the top and dregs in wine settle to the bottom. (Attraction in these cases is not caused by motion of gravity and levity only but much more by a "desire" of the homogeneous parts to collect and unite.)

Motion of the Lesser Congregation differs from Motion of Want in two respects. In the latter there is a relatively greater stimulus of a contrary nature which is present; and the former motion can take place even though there is no alien nature to arouse strife. Secondly, through the latter motion bodies which are not cognate come together, while the former brings bodies together through kindred ties and unites them as in one (*Works,* I, 494-99; VIII, 309-13).

The ninth species, Magnetic Motion, is of the genus of Motion of the Lesser Congregation. It deserves a separate name, however, as a motion which sometimes operates at great distances and without contact. The moon, for example, raises the waters; the starry heaven attracts planets to their apogees; the sun confines Venus and Mercury within a certain distance. Such motions as these cannot be satisfactorily placed under the Greater or the Lesser Congregation, for they seem to manifest, as it were, an intermediate congregation and therefore to belong to a separate sort of motion (*Works,* I, 499; VIII, 313-14).

The tenth, the Motion of Flight, is contrary to the Motion of the Lesser Congregation. By it bodies through antipathy separate themselves from, and refuse to mix with, others that are hostile. While in certain cases this motion may seem to be accidental or consequential to the Motion of the Lesser Congregation, because the homogeneous parts cannot unite unless the heterogeneous are dislodged and driven away, yet it is a motion which should be put by itself and constituted a species because in many cases the appetite of Flight is perceived to be more dominant than the appetite of Union. This Motion of Flight is especially conspicuous in the excretions of animals and not less so in objects odious to the senses, especially to the smell and the taste. A fetid odor is so thoroughly rejected by the smell that it produces in the orifice of the stomach a motion of expulsion. A bitter taste on rejection by the palate produces a shudder. In the case of quicksilver, for instance, the parts which "desire" union into a single body are kept from doing so by spittle, lard, turpentine, and the like. Oil refuses to mix with water not because of the difference of weight —for spirit of wine, which is lighter than oil, readily mixes with water— but because of the ill agreement of the bodies concerned (*Works,* I, 499-501; VIII, 314-15).

The next motion, that of Assimilation, or of Self-Multiplication, or of Simple Generation, is not to be taken as that activity by which whole or integral bodies, like plants and animals, are produced but rather as that motion by which bodies change other bodies which are akin, or at any rate well disposed, into their own substance and nature. Examples of this motion are these: Flame over vapors and oily substances multiplies itself and produces new flame; the parts of plants and animals, such as leaf, flower, flesh, bone, assimilate food. And without agreeing with the wild notion of Paracelsus that nutrition takes place merely by separation and that "in bread and meat lies hid the eye, the nose, brain, liver; in the moisture of the earth, root, leaf, flower," it may be said that "most certainly the several parts.... in vegetables and animals, first attract with some selection, and then assimilate and turn into their own nature, the juices of their food." Motion of Assimilation is not confined, of course, to organic bodies. It obviously belongs to fire, for instance. Indeed, it would seem that there is in each body a "desire" for assimilation as well as for union with homogeneous bodies. In the case of both these inclinations bodily virtue is held under a restraint, though not in the same manner in both cases. This restraint and the means of relaxing it should be made the subject of diligent inquiry, especially because it has to do with the revigoration of vital power in old age. It seems worthy of note that while, through the motions hitherto discussed, bodies seem to seek only the preservation of their nature, through this motion they seek its propagation (*Works,* I, 501–3; VIII, 315–17).

The twelfth motion is that of Excitation. This may be said to fall within Assimilation in that it is a motion diffusive, communicative, transitive, and multiplicative. Yet, while its effect agrees for the most part with that of Assimilation, Excitation manifests a special mode of operation and subject. The Motion of Assimilation proceeds as with authority and power, compelling the assimilated to turn and change into the assimilating; but Excitation moves, as it were, artfully and furtively and only invites and disposes the excited to the exciting nature. The former motion multiplies and transforms bodies and substances; the latter multiplies and transforms virtues only.

The Motion of Excitation is particularly conspicuous in the case of heat and cold. Heat does not diffuse itself in the heating-through of a body by the communication of the original heat; rather heat excites the part of the body which is heated to that motion which is the form of heat. To take another example, the magnet gives to iron a new disposition of parts and a conformable motion, but in so doing loses none of its own virtue. Similarly leaven, yeast, curd, and some poisons excite and invite successive and continued motion in dough, beer, cheese, and the human body not so much through strength exerted by the exciting body as through the predisposition and compliant yielding of the body which is moved (*Works,* I, 503–4; VIII, 317–18).

A species of motion which falls within the genus of Assimilation is the Motion of Impression. This differs specifically from what we term, respectively, Assimilation and Excitation in that it neither transforms bodies into the nature of the original mover nor continues to act after the removal of the original moving body. Its effect is produced momentarily, or at least in a very short time, through the continued agency of the original mover. We call Assimilation and Excitation the "Motions of the Generation of Jupiter," therefore, because in their case generation continues. The Motion of Impression we call the "Motion of the Generation of Saturn" because, when it is born, it is straightway, so to speak, devoured and absorbed. It manifests itself, for example, in rays of light, percussions of sound, and magnetism. If the magnet is taken away, the attached iron immediately falls. When light is removed, colors and all other presentations to sight disappear. Sound perishes if the first percussion and vibration of the body which produced it is removed. And while it would seem that when a bell is struck or a string is plucked, the sound continues after the original vibration, this is not the case; what is actually present in the continuation of sound is not the first sound but a repetition of sounds produced through a succession of vibrations. If the bell be held tightly or the string of the harp or of the spinet pressed, the resonance immediately comes to an end (*Works,* I, 505–6; VIII, 318–20).

The fourteenth species of motion is that of Configuration or Position. This topic involves questions both difficult and inadequately investigated: For example, why do the heavens revolve from east to west and not from west to east? Why do the heavens turn on poles placed near the Bears rather than about Orion or in some other part of the heaven? Is there some sort of harmony and consent of the universe which has not as yet been brought under observation? The polarity, direction, and declination of the magnet also are to be referred to this motion, as well as the collocation and positions of parts, threads, and fibers of solid bodies (*Works,* I, 506–7; VIII, 320–21).

The Motion of Transition or Motion according to the Passages is that by which the virtues of bodies are impeded or advanced, more or less, by their media, according to the nature of (*a*) the bodies concerned, (*b*) the operating virtues, and (*c*) the media themselves. One medium is adapted for light, another for sound, another for heat and cold, another for magnetic virtues, and so on (*Works,* I, 508; VIII, 321).

By Royal or Political Motion "the predominant and ruling parts in any body curb, tame, subdue, and regulate the other parts, and compel them to unite, separate, stand still, move, collect, not according to their desires, but .... as may conduce to the well-being of the governing part." This motion is particularly conspicuous in the "spirits" of animals where it imposes arrangement, order, organization, and function upon the several parts which enter into the organism. It is found also in those relatively dense and inert bodies in which the heavier parts are dominant. In the case of the latter instances there is but little hope for transforming the compositions of bodies unless the curb and yoke imposed by the heavier parts can be removed by some art or other. It may occur to the reader that when we speak of predominance here we are falling into confusion, in that we have forgotten that the subject toward whose understanding our whole list of nineteen species of motion is being presented is the relative predominance and nonpredominance of motions each to the others within bodies. It should be definitely understood, therefore, that under Royal Motion we are not considering the question of the relative predominance of any one motion or of motion as such, but rather the predominance of parts of a body through which in each particular case a dominant motion operates (*Works,* I, 508–9; VIII, 321–22).

The seventeenth species of motion is the Spontaneous Motion of Rotation. It is by this that bodies "delighting" in motion, and favorably placed, "enjoy" their own nature and conform with themselves and with no other body. Bodies seem either to move without a terminus, or to rest, or to move toward a terminus at which, according to their nature, they may either rotate or rest. Such bodies as are favorably placed and "delight" in motion have movement which is eternal and without end. Those which are favorably placed and abhor motion remain at rest. While those which are not favorably placed and desire motion move in a straight line (as in the shortest path) to consort with connatural bodies. Eternal Rotation has been commonly held from olden times to be peculiar to the heavenly bodies and has been the occasion for much dispute. The problem as to whether the earth revolves by nature or stands still is not the important one, however; the more pressing question is whether rotary motion is to be confined within the limits of the heavens or whether it descends rather and is communicated to the air and the waters (*Works,* I, 509–10; VIII, 322–23).

The Motion of Trepidation is one of "perpetual activity, that is, where bodies not altogether favourably placed according to their nature, nor yet altogether ill placed, are ceaselessly agitated and restless, neither content with their situation nor daring to proceed further." Such a motion is of necessity in all those bodies, including animal bodies, which exist in an ambiguous, unsettled state between what is agreeable and what is nonagreeable to their natures (*Works,* I, 510-11; VIII, 324).

The last and nineteenth motion may seem at first glance to be no motion at all; yet it assuredly is one. This is Motion of Repose or of Abhorrence to Move. By this, for example, the earth stands in its mass. By appetite for this motion all things of considerable density abhor motion. Their only "desire" is not to move. And though they are provoked to motion in countless ways, yet (as far as they can) they maintain their own nature; and if compelled to act, they seem always intent on recovering their rest and position (*Works,* I, 511-12; VIII, 424-25).

The most universal species or simple elements of motions, appetites, and active virtues have now been indicated. Their number makes no pretense to completeness or adequacy. It may well be enlarged and its divisions re-formed after the further investigation of nature. In any case the motions listed are not intended to be abstract and speculative but such as act within material bodies. To be speculative is easy: we might say, for instance, that bodies desire the preservation, or the exaltation, or the propagation, or the fruition of their own nature; that motions of things tend to preservation and the good either of the universe (as Resistance and Connection), or of greater wholes (as Motions of the Greater Congregation, Rotation, and Abhorrence of Motion), or of special forms, and so on. Yet even if these statements were true, they would not help us in the calculation of the predominance of any virtue or otherwise lead us to an understanding of the constitution of bodies. This calculation can follow only upon sustained observation and experiment.

Of the motions which we have listed some are invincible; some are more powerful than others, which they bind, curb, and arrange; some reach farther than others; some are more swift; some assist, strengthen, increase, and accelerate others. The Motion of Resistance is quite adamantine and invincible. Whether there is Motion of Connection still remains a question, since we cannot assert with assurance whether a vacuum, collected or interspersed, is possible. The other motions rule and are ruled in proportion to their vigor, quantity, speed, carrying distance, and also according to the aids and impediments which they encounter. There are armed magnets, for instance, which support iron sixty times their own weight; so far does the Motion of the Lesser Congregation prevail over the Motion of the Greater Congregation. A lever of a certain length will raise a certain weight; so far does the Motion of Liberty prevail over that of the Greater Congregation. Leather, when stretched to a certain tension, does not break; so far does the Motion of Continuity prevail over tension. Yet if the tension is increased sufficiently, the leather breaks, and the Motion of Continuity gives way. Water flows through a crack of a certain width; so far does the Motion of the Greater Congregation prevail over the Motion of Continuity; but, if the crack be narrower, the water does not run out and the Motion of Continuity is victorious; and so on.

The modes and manners of the yielding of motions should be carefully examined in order that discovery may be made whether on occasion they cease altogether or whether they rather struggle continually and are held in check. In bodies motion of some sort or sorts is always present. Nowhere is there a real and not apparent rest. There is motion in the scales which remain in balance when the opposite weights are equal; in water which is held in a perforated jar with a closed lid. Seemingly yielding motions actively resist. They are subject, but they are not inactive. A man bound hand and foot and pinned to the ground struggles to rise; his resistance is not less because it does not avail (*Works,* I, 512–16; VIII, 325–28).

So much for Instances of Strife or of Predominance; we come now to the last division of the Practical Instances. This includes three sorts of Propitious or Benevolent Instances, namely, Intimating Instances, Polychrest Instances, and Instances of Magic. The first of these, the Intimating Instances, are so named because they serve to intimate and designate what is useful to man. Power and knowledge, while they exalt, do not bless human nature, as do things which make for the exercise and enjoyment of life. The last are to be garnered from the whole realm of nature. The more proper time for discussing these, says Bacon, will be when we come to consider a further section of the present treatise called "Applications to Practice"—a section not included, however, in the extant *Novum organum*. Besides, adds Bacon without elucidation, there is always to be assigned within each portion or subject of the interpretation of nature a place for the Human Chart or the Chart of Things To Be Wished For (*Chartae optativae*), because to ask and to prefer wisely is a part of knowledge (*Works,* I, 516; VIII, 328–29).

Polychrest Instances are instances of general use and of frequent occurrence in varied things. When employed, they can save much labor and not a few fresh experiments. The appropriate time for discussing their contrivance will be in a treatment of Applications to Practice and Modes of Experimenting. At present we shall do no more than call attention to their general use.

Apart simply from the bringing-together and putting-asunder of natural bodies, man acts upon these bodies principally in seven ways: (1) by exclusion of those things which impede or disturb; (2) by compression and like violences; (3) by heat and cold; (4) by continuance in a convenient place; (5) by the curbing and regulating of motion; (6) by special sympathies, consents, or aversions; and (7) by due alternation, series, and succession. Ends served by the first of these practices are easily exemplified. Damage to wine and the juices of herbs is prevented by covering their surface with oil to exclude the air. Bodies are kept from the heat of the sun by being placed in subterranean caves. Powdered substances, such as flour and sand, serve to preserve grapes from the influence of atmosphere and heat. Water is excluded from diving bells and from underwater boats—of whose invention we have heard.

In the second instance, compression and violences have a most powerful effect through local motion. Compression destroys life, flame, ignition, machines, and such virtues of things as arise from the position and coarser dissimilarity of their parts. A flower, for example, has a different color when crushed; powdered amber loses the characteristics of whole amber; a pear when bruised takes on a different taste. These changes, however, manifest an obvious mutation of character. A more difficult and important problem is given in the query whether a new nature, which remains fixed and constant, can be communicated to bodies through condensation. To this end trials should be made both on bodies of nearly uniform parts, such as air, water, oil, and the like, and also on bodies whose parts are less uniform. (*Works,* I, 516–22; VIII, 329–34).

The place in nature and art of the third mode of operation, by heat and cold, is very great. In their use human power is lame on one of its feet. We have the heat of fire, which can be more intense than that of the sun (as it reaches us), and of animals. But a comparable cold is wanting. We are confined in experiment by cold mainly to wintry frost, cold of caves, and cold made by surrounding bodies with snow and ice. Besides things which are cold to the touch there are others, however, such as medicines and plasters, which have considerable power to condense bodies. And since nature applies cold sparingly, we must do as the apothecaries do when a simple is not to be had—provide a *quid pro quo;* that is to say, we must look for substitutes for cold. Those which seem likely to be available are four: simple compression; contraction of the coarser parts of body after the evaporation or escape of the finer; the union of the most solid homogeneous parts, as in the purging of metals of their dross; and "sympathies," of whose knowledge not much can be hoped for until the discovery of forms and schematisms of bodies is made.

As for heat, many varieties of this are available, heat of heavenly bodies by rays direct, or reflected, or refracted, or concentrated by lens; heat of fires, of animals, of earth, and of chemical action; gentle heats, fierce heats, regular heats; increases and decreases of heat. The effects of heat, in its several varieties, upon bodies, from bricks to human organisms, should be fully investigated to the end that not only may the actions of nature be increased and accelerated but also new works of art designed and wrought (*Works,* I, 522-28; VIII, 334-40).

The fourth manner of operation is by continuance, "the steward and almoner of nature." This takes place when a body "is left to itself for a considerable time, defended meanwhile and protected against all external force," the operations of time proving more subtle than the works of fire. Wine, for instance, is clarified by time and not by heat. For putrefaction, time is necessary. The coarse ashes produced by fire are not comparable to the powdered dust of ruins wasted by the ages (*Works,* I, 528-29; VIII, 340-41).

The fifth mode of operation is the regulation of motion. It is found in nature where one body by intervening impedes, repels, admits, or directs the free (*spontaneum*) motion of another body. It may be illustrated by the condensation of vapors in the upright cone of the alembic, by percolation, by the clarification of liquids by the whites of eggs, by molding and casting. A modern philosopher, Telesius, has gone so far as to attribute—rather rashly—the shapes of animals to the channels and folds of the matrix (*Works,* I, 528-30; VIII, 340-42).

Operation by consent and aversion, the sixth mode, often lies deeply hid. It is not to be confused, because of its "depth," with operation by so-called "occult and specific properties," "sympathies and antipathies." For consent is nothing more or less than "the reciprocal commensurateness of Forms and Schematisms." Among the more common consents found in things the principal diversity lies in this: Some bodies which differ greatly in density and rarity agree in configuration; while others which agree in density and rarity differ in configuration. Next in generality is the consent between bodies and their menstruums and foods. Therefore, inquiry should be made respecting in what climates, in what soil, at what depth of earth, the several metals are generated; in what soils and with what sorts of manure trees, shrubs, and herbs thrive best; what plants in grafting thrive better on what stocks and whether grafting will succeed in the case of the forest as well as in the orchard; what foods suit various sorts of animals best; and so on.

The interior consents and aversions, or "friendships" and "strifes," of bodies (we are almost weary of the terms "sympathies" and "antipathies" because of the superstitions and inanities associated with them) are as a rule either falsely ascribed to wrong causes or neglected. It is said, for example, that certain plants fail to thrive when grown with others, because of a disagreement or strife between the two types, while those which thrive in the same field do so because of a prevailing friendship. The proper explanation in the former case is probably the robbing of the soil by one type of what the other needs, while in the latter one sort of plant provides the earth with what the other requires.

The consents which have been established by sure experiment are but few; they are notably those between the magnet and iron, gold and quicksilver; some between certain medicines and the parts, humors, and diseases of the body; and some by chemical experiments on metals. Attention should be called here to one sort of consent of bodies of common occurrence; this is the union of bodies by coherence or simple apposition. Some bodies mix and are incorporated with others quite readily in this manner, others reluctantly. Powders mix better with water, ashes and lime with oil, and so on. Instances of the propensity and aversion of bodies toward mixture should especially be noted. A record should be made of their respective parts and of the distribution of these within the bodies concerned of "digestion" after mixture; and of their relative predominance in relation one to the other of the constituents after the mixture is completed (*Works*, I, 530–35; VIII, 342–46).

The last mode of operation is that of alternation, series, and succession of the former six. This mode, therefore, cannot be dealt with until inquiry into the earlier six has proceeded a way. The knowledge of the series or chain or alternation is the most difficult for discovery and the most effective for operation. Indeed, so far as the more considerable works of operation are concerned, this knowledge is nothing less than the Thread of the Labyrinth (*Works,* I, 535; VIII, 346).

The twenty-seventh and last Prerogative Instances, the third of the Propitious sort, are Instances of Magic. In these either the material or the efficient is scanty or small in comparison with the work and effect which follows; hence the operation effected appears a miracle. The works which appear in these Instances of Magic are, so far as we can conjecture at present, brought about in three ways: either by self-multiplication, as in the case of fire and "specific" poisons; or by "excitation or invitation" in another body, as in the case of yeast and the magnet which excites numberless needles without loss or diminution of virtue; or by "anticipation of motion," as in the case of gunpowder and cannon. Whether there is any method of changing bodies *per minima* (as they say) and of transposing the more subtle schematisms of matter, so that art may be enabled to do directly what nature undertakes through many windings, of this we have as yet no sure indications. Certainly nature's own magical effects are supplied sparingly. What she may do after the discovery of her forms and processes and schematisms will appear in future times (*Works,* I, 535–36; VIII, 346–47).

Having given this account of the Dignities or Prerogatives of Instances, Bacon admonishes his readers that in his *Novum organum,* with its scattered speculations and examples, he has been describing the beginning of a method of inquiry and not providing a philosophy of nature. He adds a brief instruction for the use of these instances. Among the twenty-seven sorts there are several whose collection, he says, should be made at the beginning of investigation, since these "either assist and set right the understanding and senses, or provide for practice generally." They are the Conformable, Singular, Deviating, Limiting, those of Power, of the Door, Intimating, Polychrest, and Magical Instances, which prove to be "as the soul among common instances of muster; and a few of them.... are worth a multitude [of the others] and therefore when we make our tables, they are to be investigated with all zeal, and submitted therein for consideration." The other sorts of instance may be neglected until Tables of Presentation are made ready for the interpretation of the particular nature concerned. These tables have, at the beginning, been introduced in a preliminary sort of way. They are still to be made the subject of further consideration after certain intervening topics have been brought under discussion (*Works,* I, 390, 536–38; VIII, 210, 349–50).

And now, says Bacon, we must proceed to the Supports and Rectifications of Induction and then to Concretes, Latent Processes, Latent Schematisms, and other parts of method which we have listed at the beginning, "that at length (like honest and faithful guardians) we may hand over to men their fortunes, the undertsanding having been emancipated—having come, so to speak, of age; from which there must necessarily ensue an improvement in man's estate, and an increase of his power over nature. For man by the fall fell at the same time from his state of innocency and from his dominion over created things. Both these losses can even in this life be partially repaired; the former by religion and faith, the latter by arts and sciences" (*Works,* I, 538–39; VIII, 349–50).

This valedictory statement of Bacon's is, unfortunately, premature. The inductive method on which his whole Instauration rests, the direction which is to guide all men who seek enlightenment and power over nature for the good of the human race, Bacon never finds time—whether he has the capacity or not—to bring to completion. Aware of the complexities of the task, as his references to accruing problems in the extant portion show, and struggling without helpers to place on record the third part of his sixfold scheme for the reform of knowledge, he abandons the remaining subjects of the *Novum organum,* turns from the second division of his Instauration to prepare for the third part a set of directions for the collecting of natural histories and then to the task of amassing these histories themselves.

CHAPTER XXII

NATURAL HISTORY: RULES AND TOPICS

THE third division of the Great Instauration is to contain, according to the plan announced in the *Novum organum,* "the Phenomena of the Universe; that is to say, experience of every kind and such a natural history as may form the foundation of a philosophy." The natural history which is now available is not sound but frivolous and, for a natural philosophy, well-nigh useless. It is literary. It is not vulgar as things themselves are vulgar. Its fables are designed to delight the curious. Its mixture of fact and fiction is calculated to compel the imagination and not to instruct the understanding. Its observations and experiments are magnified and distorted in the interests of wonder and vanity. It is the issue of the rumor of tradition, of inaccurate observation, of fortuitous experiments, of trials suspended in their initial stages, and of experiments rendered servile to immediate works (*Works,* I, 220–25; II, 196, 291; VIII, 46–50, 416, 507).

Bacon publishes his own specific directions for the collecting of natural history along with the *Novum organum* under a second title, *Parasceve ad historiam naturalem et experimentalem* ("Preparative toward a Natural and Experimental History"). In its preface he says that the proper place for the directions contained in the short work is within the Preparations for Investigation, the last but one of several parts announced but not expounded in the *Novum organum.* But a natural and experimental history, he adds, is of too great importance to be left until this section of the method is written out. Our purpose of publishing the Instauration in parts is to put some of it, at least, out of danger. This is our reason for including a delineation of the sort of experimental history which is suitable for the building of a philosophy. So necessary is this history to the Instauration that, if it cannot be provided, the scheme cannot become operative and the whole project for the reform of knowledge may as well be given up.

"What we have said on many occasions must be especially repeated;

that if all the wits of all the ages had concurred or shall hereafter concur, or if the whole human species had applied or shall hereafter apply itself to philosophy, and the whole earth had been or shall be nothing but academies and colleges and schools of learned men; still without such a natural and experimental history as we are going to prescribe, no advance worthy of the human race could have been made or can be made in philosophy and the sciences. Whereas, on the other hand, once such a history is collected and arranged, with the addition of such auxiliary and light-bearing experiments as will occur or be elicited in the course of interpretation, the investigation of nature and of all the sciences will be the work of a few years. This therefore must be done, or the business abandoned."

The history which is required is of great magnitude and cannot be collected without great labor and expense. The thought has occurred to us that it might be not amiss to see whether, once directions are available, many others may undertake the task of its collection, so that, while we continue with the carrying-through of our original design, this part may, even during our life, be made ready. Our own strength, without help from others, is not adequate to so great an undertaking. As much of the task as relates to the intellect we shall perhaps be able to master through our own effort. But the materials on which the understanding is to operate are so widely scattered that many helpers—factors and merchants, so to speak—are required to seek them out and bring them in. The immediate and chief object of our writing at present, then, is the description of the sort of history which may be used in induction, lest men who set to work on inductive knowledge may, for want of direction, go astray at the beginning (*Works,* II, 43–45; VIII, 353–55).

Having stated so much by way of preface, Bacon announces two intentions. First, he will provide certain precepts for the preparation of natural history generally; secondly, he purposes to set down an exemplary history, to which he will give the name "Primary, or Mother, History." To begin with the precepts: The assembling of data for induction is a laborious task, and the more toilsome it is, the less should it be burdened with superfluities. There are, accordingly, three points upon which collectors should be warned initially if they are to make good use of their time and energy. We mention these especially because the unnecessary recording of history may increase the mass of work immensely and add but little or nothing to its value. First, let antiquities be done away with, and citations or assents of authors, as well as altercations and opinions for disputation—everything, in fine, which is philological. Let no author be cited except in a case of doubtful credit nor any controversy be introduced except on a matter of great moment. As for ornaments of discourse, similitudes, treasury of eloquence, and inanities of this sort, let them be completely got rid of. And let all those things which are admitted be set down briefly and concisely. Secondly, let superfluity in the description and picturing of species and curious varieties of the same be avoided. Varieties of species afford pleasure of a sort; sometimes they approach to the nature of individuals. The information they furnish to science is slight and almost superfluous. Thirdly, superstitious narratives, including tales of ceremonial magic—but not accounts of "prodigies" in nature, where the record is faithful and probable—are to be rejected. For we would not have an infant philosophy—to which natural history is the nursing mother—habituated in old wives' tales. The time may come, after the searching of nature has been well furthered, for a sifting of the dregs of these tales to discover whether they contain any grains of truth. Until then they are to be set aside. Meanwhile the experiments of natural, as distinct from ceremonial, magic are to be examined with severity, especially in cases where recourse is had to "sympathies and antipathies."

These three superfluities having been avoided, let the matter which is admitted be set down briefly in a style chastened of verbiage. And let it always be remembered that the business of the historian is to make ready not a window for the display of fancy goods but a granary for the storage of things, not a dwelling place in which to stay but a storehouse to be entered on occasions when matter is required for the interpretation of nature (*Works,* II, 48–50; VIII, 359–60).

The history which we seek is of great range and must be "composed to the measure of the universe." The practice of contemplating a few things and then pronouncing on many will not do. Nature is manifold and varied. Generally speaking, she has a triplicate status, and is subject to a threefold regimen. Either she is free and displays herself in her ordinary course, or she is deprived of her usual liberty through the depravity and immoderateness of matter and the violence of impediments, or, yet again, she is constrained by art and human industry. Within these three regimens of nature fall, respectively, the species of things, monsters, and artificial things. In the third, nature is in subjugation to man, through whose labor a new form (*facies*) of bodies and, as it were, another universe or theater of things come into being.

Natural history is threefold. It treats of the liberty of nature, the errors of nature, and the bonds of nature. It may aptly, then, be divided into the history of generations, of pretergenerations, and of arts—the last customarily called "history mechanical or experimental." The history of generations consists of five parts. The first of these is the history of things celestial. (Because we segregate the heavens for purposes of observation and experiment, there is no occasion to infer that their composite parts are assumed, as with Aristotle, to be different from those of other created things.) The second part has to do with meteors, comets, and the regions of air which lie between the moon and the earth's surface; the third with the earth and sea; the fourth with the Greater Colleges, or elements—as they are called—of fire, earth, air, and water—these now being regarded not as the first principles of things but as the larger masses of natural bodies; and the fifth with the Lesser Colleges, or species of things—the main concern hitherto of natural historians.

The history of pretergenerations will contain such prodigies as are found, according to accredited observation, in fact. It will omit, at least until the investigation of nature has proceeded a considerable way, all superstitious stories of marvels and marvelous events. Accounts of monsters within the several species are sometimes to be conjoined with the histories of the species themselves, and the history of artificial things is on occasion to be set beside that of natural things. At other times the three types of history are to be kept apart. It will be best, however, to consider each individual problem as it arises; for too much stress on a fixed method, as well as on no method at all, occasions repetition and prolixity.

Of the three sorts of natural history, that which deals with the arts is of most use in that it leads the most directly to operation. It lifts the mask and veil from natural things which are generally concealed or obscured under the variety of shapes and external appearances; and it betrays the manacles and efforts of matter which refuses annihilation and accepts in preference varied bodily shapes. Upon the history of art, then, however mechanical and illiberal this may at times be, the greatest diligence—pride and fastidiousness forgotten—is to be bestowed.

Of the several arts, preference is to be given in the first instance to those which "exhibit, alter, and prepare" natural bodies and materials, such as cookery, dyeing, agriculture, chemistry, the manufacture of glass, of sugar, enamel, artificial fires, gunpowder, paper, and the like. Of less general use are the arts which manifest the delicate motion of the hands and the making of instruments, for example, weaving, carpentry, architecture, the manufacture of clocks. In the latter examples are found many things of value which pertain to the alterations of natural bodies and provide information respecting local motion.

A distinction should be kept constantly in mind between those experiments which clearly serve the end of the art under examination and those which may at first glance or through habit appear to be merely incidental. The latter can be of great use in science. For example, crabs turn red when cooked. This instance is good for investigating the nature of redness, especially since it manifests a change similar to that which takes place in other things—in bricks, for instance, when they are baked. Meat's taking less time for salting in winter than in summer provides useful knowledge for the cook; and it is also a good instance for indicating the nature and impression of cold. It would be a great mistake, then, to think that our present purpose is satisfied by collecting only those experiments which immediately serve the arts. Theirs is an end by no means to be despised; yet it is well that all mechanical experiments be considered as rivers flowing from all sides into the sea of philosophy to the provision of a general knowledge of natural body (*Works*, II, 47-48, 50-54; VIII, 357-58, 361-64).

Turning now from the three divisions of natural history, certain general precepts for its compilation may be set down. The first of these is in respect to common things. There should be received into history, if it is to be informative of nature's structures and motions, first, such ordinary things as may be and have been thought superfluous to record in writings because they are familiar; secondly, base, illiberal, even filthy things, for "to the pure all things are pure"; thirdly, things usually considered trifling and even childish; and fourthly, things which appear subtle and in themselves useless for inquiry.

Next, let everything respecting natural bodies and virtues be, as far as possible, numbered, weighed, measured, and defined. Operation, not speculation, is the final end in view. A proper combination of physics and mathematics engenders works. Therefore let there be ascertained with accurate measurement such things as the revolutions and distances of planets, the area of the earth and its amount in comparison with that of water, how much compression air will suffer without strong resistance, the relative weights of metals, and innumerable instances of this kind. It is not always possible, of course, to obtain exact measures and proportions in the case of bodies. Recourse then must be had to indefinite estimates and comparatives. And when mean proportions cannot be had, let extremes be proposed.

The statements which appear for admission into history are either true, doubtful, or false. The first sort should be set down simply. To the second should be added a qualifying note—"it is reported," or "they relate," or "I have heard from a person worthy of credit," and the like. To include arguments for and against their authenticity in each instance would be too laborious and would retard the work of the author. Nor indeed are the records themselves of much consequence to our present purpose, since, as we have noted in the first book of the *Novum organum,* errors of experiment, unless they abound everywhere, will be presently corrected by the truth of axioms. Should a doubtful instance be important either because of its use or because many other things depend upon it, the name of the author, his credibility, and the circumstances in which he gathered his information—whether from direct observation and with other witnesses or whether heard or copied (as in the writings of Pliny) from some one else, whether obtained by report from an earlier age, and so on—should be noted. The third sort, the stories of things that are manifestly untrue and yet current, the fables that prevail through tradition—for instance, that garlic weakens the magnet, that amber attracts all substances except basil—these should not be passed over in silence; they should be rejected in express statement so that science no longer may be troubled by them.

Certain minor precepts remain; these are five in number. First, there are questions as to fact—not as to causes—which should be asked in order to provoke further inquiry, for example, in the history of earth and sea, whether the Caspian Sea ebbs and flows and, if so, at what intervals; whether there is a southern continent or only islands; and the like. Secondly, when a new and nice experiment is recorded, a note should be made of the procedure employed so that the reader may estimate the trustworthiness of the information set down and human industry may be aroused to discover, if possible, more adequate methods. Thirdly, all statements of observation and experiment are to be written in truth and with religious care, as if the writer were under oath and devoid of reservation of doubt and question. This record is the book of God's works and—so far as there may be an analogy between the majesty of divine things and the humbleness of earthly things—is a kind of second Scripture.

Fourthly, it will not be amiss to intersperse in natural history occasional observations by the way (as Pliny has done). For instance, in the history of earth and sea it may be noted that the shape of the earth, so far as this is known, is narrow and pointed toward the south, broad and wide toward the north; that, except perhaps in the extreme polar regions, great oceans intersect the earth by channels running north and south and not east and west. It will be well also to set down general and catholic observations, such as, "Venus is never distant more than 46 parts from the sun, Mercury never more than 23"; and to add a sort of observation new to science, and yet of no slight importance, respecting things that are not. For example, a star is never oblong or triangular; stars are not arranged either in a quincunx, square, or any other complete figure (notwithstanding the names given their arrangements, such as delta, crown, cross, chariot, etc.), hardly ever in a straight line even, excepting perhaps the belt and dagger of Orion. Fifthly, there will be found not a little assistance to inquiry in the opinions, and their varieties, held by the several philosophic sects. These may be passed in review in order to arouse the intellect, and nothing more.

If, says the author, these rules are diligently observed, natural history will proceed directly toward its goal and not go beyond its proper bounds. If the precepts appear too restrictive, let men of learning turn their gaze upon the libraries and examine the bodies of civil and canonical laws on the one side and the commentaries of lawyers and learned doctors on the other. They may then perceive the difference in bulk and volume between law and speculation upon law and may come to grasp the reason why, for those who record the works of nature, brevity is imposed by the law of nature in things themselves; whereas, for the philosophical commentator, opinions, dogmas, and speculations are without number and without end (*Works,* II, 54–58; VIII, 365–70; See V, 440–48).

Having completed one of the purposes of the *Parasceve,* the setting-forth of precepts, Bacon now makes it clear that he cannot perform the other, which is the provision of an exemplary and basic natural history. He tells us that at present he has time only for the listing of a catalogue of titles which are to be investigated and written out—like Particular

Topics—and that he intends to reserve for himself, as he has also said in the *Novum organum,* the inquiry into the cardinal virtues in bodies. These virtues are nature's *primordia,* "the original passions and desires of matter," and include dense and rare, hot and cold, solid and fluid, heavy and light; Bacon is not prepared to hand their investigation over to others until such time as these persons have succeeded in gaining a familiarity with nature comparable to his own (*Works,* I, 223; II, 58-59; VIII, 49, 370-71; cf. VII, 294; X, 413).

The subjects which Bacon sets down for inquiry number some one hundred and thirty. The list is included here because it manifests the scope, the emphasis on utility, the interest in common things, the stress on the practical arts, and the type of humanism and humanitarianism which characterize the author's attempted reform of natural knowledge.

The "Catalogue of Particular Histories by Titles" runs as follows:

History of the Heavenly Bodies; or Astronomical History. History of the Configuration of the Heaven and its parts toward the Earth and its parts; or Cosmographical History. History of Comets. History of Fiery Meteors. History of Lightnings, Thunderbolts, Thunders, and Coruscations. History of Winds, and Sudden Blasts, and Undulations of the Air. History of Rainbows. History of Clouds, as they are seen above. History of the Blue Expanse, of Twilight, of Many (Mock) Suns, Many (Mock) Moons, Haloes, various colors of the Sun and the Moon; and of every variety of the Heavens in consequence of the appearance which results from the medium. History of Rains, Ordinary, Vehement, and Prodigious; also of Cloudbursts (as they are called), and the like. History of Hail, Snow, Frost, Hoar-Frost, Fog, Dew, and the like. History of all other things that Fall or Descend from above, and are generated in the upper regions. History of Sounds from on high (if there be any) besides Thunder. History of Air as a whole, or in the Configuration of the World. History of the Seasons or Temperatures of the Year, as well according to the variations of Regions as according to accidents of Times and periods of Years; of Floods, Heats, Droughts, and the like. History of Earth and Sea; of the Shape and Compass of them, and their Configurations relatively to each other, and of their extending widely or narrowly; of Islands in the Sea, of Gulfs of the Sea, and of Salt Lakes within the Land; of Isthmuses and Promontories. History of the Motions (if any be) of the Globe of Earth and Sea; and from what Experiments they may be inferred. History of the greater Motions and Perturbations in Earth and Sea; that is to say, of Earthquakes, Tremblings and Yawnings of the Earth, Islands springing up *de novo,* Floating Islands, Breaking off of Land through the inroad of the Sea, Encroachments and Inundations and in turn Recessions of the Sea; Eruptions of Fire from the Earth; Sudden Eruptions of Waters from the Earth, and the like. Natural History of Geography; of Mountains,

NATURAL HISTORY: RULES AND TOPICS

Valleys, Woods, Plains, Sands, Marshes, Lakes, Rivers, Torrents, Springs, and every diversity of their springing waters, and the like; omitting Nations, Provinces, Cities, and such like Civil matters. History of Ebbs and Flows of the Sea currents, Undulations, and other Motions of the Sea. History of the other Accidents of the Sea; its Saltness, its divers Colors, its Depth; also of submarine Rocks, Mountains and Valleys, and the like.

Histories of the Greater Masses Follow Next. History of Flame and of Ignited Things. History of Air, in Substance, not in Configuration. History of Water, in Substance, not in Configuration. History of Earth and its diversity, in Substance, not in Configuration.

Histories of Species Follow Next. History of perfect Metals, of Gold, of Silver; and of the Mines, Veins, Marcasites of the Same; also the things which produce these in Mines (*Operaria in Mineris ipsorum*). History of Quicksilver. History of Fossils; as Vitriol, Sulphur, etc. History of Gems; as the Diamond, the Ruby, etc. History of Stones; as Marble, Touchstone, Flint, etc. History of the Magnet. History of Miscellaneous Bodies, which are neither wholly Fossil nor Vegetable; as Salts, Amber, Ambergris, etc. Chemical History respecting Metals and Minerals. History of Plants, Trees, Shrubs, Herbs; and of their parts, Roots, Stalks, Wood, Leaves, Flowers, Fruits, Seeds, Gums, etc. Chemical History respecting Vegetables. History of Fishes, and their Parts and their Generation. History of Birds, and their Parts and their Generation. History of Quadrupeds, and their Parts and their Generation. History of Serpents, Worms, Flies, and other insects; and of their Parts and their Generation. Chemical History respecting the things which are used by Animals.

Histories of Man Follow Next. History of the Figure and External Limbs of Man, his Stature, Frame, Countenance, and Features; and of the variety of these according to Races and Climates, or other lesser differences. Physiognomical History based on the same. Anatomical History, or of the Internal Members of Man; and of their variety in so far as it is found in the Natural Frame and Structure itself, and not merely as regards diseases and preternatural accidents. History of the similar parts in Man; as Flesh, Bones, Membranes, etc. History of Humors in Man; Blood, Bile, Seed, etc. History of Excrements; Spittle, Urine, Sweats, Stools, Hair of the Head, Hairs of the Body, Hang-nails, Nails, and the like. History of Faculties; Attraction, Digestion, Retention, Expulsion, Sanguification, Assimilation of Aliment into the members, Conversion of Blood and Flower of Blood into Spirit, etc. History of Natural and Involuntary Motions; as Motion of the Heart, of the Pulses, Sneezing, Motion of the Lungs, ... etc. History of Motions mixed of the natural and the voluntary; as Respiration, Cough, Urination, Stool, etc. History of Voluntary Motions; as of the Instruments for articulation of words; Motions of the Eyes, Tongue, Jaws, Hands, Fingers; of Swallowing, etc. History of Sleep and Dreams. History of different Habits of Body, of Fat, of Lean; of the Complexions (as they say), etc. History of the Generation of Man. History of Conception, Vivification, Gestation in the Womb, Birth, etc. History of the Nourishment of Man; and of all things Eatable and Drinkable, and of all Diet; and of their variety according to nations or lesser differences. History of Growth and Increase of the Body in the whole and in its parts. History of the course of Age; Infancy, Boyhood, Youth, Old Age; of Longevity, Shortness of Life, and the like, according to nations and minor differences. History of Life and Death. Medical History of Diseases, and their Symptoms and Signs. Medical History of the Treatment and Remedies and Cures of Diseases. Medical History of those things which preserve the Body and Health. Medical History of those things which relate to the Form and Grace of the Body, etc. Medical History of those things which alter the Body, and pertain to Alterative Regimen. History of Drugs. History of Surgery. Chemical History respecting Medicines. History of Vision, and of things Visible, or Optical History. History of Painting, Sculpture, Modelling, etc. History of Hearing and Sounds. History of Music. History of Smell and of Odors. History of Taste and of Savors. History of Touch, and the objects of Touch. History of Venery, as species of Touch. History of Pleasure and Pain in general. History of the Affections; as Anger, Love, Shame, etc. History of the Intellectual Faculties; of the Cogitative Faculty, of Imagination, Discourse, Memory, etc. History of Natural Divinations. History of Diagnostics, or Secret Natural Discernments.

History of Cookery, and the subservient arts, as of the Butcher, Poulterer, etc. History of Baking and the Making of Bread, and the subservient arts, as of Milling, etc. History of Wine. History of the Cellar and of different kinds of Drink. History of Sweetmeats and Confections. History of Honey. History of Sugar. History of the Foods prepared with Milk. History of Baths and of Unguents.

Miscellaneous History respecting the care of the body; as of Barbers, Perfumers, etc. History of the working of Gold, and the subservient arts. History of the Manufacture of Wool, and the subservient arts. History of the Manufactures from Silk and from Cotton, and the subservient arts. History of Manufactures from Flax, Hemp, the Cotton-tree, Hair, and other Threads, and the subservient arts. History of Manufactures from Feathers. History of Weaving, and the subservient arts. History of Dyeing. History of Leatherworking, Tanning, and the subservient arts. History of Mattresses and Feathers. History of Ironworking. History of the Stone-Quarry or of Stone Cutters. History of Bricks and Tiles. History of Pottery. History of Cements and Hard Coverings. History of Woodworking. History of working in Lead. History of Glass and all Vitreous Substances, and of Glass-manufacture. History of Architecture generally. History of Wagons, Chariots, Litters, etc. History of Printing, of Books, Writing, Sealing; of Ink, Pen, Papyrus, Parchment, etc. History of Wax. History of Basket-Weaving. History of Mat-making, and of manufactures from Straw, Rushes, and the like. History of Washing, Sweeping, etc. History of Farming, Pasturage, Culture of Forests. History of Gardening. History of Fishing. History of Hunting and Fowling. History of the business of War, and of subservient arts; as Armoury, Bow-making, Arrow-making, Musketry, Ordnance, Ballistics, Machines. History of Navigation, and of the subservient crafts and arts. History of Athletics, and of all sorts of Exercises of Man. History of Horsemanship. History of Games of all kinds. History of Jugglers and Mountebanks. Miscellaneous History of divers Artificial Materials; as Enamel, Porcelain, various Cements, etc. History of Salts. Miscellaneous History of divers Machines, and of Motions. Miscellaneous History of Common Experiments, which have not been consolidated into an Art.

Histories of Pure Mathematics should be written; although they are rather observations than experiments. History of the natures and powers of Numbers. History of the natures and powers of Figures.

"It may not be beside the point," comments Bacon, "to suggest that, since many of the experiments necessarily fall under two or more titles (as the History of Plants and the History of the Art of Gardening will have many things almost in common), it will be more convenient to investigate them according to arts, and to arrange them according to bodies: because we have but little concern for the mechanical arts as such; only for those things which they contribute to the providing of philosophy with information. These matters, however, will be better governed in conformity with the case as it arises" (*Works,* II, 61–69; VIII, 373–81).

CHAPTER XXIII

NATURAL HISTORY: THE DATA

THAT Bacon himself could never during his natural life assemble the histories listed at the end of the *Parasceve* goes without saying. The ultimate historical requirements for his new philosophy of nature are practically endless—as wide as the natural universe. The requirements to make it operative include a history—the author tells Baranzan—six times as extensive as that of Pliny's. Yet Bacon determines to make a beginning and to publish as many natural histories as he can. Not that he is disposed to accept the task uncomplainingly; in the Preface to the *Parasceve* he opines that it is hardly fitting that the author of an undertaking like his should have to spend his time in what is available to the industry of all men. In the later *De augmentis* he writes, with some degree of reconciliation to circumstances, "I knowingly and willingly forfeit the dignity of my name and wit (if such be) while I serve human good, and, although one who should perchance be an architect in philosophy and knowledge, become workman, labourer, and what in fact you will, when I undertake and perform many things which must be done, and which others shun from an inborn pride." Rawley in his epistle, "To the Reader," which, as editor, he affixes to the *Sylva sylvarum*, tells us, "I have.... heard his lordship discourse that men (no doubt) will think many of the experiments contained in this collection to be vulgar and trivial, mean and sordid, curious and fruitless.... I have heard his lordship speak complainingly, that his lordship (who thinketh he deserveth to be an architect in this building) should be forced to be a workman and a labourer, and to dig clay and burn the brick; and more than that (according to the hard condition of the Israelites at the latter end), to gather the straw and stubble over all the fields to burn the brick withal. For he knoweth, that except he do it, nothing will be done: men are so set to despise the means of their own good." (*Works,* II, 44–45; III, 9; IV, 156; VIII, 354; IX, 193).

By 1622 Bacon has made ready and sends to the publisher his *Historia naturalis et experimentalis ad condendam philosophiam: sive phaenomena universi: quae est Instaurationis magnae pars tertia* ("Natural and Experimental History for the Foundation of Philosophy: Or Phenomena of the Universe: Being the Third Part of the Great Instauration").

Again he entreats men, as they value their fortune, to search with submissive mind for knowledge in the greater world and to forsake the trifling worlds which have issued—as from a Platonic cave—from the brains of many ancient, and not a few modern, philosophers. Men, in building universes out of their imagination, copy the sin of their first parents. The first man wished to be equal to God; his posterity would be greater. Philosophers will make worlds anew and stamp with their own image the creation, refusing meanwhile to cognize in God's works the stamp of the Creator himself; wherefore they forfeit a second time man's dominion over creatures. "If therefore," continues Bacon, "there be any humility towards the Creator, and reverence for and magnifying of his works, and charity towards men and endeavour to alleviate their necessities and tribulations; if there be any love of truth, hatred of darkness, and desire for purification of the understanding; men must be implored again and again (having quit or at least set aside for a little while those hasty and preposterous philosophies which have preferred theses to hypotheses, led experience captive, and triumphed over the works of God) to draw near with reverence and humility in order to unroll the volume of creation, to linger and reflect upon it, and, washed clean from prejudices, to meditate on it disinterestedly and with integrity."

In the epistle dedicatory to Prince Charles the author presents "the first fruits of our Natural History, a thing very little in bulk, like a grain of mustard seed, but yet a token of those things which, God willing, are to follow." He tells the Prince that he has bound himself as by a vow that every month during which God shall prolong his life he will complete and publish one or more parts of it, in so far as their relative extents and difficulties will allow. He lists the titles of six histories which are designed for the first six months—*Historia ventorum* ("History of Winds"); *Historia densi et rari* ("History of Dense and Rare"); *Historia gravis et levis* ("History of Heavy and Light"); *Historia sympathiae et antipathiae rerum* ("History of the Sympathy and Antipathy of Things"); *Historia sulphuris, mercurii, et salis* ("History of Sulphur,

Mercury, and Salt"); *Historia vitae et mortis* ("History of Life and Death").

Under the general title, "Natural and Experimental History," is included a general preface to the six histories; the "Rule of the Present History;" the "History of Winds" which is described as the "First Title in Natural and Experimental History, for the Foundation of Philosophy: Being the Third Part of the Great Instauration," with its own preface; also titles of, and short prefaces to, the remaining histories. In the "Rule of the Present History" the author explains that, since he is unable to deal with all the titles contained in the catalogue announced at the end of the *Parasceve,* he is not taking them in the order listed therein but is making a selection according to their weightiness, their usefulness, the availability of their experiments, and their difficulty and importance.

And, we gather from statements within the "Rule of the Present History," it has been Bacon's intention to place at the end of the published volume an *Abecedarium naturae* ("Alphabet of Nature") by way of supplement to the catalogue attached to the *Parasceve*. This piece, which we shall have occasion to discuss presently, is not included in the published work (*Works,* III, 211–12; IX, 375).

The "History of Life and Death, the Second Title in Natural and Experimental History for the Foundation of Philosophy: Being the Third Part of the Great Instauration," is published early in 1623. The "History of Dense and Rare" is not published by Bacon himself but posthumously by Rawley and significantly *without* the subtitle, the "Third Title in Natural and Experimental History.... the Third Part of the Great Instauration." The others of the six histories announced in 1622 survive only in their titles and prefaces. These pieces, along with the "Alphabet of Nature" published by Tenison in 1679 and the *Sylva sylvarum* published by Rawley in 1627, serve to indicate how far Bacon is able to succeed in preparing matter in representation of the third part of his Instauration.

Bacon's failure, during his lifetime, to publish, even in an imperfect form, a history of "Dense and Rare" is of considerable significance. Because, in attempting to prepare this work, he was trying without success to make good in some degree at least his promise to provide an account of the Cardinal Virtues in bodies—a promise, as we have seen, expressly given on two occasions in his publication of 1620 (*Works,* I, 223; II, 58–59; VIII, 49, 370–71).

The "History of Dense and Rare" is a revision of an earlier piece,

"Phenomena of the Universe" (*ca.* 1608). Both documents include a table of specific gravities, Bacon's only example of the consistent application of quantity to experiments. In the "History of Dense and Rare" one item of the table is omitted and six others added, there being seventy-eight items in the latter work and seventy-three in the earlier. The "History" contains a general discussion of condensation and rarefaction and records certain provisional conclusions—among these what are likely Bacon's final conclusions on the question of rarefaction, condensation, and the vacuum—a question which he believes central to a science of bodies. These run as follows: "1. The sum of matter in the universe remains constant; and there is no bringing to effect either from nothing or to nothing. 2. Of this sum [of matter] there is more in some bodies, and less in others, in the same space. 3. Abundance and paucity of matter constitute the notions of dense and rare correctly perceived. 4. There is a limit.... of dense and rare, but not in any being known to us. 5. There is no vacuum in nature, either collected or interspersed (*nec congregatum nec intermistum*). 6. Within the limits of dense and rare there is a fold of matter by which it folds and unfolds itself without a vacuum...." (*Works,* IV, 114; X, 262).

The "Alphabet of Nature" is described by Rawley as "a metaphysical piece which is lost" and listed by him among the last of Bacon's writings. The "Alphabet" is designed, we are informed in the "Rule of the Present History" attached to the "Natural and Experimental History," as a catalogue of "Titles of Abstract Natures" which are to be added to that "Titles of Concretes" which is appended to the *Parasceve*. The document has added interest because it includes the "Transcendentals" listed by the author within his first philosophy, topics which seem to have no explicit place in the *Novum organum* or the histories. The piece was found in an incomplete state among Bacon's papers by Tenison and published in 1679. That the original piece and the fragment discovered by Tenison are the same seems amply testified by the description of the former in the "Rule of the Present History" and the obvious agreement between this "Rule" and the "Rule of the Alphabet" attached to the fragment. Presumably, had the "Alphabet" been published along with the original piece one "Rule" would have sufficed. Two possible reasons for the exclusion of the "Alphabet" from the publication of 1622 suggest themselves. First, Bacon did not wish to complicate his experimental problems with considerations involving Transcendentals. As it stood, his history was not "pure" but far too "mixed" with theoretical considerations to measure up to the stipulations he had laid down for the third part of the Instauration. Again, the incompleteness of the original work may have been the cause of its being withheld. Obviously, in its extant form the fragment is only a portion of a work originally projected; for it begins with the sixty-seventh item for inquiry and ends with the seventy-eighth.

Of the titles of the "Alphabet" those numbered sixty-seven to seventy-two are the Greater Masses, earth, water, air, fire, the heavens, meteors. Bacon gives as his reason for including these subjects the following statement: "Since so many things are produced by earth and water, so many things pass through air and are received by it, so many things are changed and dissolved by fire, the other inquiries would be less clear unless the nature of those masses which occur so often were well known and explained. To these we add inquiries concerning the Heavens and Meteors, since they themselves are Greater Masses, and belong to what is universal."

The remaining subjects designated for inquiry concern "the conditions of Beings which seem as it were Transcendentals." These, notes the author, have little to do with the body of nature, yet, because of the method which is to be employed in its investigations, they will serve to throw light on other subjects. The nature of things is infinite in respect to the quantity of matter and in the variety of individuals, but in respect to its constitutive forms it is so limited that there are hardly enough of these for the mustering of a thousand. Toward the segregation of these forms negatives when taken in conjunction with affirmations can be of great assistance. Accordingly, an inquiry into nonbeing as well as into being should be instituted. After this may follow an investigation of possibility and impossibility, which are nothing other than potentiality of being or nonpotentiality of being. Next will come an inquiry into much and little, rare and usual, which are the potentialities of being in quantity; of durable and transitory, eternal and momentary, which are potentialities of being in duration; of the natural and the monstrous, which are potentialities of being by the course of nature and by its deviations; and of the natural and the artificial, which are potentialities of being, with and without the agency of man.

No title within the "Alphabet" is to be taken initially, of course, for a true and fixed division of things. There must be no assumption beforehand of a knowledge of matters which are under inquiry; for no one can divide things truly who has not a thorough experimental knowledge of their inmost nature. Let it be sufficient, then, if the titles are well adapted to the order of inquiry—which is the matter in hand—and not to final conclusions respecting the objects investigated (*Works,* III, 211-13, 306-11; IX, 375-77, 475-79).

The "History of Winds" and the "History of Life and Death" include "particular topics" for inquiry, histories bearing on these, observations, and provisional canons (*canones mobiles*) or conclusions.

In the "History of Winds," Bacon undertakes the naming specifically and inquiry into the nature of many types of winds. He includes the winds named according to the points of the compass; general winds, regular winds, frequent winds, free winds—which blow from every quarter of the heavens; vehement winds, gentle, steady, variable, hot, cold, moist, dry; winds from the sky, from the earth, in the region of the air; from compressions, percussions, and repercussions of air; prodigious winds, whirlwinds, hurricanes; subterranean winds, vaporous winds in mines, sulphurous winds from volcanoes; factors which enter into the making of winds—more than concomitants and less than efficients; the limits of winds in altitude, extension, and duration; what succeeds winds —rains or showers; the motions of winds in addition to those which are upward, downward, sideways, and of compression; motion of undulation, of conflict, and of organs and man-made machines; strength and power of winds on currents of water, in bringing locusts and blights, in purifying or contaminating the air, in communicating sounds, and the like; prognostics of wind according to skies, waters, instinct of animals; and, finally, the imitations of winds in natural or artificial things (*Works,* III, 217-24; IX, 382-90).

Such are the topics for inquiry listed by Bacon within a history of winds. He chooses, he tells us, to deal with the subject partly because of the part winds play in the lives of men. Winds, while they do not always work to man's benefit, do enable him to carry on his commerce over the seas; they drive his mills; they purify his air. Yet they have always been regarded as a mystery. To dispel this ignorance by inductive investigation and to apply a knowledge through natural causes of winds to agriculture, navigation, commerce, and the like, is the design of an inquiry of which the present history represents an early stage.

There can be nothing but regret that Bacon has neither the time nor other means at his disposal to obtain answers to the questions which he puts, like a lawyer—to use his own expression—to nature. He is forced to turn from what he calls the books of nature itself to the writings of other men for historical data. His "history" is inevitably literary. Neither its detailed items nor its general observations and provisional canons which are based upon these need detain us here. Nor shall we linger over his next history, which concerns "Life and Death," a subject which, along with the prevention and the cure of disease, he accounts a major division of medicine. He takes great pains with the assembling of the content of this second work; and occasionally he is able to rely on his own observations; but mainly he depends on the writings of others for stories and legendary examples of longevity and the circumstances, such as birth, diet, clothing, anointing, passions, and sundry other things, which are alleged to be attendant upon shorter and longer spans of life.

Several of the sources of these two histories are obviously the commonly accepted literary repositories of the lore of natural history. Not a few of the others are doubtless beyond the discovery of the most ardent and meticulous searcher. To the *Historia ventorum,* the writings of Aristotle, Pliny, and Acosta contribute in large measure. Much of the historical part of the *Historia vitae et mortis* is garnered from the works of Aristotle, Pliny, Egnatius, Marsilius Ficinus, and Valerius Maximus.

Another work which Bacon leaves in representation of the third part of the Instauration is the *Sylva sylvarum,* published by Rawley in 1627, following the author's death. This collection of material is the result of a feverish attempt on Bacon's part to collect against time data on as many as possible of the topics listed within the catalogue of 1620. Rawley tells us in the epistle "To the Reader," "I have heard his lordship often say, that if he should have served the glory of his own name, he had been better not to have published this Natural History: for it may seem an indigested heap of particulars, and cannot have that lustre which books cast into methods have; but that he resolved to prefer the good of men, and that which might best secure it, before anything that might have relation to himself. And he knew well that there was no other way open to unloose men's minds, being bound and, as it were, maleficiate by the charms of deceiving notions and theories, and thereby made impotent for generation of works, but only nowhere to depart from the sense and clear experience; but to keep close to it, especially in the beginning: besides, this Natural History was a debt of his, being designed and set down for a third part of the Instauration."

The *Sylva sylvarum* ("Forest of Materials") contains a thousand paragraphs of observations and experiments. Its materials are collected but hardly ordered. Its content is of wide range and includes such subjects as air, flame, water, gravity, flight, chemical constituents of bodies, germination, growth, ripening, putrefaction, parts and functions of animals, insects and vegetables, soils, fruits, trees, vines, foods, assimilations, diets, disease, medical treatments, mineral waters, medical herbs, sounds and tones in production and transmission, vision, colors, luminosity, and so on.

The work, while it undoubtedly contains some observations made by Bacon himself, abounds in statements accepted on the spoken or written reports of others. It is "bookish" throughout. A very large portion of it is taken from such sources as Aristotle's *De mirabilibus* (spurious) and *Problems* (perhaps spurious), Cardan's *De subtilitate* and *De rerum varietate,* Pliny's *Natural History,* Porta's *Natural Magic,* Scaliger's *Exercitationes adversus Cardanum,* and Sandys' *Travels.* So feverish is Bacon's haste to assemble the contents of this work that Ellis, who has traced much of the author's historical material back to its origins, has found it fitting to observe that in paragraphs 701–783 of the collection one can trace the route taken by Sandys—so literally does Bacon use his sources—in his travels between Lemnos and Vesuvius (*Works,* IV, 155; V, 7–51)!

The *Sylva sylvarum* is the work of a man failing in strength, lacking assistants, and pressed by time, who in desperation strives to prepare something in representation of a part of a scheme for knowledge which he hopes may through his efforts be given means for survival. The document, needless to say, does not meet the requirements for natural history which are set down in the *Parasceve.* None of his histories does. Yet, a generation after Bacon's death his preliminary attempts to compile data according to his own stipulations arouse others to succeed where he fails. Historians of nature with time and means at their disposal are able to perform in co-operation what Bacon by himself is not able to do. Bacon becomes their prophet, and his works the symbol of a new science. The "Catalogue of Particular Histories" attached to the *Parasceve* furnishes subjects for inquiry by members of the Royal Society and others who investigate the constitution of things from minerals to human faculties by means of a "historical" method. Sprat, in his official *History of the Royal Society,* is able to say that in the works of Bacon "are everywhere scattered, the best Arguments that can be produc'd for the defence of experimental Philosophy; and the best Directions that are needful to promote it..... If my Desires could have prevail'd .... there should have been no other Preface to the *History* of the *Royal Society,* but some of his Writings." And Cowley in his salutation to this same society significantly climaxes his verses with this reference to its recognized prophet:

> *Bacon* like *Moses,* led us forth at last,
> The barren Wilderness he past,
> Did on the very Border stand
> Of the blest promis'd Land,
> And, from the Mountain Top of his exalted Wit,
> Saw it himself, and shew'd us it.
> But Life did never to one Man allow
> Time to Discover Worlds, and Conquer too.

CHAPTER XXIV

LADDER OF THE INTELLECT: FORERUNNERS OF THE NEW PHILOSOPHY: THE NEW METAPHYSICS

OF THE fourth part of Bacon's Great Instauration nothing survives beyond (*a*) an announcement which precedes the *Novum organum* proper, (*b*) scattered references to its character and range in the *Novum organum* and the *Historia naturalis et experimentalis,* and (*c*) an introductory fragment called *Scala intellectus sive filum labyrinthi* ("Ladder of the Understanding or Thread of the Labyrinth"). The argument of this fragment runs as follows: It would be difficult to pass censure on those who are satisfied that nothing is known, were they to accept the propositions that science is knowledge through causes; that in science the understanding rises continuously by sequence and concatenation to the heights, as it were, of nature; and that therefore the knowledge of a particular thing is not properly complete without an accurate comprehension of the whole of nature. The skeptics refuse, however, to argue on these grounds. Rather they deprive the senses of their status, introduce a theoretical distinction between the true and the probable, turn discovery into an exercise of wit and disputation, and, finally, cut the sinews of human discovery.

Not that we are in complete disagreement with the skeptics; indeed, we are one with them in their refusal to accept the competency of the unaided senses and intellect to know things. But while they contend that nothing can be truly known, we on the other hand maintain that nothing can be truly known by the methods which traditional investigators have employed. The skeptics assert the utter incompetency of the human intellect; we ascribe to it a limited competency. They discount the senses completely; we, with a new method of inquiry, undertake to control and correct the errors of both sense and intellect. They, having decided that the question of knowing has been disposed of once and for all, like a die that has been cast, betake themselves to the unimpeded and pleasant ramblings of wit; we, because of our belief in knowledge, enter a difficult and remote province which we pray may bring happiness and good fortune to mankind.

The beginnings of the paths to knowledge we delineated in the second book. And, having entered upon these, we proceeded in the third book to investigate the phenomena of the universe and history. There we began to penetrate and traverse the forests of nature, made dark and intricate by the endless variety of experiments as by foliage and enveloped by the subtlety of observations as by thickets and thorns. And now, having emerged from the woods to the foot of the mountains, so to speak, we are about to undertake what is more open and yet more difficult travel. For we are to proceed without deviation from the particulars of history by a new and steadfast course—untried as it is—to universals. The old way of tradition is level and easy at the entrance; but it leads the traveler to broken and impassable places. The new course is arduous in the beginning; but it ends on level ground. The wayfarer who, following the old road, undertakes to ascend to knowledge by way of settled principles in the sciences will fail to reach his destination. But the traveler who, remaining steadfast to the second way, holds his judgment in check and is content to climb step by step, to attain one summit, then another, and yet others in succession, will arrive in due time at the heights of nature. Here his station will be serene, his prospect of things most fair, and his descent to all practical arts easy, as along a gentle slope.

We are ready with this warning, then, to undertake our first ascent in knowledge. In the second book we have already set down the precepts of the true and legitimate investigation of things. Here we shall expose and describe examples of knowledge reached through its use and in the manner which we think most agreeable to truth (*Works,* V, 177–81).

The "examples" of which Bacon speaks in the *Scala intellectus* are also mentioned in the first book of the *Novum organum* and there described as "particulars digested and set in order (which belong partly to the Second, but much more to the Fourth division of our Instauration) . . . . not merely the expectation of something, but the thing itself." And in the "Plan of the Work" which precedes the *Novum organum* they are said to be "actual types and models, which would set before our eyes the entire process of the mind and the continuous art and order of discovery in certain subjects, and these varied and prominent" (*Works,* I, 225, 303, 310–11; 323; VIII, 51, 129, 136, 148).

The author fails, however, to expose and describe in his extant works any examples of the "types and models" which are to constitute the fourth part of his Instauration. The reason for this is clear. These are resultant upon the operation of the inductive method on materials provided by natural history; and the fact is, the author has no adequate natural history collected and no method completed.

Yet, while Bacon is unable to delineate "models" of inductive knowledge, he does indicate the breadth of the subject matter in which they ultimately are to be found. Aphorism CXXVII of his first book of the *Novum organum* contains the following statement: "Some one will raise the doubt, rather than the objection, whether we speak of reaching conclusions by our method not only in natural philosophy but in the other sciences, Logic, Ethics, Politics, as well. Now we certainly understand that what we have had to say refers to all the sciences. And just as the common logic which governs things by means of the Syllogism extends not only to the natural sciences but to all, so ours also which proceeds by Induction, embraces everything. For we prepare history and Tables of Discovery concerning Anger, Fear, Shame, and the like; and also concerning Political Precedents; and concerning the mental operations of Memory, Composition and Division, Judgment, and the rest, not less than Heat and Cold, or Light, or Vegetation, or the Like."

Again, in the "Rule of the Present History" within the *Historia naturalis et experimentalis* the author makes further reference to the range of subjects which are to be brought within the jurisdiction of the new induction. "The present history," he there says, "not only makes good the Third Part of the Instauration but in turn is a preparation of no small value for the Fourth by reason of the titles from the Alphabet, and the Topics." The "Topics" to which he refers on this occasion includes types of winds and their causes; and these clearly fall within physics. The "Alphabet of Nature," we learn from the second paragraph of the "Rule," includes schematisms of matter, simple motions, and sums of motion, which also belong to physics. It includes also measures of motion, which fall within an appendix to physics, and Transcendentals which belong to first philosophy. It may be concluded, therefore, that it is Bacon's intention to bring the subject matter of his three sciences of natures and bodies, first philosophy, physics, and metaphysics under the jurisdiction of one inductive method (*Works*, I, 333; II, 257, 281-84, 289-90; III, 211, 213, 308; VIII, 159, 475, 498-500, 505-6; IX, 375, 377, 476).

So much for the available account of the fourth part of the Instauration. We learn from a portion of a letter of Bacon's to Fulgentius which respects the several divisions of the Instauration that another fragment, *Prodromi sive anticipationes philosophiae secundae* ("Forerunners or Anticipations of the New Philosophy"), constitutes an introduction to the fifth part. The argument of this piece is simple. That legislator, says the author, was a patriotic and prudent man who, when asked whether he had given the best laws to the citizens, replied, "The best they were able to bear." In the kingdom of learning, leaving aside mere contemplation—which is no better than dreaming unless it issues in operation—there may be said to be two sorts of conclusion, one greater and not always possible, one lesser and often practicable. Of these two we must not scorn the lesser, which lies at hand, while we contend for the greater, which remains remote. The greater is to be attained through the application of our method of interpretation. The other follows from the application of ordinary reason to the experimental study of nature; and, beyond a doubt, if any man of mature mind, who does not proceed according to the manner of our interpretation, is yet willing and able to put away his Idols or false fantasies and to resolve anew on abiding attentively, diligently, and freely among the reckonings and truths of natural history—that man, whoever he may be, will, by his own native powers and with his own anticipations, penetrate more deeply into nature than he ever could by reading all sorts of authors or engaging constantly in abstract meditation or disputation. The reflections on things which can be gathered in this manner are many and useful. It will be well to leave such scattered about and not to bind them together methodically. This is a better plan for pubescent knowledge, where the object is not to constitute an organized body of science but to institute an unimpeded inquiry into relatively isolated separate things (*Works,* V, 182–84).

The fifth part, then, is to contain such anticipations or forerunners of the new philosophy as are based on mere experiment without the application of the new induction. It is, Bacon tells us in the "Plan" which precedes the *Novum organum,* "for temporary use only, until the rest are completed; and is rendered as interest until the principal may be had. For we do not make so blindly for our object as to neglect anything useful that may turn up in the way. And therefore we make up this fifth part of the work out of such things as we have ourselves discovered, proved, or added—this not according to the methods and rules of interpretation, but by that use of the intellect to which others in investigation and discovery are accustomed to adhere..... They will serve for wayside inns in which the mind may rest for a while on its journey to more certain things. Nevertheless we wish it to be understood in the meantime (because they are not discovered and proved by the true form of interpretation) we do not pretend to be bound by them. Nor indeed need anyone be alarmed at such suspension of judgment in the teaching which asserts not simply that nothing can be known, but that nothing can be known except in a certain order and method; and yet establishes provisionally certain degrees of certitude for use and alleviation until the mind shall rest in an explanation of causes" (*Works,* I, 226; VIII, 51–52).

The inclusion by Bacon of this second-best fifth part within a scheme for learning which begins with a refutation of past philosophies and methods and is to end with a body of truth established by true induction has occasioned comment. Spedding, for instance, considers the fifth part, and the first part as well, extraneous to the Instauration. He contends that the author's design for the Instauration is announced in the *Temporis partus masculus,* in which it is said to consist of three books concerning the interpretation of nature, namely, (1) The Refinement and Direction of the Intellect; (2) The Light of Nature, or Method of Interpretation; and (3) Nature Illuminated, or the Truth of Things. He conjectures that the first and the third divisions of the Instauration are added by Bacon some time after the writing of this piece in order to render possible the inclusion within his scheme of miscellaneous writings which would otherwise fall without the original design.

This view is open to great objection. To begin with, Bacon does not include his many miscellaneous writings within his Instauration. That he does not intend to do so is clear from his letter written one year before his death to Fulgentius in which he lists the pieces which fall within the several divisions. Again, the *Temporis partus masculus* is a very early work. Even Spedding, who, erroneously as we believe, is inclined to assign the main portion of it to a middle period somewhere about 1608, admits that the part which contains the threefold partition, as above, is one of the author's earliest philosophical statements. And if we cannot take a piece like the *Valerius Terminus,* for instance, as a statement of Bacon's mature description of method, there seems but little justice in holding the author to a relatively juvenile utterance respecting a design which takes final shape as the Great Instauration announced in 1620.

Actually, of course, Bacon's sixfold scheme is mentioned in the *Delineatio*, a work written about 1607 when very few of the philosophical pieces have been written. In this document the nature of the fifth part is definitely indicated. After stating there that "the better and more perfect use of reason" is to be set forth in the second of six parts, the author goes on to say, "To the Interpretation of Nature we have assigned three books, the third, the fourth and the sixth; since the fifth which consists in Anticipations following the ordinary use of reason is to be taken as temporary, and later when its direction and verification by the legitimate use of reason shall have begun it is transferred and enters the sixth" (*Works*, V, 174–75; VII, 11, 16, 41).

So far from being a doubtful procedure, the author's inclusion of the fifth part within the design for the reform of the sciences seems both prudent and necessary. Bacon, it must be borne in mind, has rejected from his scheme of induction all conclusions which have been or shall be reached through the use of other methods. Yet he cannot hope that all fields of science and operation can be brought immediately, or indeed for a long time, within the scope of that knowledge of nature which is begun in natural history and then pursued through a most rigorous induction to comprehensive metaphysics. Meanwhile the arts must be plied and nature used for the service of mankind. The methods of tradition are, he believes, futile. The alternative left consists in more or less empirical observation and experiment. These must do, since nothing better is to be had, until the Instauration itself becomes operative.

Thanks to Bacon's habitual repetition of descriptive phrases, we are not left in the dark concerning the nature of this intermediate kind of knowledge nor are we without directions for its use. It is to consist of Learned Experience. In the "Plan of the Work" he tells us that "The Fifth Part is for temporary use only, until the rest are completed; and is rendered as interest until the principal may be had (*tamquam foenus redditur, usque dum sors haberi possit*)." In the *Novum organum* he cautions against a premature turning-aside from experiment of natural history for the preparation of tables, and yet he advises, "if there be any one more apt and prepared for mechanical pursuits, and sagacious in hunting out works (*sagax ad venanda opera*) by mere intercourse with experiments, we commit and bequeath to him that industry, that he gather from our history and tables many things as by the way, and apply them to works, and receive them as interest for a time until the principal may be had (*ac veluti foenus recipiat ad tempus, donec sors haberi possit*)." This procedure he alternately calls "Learned Experience," "a kind of Sagacity" and "borrowing the name from fable"—the Hunt of Pan (*pro Sagacitate quadam; unde etiam eam Venationem Panis—hoc nomen ex fabula mutuati—quandoque appellemus*). He describes it as "a thing more ingenious and sagacious than it is philosophic (*magis ingeniosa quaedam res .... et sagax, quam philosophica*)" (*Works*, I, 226, 311, 318, 321-23; II, 298, 371; VIII, 51, 137, 143, 147-49, 513; IX, 71-72).

In the early *Advancement of Learning* the author tells us that he purposes to "propound" scientific invention or discovery in "two parts; whereof the one I term *Experientia literata*, and the other *Interpretatio Naturae:* the former being but a degree and rudiment of the latter. But I will not dwell too long, nor speak too great upon a promise." Later in the *Phaenomena universi* he speaks of the most worthy design of bringing men into a close association with things through Learned Experience. In the *Redargutio philosophiarum* also he mentions *literata experientia* along with a true method of interpreting nature (*ratio naturam sincere interpretandi*); and in the late *De augmentis* he divides the art of discovery into "Learned Experience" and the "New Organon," contrasts the two, and proceeds to give an exposition of the former. The New Organon, he says, is the most important part of the Instauration; yet the other method, Learned Experience, is not to be despised. It is a means of "bringing down as from heaven a shower of inventions at once useful and new. For though the rational way by the Organon gives assurance of greater things in the distance, yet this sagacity by Learned Experience will in the meantime yield the human race and scatter upon them (like largess thrown upon the ancients) many inventions which are near at hand."

Learned Experience is not a mere groping in the dark; it is a kind of wisdom, even if it is not lighted by a true scientific method. It is the following of a degree of direction in experimenting, as if the searcher, unsure of his way and direction, were to be led by the hand of another. As a method of investigation it proceeds by way of the Variation of Experiment, the Production, the Translation, the Inversion, the Compulsion, the Application, the Coupling, and the Chances of Experiment (*Works*, II, 362, 370-72; VI, 268; VII, 78, 229; IX, 64, 71-72).

Variation of Experiment has regard to the matter, the efficient, and the quantity under investigation. An example of variation in matter is seen in the attempt to make paper—in whose manufacture linen has been previously used—from silks, wools, cotton, skins, and hair. To take another example, grafting is common in fruit trees, and the query occurs: Should it not be tried on wild trees, and on flowers generally, and through inserting seeds in roots?

An instance of the variation of the efficient is the investigation, after observation that the heat of the rays of the sun is intensified by burning glasses, whether the rays from the moon can be concentrated by similar means to the production of any degree of heat. Again, amber when rubbed becomes warm and attracts straw. Will it have this efficacy when warmed by fire?

Variation in quantity should be treated with great care. It is easy to believe that an increase in matter or a causal agent will increase proportionately an effect which is sought. Yet this is not so. For example, if a leaden ball of a pound weight when dropped from a certain height reaches the ground in, say, ten seconds, it does not follow that a ball of double this weight will fall in half the time.

Production of Experiment is twofold, including as it does repetition when the experiment is done again and extension when the experiment is tried on something which is more complex than the original object. An instance of the former is a proposed experiment on spirit of wine. If the spirit is originally made by distillation and the distillation is repeated, will the final spirit be doubly stronger than the original distillation? An example of the latter is this: The magnet attracts a solid piece of iron; will it when immersed in a dissolution of iron attract the iron and so obtain a coating of iron?

Translation of Experiment is possible in three ways: from nature or chance into art, from one art or practice into another, and from one part of an art into a different part of the same art. Of translation from nature into art innumerable examples present themselves. Distilling, for example, may have sprung from observing either the dew or the adhering of drops of boiling water to the lid of a vessel. The production of artificial rainbows follows easily from the observation of the formation of the natural rainbow by a dewy cloud. The adage that one cluster of grapes ripens faster when it lies by the side of another has suggested to the cidermaker the practice of leaving apples in heaps. Most of the arts have sprung from such simple observations of nature's operations as these.

Men, therefore, who would invent useful things "ought to observe attentively, minutely, and systematically natural works and operations one by one, and be perpetually and earnestly considering which of them may be transferred to the arts. For nature is the mirror of art."

The Translation of Experiment from one art to another or from one part of an art to another part is of no less importance; for by this "the arts can mutually cherish and as it were kindle one another by mingling rays." The practice of sealing upon wax, cements, and lead is ancient; and out of it has come the modern art of printing. Why within the art of medicine, for instance, could not experiments relating to the curing of diseases be applied to the preservation of health and the prolongation of life? Why, again, since spectacles have been invented for the improving of weak sight, cannot some instrument be devised to aid ears that are dull of hearing? In artificial freezing, salt has been found to have great power of condensation. Why can its efficacy not be tested for the condensation of metals?

Inversion of Experiment is the trial of the contrary of that which has been established by the original experiment. Heat, for instance, is increased by burning glasses; is cold also? The rays of the sun are collected on black and reflected from white. Are its shadows collected on white and lost on black?

Compulsion of Experiment is the extension of an experiment to annihilate a power originally made manifest by the experiment. The magnet attracts iron. Suppose then we "work" the magnet until it can attract no more; or try to discover a medium through which it can no longer attract iron, using oil, gum, ignited coal, and other things hitherto untried. Magnifying glasses enable one to see minute objects. Diminish the size of objects under experiment until they become so small that glasses cannot reveal their structures to the eye. Examples of Compulsion of Experiment usually fall, however, outside learned experience; for they are likely to involve a knowledge of general axioms. Generally they require for their examination that negation or exclusion which throws light on the discovery of forms. They are, therefore, generally to be referred to the treatment of causes and axioms which falls within the New Organon.

Application of Experiment is nothing more than the ingenious translation of one experiment to another. For example, since silver has less weight and more dimension than gold, and wine than water, the experiment of examining the bulks and weights of these substances may lead to the discovery of the amount of silver which, in an instance, has been mixed with gold or the amount of water which has been added to wine.

Coupling of Experiment is the making of a series of applications which, while relatively incapable singly, are effectual through conjunction. To have late roses or fruit, for example, one can either pluck the earlier buds or not uncover the roots until late in the spring; but the end is most successfully achieved if both courses of action are conjoined. Again, either ice or niter has some power of refrigeration; the two are much more effective when mixed. The caution should be given, however, that in the Coupling of Experiment within learned experience, where a knowledge of axioms is wanting, care must be exercised lest there be a uniting of things which act in contrary ways.

The Chances of Experiment remain for consideration. In these instances we have a kind of trial which is irrational, so to speak, "mad." For here one experiment is conducted not because another suggests it but simply because it has never been tried. In this case the investigator, aware that the great and important things of nature generally lie away from the common roads and beaten paths, leaves no stone unturned in his path. He is not disheartened if his experiments disprove the discovery he would make, for he knows that while a successful experiment is more agreeable, an unsuccessful one can be more instructive. He is prepared to wait for results because he is not pursuing experiments which enable him to pluck the fruit of immediate practice but those which furnish permanent light (*Works,* II, 372–85; IX, 72–83).

Of the sixth, and final, part of the Great Instauration no work of the author, not even a fragment, is given over to an exposition. Its character is indicated only by occasional references throughout his writings. Its design is stated briefly in the "Plan of the Work" in the following words: "The sixth part of our work, to which the other parts are subservient and ministrant, discloses and sets forth a philosophy which is raised and established by a legitimate, pure, and severe method, such as we have previously exhibited and provided. But truthfully speaking to complete and conclude this last part is a thing beyond both our powers and our expectation. We have made (we hope) no mean beginning. The fortunes of the human race will provide the issue—and of such a kind, it may be, as men in the present state of their affairs and of mind cannot easily comprehend or estimate. For the matter under discussion is no mere felicity of speculation, but in truth the affairs and the fortunes of humanity, and all power of operation. Man, the servant and interpreter of nature, does and understands as much as he has observed of nature's order.... more than this he neither knows nor can perform. For no powers can loose or break the chain of causes; nor is nature conquered except by obedience. And so these twin designs, human Knowledge and human Power actually meet in the same thing; and the failure of works arises from ignorance of causes.... God forbid then that we should publish a dream of our imagination as a model of the world; but rather may he benignantly grant us to write a revelation (*apocalypsim*) and true vision of the footsteps and marks of the Creator upon his creatures" (*Works*, I, 226-27; VIII, 52-53).

The reason for Bacon's failure to describe the sixth part, except in the barest of outlines, is obvious. No account of this part can be given while the natural histories of the third part, which are to furnish the materials of knowledge, remain uncollected; while the second part, which is to provide the method of interpretation, remains far from complete; and while the fourth part, which is to furnish exemplary "Tables of Discovery" in varied fields of investigation, must remain completely barren.

We gather from those scattered references which have come under our observation that the final part of the Great Instauration consists in a unified knowledge, inductively discovered, of God, nature, and man. It is designed to be a thoroughly materialistic philosophy, which construes nature, including man, in terms of the virtues, structures, and motions of body. It does not attempt to deal with that part of man which is made in the Divine Image, or with the nature, being, and will of God. These subjects it consigns to revealed theology, while it includes within its orbit only so much of God's power and skill as is made manifest in his creatures.

The end of this philosophy is knowledge in operation for the good and happiness of mankind and the relief of his present estate. So much of it as the author has been able to achieve is, he believes, a "planting for future generations and the Immortal God." It will establish in the human intellect "a holy temple after the model of the world." It will contain the Ideas of the Divine Mind, that is to say, not the thoughts of God as a thinking being—these belong to faith—but "the true seals (or signet

—*signacula*) of the Creator upon creatures, impressed on and determined in matter by real and exquisite lines." It will discover those universal natures from whose combinations, even as a language is composed of letters, all things in the created universe, which bear the Creator's stamp, are composed (*Works,* I, 326, 330-31; III, 186; VIII, 151, 156; IX, 356).

The method through which this philosophy is achieved is a directive logic designed to guide the human mind from its first perception of things onward. Knowledge under the control of this logic, while observational, is never purely empirical in character. From the beginning, induction makes provision for a conjunction between sense and understanding, between the experimental and the rational. Simple observation of particulars is a "groping," which hinders men rather than informs them. Empiricists are like ants which merely amass; rationalists are as spiders which spin light cobwebs. The inductive scientist, like the bee, gathers, digests, and fashions by faculties, fitted for knowing, the materials collected from things. Particulars perceived by the senses are transformed in his memory and set by his understanding in the due and proper order of knowledge.

Science proceeds from natural history through physics to metaphysics, drawing much of its initial strength from first, or primary, philosophy. Metaphysics is physics made general. At every stage of discovery procedure is methodically controlled. In natural history the data, even during their collection, are being prepared for Tables of Discovery. Scientific experience is thus both "ordered and digested" from the beginning. All along the way inquiry proceeds according to Topics, or questions put to nature according to Prenotions; and throughout its course, even from the beginning, there is a delimitation of the infinity of particulars by classification. Investigation brings under universals more and more particulars, ascends to higher and higher generalities of axiom, until finally it arrives at the apex of knowledge, the summary law of nature, the Great Form or Fabric of the Universe, the "first cause" within nature (*Works,* I, 289, 306; VIII, 114-15, 131-32).

For the principles of nature may be regarded as laws, as forms, or as causes. The form is the law of nature's operation. What in contemplation is the form is in operation the cause. Knowledge moves from those lesser and more restricted laws of operation which are described in physics to the most general and universally prevalent laws of things, even up to the summary law of nature, which marks the final stage of metaphysics. And, since science is knowledge through causes, inquiry passes from the lesser causes to the first cause within nature.

In the "Rule" of his "Natural and Experimental History" Bacon tells us that this history is no mean preparation for the sixth part of his Instauration because of the speculations and major observations; and explains that these speculations are to be regarded "as rudiments of interpretations concerning causes." The rudimentary principles of the third part are to become a full doctrine of causes in the sixth. The philosophy of nature begins with the discovery of causes, goes on to discover the causes of causes, and finally ends with the first cause within nature—for to look for a first cause beyond the chain of natural causes is to abandon the principle of causation and to fly from solid knowledge into a realm of fantasy. Since natural causation is a chain which must not be loosed or broken in the ascent from the least to the greatest axiom and since scientific knowledge culminates in one most general principle, it follows, according to Bacon, that the final and real understanding of each particular thing is to be attainable only through a knowledge of the whole of nature (*Works,* III, 213; IX, 377).

CHAPTER XXV

BACON'S INFLUENCE

THE framework of a philosophy which remains in Bacon's extant writings appears unimpressive in comparison with the great designs of his Instauration. Yet the fact remains that when regarded as a performance in his own century, what the author has done toward changing the course of knowledge is indeed great; and when considered as an influence upon the future of British thought in particular and of European thought in general, the importance of his work can hardly be overestimated.

Bacon's right to be called a significant thinker has been the subject of an intermittent controversy which is perhaps without parallel in the history of learned discussion and one into which, it must be admitted, both national and racial prejudices have entered. Admirers would make him —what no one man could possibly be—the founder of modern science and the inventor of experimental induction. Detractors have called him an exponent of feeble thoughts and the declaimer in resourceful language of philosophical commonplaces. Many have assessed his opinions without reading what he has had to say. His reputation has often been made to rest solely upon his partial statement of a method of experimental investigation in the *Novum organum,* while his multiple projects for the reform of learning and systematic philosophy have been forgotten. He has suffered through comparison with Copernicus, Galileo, and Gilbert—discoverers with whom he has little in common—and been condemned as a philosopher because he was not a mathematician. He has been called an empiricist because he rejected theoretical constructions and did not dilate upon hypothesis or enthrone a dialectical reason. He has been assigned an inferior status by many who find the main source of "modern thought" in the rationalism of Descartes, Spinoza, and Leibniz.

This is not the time or the occasion to enter into the details of the several controversies from which this disagreement has issued. We must be content merely to indicate the bearing which our interpretation of the works of Bacon has upon them by amplifying slightly the claim which we made at the beginning of the present study, namely, that our author set much of human knowledge on a new way by (1) freeing science from learning and the practices and privileges of the learned; (2) separating completely truth which is humanly discoverable from the dogmas of revealed theology; and (3) propounding a philosophy which is to be achieved by (*a*) a new sort of scientific organon, (*b*) a "modern" interpretation of nature, and (*c*) the identification of metaphysics with a generalized natural science based on natural history. These three we shall consider briefly in turn.

The part played by Bacon in changing the course of knowledge is to be seen most readily in the first instance, the tributes of Continental thinkers like Mersenne, Descartes, and Leibniz notwithstanding, in the specific effects of his writing on his own countrymen from a quarter of a century after his death onward, and then in the more general effects which become evident in later philosophy throughout the Western world.

Bacon's reputation underwent a great increase in England some score of years following his death. Shortly after the middle of the century the "Advancement of Learning" became a major crusade. "Experimental philosophy," with varying interpretations—and sometimes with no interpretation at all—of its implications and consequences, was accepted by a legion as the only "real" and "solid" learning. Bacon was greeted as the "secretary of nature," hailed as the "modern Aristotle," and praised as the "restorer of physics" and, therefore, as the "architect" of future philosophy. Virtuosi quoted his works by page, paragraph, sentence, and phrase; and the topics which he had listed for investigation became prescriptions for marking the area and the boundaries of human knowledge. By the beginning of the third quarter of the century, so considerable had his authority become in matters of experimental truth-seeking that he was not unjustly dubbed by his opponents a "dictator" of philosophy.

In an estimation of Bacon's actual achievement it should not be assumed, of course, that in England, where an author could openly make announcement of attacks upon the ancients with impunity, while Bruno was on trial for a like cause on the Continent, religious reform had brought the emancipation of science from the domination of the "learned," especially of learned theologians. Nor should it be forgotten that the revival of pagan authors at the Renaissance had resulted in an authoritarianism imposed by ancient texts. Bacon's struggle for the reform of knowledge was waged in a country whose science was identified with learning. Learned men, mainly theologians, dominated and directed colleges and universities. Those who followed learning possessed the rights, privileges, and prerogatives which membership in ecclesiastical and other royal foundations conferred. The universities recognized the liberal arts and the two professions of theology and medicine. Professors and tutors edited texts, both secular and religious, of accepted authors. Medicine was literary and sometimes practiced as an avocation by poets, divines, rhetoricians, antiquaries. Ability to quote such authors as Hippocrates, Dioscorides, and Galen on the nature and care of diseases was enough to make a man a physician, to fit him for membership in the Royal College, and to equip him for the writing of acceptable discourses on the character and cure of diseases.

To Bacon belongs in large measure credit for implementing the dissociation of British science from magisterial learning. He undertook this in the first instance by attacking the universities. This attack, conceived during his youthful sojourn at Cambridge, was never lessened or abated even to the day when the rebellious student had become Lord Chancellor of England. It was addressed to none other than the sovereign head of the church and the state and was repeatedly pressed without hesitancy and without compromise. It was undertaken on the assumption that the strongholds of learning could not be reduced by mere satire, however subtle, or by intellectual buffoonery, however brilliant. The inhabitants therein had shown marked capacity to resist the effects of these weapons. It included a denunciation of the prevailing ends of education, the vehicles of learning, the exercises of colleges, and the administration of universities. And it made insistent and specific demands for the immediate provision of a new sort of foundation in which only natural science and the "mechanical" arts might be given place.

This attack on learned practice and opinion was not conceived in a mere attitude of doubt, and it was not resultant upon any dramatic discovery by its author or dependent upon any specific or general mathematical, astronomical, or physiological theory. It was positive and—in its own way—complete in character. It began with a matter-of-fact account of the barren places of knowledge. Then it overran with assurance the accepted boundaries and divisions of investigation. Next, it overruled the authority and disallowed the method exercised in each of the several internal jurisdictions within the realm of human knowledge. And, finally, it undertook to provide a new rule for the attainment of new ends. It was designed to force, once and for all, a definite parting of the ways between philosophical learning, with its maxims, deductive demonstration, ontology, and meditation, on the one hand, and, on the other, experimental philosophy, with its inductive observation of facts and things, its assignment of primacy to natural history, its distrust of logical principles, its fruition in useful inventions and great mechanical works, and its search from the beginning to the end for the processes, schematisms, and laws of operation in matter.

The attack was inordinately successful; indeed, it was more than anyone without the enthusiasm of a Bacon could have expected or have prophesied. The author called the new scheme for learning "the birth of time." Certainly the plea for the reform of knowledge fell some twenty years after his death on very willing ears. Natural philosophy by then not only found the universities inadequate but it left them. In an "experimental" role it flourished outside them; and it did not return until the universities had modified their earlier attitude to meet its terms. When it came back, it brought a new vocabulary of learning, new methods of thinking, new educational emphases, and, not least in importance for the future of knowledge, many exponents who thought it possible to base a complete philosophy on the results of natural history.

Bacon had called on all and sundry, whether learned or unlearned, to pursue observational and experimental investigation. At his bidding, data of earth, air, sea, and sky were recorded in natural histories; and chemists' shops and kitchens became improvised laboratories. The "invisible" or "philosophical college," which shortly after its inception became the Royal Society, was organized to perform what the universities would not do. Other groups of chemists, physicists, and physicians were formed to carry on experiments. A new "liberty" and "latitude" in the pursuit of "real" and "solid" learning stirred the imaginations of many. Exponents of educational theory and practice, taking the *New Atlantis* as a model, organized or designed *gymnasia mechanica* in which technical training was to supplant traditional book learning. By these revolutionaries skill in operation, in the tilling of fertile soil, in the making of tools, carriages, artillery, in spinning, printing, and the like was considered a more fitting achievement in education than a knowledge of ancient—and therefore useless—languages and the re-editing of outworn and outmoded texts. So seriously were their views entertained that during the Cromwellian regime not a few Reformers hoped to have the universities either closed or turned into technical schools and a many-sided controversy—which has never abated since—was introduced into educational theory, both within and without the universities, over the relative merits of "classical" study, on the one hand, and "technical" training, on the other.

Bacon had defined the ends of education in terms of high utility, meaning thereby the happiness and the relief of mankind. Consideration of means for the public good supplanted in the minds of his disciples the contemplation of pure being, and with them knowledge passed from speculation to the historical recording of fact whose culmination was to lie in works and operations. Operative "realism" was set in sharp contrast to the "shadows" and "phantoms" of Plato and Aristotle. This new philosophy, with its simple objectives, was made a model for guidance by many Reformers under Cromwell and Charles. It was espoused by churchmen and acclaimed by humanitarians. Christ, the church's founder, came to be regarded as an experimenter who proved himself not by theories but by works. Nature ceased to be sundered from art and was now construed as the artistic production of God himself.

The effect of the polemic against learning soon became apparent within the universities. By the middle of the century heads of colleges were answering the attack with the claim that the logical and metaphysical works of Aristotle were no longer read in course by undergraduates. The relative importance of libraries and of laboratories became the subject of debate within the universities themselves. Authorities undertook to make adjustments between the respective claims of experimental observation and textual scholarship—even though most of them thought the former could never make a man learned or wise. Formal disputations all but disappeared and were generally acknowledged to be but a "battle of words." An assault on learned terms was maintained with asperity. *Materia prima,* privation, potentiality, and the like were condemned as unintelligible "sound," "trumpery," "rubbish." The Baconians, especially, placed the language of artisans before that of the learned. The Royal Society appointed a committee to prepare a new and exact "philosophical" language through whose use the connotations and denotations of traditional Latin and Greek nomenclatures would be escaped. The result of this action of the Royal Society was the beginning of a traditional use within British philosophical scholarship of plain, simple, and concrete terms in which the resources of a rich, varied, and flexible language have been drawn upon in order to escape both the aridity and obscurity which readily attach themselves to philosophical writing.

Hardly of less moment than his attack on the universities for the future course of knowledge was Bacon's complete separation of a knowledge which includes conceptions and doctrines traceable to revelation from a knowledge reached through the observation of nature and her ways. This separation has led to a rather curious type of reflection upon the author's integrity. The French Encyclopedists have seen beneath it a brand of atheism which paraded under a mask in order to deceive and to escape the wrath of ecclesiastical authorities. And many others have debited the author with similar motives and equal awkwardness in his tactics. Yet the fact is patently obvious to any person who reads Bacon's works fully and consistently that the classification of the sciences on which his philosophical argument rests cannot be entertained without the segregation concerned. This surely is reason good and sufficient for accepting the author's account of the matter at its face value.

Despite his complete emancipation of natural knowledge from the dominant conceptions of traditional theology, the charge of atheism was only on the rarest of occasions leveled against the author. This is the more surprising when we recall that Hobbes was labeled an atheist by his contemporaries, likewise Spinoza, while the theological implications of the doctrines of Descartes were held in increasing suspicion. Bacon had not plunged *more geometrico* into discoursing of God's essence but had founded his distinction between truths discovered by natural faculties and revealed dogmas concerning God's nature on a definite reclassification of the sciences and, with this scheme, the faithful, found it necessary to cope before uttering their anathemas. Few of them, in fact, showed a disposition to undertake the task.

The age of Bacon's writing and initial influence was dominated by theological preoccupations not only on the part of those who wrote under Platonic or Aristotelian influences but on the part, as well, of "moderns" who variously had turned upon tradition and had set themselves up as "novel" investigators of nature and independent thinkers. The Paracelsans, for instance, indulged in mystery-mongering about supernatural influences. Chemists felt it necessary to introduce the Word of God into the interpretations of their experiments. Astrologers mixed the human and the divine in fantastic measure. Alchemists construed their fantastic promises as "miracles" which would break the bonds of nature. Even a thinker like Kepler still could construe the movements of the planets according to the acts of suprahuman intelligences.

Among systematic philosophers Bruno conceived the world as infinite space filled with matter which might be regarded either as things in its extension or as God in its form and movement. He thus undertook to bring into union the doctrines both of God's immanence and of God's transcendence. Descartes and Spinoza identified the only real substance known to philosophy with God. Spinoza equated nature with the Deity, making mind and matter God's attributes, and finding in both *natura naturata* and *natura naturans* the manifestation of the Divine Being. Occasionalists solved the problems of causation, motion, and continuity by the doctrine of the incessant intervention of Providence. Newton construed space as the *sensorium* of God; while Leibniz organized the motions attendant upon the appetitions of monads according to a divinely pre-established harmony and, along with Spinoza, employed the notion of God as the means to achieve unity of explanation.

With all and any of such theological presuppositions as these Bacon would have nothing whatever to do. He asserted that since revelation informs men that God made the world—they could never, as reasonable creatures, argue to a First and noncaused Cause which would lie without the chain of causation in such a way that it would not itself be the effect of any other cause—they can assume that His stamp and signature are to a degree upon it. They can discover these, and no more, through their investigation of nature's forms, processes, and schematisms. There is, nevertheless, nothing of God's nature and essence to be found through a study of the world. There is no divine mind in nature or indeed a rational mind. Nature shows no divine efficiency in its movements or divine form in its structures. It possesses no divine causation, divine motivation, divine appetition, or any attributes of divinity. It is formed matter acting through varieties of local motion inherent within itself and nothing more. Bacon thus repudiates pantheism, theism, immanence, and transcendentalism. God as Being or Essence or Cause is neither immanent within his system of nature nor transcendental to it but lies altogether outside it.

Needless to say, not all Bacon's disciples followed their master to his extreme naturalistic conclusions. Yet the more central implications of his teachings were soon to reveal themselves in far-reaching consequences. Aristotelianism, by the third quarter of the century, had fallen into disrepute. Platonism became either cabalistic or Cartesian and suffered neglect. Among those who discussed the relation between the creation and the Creator the argument from design in nature to the mind and will of Deity supplanted "proof" of an ontological sort, namely, that which was based on the contention that the notion of God is such that the existence of the Being affirmed therein is necessarily involved in the essence which the notion contains. In place of theological Aristotelianism and Platonism many Reformers substituted the simpler dogmas of Holy Writ and demanded of the pious instead of meditation the practice of humanitarianism in the operation of good works for the relief of human misery and for the public good. Certain extremists, having repudiated all human learning and philosophy as heathenish and carnal, took refuge in individually communicated prophecies from the Most High. Theologians and others who believed in the efficacy of systematic learning had occasion for alarm when Enthusiasts went so far as to include all human knowledge under the Pauline term "vain philosophy" and showed a disposition to have the traditional university disciplines removed from the curriculum for training clergy.

Men of less extreme opinions, not a few of them with but little interest in theology, were greatly impressed by the fact that under a new intellectual regime the study of nature could be carried on without considerations of theological consequence. Physics underwent emancipation from the rule of ontology. Experimental investigators became aware of a new freedom. Locke, Bacon's first considerable philosophical disciple, divided all human knowledge into the doctrine of signs, or logic; the calculating of pleasures and pains, or ethics; and physics. Naturalism became established and habilitated as a free philosophy with station, rights, and privileges.

It is not on any specific investigation or discovery either in natural history or in physics that Bacon's importance for succeeding philosophy rests but on his thoroughgoing naturalism. This naturalism includes three factors: first, an organon or method, secondly, an interpretation of nature; and, thirdly, the identification of generalized experimental physics with metaphysics.

More often than not the author's reputation as a philosopher has been made to rest in the degree of adequacy of that inductive method partially described in the *Novum organum,* while his other contributions to thought and learning have been overlooked. This is unfortunate, especially because the estimate of any philosopher of induction is rendered difficult, even precarious, by the obscurity of the whole matter with which he is presumed to deal. If one interprets the content of the division of philosophy which is called "induction" as psychological history in terms of human sensation or animal behavior or as Scholastic discussions of the relation between the particular and the universal, whether under semantic or any other guise, then, it must be admitted, Bacon has but little to contribute. Again, if one considers the function of inductive logic to be the provision of directions for procedure in laboratories, it may be said that Bacon's *Novum organum* is no worse and probably much better than other comparable treatises prepared by philosophers. Certainly Bacon's own directions were seldom employed by those who professed allegiance to him. Actually these directions include all and more than all that is to be found in Mill's five canons, through comparison with which the careless reader is sometimes prone to question their adequacy.

Bacon's *Novum organum* is nevertheless a document of extreme importance in that it marks a turning-point in experimental, as distinct from theoretical, science. It served to impress upon men of the seventeenth century in pursuit of a knowledge of things that some new organon or other, beyond that contained within the Analytics, the Topics, and the Categories of Aristotle, had to be provided. The author's purpose in writing the work was to endeavor to show how one can pass from facts to axioms and also to impress on his contemporaries and future generations that the passage had to be made. Its directions proved to be inadequate, but its effect was more than salutary—just as most of the data of the author's natural histories were badly assembled, although the topics under which they were brought proved to be excellent by way of example and suggestion.

Quite apart from the question of laboratory directions, Bacon's inductive philosophy can hardly be compared with that of Mill and his followers. Mill is concerned with predicting repetition of contiguous phenomena in recurring situations, while Bacon seeks the elements which constitute the system of nature, governed by settled law and moved by identical causes. Mill is an empiricist for whom the universal is but a product of mental association. Bacon is a rationalist and a realist for whom particulars are constituted of universal natures and for whom the science by which they are known is the rational cognition of natures as they really are.

To interpret Bacon properly as a rationalist is to ascribe to him certain implications and to deny him others which belong to the term. Bacon is not a thoroughgoing inductive empiricist, as many historians assert. He brought an active mind to nature; and if he thought that both its sensuous and intellectual activities needed control, he knew that neither could be extirpated without the destruction of knowledge. He accepted the principle of identity as well as the principles of contradiction and excluded middle even if, unlike many of his predecessors and successors, he did not choose to build a whole philosophy of being on one or more of the three. He, as well as Aristotle, recognized that in both mathematics and logic things which are equal to the same thing are equal to one another; yet he did not think that this truth, when displayed in the syllogism, is sufficient to typify all manifestations of knowledge. He assumed a unity in nature, as well as universal causation and recurring identical causes in ordered sequence. He affirmed the principle of limited universal natures in the universe, made investigation proceed by way of the definition of these, and assumed that nature would respond to the questions put to her in proof of axioms or established hypotheses. And, while he accepted the unity of nature and sought a universal natural science from which the sciences and the arts might be nurtured, he refused to base a whole philosophy on the results of experiments on the loadstone or to construct one out of ideas or any astronomical theory. Bacon's hesitation to accept the far-reaching conclusions of Copernicus and Galileo springs from the fact that he considered it necessary to treat with the greatest caution a theory which explained occurrences which could also be accounted for by another theory, in this case the Ptolemaic. It is not surprising, in view of this caution, that he was more appreciative of Agricola's accounts of mines than of mathematical constructions according to which the movements of the planets were aligned by astronomers. He suspected mathematics. It had a way of departing from facts and creating notional systems of its own. He thought it best, so far as natural philosophy is concerned, to regard mathematics as an instrument, yet such an instrument that it may be truly affirmed that the best knowledge is that which, having begun in natural history, ends in mathematics.

Bacon's attack on what he himself called rationalism had marked effect in his own country. Aristotle's theoretical interpretations of being were disregarded. Copernicus and Galileo, however greatly extolled for their refutation of the Stagirite's theory, were not accepted as the founders of experimental philosophy. Descartes's *res cogitans* and *res extensa*, greeted at the beginning with enthusiasm, were gradually recognized as the creations of logical definition and then repudiated by his erstwhile disciples, such as the Platonist More and the popularizer of scientific opinions Glanvil. Locke, having refused to accept the results of Cartesian definition, undertook to describe the processes of the human mind by that plain, laborious, historical method which other Baconians had employed in investigating the nature of inanimate and animate bodies.

Bacon's departure from Aristotle marked a complete reversal in the recognition of supremacy not only so far as the instruments of knowledge were concerned but also in the organization of their products. The scale of knowledge, according to Aristotle, descends from metaphysics through mathematics to physics. Descartes with his analytical geometry and Leibniz and Newton with their differential calculus brought metaphysics and physics within the middle orbit of mathematics. Bacon, however, in his search for human knowledge went down to physics, incorporated metaphysics within this lowest domain, and brought mathematics into the service of both physics and metaphysics. Having done so he propounded a theory of nature. How novel Bacon's theory of nature is remains a matter of dispute. Certainly parts of his doctrine, according to his own admission, were suggested to him, respectively, by Pythagoras, Democritus, Plato, Telesius, and others. Yet certain it is that, if the author's doctrine of nature was not altogether "novel" with him, it was thoroughly "modern" and, through the impact made on investigation generally by Baconian virtuosi both within and without the Royal Society, determinative of succeeding thought. What he borrowed from predecessors and contemporaries he transformed. He rescued the forms in Pythagorean doctrine from purely theoretical quantity and rendered the forms of Plato materiate. He multiplied the motions of Democritean atoms and freed the heat and cold of Telesius from the obscurantism of indeterminate matter. He looked for no transcendental factor in nature and refused to inquire even into the nature-as-such of matter itself. He described matter in terms of kinematical design. This is what matter manifests and, therefore, what it is, even as nature is what it does.

Bacon's naturalism was properly described by his followers as "mechanical," "experimental," and "materialistic." It was mechanical in that it interpreted nature, including "spirit," in terms of the local motions of adjacent bodily parts; experimental in its recognition only of such conclusion as could be based on natural history; and materialistic in its being content to find the explanation of all processes amenable to scientific treatment in the "motion, figure, and magnitude" of bodies. The author construed the soul, as an object of investigation, in materialistic terms—here Locke somewhat furtively followed him. Universal forms he regarded as material. Incidentally, thinkers of the seventeenth century were not disposed to consider Bacon an Aristotelian because he employed the term "forms" along with his account of motion in terms of bodily contiguity in local motion. Really significant teleology had obviously become otiose for the author. There are recent writers who cavil at Bacon's use of the term "forms"; they probably would prefer such a nomenclature as "point-instants" or "neutral entities." Which one of the three is best it is difficult to say. All carry the difficulties inherent in the cultivated mythology or the barrenness, as the case may be, which belongs to any linguistic symbol, however carefully defined and hedged.

Inherent within Bacon's philosophical outlook is a refusal to accept all ontological doctrine. His philosophy professedly admits only naturalistic methods and subjects. Locke, with his "historical, plain" treatment of knowledge, is Bacon's first outstanding descendant. Then comes Hume, who interprets the structure of all experience in terms of psychological history so effectively that he awakens Kant from a rationalistic slumber induced by the reading of Leibniz and his school. After Hume come countless others who identify the whole content of philosophical reflection with a universalized natural science, such as psychology, mechanics, or biology. Such ascendancy does experimental naturalism achieve that first philosophy ceases to be ontology and becomes an elaborated cosmology based on physics and biology or an epistemology which undertakes in many instances a psychological examination of the presuppositions of experience; and metaphysics as the Aristotelians construe it finally all but disappears from British and European philosophy.

PROPER NAME AND TITLE INDEX

Abecedarium naturae, 35, 272–74
Academy, 111, 126, 133
Achilles, 56
Acosta, 276
Advancement of Learning, 10, 14, 16–17, 19, 22, 28, 34, 40, 41, 42, 45, 47, 48, 53, 55, 56, 78, 98, 112, 128, 129, 146, 147, 148, 157, 285
Advertisement touching an Holy War, 146
Agricola, 301
Agrippa, 47, 110
Albertus Magnus, 135, 136
Alexander the Great, 15, 190
"Alphabet of Nature," 35, 272–74
Anaxagoras, 9, 48, 109
Anaximenes, 69
Andrews, 23, 42, 146
Anytus, 121
Aphorismi et consilia, 40, 41, 42
"Aphorisms and Counsels," 40, 41, 42
Aquinas, 50, 107
Arabians, 108, 114, 135
Aristotle and Aristotelians, v, 15, 20, 29, 49–50, 63, 65, 68, 69, 74, 82, 83, 84, 90, 92–93, 95, 101, 105, 106, 107, 113, 114, 116, 117, 118–24, 126, 127, 130, 131, 133, 134, 135, 136, 138, 140, 153, 163, 174, 175, 176, 177, 178, 180, 182, 190–216, 237, 262, 276, 277, 296, 300, 301, 302–3
Arnoldus de Villa Nova, 108
Ascham, 91
Atalanta, 62, 96, 143
Atlantis, 182
Atlas, 200
Augustine and Augustinians, 50–53, 121, 128

Bacchus, 58
Bacon, Anthony, 3, 4
Bacon, Sir Nicholas, 2
Bacon, Roger, 108
Baranzan, 270
Boccaccio, 56
Bodley, 41
Bruno, 293, 298
Burghley, 3, 4, 5, 9, 13, 14, 46

Caesar, 15
Calor et frigus, 29, 40, 42
Cambridge, 3, 5, 7, 20, 23, 91, 294
Canterbury, Archbishop of, 23
Car, 91
Cardan, 107, 135, 136, 277
Carneades, 122
"Catalogue of Particular Histories," 34, 273, 277
Catalogus historiarum particularium, 34, 273, 277
Cato, 174
Charles, 296
Christian Fathers, 50, 95, 116
Chrysippus, 56, 122
Cicero, 91, 107, 110, 116, 117, 123, 134, 174, 180
Coelum, 57, 60
Cogitata et visa, 19, 32, 33, 40, 41, 42, 47, 48, 80, 90, 113, 124, 127
Cogitationes de natura rerum, 39, 41, 43, 56, 70, 75, 78, 120
Cogitationes de scientia humana, 39, 41, 57
Coke, 5
Columbus, 182
Comes, 56
Commentarius solutus, 23, 29, 31, 42, 45, 46, 75, 146
"Concerning Principles and Origins," 36, 39–40, 44, 57, 64, 66, 78, 120
"Concerning the Wisdom of the Ancients," 39, 41, 42, 44, 46, 53, 56, 57, 64, 78, 113
Conference of Pleasure, 9, 46
Cooke, Anne, 2–3, 5
Copernicus, 132, 136, 137, 292, 301, 302
Cowley, 7, 278
Cromwell, 296
Cupid, elder, 64, 65, 66, 67, 68, 69, 78
Cupid, younger, 57, 64, 66

De augmentis, 3, 8, 10, 14, 16, 19, 28, 33, 34, 39, 40, 41, 53, 57, 97, 98, 112, 128, 130, 146, 147, 148, 157, 180, 245, 270, 285
De fluxu et reflexu maris, 29, 40, 42, 43

De interpretatione naturae prooemium, 10–12, 13, 16, 39, 40, 81
De interpretatione naturae, sententiae XII, 40, 41
De principiis atque originibus, 36, 39–40, 44, 57, 64, 66, 78, 120
De sapientia veterum, 39, 41, 42, 44, 46, 53, 56, 57, 64, 78, 113
Delineatio, 31, 32, 33, 40, 42, 43, 85, 90, 98, 129, 284
Democritus, 48, 49, 60, 65, 67, 69, 70, 72, 73, 77, 92, 102, 109, 110, 115, 116, 117, 118–20, 132, 216, 228, 302
Demosthenes, 91, 180
Descartes, 292, 293, 297, 298, 302
Descriptio globi intellectualis, 29, 30, 39, 40, 42, 43, 72, 75, 77, 78, 79, 120
"Description of the Intellectual Globe," 29, 30, 39, 40, 42, 43, 72, 75, 77, 78, 79, 120
Device, *On the Queen's Day*, 9–10
Diagoras, 100
Dindamus, 110
Dionysius, 122
Dioscorides, 135, 294
Donius, 138, 169

Echo, 61
Egnatius, 276
Egyptians, 15, 183
Elizabeth, 3, 5, 13, 16
Ellis, v, vi, 43, 57, 277
Empedocles, 48, 60, 63, 109, 117
Encyclopedists, 297
Enthusiasts, 51, 52, 299
Epicurus and Epicureans, 65, 110, 116, 122, 132
Erasmus, 91
Eros, 57
Essex, 4, 5, 47
Euclid, 63, 113
Euthydemus, 122

Fernelius, 108
Ficinus, 276
Filum labyrinthi, sive formula inquisitionis, 19, 40, 41, 56, 127
Filum labyrinthi; sive inquisitio legitima de motu, 29, 40, 75, 78
"Forerunners or Anticipations of the New Philosophy," 36, 43, 145, 282
"Forest of Materials," 29, 35, 44, 270, 272, 276, 277
Fulgentius, 29, 44, 282, 283

Galen, 46, 107, 108, 109, 113, 119, 294
Galileo, 132, 136, 138, 292, 301, 302
Gesta Grayorum, 13–16
Gilbert, 101, 120, 132, 136, 292
Glanvil, 302
Gray's Inn, 3, 13
"Greatest Birth of Time," 44
Greeks, 113, 133
Gymnosophists, 15

Hammond, 23
Harriot, 23
"Heat and Cold," 29, 40, 42
Heraclitus, 69, 109, 110, 117
Hero, 70, 71, 120
Hesiod, 57
Hippias, 122, 125, 126
Hippocrates, 109, 113, 114, 120, 168, 174, 294
Hippomenes, 62
Historia densi et rari, 34, 35, 44, 120, 271, 272, 273
Historia gravis et levis, 35, 77, 271
Historia et inquisitio prima de sono et auditu, 29, 40, 77
Historia naturalis et experimentalis, 14, 29, 34, 35, 77, 180, 270–73, 279, 281, 290
Historia sulphuris, mercurii, et salis, 35, 271–72
Historia sympathiae et antipathiae rerum, 35, 271
Historia ventorum, 34, 35, 271, 272, 275, 276
Historia vitae et mortis, 34, 44, 272, 275, 276
"History of Dense and Rare," 34, 35, 44, 120, 271, 272, 273
"History and First Investigation of Sound and Hearing," 29, 40, 77
"History of Heavy and Light," 35, 77, 271
"History of Life and Death," 34, 44, 272, 275, 276
"History of Sulphur, Mercury, and Salt," 35, 271–72
"History of the Sympathy and Antipathy of Things," 35, 271
"History of Winds," 34, 35, 271, 272, 275, 276
Hobbes, 297
Homer, 57, 125, 144
Hume, 1, 303

"Inquiry concerning the Lodestone," 35, 44
Inquisitio de magnete, 35, 44

INDEX

James, 5, 7, 16, 17, 19, 21, 22, 23, 24, 27, 28, 145, 147
Jupiter, 60, 63, 96, 138, 250

Kepler, 298

"Ladder of the Understanding or Thread of the Labyrinth," 36, 43, 145, 279, 280
Leibniz, 292, 293, 298, 302, 303
Letter and Discourse touching Helps for the Intellectual Powers, 47
Leucippus, 102, 117, 120
Locke, 299, 302, 303
Lucretius, 116
Lully, 132, 134, 135, 136
Luther, 50

Machiavelli, 56
Macrobius, 56
"Masculine—or Fertilizing—Birth of Time," 31, 40, 44–47, 48, 53, 56, 80, 97, 106, 112, 283
Mersenne, 293
Mill, J. S., 1, 300
Minerva, 59, 61, 163
More, 302
Mountjoy, 192

"Natural and Experimental History," 14, 29, 34, 35, 77, 180, 270–73, 281, 290
Neo-Platonists, 132
Neptune, 59, 100
New Atlantis, 24, 36, 40, 42, 295
"New Organon or True Directions"; see *Novum organum*
Night, egg of, 67
Novum organum, 14, 19, 27, 28, 29, 31, 33, 34, 35, 39, 40, 41, 42, 43, 44, 75, 77, 97, 98, 99, 120, 127, 130, 145, 146, 147, 148, 157, 158, 181, 217, 222, 224, 228, 231, 253, 257, 258, 259, 266, 273, 279, 280, 281, 282, 284, 292, 300

Occasionalists, 298
Oedipus, 62
"Of the Dignity and Advancement of Learning"; see *De augmentis*
"Of the Ebb and Flow of the Sea," 29, 40, 42, 43
"Of the Interpretation of Nature: Proem," 13, 16, 39, 40, 81
Olympus, 154
"On the Interpretation of Nature, XII Judgments," 40, 41

Oracle of Delphi, 122
"Outline and Argument of the Second Part of the Instauration," 31, 32, 33, 40, 42, 43, 85, 90, 98, 129, 284
Oxford, 7, 23

Pan, 60, 61
Paracelsus and Paracelsans, v, 46, 108, 109, 111, 141, 167, 249, 297
Parasceve, 14, 28, 33, 34, 42, 75, 146, 180, 259, 265, 270, 272, 273, 277
Paris, 3, 55, 113
Parmenides, 63, 69, 117, 130, 138
Pentheus, 58, 59
Peripatetics; see Aristotle, Schoolmen
Persians, 15, 161
Phaenomena universi, 40, 41, 145, 273, 285
"Phenomena of the Universe," 40, 41, 145, 273, 285
Philo, 116
Phocion, 191
Pindar, 165
Pius, Antoninus, 102
Plato and Platonists, v, 51, 56, 68, 101, 107, 113, 114, 115, 116, 117, 119, 120, 121, 122, 123, 124–26, 127, 128, 130, 133, 134, 150, 182, 190, 192, 233, 296, 302
Playfer, 146, 147
Pliny, vi, 135, 136, 264, 265, 270, 276, 277
Plutarch, 56, 107
Polus, 122
Polyphemus, 112
Porta, 136, 277
Post-Aristotelians, 132–43
"Preparative toward a Natural and Experimental History," 14, 28, 33, 34, 42, 75, 146, 180, 259, 265, 270, 272, 273, 277
Pre-Platonists, 116–23, 124
Proclus, 101
Prodromi sive anticipationes philosophiae secundae, 36, 43, 145, 282
"Proem"; see "Of the Interpretation of Nature: Proem"
Prometheus, 59, 62, 203
Protagoras, 122, 126
Proteus, 59, 60, 61, 74, 151
Ptolemies, 15
Ptolemy, 63, 113, 137
Pyrrho, 111, 126, 133
Pythagoras and Pythagoreans, 48, 72, 110, 115, 116, 120, 121, 164, 302

Ramus and Ramists, 47, 83, 107, 132, 134, 135, 136

Rawley, 6, 24, 35, 36, 42, 43, 44, 147, 181, 270, 272, 273, 276
Redargutio philosophiarum, 29, 41, 42, 46, 48, 55, 56, 113, 285
"Refutation of Philosophies," 29, 41, 42, 46, 48, 55, 56, 113, 285
Romans, 113, 114, 117

Salisbury, 4, 17
Sandys, 277
Saturn, 60, 250
Savill, 47
Scala intellectus sive filum labyrinthi, 36, 43, 145, 279, 280
Schoolmen, 50, 80, 114, 116, 127, 132, 133, 134, 165, 192, 199, 215, 245, 247
Scotus, 107
Scylla, 134
Seneca, 107
Severinus, 108, 111
Skeptics, 126, 132, 133, 279-80
Socrates, 96, 120, 121, 122, 125
Solomon, 15, 167
Sophists, 106-9, 120, 121, 122, 126
Spedding, v, vi, 44-47, 57, 147, 283
Sphinx, 62
Spinoza, 292, 297, 298
Sprat, 277
Stoics, 132, 176, 183
Sylva Sylvarum, 29, 35, 44, 270, 272, 276, 277

Tacitus, 157
Telesius, v, 69, 109, 120, 132, 136, 138, 140, 141, 169, 240, 255, 302

Temporis partus masculus, 31, 40, 44-47, 48, 53, 56, 80, 97, 106, 112, 283
Temporis partus maximus, 44
Thales, 69, 114
Thema coeli, 29, 30, 39, 40, 42, 75, 76, 79
Theophrastus, 122, 135, 136
"Theory of the Heaven," 29, 30, 39, 40, 42, 75, 76, 79
"Thoughts on Human Knowledge," 39, 41, 57
"Thoughts and Impressions," 19, 32, 33, 40, 41, 42, 47, 48, 80, 90, 113, 124, 127
"Thoughts on the Nature of Things," 39, 41, 43, 56, 70, 75, 78, 120
"Thread of the Labyrinth; or the Legitimate Investigation of Motion," 29, 40, 75, 78
"Thread of the Labyrinth, or Rule of Inquiry," 19, 40, 41, 56, 127
"Topic of Inquiry concerning Light and Illumination," 35, 44
Topica inquisitionis de luce et lumine, 35, 44

Valerius Maximus, 276
Valerius Terminus, 13, 16, 32, 33, 39, 40, 41, 42, 45, 47, 48, 53, 77, 78, 81, 90, 98, 129, 283
Velleius, 110
Virgil, 174
Vulcan, 61, 163

Wilkins, 179

Zeno, 122

SUBJECT INDEX

Abstract notions, 57, 65, 103, 200
Abstraction, 118, 192, 193, 211, 215, 216
Acatalepsia, 126, 133
Adventitious Conditions of Beings, 153–54, 156, 196, 209, 214–15, 273, 274, 281
Alchemy, 21, 105, 142–43
Allegory of the Cave, 101, 124, 271
Analytic, 36, 183, 194, 300
Anatomy, 162, 168
Anticipations, 31, 81, 93, 282
Application of Experiment, 285, 287–88
Art and motion, 73, 77
Art and nature, 55, 61–62, 64, 77, 151, 202, 239, 257, 261–63, 296
Art and science, 58, 183–84, 202–3
Ascending and Descending Scale of Axioms, 218
Astronomy: to be advanced by a philosophy of nature, 137, 301; and mathematics, 164, 301; traditional theories of, 164, 301
Athletic, 166
Atoms, 66–67, 120; definition of, 70–73
Axioms, 81, 83, 88, 90, 135, 148, 183, 218, 219, 288, 290, 291; convertible, 82–83; middle, 32, 81, 85–86, 101, 130, 187, 188

Base and common things, 94, 125, 263
Being, 49, 153, 193–94, 206, 209, 212, 216, 231, 274, 301
Bodies: Aristotelian doctrine of, 71; celestial and terrestrial, 72, 137, 208–9, 237
Bringing Down to Practice, 218

Categories, 103, 118, 194, 207, 212, 215, 300
Causes, 289, 290, 291, 300, 301; final, 48, 54, 88, 118, 127, 156, 208, 209–10, 211; First Cause, 15, 153, 290, 291; four traditional, Bacon's use of, 156–58, 212; in metaphysics, 14; natural, and First Cause, 58, 66–67, 213, 291; in physics, 14
Certainty in direction, 82
Chances of Experiment, 285–88
Chemical experiments, 21, 61, 143, 167
Civil history, 150–52
Civil philosophy, 165 ff.

Classification of the sciences, 49, 297, 302; Aristotle on the, 130–31, 192–93; Plato on the, 130–31
Color, 77
Compulsion of Experiment, 285, 287
Condensation and rarefaction, 71–73, 273
Conservation of matter, 41, 60
Contemplation, 85, 121, 161, 184, 290, 295; and knowledge, 96, 220; and operation, 87, 89–90, 161
Continuation of Inquiry, 88
Contraction of Inquiry, 88–89
Contradiction, law of, 194, 196, 301
Convertible propositions, 66, 82–83, 90, 135, 196, 215
Cosmetic, 166
Cosmography, 152, 164
Coupling of Experiment, 285–88

Dates of Bacon's works, 41–47
Definition and division, 84, 88, 103, 127, 128–30, 222–23, 281
Density and rarity, 71–73, 266, 271, 273
Determination, principle of, 85, 90, 128–30, 187, 234, 235, 290
Dialectic, 182–83
Disputation, 20, 68, 103, 148, 278, 294, 295
Dissection versus abstraction, 118, 193

Elements, 69, 104, 118, 138–39, 143, 205, 207–8, 246, 262
Elenches, 97–98, 122
Empiricism, 21, 62, 64, 85, 105, 130, 143, 144–45, 161, 167, 183, 187–89, 198, 212, 219, 290, 300–301
Epistemology: Aristotle's, 2, 10–11; Bacon's, 214
Ether, 206, 209
Ethics: dispositions of the mind, 75–77; precepts of, respecting habit, 177–78; subsidiary to revealed theology, 171–72, 193–94
Excluded middle, law of, 194, 196, 301
Exemplar of Good, 171, 173 ff.
Experiments of light and experiments of fruit, 143, 183, 260

309

Fables: Bacon's interpretation of, 56–69; as a vehicle of knowledge, 56
Fabric of the Universe, 232, 234, 290
Faith and knowledge, 95
First Moved, 206, 209
First philosophy, 152–53, 156, 281, 290; not equivalent to metaphysics, 214–16
First principles, 80, 86, 129, 173, 184, 186, 188, 199, 200
First Vintage, 218, 222, 223, 224
Forms, 88, 124, 127–28, 160–62, 218, 219, 220, 221, 229, 230, 231, 236, 243, 287, 303; abstract, 48, 68–69, 128, 160; as causes, 84, 156, 290; as exemplars, 51; few in number, 130; of the First Class, 159; as laws of action, 118, 156, 236, 290, 295; Lesser, 233, 234; limited as the alphabet of nature, 75, 79, 159, 217–18, 274, 290; Pure Form, 153, 209–10, 211

Genus and species, 85, 222, 235, 237
God, knowledge of his nature, will, and thoughts, 51–55, 58, 61, 118, 153, 211, 289, 297–99
Good, the, 51–54, 127
Great Form, the, 234, 290

Heat, 29, 40, 77, 139–41, 158, 160, 217–18, 222, 237, 254–55, 266, 281; definition of, 136, 223; investigation of, 219–23; as motion, 27, 222–23, 249
Heresy, 95, 122, 127

Identity, law of, 194, 196, 209–10, 212, 301
Idols, 39, 97–99, 106–7, 109–10; of the Cave, 101–2; of the Market-Place, 102–4; of the Theatre, 104–5; of the Tribe, 99–100
Imagination, 170–71
Induction, 300; Aristotelian account of, 197–98; Bacon's, not pure, 219, 290
Indulgence of the Understanding, 218, 222, 223, 224
Instances; *see* Prerogative Instances
Instauration: its parts and ends, 31–33, 145; first part, 34, 144–80; second part, 34, 181–89, 217–58; third part, 34–35, 259–69; fourth part, 36, 279–82; fifth part, 36, 282, 288; sixth part, 288, 289; works in representation of the, 34–37; works which fall without the, 39–41
Intellect; *see* Reason
Invention of Argument, 179
Inversion of Experiment, 285–87

Knowledge, its division according to natural faculties, 193; its motive, 95–96

Language (*see also* Words), 110, 126, 295, 296–97; Latin, 19, 146–47, 179; Real, 179; science as verbal, 84; terms of syllogism, 187; verbal demonstration, 134–35, 199, 201
Latent process, 154, 158, 162, 257, 258
Latent schematism, 154, 158, 161–62, 163, 257, 258, 281, 295
League of Common Bond, 165–66
Learned Experience, 32, 180, 284–88
Learning: Bacon's attack upon, 2, 17–21, 293; contentious, 91–92; delicate, 92–93; discredits of, by politicians and divines, 18–19, 39, 49, 55, 95; fantastical, 91–92; history of, 39–40, 92, 109, 112–117, 191; and politics, 8–12, 19; refutation of, 39, 40–41
Liberty in direction, 82
Light of Nature, 58–59, 102, 172
Limits of Investigation, 218, 219
Logic: of abstraction, 117; Baconian, 198; and rhetoric, 123; traditional, 94, 101

Magic, 154, 158, 161
Materialism (*see also* Matter, Motion), 2, 48–79, 132, 289, 302; of poets, 57
Mathematics, 163–64, 192–93, 281, 292, 301, 302; handmaid of physics, 121, 166
Matter: as active, 48, 141; conservation of, 73; constraint of, 61, 64; eternity of, 60; as formed, 48, 58, 67–69, 78, 88, 118–19, 141; inherent motion of, 64–65, 73, 78, 118, 207; oldest created thing, 58; properties of, 78; source of all natural species, 59–60, 65
Mechanics, 154, 158, 161
Medicine, 166; defects of, 167–68
Memory, 188, 234, 281; aids to, 86, 87, 179, 217
Metaphysics, 154, 156, 158, 163, 196; objects of, 14, 159, 218; identified with generalized physics, 2, 55, 193, 206–7, 212, 290, 293
Method, inductive, development of, 33, 39–42
Middle term, 90, 194, 199, 201
Modern times, the ancient times, 115–16
Motion, 29, 160; and color, 77; and heat, 77, 222–23, 249; local, predominance of, 76–78, 206, 302, 303; natural and violent, 74, 208; and primary natures, 75; and

INDEX

sound, 77; traditional theories of, 65, 74, 77, 104, 118–19, 204–5, 207–9, 245–53; types of, 74–75, 79, 155–56, 205, 245–53, 281

Natural faculties, their use and limitation, 18, 52–53, 57–59, 63, 113, 213
Natural history, 17, 39, 40, 148; Bacon's, as derivative, 276–77; the basis of knowledge, 14, 28–30, 81, 86–87, 88, 217, 219, 259–60, 271, 295, 302; defects of extant, 259–61, 264, 270–71; divisions and uses of, 30, 32–34, 136, 151, 260, 261, 271; precepts concerning, 258, 260–65; range of, 14, 18, 29, 32, 260, 261, 270; titles of, for inquiry, 266–69; traditional, 135
Natural theology, 196; objects and range of, 49, 54–56, 153, 156, 193, 209, 212, 213
Nature, 156, 160–61, 162; Light of, 58–59, 102, 172; modern interpretation of, 2, 293; threefold manifestation of, 75, 135, 150–51, 201–2, 261–62
Natures, 159, 219, 231, 240; as alphabet, 75; constitutive of things, 75, 78, 81, 83, 85; Prerogative, 218
Ne plus ultra, and *plus ultra,* 29, 115, 152, 182, 287
Negation, 67, 78, 88, 100, 127, 186, 198, 200, 220–21, 231
New method, 181, 182, 293; Bacon's description of, 80–81, 145–46; early interpretation of, 81–85; eleven directions for, 218, 219; importance of, 181–82; incompleteness of, 219, 228, 231, 253, 258; levels men's wits, 185–86, 214; middle interpretation of, 86–90; purpose of, 81–82, 85, 295; range of subjects of, 281
Notion, 85, 86, 88, 90, 103, 135, 188

Operation: aids toward furthering of, 224; and science, 20–21, 58, 80, 81, 84, 86, 144, 154, 159–60, 161, 193, 223, 263, 295

Particular proposition, 231
Particulars, 32, 81–82, 85–86, 90, 103, 127, 129–30, 187–88, 199, 280, 290
Perception in bodies, 169–70
Philosophy: and revelation (*see* Revelation); and the special sciences, 21, 63, 92, 195–96, 200–201, 211–12
Physics: of abstracts, 155; of concretes, 154–55; generalized, equivalent to metaphysics, 2, 55, 193, 206–7, 212, 216, 290, 293, 299; objects of, 14, 154–55, 159
Pleasure: servant of virtue, 132; types of, 125
Poetry, 149–50, 152
Poets, 56, 175
Power and knowledge, 62, 94, 115, 161, 181–83, 185, 253, 289
Prenotions, 180, 290
Preparations for Investigation, 218
Prerogative of the Instance, 89
Prerogative Instances, 218; classification of, 224–25; of Alliance, 237; Bordering, 238; Clandestine, 235–36; of Companionship, 231; Conformable, 232; Constitutive, 233; of the Course, 243–44; Deviating, 238; Dissecting, 228–29; of Divorce, 240, 241; of the Door, 225; of Enmity, 231; of the Fingerpost, 239; Intimating, 253; of the Lamp, 224–28; of Magic, 253, 257; Mathematical 242, 243–53; of Migration, 229, 231; Polychrest, 253, 254; of Power, 242–43; Propitious, 242, 253; of Quantity, 244; of the Road, 226–27; of the Rod, 243; Singular, 236; Solitary, 228; of Strife, 244–45; Striking, 230; Subjective, 231, 232; Summoning, 225–26; Supplementary, 227–28; their order in use, 257–58
Prerogative of That Inquired Into, 89
Presentation of Instances to the Understanding, 35, 218, 219, 258
Prime Mover, 54, 104, 153, 206, 209–10, 211
Privation, 65, 157, 207
Production of Experiment, 286
Promptuary, 179–80
Pyramid: of knowledge, 14, 131, 154, 206, 212; of nature 60–61, 291

Quantity, 72, 110, 121, 156, 163–64, 263–64, 273, 281
Quintessence, 206, 209

Rationalist school, 104–5
Reason, 87, 118, 127, 143, 149, 155, 214, 279; aids to, 70, 86–90, 217, 224, 229–40; deficiencies of, 99, 188, 279; divine source of, 59, 171, 193, 214; dominance of, 149–50
Rectification of Induction, 218, 258
Regiment of mind, 173 ff.
Reminiscence, 128
Rest, nonexistent, 73

Revealed theology, and natural knowledge, 18, 50, 53, 58, 61, 95, 119, 138, 149, 151–52, 153, 169, 171–73, 193, 212–13, 293, 297

Revelation, and carnal knowledge, 49, 51, 52–53, 299

Rhetoric, 121, 123, 124; and logic, 123

Rule: of prudence, 82–83; of truth, 82–83

Sapience; *see* First philosophy

Scala naturae, 210

Scala universi, 210–12

Senses, 85, 118, 127, 128, 155, 170, 186–88, 199, 214, 217, 222, 279; aids to the, 86–87, 224; deficiencies of the, 86, 99, 187, 225–28, 279

Signet of Creator, 185, 289–90

Skeptics, 126, 133, 278, 279

Soul: dual theory of, 128, 138, 149, 169, 193, 213–14, 303; Peripatetic account of the, 213; rational, as determinative of knowledge, 213

Sound, 77

Species, 59–61, 195–96, 200, 202, 209, 234–35, 238, 261

Spiritus mundi, 124–25

Summary law of nature, 65, 67, 154, 212, 290, 291

Sun (Platonic), 51–52

Supports of induction, 218, 258

Syllogism, 90, 130, 186, 194, 198, 199, 201, 233, 301

Systems of philosophy, traditional, 24, 126

Tables, 32, 75, 87, 217, 280–81, 289, 290; of Degrees, 35, 221, 230; of Deviation, or of Absence in Proximity, 35, 220; of Essence and Presence, 35, 219

Technical education, 15, 22–27, 40, 294, 295–96

Teleology, 2, 48, 66, 77, 126–27, 303

Titles: from the Alphabet, 274, 281; for natural history, 266–69, 295

Topics, 87, 179–80, 265–66, 290

Transcendentals, 153–54, 156, 196, 209, 214–15, 273–74, 281

Translation of Experiment, 285, 287

Truth, tests of, 32, 33, 81–82, 90, 145

Understanding, disposed to error, 81, 98–105; and nature, 80, 189

Unity and multiplicity, 129–30

Universals, 128, 214, 280, 290, 300–301

Universities: criticism of, 17–22, 294–97; dominated by theologians, 48–49; as repositories of learning, 20; and the sciences, 20–21

Utility and science, 62, 64, 80, 81, 96, 143, 184, 259, 288, 296

Vacuum, 66, 70–71, 76, 120, 273; Aristotelian account of, 206; Bacon's problem concerning, 120, 273

Variation of Experiment, 285–86

Variation of Inquiry, 88; according to the Nature of the Subject, 218

Virtue, 123, 124, 173

Virtues, cardinal, 266, 272

Voluptuary, 166

Whiteness, investigation of, 83–84, 158–59

Will, 170, 171

Winds, 275

Words (*see also* Language): and abstraction, 74, 103; as coins, 102–3; and definition, 103, 199, 302; and matter, 91–92, 122; perpetuate errors, 102–4; as symbols of thought, 192, 195, 303